Y0-DLF-647

Crime and Justice
An Introduction

Nelson-Hall Series in Law, Crime, and Justice
Consulting Editor: Jon R. Waltz,
Northwestern University School of Law

Crime and Justice
An Introduction

Howard Abadinsky

Nelson-Hall Publishers/Chicago

To Donna, Alisa, and Sandi

Copy Editor: Barbara Armentrout
Designer: Claudia Von Hendricks
Production Manager: Pamela Teisler
Photo Editor: Stephen Forsling
Illustrations: Sally A. Ireland
Cover Design: Jane Rae Brown

ACKNOWLEDGMENTS

Cover: *Tres Lindos* by Ed Paschke, 1982, oil/canvas, 42" × 80". Collection of A. Goldberg, New York. Courtesy of the Phyllis Kind Gallery–Chicago/New York. Photo: William H. Bengtson.

Photo credits appear on p. 553.

LIBRARY OF CONGRESS CATALOGING-IN-PUBLICATION DATA

Abadinsky, Howard, 1941-
   Crime and justice.

  Bibliography: p.
  Includes index.
  1. Crime and criminals—United States. 2. Criminal justice, Administration of—United States. I. Title.
HV6025.A17   1987   364'.973   86-18093
ISBN 0-8304-1134-8

Copyright © 1987 by Nelson-Hall Inc.   Reprinted 1991

All rights reserved. No part of this book may be reproduced in any form without permission in writing from the publisher, except by a reviewer who wishes to quote brief passages in connection with a review written for broadcast or for inclusion in a magazine or newspaper. For information address Nelson-Hall Inc., Publishers, 111 North Canal Street, Chicago, Illinois 60606.

Manufactured in the United States of America

10   9   8   7   6   5   4   3

∞ ™ The paper used in this book meets the minimum requirements of American National Standard for Information Sciences—Permanence of Paper for Printed Library Materials, ANSI Z39.48-1984.

Contents in Brief

PART ONE **Crime, Criminals, and Criminal Justice**   **1**

Chapter 1   Crime: Problems of Definition and Law   2
Chapter 2   Of Crime and Criminals   22
Chapter 3   How Much Crime? The Problems of Perception and Statistics   46
Chapter 4   Why Crime? Theories of Causation   76
Chapter 5   The System of Criminal Justice   110

PART TWO **Reacting to Crime**   **153**

Chapter 6   The Police: History, Goals, and Organization   154
Chapter 7   Police Operations   178
Chapter 8   Issues in Policing   208
Chapter 9   Federal Law Enforcement   242
Chapter 10   Federal and State Courts   272
Chapter 11   The Lawyers: Judge, Prosecutor, Defense Counsel   300
Chapter 12   Plea Bargaining and Trials   332

PART THREE   Reacting to Criminals   **365**

Chapter 13   Sentencing and Probation   366
Chapter 14   The Question of Punishment: Jails and Prisons   394
Chapter 15   The Question of Punishment: Corrections and Capital Punishment   414
Chapter 16   Parole and Community-Based Corrections   448

PART FOUR: Juvenile Justice   **479**

Chapter 17   Juvenile Justice and the Juvenile Court   480

Contents

Preface xv

Acknowledgments xvii

PART ONE: Crime, Criminals, and Criminal Justice 1

Chapter 1 Crime: Problems of Definition and Law 2

DEFINING CRIME 2

LAW AND ITS SOURCES 6

CIVIL LAW 6

CRIMINAL LAW 7
Objectives
  Punishment
  Deterrence
Categories of Crime

CORPUS DELICTI 11
Actus Reus
Mens Rea
Concurrence

CRIMINAL RESPONSIBILITY 13
Infancy
Insanity

AFFIRMATIVE DEFENSE 18
Self-Defense
Entrapment

REVIEW QUESTIONS 21

Boxes

The Law: Where to Find It

Chapter 2 Of Crime and Criminals 22

VIOLENT PERSONAL CRIME 25

OCCASIONAL CRIME 27

FRAUD 28

EMPLOYEE CRIME 28

CAREER CRIME 29

POLITICAL CRIME 30

CORPORATE CRIME, OR "CRIME IN THE SUITES" 32

PROFESSIONAL CRIME 34

VICTIMLESS CRIME 37

ORGANIZED CRIME 38

REVIEW QUESTIONS 45

Chapter 3 How Much Crime? The Problems of Perception and Statistics 46

CRIME: A MATTER OF PERCEPTION 46

UNIFORM CRIME REPORTS 49
Problems with the UCR

vii

NATIONAL CRIME SURVEY 60
Findings of the NCS
Problems with the NCS

HOW MUCH CRIME? 71

REVIEW QUESTIONS 75

Boxes ─────────────

Politics and Crime Statistics
Victimization Study

QUALITATIVE RESEARCH 106
Case Study
Participant Observation

REVIEW QUESTIONS 108

Boxes ─────────────

Smithkline Pleads Guilty
E.F. Hutton Pleads Guilty
General Electric Pleads Guilty
Sample Self-Report Instrument

Chapter 4 Why Crime? Theories of Causation   76

WHAT IS A THEORY? 77

THEORIES OF CRIME 78
Classical Theory
   Criticisms of the Classical Theory
Positivism
Biological Theory
   Criminal Man
   XYY Chromosome Theory
Psychological Theory
   Psychoanalytic Theory
   Behaviorism
Sociological Theory
   Anomie
   Cultural Transmission
   Differential Association
   Differential Opportunity
   Subcultural Theory
   Neutralization
   Delinquency and Drift
   Labeling
   Conflict Theory
   Functionalism

THE "MAGIC BULLET" 99

QUANTITATIVE RESEARCH 104
Survey Research
Experimental Design

Chapter 5 The System of Criminal Justice   110

THE PROBLEM OF GOVERNMENTAL COMPLEXITY 110
The Law and Jurisdiction
Law Enforcement and Jurisdiction

CRIME CONTROL VERSUS DUE PROCESS 113

DUE PROCESS OF LAW 118
The Right to Remain Silent
   Exceptions
The Right to Legal Counsel
The Right to Bail
The Right to a Jury Trial
The Right to Confront Witnesses
Double Jeopardy
The Exclusionary Rule
   Exceptions

THE CRIMINAL JUSTICE PROCESS 134
Preliminary Investigation
Arrest
Booking
Pretrial Hearings
Grand Jury
Plea Bargaining
Trial

Sentencing
Probation
Jail/Prison
Parole
Appeals

REVIEW QUESTIONS   150

Boxes

Cases of Mistaken Guilt
Miranda Warnings
Mapp v. Ohio
United States v. Leon
Crime Victims

PART TWO: Reacting to Crime   153

Chapter 6 The Police: History, Goals, and Organization   154

STATE POLICE   155

SHERIFF   155

MUNICIPAL POLICE HISTORY   159

POLICE GOALS AND OBJECTIVES   168
The Dilemma of Law Versus Order

STYLES OF POLICING   170

POLICE ORGANIZATION   172

REVIEW QUESTIONS   177

Boxes

New Jersey State Police
The Boston Police Strike of 1919
Vollmer and Wilson: Pioneers in Police Administration
Organization of the Minneapolis Police Department

Chapter 7 Police Operations   178

PATROL   178
Calls for Service
Preventive Patrol
Officer-Initiated Activities
Administrative Tasks

SPECIALIZED PATROL   184
Uniformed Tactical Patrol
Decoy Operations
Stakeouts
Covert Surveillance

INVESTIGATION   192
Proactive Investigation
Reactive Investigation

TRAFFIC   196
Sobriety Checkpoints

INTERNAL AFFAIRS   200

SPECIAL WEAPONS AND TACTICS (SWAT) TEAMS   201

POLICE AUXILIARIES   203

OTHER SPECIALIZED BUREAUS AND UNITS   206

REVIEW QUESTIONS   207

Boxes

Decoy
Street Crime Unit

Chapter 8 Issues in Policing   208

LIMITATIONS OF POLICING   209
Structural Limitations
Resource Limitations
Legal Limitations

POLICE DISCRETION 211

CONTROLLING THE POLICE 214
Police Alienation, Authoritarianism, and Solidarity

POLICE DEVIANCE 216
Corruption
Brutality
Deadly Force
Common Law Statutes
Modified Common Law
Model Penal Code

PROFESSIONALISM 226

POLICE UNIONISM 229

AFFIRMATIVE ACTION 232

PRIVATE SECURITY 233

LEGAL ISSUES 235
Search and Seizure

REVIEW QUESTIONS 240

Boxes

Homicide
Patterns of Police Corruption
Terry v. Ohio

Chapter 9 Federal Law Enforcement 242

UNITED STATES MARSHALS SERVICE 243

SECRET SERVICE 247

BUREAU OF ALCOHOL, TOBACCO AND FIREARMS 250

IMMIGRATION AND NATURALIZATION SERVICE 251

CUSTOMS SERVICE 253

GENERAL SERVICES ADMINISTRATION 255

INTERNAL REVENUE SERVICE 255

POSTAL INSPECTION SERVICE 256

DRUG ENFORCEMENT ADMINISTRATION 257

FEDERAL BUREAU OF INVESTIGATION 259

COAST GUARD 264

MILITARY LAW ENFORCEMENT AGENCIES 264

OFFICES OF INSPECTOR GENERAL 266

MISCELLANEOUS AGENCIES 266

INTERPOL 268

REVIEW QUESTIONS 271

Chapter 10 Federal and State Courts 272

U.S. DISTRICT COURTS AND MAGISTRATES 273

U.S. COURT OF APPEALS 277

U.S. SUPREME COURT 278

THE STATE COURTS: EARLY HISTORY 282

THE STRUCTURE OF STATE COURTS 284

LOWER COURT/COURT OF LIMITED JURISDICTION 285

**SUPERIOR COURT/
COURT OF GENERAL
JURISDICTION**   287

**INTERMEDIATE COURT OF
APPEALS/APPELLATE
JURISDICTION**   287

**COURT OF APPEALS/COURT
OF LAST RESORT**   288

**THE APPELLATE
PROCESS**   289

**ADMINISTERING THE
COURTS**   294

COURT REFORM   295

REVIEW QUESTIONS   299

Chapter 11 The Lawyers:
Judge, Prosecutor, Defense
Counsel   300

LEGAL EDUCATION   301
Langdell and Twentieth-
   Century Legal Education
Legal Education Today

**THE LEGAL
PROFESSION**   306
National Law Firms
Stratum IV Lawyers

**THE JUDGE: ROLES AND
RESPONSIBILITIES**   312

SELECTING JUDGES   313
Executive Appointment
Partisan Election
Nonpartisan Election
Merit/Missouri Plan

PROSECUTORS   319
Horizontal Prosecution
Vertical Prosecution
Mixed Prosecution

DEFENSE COUNSEL   323
Private Defense Counsel
Public Defender
Assigned Counsel
Attorney Competency

REVIEW QUESTIONS   331

Chapter 12 Plea Bargaining and
Trials   332

PLEA BARGAINING   332

**PLEA BARGAINING IS
UNJUST**   335

**PLEA BARGAINING SERVES
JUSTICE**   340

**PLEA BARGAINING: THE
PROCESS**   342

**PLEA BARGAINING: LEGAL
ISSUES**   347

JURY TRIALS   349
Jury Selection

**THE TRIAL
PROCESS**   353
Opening Statements
Prosecution's Case-in-Chief
Cross-Examination
Defendant's Case-in-Chief
Closing Arguments
Charge to the Jury
Jury Deliberations

REVIEW QUESTIONS   362

Boxes

*A Plea Bargaining Session
Selection for a Criminal Trial
   Jury, Cook County, Illinois
Impeaching Witness Credibility*

PART THREE: Reacting to Criminals 365

Chapter 13 Sentencing and Probation 366

THE OBJECTIVES OF SENTENCING 366

THEORIES OF CRIME AND SENTENCING 368
The Classical School
The Positive School

DETERMINATE SENTENCES 371

INDETERMINATE SENTENCES 373

SENTENCING GUIDELINES 374

PRESENTENCE INVESTIGATION 377

PROBATION 383
Factors in Granting Probation
Advantages and Disadvantages
Probation Supervision
The Probation Officer

REVIEW QUESTIONS 392

Boxes

Felony Sentencing Guidelines
Victim Restitution and Community Service
The Probation Officer

Chapter 14 The Question of Punishment: Jails and Prisons 394

HISTORY OF THE AMERICAN JAIL 394
The Modern American Jail
Problems of Jail Maintenance

HISTORY OF THE AMERICAN PRISON 402
The Pennsylvania System
The Auburn System
Elmira Reformatory
Prison Labor
The Big House
Prisonization
Maintaining Control

REVIEW QUESTIONS 413

Chapter 15 The Question of Punishment: Corrections and Capital Punishment 414

CORRECTIONAL INSTITUTIONS 415
Classification
Treatment

DIVISIONS, REBELLIONS, AND RIOTS 419
Attica
Riot at Attica

MODERN AMERICAN PRISONS 426
Prison Violence
Gangs
Types of Prisons
Maximum-Security
Medium-Security
Minimum-Security
Prisons for Women
Privately Owned Prisons

THE PRISON AND THE COURTS 436
Freedom of Religion
Habeas Corpus
Right of Access to the Courts
Prison Conditions
Other Prisoners' Rights

CAPITAL PUNISHMENT 440
The Arguments Pro and Con

REVIEW QUESTIONS 447

Boxes

Inmate Rules
The Correction Officer
Valley Women
Death Penalty Reversals
The Death Penalty as Deterrent

Chapter 16 Parole and Community-Based Corrections 448

THE HISTORY OF THE INDETERMINATE SENTENCE AND PAROLE 448
Elmira Reformatory

THE MEDICAL MODEL 451
Criticisms of the Medical Model

THE PAROLE BOARD 453
Parole Guidelines

PAROLE SUPERVISION 456

PAROLE VIOLATIONS 460
Parole Violation Hearings

THE ABOLITION OF PAROLE 461

INTENSIVE SUPERVISION 462

EXECUTIVE CLEMENCY 462

COMMUNITY-BASED CORRECTIONS 464
Diversion
Pretrial Release
Deferred Sentencing
Halfway Houses
Work Release

THE DEMISE OF COMMUNITY CORRECTIONS 474

REVIEW QUESTIONS 476

Boxes

The Parole Officer
The Pardon in California
Brooke House Multi-Service Center

PART FOUR: Juvenile Justice 479

Chapter 17 Juvenile Justice and the Juvenile Court 480

THE HISTORY OF JUVENILE JUSTICE 480
The Child-Savers

JUVENILE COURT 484

THE RIGHTS OF JUVENILES 487
Due Process
Standards of Evidence
Jury Trial
Double Jeopardy
Preventive Detention

THE JUVENILE JUSTICE PROCESS 491
Delinquency
Status Offenses
Neglect, Abuse, and Dependency

JUVENILE COURT PROCEDURES 494
Preliminary Hearing
Adjudicatory Hearing
Dispositional Hearing
  Delinquents
  Status Offenders
  Abused or Neglected Children
  Dependent Children

JUVENILE INSTITUTIONS 500

REVIEW QUESTIONS 503

Postscript 505

Glossary 507

References 523

Case Index 543

Author Index 545

Subject Index 549

Preface

This book is designed as a teaching tool; its purpose is to provide the instructor with a basis for presenting a course on crime and justice in the United States. It utilizes a curriculum format that has been classroom-tested for several years and is designed to provide the basics of crime and justice in a manner that facilitates classroom instruction.

Many textbooks dealing with issues of crime and justice are presented by authors with little or no practical experience in the field. The result is often a level of abstraction that fails to provide the student with a real picture of crime and justice in America. On the other hand, some textbooks are written by authors who have extensive practitioner experience, but who fail to relate the specific to the general, or to abstract theory, so that the classroom provides an educational—as opposed to a training—experience. This book blends the practical experiences of those working in the field of criminal justice with the scholarship of the criminologist; it is an approach that will interest and stimulate students.

The problems inherent in trying to define criminality, to measure crime, and to explain its causes are dealt with in *Part One*. *Part Two*, the societal reaction to crime, includes chapters on federal, state, county, and municipal law enforcement agencies, on federal and state court systems, on the role of lawyers—judges, prosecutors, defense counsel—on plea bargaining and trials. Reacting to criminals—sentencing, probation, jails, prison, parole, community-based corrections—is the topic of *Part Three*. *Part Four* deals with the issues and structures of juvenile justice.

In order to avoid the ahistorical approaches of many introductory textbooks, each substantive aspect of crime and justice is introduced with a review of its historical context. In addition, the often outdated and quite meaningless data dumped into many criminology and criminal justice textbooks have been avoided in favor of narrative. While there is a detailed discussion of the Uniform Crime Report and the National Crime Survey, the instructor and student are not burdened by pages of data listed from these reports, which only serve to "fatten up" a text. Instead, there is a simplified version of a victimization study designed for student participation; each student can complete the study in a few minutes, and the results can serve as a basis for classroom discussion. Footnotes have also been deliberately kept to a minimum—less than a dozen—in order to let the material flow more easily. If information is important, it appears in the narrative and not as a note.

Distinctive Features

1. The book is organized on a curriculum format.

2. Each chapter opens with a list of topical headings contained in the chapter, and ends with a list of key terms and with review questions that cover every salient point and can serve as a basis for ongoing discussion and as a chapter summary.

3. There is an entire chapter devoted to law enforcement agencies at the federal level. There is also a thorough discussion of legal education and the practice of law, and their impact on the system of criminal justice.

4. There is an index of case decisions referred to in the text and a glossary of terms to familiarize students with the vocabulary of criminal justice.

Acknowledgments

The author would like to thank the educators who reviewed and critiqued earlier versions of this book, and whose suggestions improved the quality of the final work: Robert G. Culbertson, Eastern Montana University; George Evans, William Rainey Harper College; and Lawrence F. Travis, University of Cincinnati.

A special acknowledgment and thanks is extended to Jon R. Waltz of Northwestern University School of Law, who reviewed the legal materials contained in the book, and who generously lent his own writings on this topic for use by the author.

Kristen Westman is thanked for her careful and patient concern with all of the myriad of editorial details that went into producing this book. Special recognition goes to Barbara Armentrout, who proved to be the most proficient copy editor this writer has ever had the pleasure to work with. The photos and cartoons that enhance the book are the result of the efforts of photo editor Stephen Forsling. Finally, special thanks go to Ronald F. Warncke, Nelson-Hall vice president, for his confidence in the author.

Ed Paschke, Purple Ritual

PART ONE

Crime, Criminals, and Criminal Justice

1 **Crime: Problems of Definition and Law**

2 **Of Crime and Criminals**

3 **How Much Crime? The Problems of Perception and Statistics**

4 **Why Crime? Theories of Causation**

5 **The System of Criminal Justice**

CHAPTER 1

Crime: Problems of Definition and Law

DEFINING CRIME

LAW AND ITS SOURCES

CIVIL LAW

CRIMINAL LAW
Objectives
  Punishment
  Deterrence
Categories of Crime

CORPUS DELICTI
Actus Reus
Mens Rea
Concurrence

CRIMINAL RESPONSIBILITY
Infancy
Insanity

AFFIRMATIVE DEFENSE
Self-Defense
Entrapment

REVIEW QUESTIONS

Boxes

The Law: Where to Find It

In this chapter we begin a journey over the landscape of crime and justice in the United States. But first we need to define the seemingly obvious—what is a crime? Crime, as we shall see, is often a matter of perspective—for example, under certain circumstances, the killing of women and children may be defined, not as a crime, but as the heroic action of "freedom fighters." Furthermore, the law which defines certain harmful behavior as criminal, defines even more harmful behavior as a civil wrong. What accounts for these differences?

DEFINING CRIME

Societal concern with the "crime problem" has an ancient history that includes divine intervention: "Thou shalt not kill!" Every recorded society has had some version of that prohibition, but nearly all also make some kind of exception to it, and the exceptions have often led to the destruction of entire populations. Thus, for ancient Hebrews the prohibition against killing did not extend to Amalekites; for Catholics during the Thirty Years' War (1618–48) the prohibition did not extend to Protestants, and vice-versa; it did not extend to Armenians under the Ottoman Empire; it did not include Jews under Nazi rule. Even a cursory review of history will cause the reader to conclude that crime and justice are not objective realities—they are human constructs that must be understood against the backdrop of time and place.

A legal dictionary (Gifis 1975: 50) defines crime as "any act which the sovereign has deemed contrary to the public good." While sufficient in a legal sense—it permits lawyers to "do their thing"—this definition is problematic. We know, for example, that throughout history a variety of religious beliefs and practices have been "deemed contrary to the public good." At various times in various places merely being a Moslem, a Jew, or a Christian was a crime. Vestiges of such "crimes" remain in nations ruled by fundamentalist religious doctrine. In 1984, for example, the Italian and Vatican embassies protested the public flogging of an Italian Roman Catholic priest in Sudan; his crime: possessing an alcoholic beverage (*Chicago Tribune*, June 4, 1984). Certainly, the treatment of religious minorities in the Soviet Union, particularly Jews, indicates that certain religious activity is "deemed contrary to the public good."

Closer to home, this definition proved quite flexible, allowing for black persons to be defined as property, and enabling Congress ("the sovereign") to enact the Fugitive Slave Act, which in 1850 made it a crime to be a "fugitive from service or labor." In our more recent past there were laws that made it a crime for a black person to sit in the front of buses or to utilize certain public facilities, and in many of these United States it was "deemed contrary to the public good," a crime, for black children to attend school with white children.

Crime can be divided into two broad categories:

1. *Mala in se*, Latin for "evil in itself," refers to crimes that by their very nature are evil, such as murder. As we have already noted, while societies may differ on what behavior actually constitutes "murder" (as opposed to self-defense or justifiable manslaughter, such as carrying out a judge's sentence of execution) every society deems murder "contrary to the public good" and prohibits it.

2. *Mala prohibita*, Latin for "wrong because it is prohibited," refers to activities that have been *defined as criminal*, not be-

Throughout history, there have been times when merely being a Moslem, a Jew, or a Christian was considered a crime. *Right,* a gas chamber door at Auschwitz–Birkenau in Poland, where as many as 4,000,000 prisoners, mostly Jews, were executed during World War II.

cause they are inherently evil, but because they violate standards of public decency or endanger the public welfare. Examples are laws governing public attire or consumption of alcoholic beverages.

While the *mala in se/mala prohibita* dichotomy can be useful, the difference between them is sometimes unclear. For example, how would laws making abortion a crime be categorized? What is clear, however, is that the acts or omissions a society defines as criminal often reflect power relationships within that society. Barbara Ann Stolz (1984) provides an example: corporate interests defeated legislation that would have made it a crime ("reckless endangerment") for businesses to engage in conduct they knew could imperil someone's life, such as selling toys contain-

1 ▪ CRIME: PROBLEMS OF DEFINITION AND LAW

ing toxic substances. A well-organized minority can also impose its own definition of crime on the majority; an example is the Eighteenth Amendment to the Constitution, which inaugurated the era of Prohibition (1920–1933). William Chambliss (1973: 10) states that Prohibition was accomplished by the political efforts of a determined segment of the American middle-class: "By effort and some good luck this class was able to impose its will on the majority of the population through rather dramatic changes in the law." The effect was indeed dramatic—large segments of the population refused to accept this minority-imposed definition of crime; and this led to rampant lawlessness and a form of organized crime heretofore unknown in the United States (see Abadinsky 1985).

Well-organized minorities occasionally succeed in imposing their definitions of crime on the larger population. During Prohibition (1920–33) many people refused to accept such a minority-held view, resulting in widespread lawlessness and large-scale organized crime.

Because there is not universal agreement on what behaviors are "contrary to the public good," we must turn for a definition of **crime** to the simple legal construct: *A crime is an intentional act or omission that violates the criminal law.*

Law and its sources

Like crimes, laws are not universal; they are not the same in all societies. The simplest definition of law is *a body of rules governing a social order;* as Lawrence Friedman (1973: 14) points out, "it does the bidding of those whose hands are on the controls," be they Democrat or Republican, Nazi or Communist. The first code of laws established in New England, the "Body of Liberties" (1641), contained criminal provisions based on the Bible (Eliot 1910); for example, "If any man after legall [*sic*] conviction shall have or worship any other god, but the lord god, he shall be put to death." The code also provided the death penalty for blasphemers, kidnappers, witches, adulterers, and homosexuals. Thus, an understanding of "law and order" requires an answer to the question, "Whose law, what order?"

In the United States law has two basic sources.

1. Statutory Law is enacted by legislative bodies such as Congress or a state legislature.

2. Case Law is derived from the courts as a result of litigation. It is based on the English tradition referred to as **common law**, utilizing the precedent established by prior cases to decide the outcome of current litigation.

Each of these sources is divided into civil and criminal law.

Civil law

Civil law provides for the redress of *private* wrongs, or **torts**, and has as its primary objective the resolution of disputes between individuals and/or organizations; government may also be a defendant or plaintiff in a civil action. Civil law aims to resolve disputes that the parties cannot peacefully work out or settle between themselves and to provide the injured party with a nonpunitive remedy, such as money damages, for the harm done.

As opposed to criminal law, civil law is not restricted to conduct that can be labeled intentionally wrongful. For example, it applies to conduct that is merely negligent (carelessness); lawsuits arising out of automobile accidents are an example. Civil law also deals with behavior that does not involve a question of "fault" or "wrongdoing"; it includes rules about permissible forms of business organization, for example, corporate law and laws relating to business partnerships.

The primary goal of civil law is compensation and reimbursement—persons are not imprisoned in civil cases. Civil law, however, can also serve to redress the harm caused by wrongful conduct, actions that range from libel to assault. The court may impose punitive (in legal terminology, *exemplary*) damages in cases of malicious and willful conduct. Thus, a criminal assault may give rise not only to a criminal prosecution, but also a civil lawsuit based on damages for personal injuries.

CRIMINAL LAW

Criminal law reflects society's interest in controlling the "wrongful" behavior of its citizens. Unlike civil laws, the criminal law is not available to individuals; it is invoked by government on behalf of all of the people. That is why criminal cases are identified as *United States v. Smith* or *State of California v. Jones*.

Because it is such a powerful mechanism—one that mobilizes the law enforcement resources of government—whenever the criminal law is invoked, a host of legal protections automatically become available to the accused person, such as the right to remain silent and the right to counsel. These rights will be discussed in chapter 5.

Objectives

The criminal law has two specific objectives, punishment and deterrence.

THE LAW: WHERE TO FIND IT

The law—federal or state, statutory or case—comprises a staggeringly large body of literature, as anyone knows who has ever visited a library in a law school or courthouse. First there are the "true" sources of law: the innumerable statutes and judicial opinions, as well as local ordinances and administrative regulations. All federal and state statutes and regulations, all municipal ordinances, and all but the most unimportant judicial opinions are published in full, officially or unofficially (that is, by a nongovernment source), in one place or another, and sometimes in several. For example, the *Federal Register* publishes federal agency regulations on a daily basis, and the *U.S. Tax Court Reports,* issued each month, contains Tax Court decisions.

Lawyers refer to published statutes, ordinances, regulations, and court opinions as *primary authority* since they constitute the law to which citizens must adhere and which government is obligated to enforce. Then there is a mass of *secondary authority* that expounds and interprets the primary sources of law: legal encyclopedias, treatises, dictionaries, law reviews and journals published by the nation's law schools, and other legal periodicals. There are also elaborate indices, digests, citators, and computer programs that aid judges and lawyers in locating relevant primary and secondary authorities.

State statutes, the enactments of state legislatures, are

Punishment

This is an ancient notion expressed as *lex talionis*—"an eye for an eye." It is the basis of such concepts as the theological concern with expiation, retribution, vengeance, and just desserts—all of which imply that one should "pay" for one's wrongful behavior. (In biblical days *lex talionis* referred to financial compensation for injuries caused—it was a concept of civil rather than criminal law.) The Eighth Amendment to the Constitution of the Unit-

> first published in volumes called *session laws* because they are prepared at the end of each legislative session. They are later printed in volumes that are arranged by subject matter and have different names in different states: *Statutes, Statutes at Large, Compiled Statutes, Consolidated Statutes, Code,* and *Revised Code.* In this chapter, for example, we frequently cite *Illinois Revised Statutes,* Chapter 38, the criminal law in Illinois. *Federal statutes,* the enactments of Congress, appear in several forms, the most convenient being the compilation authorized by Congress in 1925 and referred to as the *United States Code* (U.S.C.). There is also the *United States Code Annotated* (U.S.C.A.), which includes commentary on judicial decisions relating to the statutes contained in the code.
>
> *State court opinions,* those of the state appellate courts, are found in the *National Reporter System* which is divided into seven regional volumes, such as Atlantic or South Western, and additional volumes for New York and California.
>
> *Federal court opinions* are to be found in a series commissioned by the U.S. Supreme Court, *United States Reports.* Supreme Court decisions can also be found in several other publications, for example, *Supreme Court Reporter,* and decisions of the United States Court of Appeals can be found in the *Federal Reporter.* Occasionally federal court judges in trial courts, United States District Court, produce written opinions and these are published in the *Federal Supplement* series.

ed States prohibits cruel and unusual punishment, thus limiting punishment to fines, imprisonment, and "humane" forms of execution.

Deterrence

The purpose of deterrence is to prevent crime. It involves fear of punishment and the knowledge that each criminal act has penalties attached.

There are two types of deterrence. *Individual deterrence* refers to the offender who, once punished according to law, is less likely to offend again (**recidivate**). *General deterrence* refers to "intimidation" (Packer 1968); in other words, the law creates a risk for those who would commit a crime. The punishment inflicted on the individual offender serves to reinforce the strength of general deterrence.

Categories of Crime

The criminal law divides crime into two basic categories, misdemeanors and felonies; the difference has to do with the seriousness of the offenses, which is reflected by the penalties that are attached. Generally, a **misdemeanor** is any crime that can be punished by no more than one year of imprisonment. (Some states, such as North Carolina, have two-year maximums for misdemeanors.) A **felony** is any crime that can be punished by more than one year of imprisonment (or two years in certain states). Since each state (and the federal government) determines the penalties for each offense contained in its criminal law, a misdemeanor in one state may constitute a felony in another. In addition to these two major categories, there are also *offenses*, violations of local ordinances such as jay-walking or littering, or motor-vehicle-related violations.

Both felonies and misdemeanors are usually subdivided into grades—classes or degrees. Thus, in one state a person who takes money from another by threatening him or her with a firearm can be found guilty of a *class B* felony, armed robbery; in another state this same offense may be referred to as armed robbery, *first degree*. The difference is in the language and not the substance of the law.

We have already determined that (*a*) what constitutes a crime depends on the law; (*b*) the law is derived from two sources, statutes and court decisions; (*c*) the law is divided into the civil and the criminal; (*d*) the purposes of the criminal law are punishment and deterrence; and (*e*) criminal law differentiates between misdemeanor and felony crimes. We will now examine the conditions that must be met under our system of law in order for behavior to constitute a crime: the *corpus delicti*.

Corpus Delicti

The Latin term **corpus delicti** literally means the "body of the crime." It has nothing to do with the body of a murder victim, although proving that the alleged victim is indeed dead is one of the elements of the *corpus delicti* in a case of murder. In legal parlance it refers to the three basic elements required to constitute a criminal offense: the first *(actus reus)* is physical and objective; the second *(mens rea)* is psychological and subjective, and the third is a timely combination of the two.

Actus Reus

Literally a "guilty act," **actus reus** refers to the need to prove that a crime has actually occurred. In the criminal law it is the description of a crime; for example, according to the criminal law of Illinois, "A person commits residential burglary who knowingly and without authority enters the dwelling place of another with the intent to commit therein a felony or theft" (*Illinois*, Chapter 38: 19-3a). Thus, in order for *actus reus* to be legally present, the prosecution must prove "beyond a reasonable doubt" that the defendant entered the dwelling place of another without permission of the legal occupant for the purpose of taking property or harming the occupant. In Illinois "A person commits robbery when he takes property from the person or presence of another by the use of force or by threatening the imminent use of force" (*Illinois*, Chapter 38: 18-1a). Evidence of the display of a firearm and subsequent lifting of the victim's wallet would indicate *actus reus*.

An act of omission (as noted above in our definition of crime) can also be *actus reus*, as in the case of child neglect. According to Illinois law:

> Those who are neglected include any minor under 18 years of age whose parent or other person responsible for the minor's welfare does not provide the proper or necessary support, education, as required by law, or medical or other remedial care recognized under State law as necessary for a minor's well-being, or other care necessary for his or her well-being, including adequate food, clothing and

shelter, or who is abandoned by his or her parents or other persons responsible for the minor's welfare. (*Illinois*, Chapter 37: 702-4)

Even a *legal impossibility* can amount to *actus reus*. For example, while it is obviously impossible to murder someone who is already dead, it is a crime to solicit a person to murder another even if, unknown to the solicitor, that person is already deceased. In Illinois, "It shall not be a defense to a charge of attempt that because of a misapprehension of the circumstances it would have been impossible for the accused to commit the offense attempted" (*Illinois*, Chapter 38: 8-4b).

Mens Rea

Literally a "guilty mind," **mens rea** refers to the question of "intent," the mental state accompanying the prohibited behavior. There are four *criminal states of mind* (definitions below are from *Illinois*, Chapter 38: 4):

1. *Intentional.* "A person intends, or acts intentionally or with intent, to accomplish a result or engage in conduct described by the statute defining the offense, when his conscious objective or purpose is to accomplish that result or engage in that conduct."

2. *Knowing.* "A person knows, or acts knowingly or with knowledge of:

(a) The nature or attendant circumstances of his conduct, described by the statute defining the offense, when he is consciously aware that his conduct is of such nature or that such circumstances exist. Knowledge of a material fact includes awareness of the substantial probability that such fact exists.

(b) The result of his conduct, described by the statute defining the offense, when he is consciously aware that such result is practically certain to be caused by his conduct."

3. *Reckless.* "A person is reckless or acts recklessly, when he consciously disregards a substantial and unjustifiable risk that circumstances exist or that a result will follow, described by the statute defining that offense; and such disregard constitutes a gross deviation from the standard of care which a reasonable person would exercise in the situation."

4. *Negligent.* "A person is negligent, or acts negligently, when he fails to be aware of a substantial and unjustifiable risk that circumstances exist or a result will follow, described by the statute defining the offense; and such failure constitutes a substantial deviation from the standard of care which a reasonable person would exercise in the situation."

A person who kills another by accident has committed a crime if his or her actions were *reckless* or sufficiently *negligent,* for example, while driving under the influence of alcohol or drugs (vehicular homicide), even if he or she had no intention of harming the victim.

Concurrence

For the *corpus delicti* to be present there must be concurrence of act and intent, a timely relationship between *actus reus* and *mens rea*. For example, if two or more persons plan a bank robbery, they are involved in conspiratorial behavior. The law, however, usually requires an overt action in furtherance of the conspiracy, such as the purchase of a revolver, for the behavior to constitute the crime of *conspiracy.* If considerable time elapses (two years, three years, . . . ten years) between the planning and the purchase, concurrence is not evident. If, several years after the planning, however, a revolver is purchased and the participants meet again to review their plan, there is concurrence and, thus, criminal conspiracy. There is an exception to the requirement of concurrence. Certain offenses carry strict or *absolute liability,* and mental state is not an issue—for example, vehicular homicide or crimes that are *mala prohibita,* such as violations of controlled-substances statutes.

CRIMINAL RESPONSIBILITY

The absence of *mens rea* may be the result of impaired or diminished mental capacity. Traditionally, the law has recognized certain persons as not having responsibility for their behavior, or as being ineligible for trial or punishment for their criminal acts. The Bible (I Samuel 21:11-16) refers to an incident in which David, in the court of the Philistine king, was recognized as the slayer of Goliath. In order to escape the king's wrath, David feigned madness. Since ancient times, madness and the age of an offender have been reasons for mitigating or annulling culpability and punishment. In our modern criminal codes the terms for these reasons are *infancy* and *insanity*.

Infancy

Infancy, or not having yet reached the age of legal majority, prevents a person from being convicted of a crime. In Illinois, for example, "No person shall be convicted of any offense unless he had attained his 13th birthday at the time the offense was committed" (*Illinois*, Chapter 38: 6-1). The response to juvenile offenses, those committed by persons beyond infancy but short of adulthood (generally ages thirteen to seventeen) will be discussed in chapter 17.

Insanity

Insanity may refer to a lack of criminal responsibility—"not guilty by reason of insanity"—or to the inability (incompetence) to stand trial. A person who is ruled legally sane at the time he or she committed an offense, but who is later found to be incompetent, is still criminally responsible, although he or she cannot be tried until competent to stand trial. This requirement of competence is based on a concern for the defendant's ability to understand the nature of the charges and to be able to cooperate with defense counsel in preparation of his or her own defense. The **insanity defense**, on the other hand, is based upon the proposition that the accused did not have the capacity to understand the nature of the criminal act or to understand that the act was wrong.

Illinois criminal law states, "A person is not criminally responsible for conduct if at the time of such conduct, as a result of mental disease or mental defect, he lacks substantial capacity to appreciate the criminality of his conduct or to conform his conduct to the requirements of law" (*Illinois*, Chapter 38: 6-2a). This is known as the **substantial capacity test** for criminal responsibility, and in Illinois and many other states it has replaced the so-called **M'Naghten Rule**. Daniel M'Naghten attempted to assassinate British Prime Minister Robert Peel, but mistakenly killed Peel's secretary, Edward Drummond. The defense counsel claimed that his client was insane and, therefore, should not be held accountable for his actions. In rendering a decision in this case a British court established the M'Naghten Rule:

> Every man is presumed to be sane, and ... to establish a defense on the grounds of insanity, it must be clearly proved that, at the time of the committing of the act, the party accused was labouring under such a defect of reason from disease of the mind, as not to know the nature and quality of the act he was doing; or if he did know it, that he did not know he was doing what was wrong. (8 Eng. Rep. 718, 1843)

The M'Naghten Rule requires evidence of mental defect resulting in an *inability to distinguish between right and wrong.* This restrictive legal concept was replaced in some jurisdictions by the **Durham Rule:** the accused is not criminally responsible if his or her unlawful act was the product of a mental disease or defect. Some states use a combination of the M'Naghten Rule and the **irresistible impulse test.** This permits the accused to use the insanity defense if a mental disease has rendered the defendant incapable of *choosing* between right and wrong, even though he or she can recognize the difference. Sue Titus Reid (1985: 128) notes that this is sometimes referred to as **temporary insanity** and "means that a defendant cannot control his or her behavior and conform to the law."

Once a defendant has presented evidence raising doubt as to his or her sanity, the government (represented by the prosecutor) has the burden of proving the defendant's sanity "beyond a reasonable doubt." The government can ask the judge (in legal jargon, "motion the court") to order the defendant to submit to a psychiatric examination. However, any statements made by the defendant during the course of the examination cannot be admitted into evidence at any subsequent trial on the issue of the defendant's guilt. If a defendant ultimately decides to forego the insanity defense before trial, any statements made to the government psychiatrist cannot be used by the government for any reason. In 1984, a revised federal criminal code shifted the burden of proof to the defense, and some states are following the federal lead in this area.

It should be noted that *insanity* is a legal, not a medical, term. Psychiatrists refer to conditions of diminished mental capacity: psychosis, mental illness, or retardation. When they testify as expert witnesses in cases involving the insanity defense, psychi-

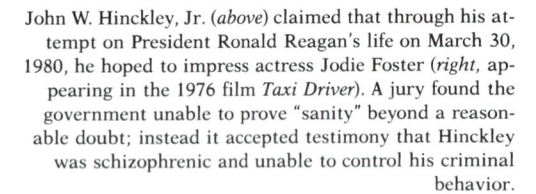

John W. Hinckley, Jr. (*above*) claimed that through his attempt on President Ronald Reagan's life on March 30, 1980, he hoped to impress actress Jodie Foster (*right*, appearing in the 1976 film *Taxi Driver*). A jury found the government unable to prove "sanity" beyond a reasonable doubt; instead it accepted testimony that Hinckley was schizophrenic and unable to control his criminal behavior.

atrists (who are medical doctors) and psychologists (who have Ph.D.s but are not medically trained) provide evidence and/or professional opinions about the possible influence of mental conditions on the capacity of the accused to form criminal intent—*mens rea*.

It is the jury (or judge if no jury is being used) that decides the question of criminal responsibility. If the jury (or judge) decides that the defendant is not guilty by reason of insanity, the defendant is committed to a mental institution where he or she remains under the jurisdiction of the court until institutional authorities certify that the defendant is not mentally ill. At that time the subject is returned to court for a subsequent disposition.

Because a successful insanity defense spares criminal offenders from prison, it has always been controversial. The attempted assassination of President Ronald Reagan by John W. Hinckley, Jr. on March 30, 1981, has added fuel to that controversy. Hinckley claimed that his action—which wounded the president, his press secretary, James Brady, a Secret Service agent, and a policeman—was an attempt to impress a movie actress, Jodie Foster, whom he had never met. His defense attorney argued that Hinckley had been affected by the film *Taxi Driver*, in which Miss Foster appeared; it was about a disturbed taxi driver whose violent fantasies caused him to arm himself and stalk a political candidate. As is typical of these types of cases, defense psychiatrists contradicted prosecution psychiatrists. The jury, twelve lay persons, was left with the task of determining which doctors were to be believed. In the end they accepted expert testimony that indicated Hinckley suffered from a serious form of schizophrenia that caused him to be unable to appreciate his actions or control his criminal behavior—an "irresistible impulse." The government was unable to prove sanity beyond a reasonable doubt, at least to the satisfaction of the jury.

In response to the public reaction over persons who commit crimes and are subsequently saved from imprisonment by reason of insanity, a number of states have added the verdict **guilty but insane**. In Illinois, "a person who, at the time of the commission of a criminal offense, was not insane but was suffering from a mental illness, is not relieved of criminal responsibility for his conduct and may be found 'guilty but mentally ill'" (*Illinois*, Chapter 38: 6-2c). Typically, psychiatrists offer opinions as to whether or not the defendant was sane at the time of the crime. In 1984, Congress passed the Insanity Defense Reform Act which restricts the testimony of expert witnesses to presenting and explaining their diagnoses; the jury determines whether the defendant was sane in federal cases.

Another controversial aspect of criminal insanity is the inability of psychiatrists and psychologists to predict "dangerousness." It is beyond current medical knowledge and competence to determine if any particular person, despite a history of stability and sanity, or a history of mental illness, will commit future acts of criminal violence. As we know, most violent criminals do not have any history of mental illness, and most persons with a history of mental illness do not commit criminal acts, violent or otherwise.

Affirmative Defense

In addition to infancy and insanity, there are other legal excuses that can result in a finding of not guilty; in legal terminology they constitute an **affirmative defense**. In such instances, the burden of proof rests with the defendant, who must present arguments and evidence to legally justify or excuse the behavior. The two most important categories of affirmative defense are *self-defense* and *entrapment*.

Self-Defense

Self-defense refers to the historic right to protect one's person or members of one's family, and, to a lesser degree, one's property, from harm by another person. The criminal law of Illinois provides:

> A person is justified in the use of force against another when and to the extent that he reasonably believes that such conduct is necessary to defend himself or another against such other's imminent use of unlawful force....
>
> With respect to the protection of a dwelling: A person is justified in the use of force against another when and to the extent that he believes that such conduct is necessary to prevent or terminate such other's unlawful entry into or attack upon a dwelling....
>
> With respect to the defense of other property: A person is justified in the use of force against another when and to the extent that he reasonably believes that such conduct is necessary to prevent or terminate such other's trespass on or other tortuous or criminal interference with either real property (other than a dwelling) or personal property, lawfully in his possession or in the possession of another who is a member of his immediate family household or of a person whose property he has a legal duty to protect....
>
> *(Illinois*, Chapter 38: 7, 1-3)

In any event, a person "is justified in the use of force which is intended or likely to cause death or great bodily harm [such as the use of a firearm] only if he reasonably believes that such force is necessary to prevent imminent death or great bodily harm to himself or another, or the commission of a forcible felony."

The affirmative defense of self-defense has three components:

1. The defendant must be free from fault—must not in any way provoke the attack.
2. There must be no safe or convenient way to avoid the use of force by escape or retreat.
3. There must be a reasonable belief of impending peril.

Entrapment

A defense of **entrapment** requires the defendant to prove that the government used trickery to get him or her to commit a crime. In Illinois:

> A person is not guilty of an offense if his conduct is incited or induced by a public officer or employee, or agent of either, for the purpose of obtaining evidence for the prosecution of such person. However, this Section is inapplicable if a public officer or employee, or agent of either, merely affords to such person the opportunity or facility for committing an offense in furtherance of a criminal purpose which such person has originated. (*Illinois*, Chapter 38: 7-12)

In raising this defense, the defendant must show that but for the behavior of government agents, he or she would not have committed the offense. In determining whether or not there was entrapment, the judge or jury must decide if the defendant was *predisposed* to commit the offense, as weighed against the conduct of the government (agent). The most celebrated case in which this defense was raised was Abscam, in which an agent of the Federal Bureau of Investigation pretended to be a wealthy Arab seeking favors from government officials.

In this chapter we looked at the problems inherent in defining crime, the sources and categories of law, and the concept of criminal responsibility. In chapter 2 we will examine specific types of crime and the activities of the criminals they define.

KEY TERMS

mala in se
mala prohibita
crime
statutory law
case law
common law
civil law
torts
criminal law
recidivate
misdemeanor
felony
corpus delicti
actus reus

mens rea
infancy
insanity
insanity defense
substantial capacity test
M'Naghten Rule
Durham Rule
irresistible impulse test
temporary insanity
guilty but insane
affirmative defense
self-defense
entrapment

REVIEW QUESTIONS

1. Defining crime as "any act contrary to the public good" is problematic. Why?
2. What is meant by crimes that are *mala in se?* Provide examples.
3. What is meant by crimes that are *mala prohibita?* Provide examples.
4. What is the danger of criminal legislation that lacks sufficient popular support? Provide an example.
5. What is the difference between *statutory law* and *case law?*
6. There are a number of differences between *civil law* and *criminal law.* What are they?
7. What are the two major objectives of the criminal law?
8. What is the difference between a felony and a misdemeanor?
9. What are the three elements of the *corpus delicti?*
10. What is meant by a "legal impossibility"?
11. What are the four criminal states of mind?
12. What factors can legally mitigate or limit "criminal responsibility"?
13. What is the M'Naghten Rule?
14. What is meant by the verdict, "guilty but insane"?
15. If the defendant raises the insanity defense, what must the government (prosecutor) prove beyond a reasonable doubt?

CHAPTER 2

Of Crime and Criminals

VIOLENT PERSONAL CRIME

OCCASIONAL CRIME

FRAUD

EMPLOYEE CRIME

CAREER CRIME

POLITICAL CRIME

CORPORATE CRIME, OR "CRIME IN THE SUITES"

PROFESSIONAL CRIME

VICTIMLESS CRIME

ORGANIZED CRIME

REVIEW QUESTIONS

It is 8 P.M. on a summer evening in an exclusive residential area. In the home of a wealthy publisher, servants prepare to serve dinner to the man and his wife. Several miles away, two men wearing dark clothing drive into a shopping center and park their car. Without being noticed, they slip into the wooded area adjacent to the parking lot and begin trotting through the woods. The publisher and his wife are enjoying hors d'oeuvres and cocktails. The two men quickly scale the wall surrounding the estate and silently move toward the main house, using trees and bushes to shield their approach. The main course is being served as the publisher and his wife discuss the day's events. Upstairs, in the master bedroom, one of the men in dark clothing has put his tools aside and is placing jewelry into a pillowcase, which he lowers to his partner who has been outside watching the dining room in case someone left to go upstairs. Before dessert is served, the two men leave the estate as quickly and quietly as they had entered. As the publisher and his wife rise to leave the table, the two men reenter the parking lot. Their tools have been buried in the woods, and the jewels are in a secluded spot near the road from which they will be retrieved later and brought to a *fence* (a dealer in stolen merchandise). As they enter their car, neither of the men has anything that will connect him to the theft at the estate (Abadinsky 1983).

The following day, in a less affluent section of a large city, two young men force open the door of a ground-floor apartment. They enter quickly and begin rifling through closets and dressers. With a portable color television, several suits and some bottles of whiskey, the two make their exit, just as a police cruiser pulls to the curb.

Similar crimes—residential burglary—but contrasting criminals. The first set of burglars ("jewel thieves") represent a criminal elite, persons at the pinnacle of the "world of crime"; they are often referred to as "professionals." Their less successful counterparts represent the vast majority of criminals whose skills are minimal and whose arrests are numerous.

In this chapter we will examine a variety of crime categories and the criminals who inhabit them. These are not *legal* categories; they do not necessarily reflect divisions normally appearing in the criminal law. Instead, they group criminals according to characteristics that they share, such as how much of one's life is devoted to criminal activity and the level of one's skill as a criminal.

In examining these characteristics and categories we assume the role of criminologist; **criminology** is a field within the social sciences devoted to the study of crime and criminals. Criminologists attempt to explain the legal process, why certain behavior is labeled "criminal," why persons engage in law-violative behavior, and the societal reaction—criminal justice—to persons who violate the law.

One of the characteristics that criminologists use to differentiate criminals is the role of criminal activity in the offender's life: *commitment*. Is the offender a full-time criminal, a person for whom crime is the primary means of support; an offender who spends much of his or her waking time planning or carrying out criminal activity? Or is the offender a part-time criminal, a person for whom crime provides a financial supplement to regular or irregular employment? The offender may be an **opportunistic criminal**, a person who violates the law when opportunity—"temptation"—presents itself, but does not plan or seek out criminal opportunities. For the **situational criminal**, particular momentary circumstances trigger criminal behavior; these include excessive alcohol, personal disputes, and peer pressure, or

Criminals may be categorized according to their level of skill. *Below,* a guard from the Marmottan Museum in Paris points to an empty space where—until October 27, 1985—Claude Monet's *Impression, Sunrise* (*right*) hung. On that day five armed men posing as tourists bought museum tickets. Shortly after entering, they pulled revolvers on seven guards and a stunned group of visitors and made a bank-robber style getaway with nine Impressionist masterpieces. The heist, which took a total of five minutes, represented a loss of $12.5 million. None of the paintings was insured.

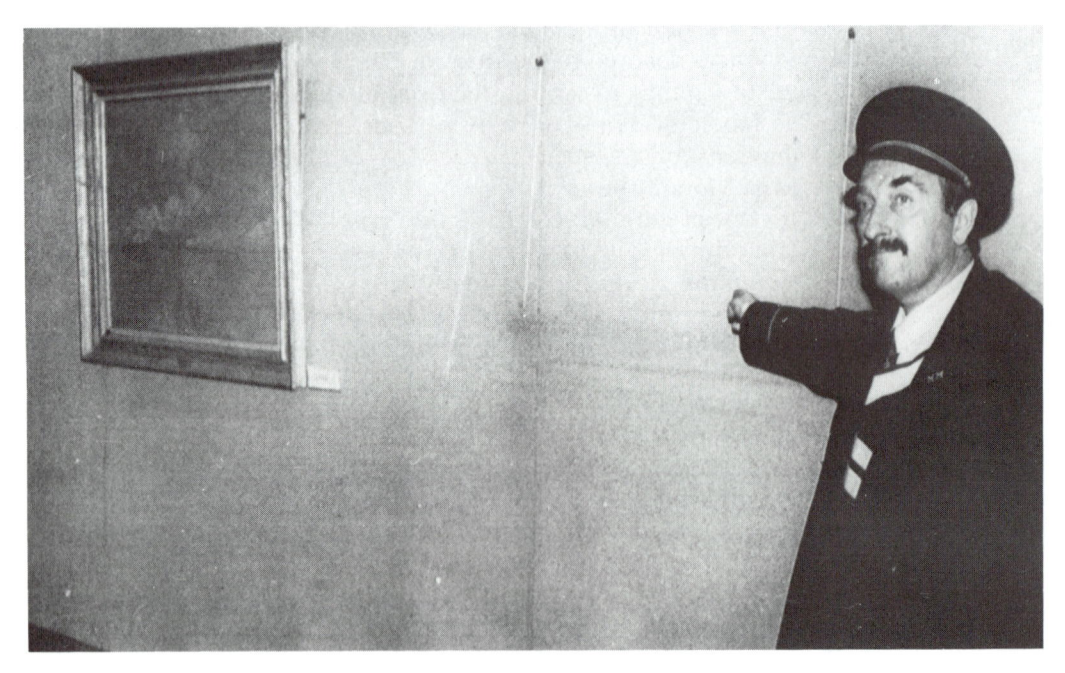

a need to conform to the deviant activities of associates (such as a street gang).

A second characteristic that can be useful in distinguishing one type of criminal from another is the *level of skill* with which the law-violative behavior is accomplished. One way to measure skill is by the amount of income derived from the criminal activity (which precludes certain types of crime such as rape, from this type of comparison). Skill is also evaluated subjectively—for example, do the crimes appear to be well-planned and executed? It is also measured by comparing the amount of income derived from the criminal activity with the amount of time the offender spends in prison.

The sequence in this chapter begins with criminals for whom skill is not a factor, persons whose criminal behavior is devoid of an economic motivation. It ends with persons whose entire lifestyle involves crime and criminals; persons whose activities are skilled and well-organized. In between these two extremes we will examine criminals with varying degrees of criminal commitment and skill.

VIOLENT PERSONAL CRIME

Although **violent personal crimes**—murder and assault—are those toward which society has the strongest reaction, Marshall Clinard and Richard Quinney (1967) state that the offenders do not consider themselves criminals—to them, a criminal is someone who *steals*. The assaults and homicides committed by criminals in this category are without an economic motivation. The offenders typically do not have serious criminal histories and commit the offense because of "circumstances"; they are situational offenders. The "crime of passion" (for example, a husband who murders an unfaithful wife or girlfriend) is part of this category of crime. Clinard and Quinney (1967:22) include rapists in this category, although they note that these offenders "are reported by some to have a fairly extensive criminal record for other offenses."

Personal violence is an unfortunate tradition in the United States. In urban America, violent personal crime is typically committed by young working-class males whose social milieu accepts the use of violence for resolving personal disputes. There

Two of the most celebrated murder cases in recent history involved "situational" offenders with no previous criminal record. In 1979 Jeffrey MacDonald (*above right*, with his lawyer Bernard Segal), a Princeton-educated Green Beret Army physician, was found guilty of the brutal slaying of his pregnant wife and two young daughters. In 1981 Jean Harris (*below right*), headmistress of a prestigious girls' school in suburban Washington, D.C., was convicted in the fatal shooting of Scarsdale Diet author Dr. Herman Tarnower, with whom Harris had been romantically linked. Harris was sentenced to a fifteen-year-to-life term; MacDonald is currently serving three consecutive life sentences.

is an emphasis on macho behavior which, when mixed with alcohol and sexual adventures, can lead to physical confrontations that sometimes end in serious injury and police intervention. Much violent personal crime in urban areas is associated with the activities of street gangs. The highest rate of homicide, however, has traditionally been in the South, and the widespread ownership of firearms offers only a partial explanation; family feuds (such as the legendary one between the Hatfields and the McCoys), vigilantes, and lynchings are all part of Southern history.

Included in this class of criminality is **domestic violence**, a problem that has received increasing attention during the 1980s. It includes assaults against spouses and girlfriends and the abuse of children by adults who are related by blood, marriage, or cohabitation. In more serious cases, child abuse results in infanticide. Unfortunately, domestic violence has a long history in the United States, where women were once considered chattel, the property of their husbands to whom they owed honor and obedience, and where children have traditionally been denied many basic rights.

Occasional crime

For offenders who commit **occasional crime**, it is "incidental to their way of life" (Clinard and Quinney 1967: 90). Persons in this category include juvenile and adult shoplifters, who can hardly be said to have a "criminal career," since they shoplift only occasionally; it is not the way they make their living and they do not play criminal roles. Their thefts are often rationalized: "everybody takes a little something," or "that big store can afford it," or "they deserve it for charging such high prices."

Persons in this category are opportunistic criminals, that is, they commit crimes when either opportunity or need, or both, is present. Occasional criminals will often hold conventional jobs but, due to marginal economic conditions, drinking, or gambling, may be motivated to take advantage of a criminal opportunity. These persons are not committed to a "life of crime"; they are intermittent or even one-time offenders. Their crimes range from petty theft to (less frequently) armed robbery.

FRAUD

Fraud is most often committed against the government; this takes the form of tax evasion and deceit in filing tax returns. Fraudulent returns have been estimated to cost about $100 billion annually, and another $100-billion loss in tax revenue is ascribed to the "underground economy," or business—legal and illegal—that is conducted in cash. Fraud against the government may be perpetrated by medical and other practitioners in submitting Medicare and Medicaid bills, by persons who secure government benefits fraudulently, by students who default on government loans, or by veterans who receive benefits for schooling and who fail to attend school.

Second to the government as victims of fraud are insurance companies. Some people falsely report that their cars have been stolen when in reality they may have been sold to a "chop shop"; others report thefts and burglaries that have never occurred, or claim more than what was actually stolen; and property is "torched" (arson) to collect insurance.

Consumer fraud is also common. It has plagued the automobile repair and home improvement industries, where, too frequently, customers have been charged for repairs that were either not needed or not performed. Recently, exposés have centered on unneeded surgery or treatment by physicians and related practitioners. Also included in this category are an assortment of miscellaneous frauds involving the sale of land (uninhabitable property offered as prime real estate), medical quacks offering cures for everything from baldness to cancer, charity frauds, and a variety of pills and devices for dealing with maladies ranging from obesity to small breasts. A number of years ago, this author was almost the victim of a fraudulent car sale—the odometer had been turned back and a used car was offered as a new vehicle. In 1976, legislation was enacted that makes tampering with odometers a federal crime.

EMPLOYEE CRIME

This category refers to crimes committed by employees against their employers. The employee takes advantage of a position of trust to enrich himself or herself at the expense of the employer. The simplest form of **employee crime** is minor pilferage, ranging from pencils and staplers to more expensive items such as typewriters and personal computers. Employees may rationalize this form of crime as being too petty to be important, or as being justified by the low wages they are receiving for their labors. An employer may tolerate this type of activity as a way of keeping employees contented without having to substantially improve working conditions. Along a thin line dividing lawful activity from criminal behavior are various forms of "gratuities" from vendors to employees who influence company purchases. These can range from routine Christmas gifts to systematic kickbacks based on a fixed percentage of the purchase price.

Embezzlement involves the systematic appropriation of the financial resources of an employer by an employee, usually over a long period of time. It requires extensive knowledge of the financial aspects of the business and, thus, is usually a crime perpetrated by an employee with some control over the financial records of a business—a bookkeeper or bank teller, for example. The routine use of computers has added another dimension to employee theft. The persons in charge of these devices are often well-educated and their knowledge of computers usually exceeds that of their employer or fellow employees. This makes computer-based embezzlement quite difficult to detect—and if detected, difficult to prove for purposes of prosecution. In general, the penalties for embezzlement are minimal as employers are often eager to avoid the publicity involved in prosecution or are more interested in recovering some of their loss than in having the perpetrator imprisoned.

CAREER CRIME

Career criminals commit a variety of serious crimes. They may be partial to burglary or armed robbery, or they may show a mixed pattern of criminal activity. In either event, crime is a *career* for persons in this category; they commit crimes for economic benefit, and the fruits of their criminal activity represent at least a substantial portion of their income. Marshall Clinard and Richard Quinney (1967: 320) point out that criminal activity is a way of life for the career criminal.

A career in crime involves a life organization of roles built around criminal activities, which includes identification with crime, a conception of the self as a criminal, and extensive association with other criminals. In career crime there is a progression in crime which includes the acquisition of more complex techniques, more frequent offenses, and, ultimately, dependence on crime as a partial or sole means of livelihood.

These persons usually act in concert with others having similar, that is, very limited, criminal skills. As opposed to those of the professional criminal, the activities of these career criminals are often poorly planned and executed, and their crimes may involve unplanned violence. Those who acquire more complex techniques may pass into the ranks of the "professional." Career criminals display a great deal of personal animosity toward police officers; they frequently view themselves as "victims" of society and see criminality as a result of shortcomings of society—unequal educational and employment opportunity, prejudice, and so on. Because these criminals are arrested frequently, they spend much of their lives incarcerated.

There is a widespread belief that a relatively small core of career criminals is responsible for most crime. Mark Moore and his colleagues (1984: 1) argue that "persuasive evidence has been compiled indicating that serious criminal offending is highly concentrated: 5 percent of criminal offenders account for half of the serious violent crime in the United States." Moreover, they state, each of the worst one percent commits more than fifty serious crimes per year. This belief in a small "hard core" of career criminals has generated a great deal of research, often federally funded, designed to separate the occasional criminal from the career criminal. The implications of this strategy will be discussed later in chapters dealing with theories of crime and the response to criminal behavior.

Political crime

In the first chapter we examined the problem of defining crime and the reality that crime is what those in power say it is—*power defines crime*. Thus, what is an outstanding achievement in capitalism may be defined as a capital crime (for example, "profiteering") under a communist regime. **Political crime** has as its purpose a challenge to existing definitions of crime or the more far-reaching goal of reordering the legal system. Political and economic systems are defined by the legal system. Political crime may seek to overthrow existing power relationships for the purpose of reordering a legal, and thus, political and economic, system. Clinard and Quinney (1967: 178) state that "violating behaviors are political in that the violators are attempting to express their opinions and beliefs about the proper structure of the state, with a possible attempt to bring about change." The law-violative behavior of the political criminal is for a "higher" purpose; it is not simply self-serving, and the political criminal does not view himself or herself as a "criminal." (For a discussion of the problem of defining political crime, see Schafer 1974.)

The difference between a "hero" and a "criminal" may be political, depending upon the definer's perspective. If the American Revolution had failed, George Washington and Thomas Jefferson would have been political criminals instead of patriots and presidents. Perhaps the only way to determine if a law-violative act constitutes a conventional or political crime is to test the perpetrator's motivation: is it personal or ideological? Political crime is crime based on an *ideology*. Using this test, a wide variety of criminal behavior becomes political, including the law-violative activities of civil rights activists who challenged segregation, and the crimes committed by racists such as the Ku Klux Klan.

During the 1960s and 1970s the public was exposed to the criminal exploits of groups such as the Symbionese Liberation Army (of Patty Hearst fame) and the Weathermen. In the 1980s organizations at the other end of the political spectrum grabbed headlines: The Order, White American Bastion, Bruder Schweigen, Church of Jesus Christ Christian, Posse Comitatus, and the Aryan Nations. Members of these right-wing groups have been accused of committing armed robberies and murdering law enforcement officers as part of their effort to overthrow the United States government and to destroy Jews and blacks.

Julian Roebuck and Stanley Weeber (1978) also term crimes committed by the government, such as those disclosed during the Watergate hearings, "political crimes." Another example is crimes committed by the FBI in an effort to neutralize or defeat domestic organizations that J. Edgar Hoover deemed subversive. One target of these efforts in the 1960s was the Reverend Martin Luther King, Jr., and his Southern Christian Leadership Conference (see Garrow 1981).

Corporate Crime, or "Crime in the Suites"

Edwin Sutherland noted back in 1940 that although **corporate crime** (he used the term "white collar," which included embezzlement) is rather extensive, punishment is quite rare. Irwin Ross (1980) reported that since 1970, of the over 1,000 major corporations in the United States, 11 percent have been involved in major delinquencies such as antitrust violations and bribery (this does not include crimes they might commit in foreign countries). Marshall Clinard and his associates (1979: xix) point out:

> A single case of corporation law violation may involve millions and even billions of losses. The injuries caused by product defects or impure or dangerous drugs can involve thousands of persons in a single case. For example, in one case, the electrical price-fixing conspiracy of the 1960s [involving such corporations as General Electric and Westinghouse], losses amounted to over $2 billion, a sum far greater than the total losses from the 3 million burglaries in any given year. [See R. Smith, 1961a, 1961b, for a discussion of this case.] At the same time, the average loss from a larceny-theft is $165 and from a burglary $422, and the persons who commit these offenses may receive sentences of as much as five to ten years, or even longer. For the crimes committed by large corporations the sole punishment often consists of warnings, consent orders, or comparatively small fines.

The harmful activities of corporations may not even be defined as "criminal," but may instead constitute only a civil wrong. For example, the Eleventh U.S. Circuit Court of Appeals overturned the fraud convictions of five Texas oilmen involved in a Florida fuel-oil pricing conspiracy that occurred in the mid-1970s. As a result of the scheme customers of the Florida Power Corporation paid as much as $7.5 million in overcharges. The Circuit Court ruled that although the actions may have been "against the public interest," they were *not illegal* (*Chicago Tribune,* December 17, 1981: sec. 2: 3). In 1980, a number of corporations were accused of being part of an eighteen-year nationwide conspiracy to fix the prices of corrugated containers and sheets, a multibillion-dollar scheme that defrauded American consumers. Thirty-four manufacturers merely settled out of court (*New York Times*, June 17, 1980: D1).

Between 1971 and 1974, the A. H. Robbins Company marketed the Dalkon Shield as a safe and effective contraceptive. The inventor produced false and misleading test results, while company representatives disregarded mounting evidence of serious injuries and continued to market the product. Company officials destroyed documents and misled physicians and federal officials who inquired about the Dalkon Shield and the mounting reports of injuries. At least 110,000 women became pregnant while using the device, most of them miscarried, and 32 died as a result of septic abortions and pelvic inflammation. Thousands of women suffered pelvic infections that left many of them infertile, while deformed children were born to those who left the shield in during pregnancy. Not a single person was imprisoned as a result of these criminal actions (Mintz 1986).

Sutherland's (1949) study of white-collar crime examined the illegal activities of 70 of the 200 largest nonfinancial corporations. He found, as subsequent researchers have also discovered, that corporate crime usually goes either unpunished or underpunished. Marshall Clinard and Peter Yeager (1980) note that fines are usually minimal and imprisonment quite rare. For example, between 1890 and 1970, in only three cases did businessmen actually go to jail for antitrust violations.

There are important reasons for the lack of vigorous prosecution of corporate criminality. First, corporate crime is, for the most part, invisible. That is, the victims—us—do not usually realize that we have been victimized. While the victim of a burglar or a robber is only too aware of having been victimized, the victim of corporate criminality is usually oblivious to the crime. The second reason is the cost of prosecuting corporate crime. David Simon and Stanley Eitzen (1984) state that the laxness with which antitrust laws are enforced is in part attributable to the meager resources devoted to such enforcement. The investigation of corporate crime requires highly sophisticated investigators, and prosecution can cost millions of dollars. Third, corporate defendants are invariably represented by the best legal services that money can buy, so convictions are rare, and when a corporate executive is convicted, the judge is often reluctant to send an older, white, well-educated "pillar of the community" to the prison jungle.

White Collar Crime and Punishment

Crime	Sentence
Eli Lilly and Company executives plead guilty to failing to report the dangers of an arthritis drug which was linked to twenty-six deaths.	$25,000 fine
Smithkline Beckman Corporation executives plead guilty to withholding information about adverse effects of a product that has been linked to the death of thirty-six persons.	$100,000 fine
The multimillion-dollar swindles of a Houston banker shook the Texas state government and forced the	

PROFESSIONAL CRIME

Edwin Sutherland (1937/1972) pointed out that among criminals a few distinguish themselves by a high degree of skill and success; he called them "professionals." Sutherland compared these criminals to professionals in legitimate occupations such as bricklayers and lawyers. He found that they take pride in their skills and status among other criminals. **Professional criminals** are contemptuous of the "amateur" in crime, and they have their own argot (language) and connections with an underworld that can provide assistance in the event of an arrest. As opposed to the often-violent career criminal, the use of violence by professional criminals is quite rare. Sutherland was particularly interested in the method by which a criminal becomes a "professional," the learning process that he called *differential association* (to be discussed in chapter 4). In short, professional criminals learn their trade and its norms from criminals who have already achieved the "professional" status. Sutherland (1937/1972: 207) also observed that "the group defines its own membership. A person who is received into the group and recognized as a professional thief is a professional thief."

Crime	Sentence
resignation of the head of the Criminal Division of the Justice Department.	3 years probation and a $5,000 fine
A wealthy drug manufacturer diluted an antidote for poisoned children with a worthless look-alike substance.	One year probation and a $10,000 fine
The portfolio manager of two mutual funds bilked clients out of nearly $10 million.	6 months in prison and 5 years probation.
An executive vice-president of American Airlines accepted $200,000 in kickbacks from contractors.	6 months in prison and 2 years probation.

What types of crime do "professionals" commit? Sutherland's study centered on the life history of a "booster" (professional shoplifter). David Maurer (1940) studied the "confidence man"—an elite criminal whose technical skills are quite impressive (as portrayed in the popular motion picture, *The Sting*). Neal Shover (1971) looked at professional burglars; William Chambliss (1972) followed the career of a "box-man" (safecracker); James Inciardi (1977) studied the "cannon" (pickpocket); Peter Letkemann (1973) studied safecrackers and bank robbers; and this author (Abadinsky 1983) looked at the career of a jewel thief. These studies reveal that professional crime, which has its origins in earlier centuries, continues in our society as older criminals pass on criminal skills and norms to younger protégés.

Professional criminals are a particular problem for law enforcement. They are quite mobile, moving from one area to another across jurisdictional boundaries, traveling throughout the country in search of victims. Their skills and connections (which enable them to "fix" encounters with law enforcement authorities) make arrests and convictions relatively rare, while the size of their "takes" belies the fact that professionals are few in number. The Pennsylvania Crime Commission (1980), for example, estimates that gangs of professional criminals are responsible for only about ten percent of the incidents of burglary in that state, but they account for about 90 percent of the dollar value of the objects stolen.

Mafia hitman Charley (Jack Nicholson) met his match in free-lance killer Irene (Kathleen Turner) in the 1985 film *Prizzi's Honor*. Here the enforcers dispose of a victim who had the bad luck to witness an assignment being carried out.

VICTIMLESS CRIME

The term **victimless crime** usually refers to unlawful acts that are *mala prohibita*, such as drugs, gambling, and prostitution. This does not mean that such crimes do not have a victim; however, the drug addict, gambler, or prostitute usually does not view himself or herself as a "victim." Moreover, such persons, as opposed to victims of *mala-in-se* crimes such as burglary and robbery, do not report their victimization to the police. Thus, "victimless crimes" are actually *crimes without complainants*. This, of course, makes law enforcement efforts against such activities quite problematic; legislators and judges are reluctant to impose severe penalties on **consensual crimes** such as gambling and prostitution, and the police must initiate their own investigations—find crime—since they do not have a complainant. Investigating victimless crime involves the use of informants and undercover operatives, and enforcement of laws against vice has been associated with a great deal of corruption. The reasons for this will be discussed in later chapters on policing.

There has been support for decriminalizing gambling, drug abuse, and sex for pay, to reduce illegal markets and/or raise tax revenue. The English provide some basis for comparison. In England heroin addicts who are registered with the government are able to receive controlled doses under medical auspices, and certain forms of prostitution (not streetwalking) are permitted. England also permits all forms of gambling under government license. As a result, England has been able to avoid the problem of large-scale criminal syndicates which have plagued the United States.

In the United States, a few states have decriminalized possession of small amounts of marijuana; one state (Nevada) permits prostitution (licensed bordellos on a county-option basis); and a majority of states permit some form of gambling such as horse or dog racing, lotteries and gambling casinos. As opposed to the English approach, however, in the United States advertising and entertainment are used to encourage people to gamble. This is not permitted in England, where gambling is considered harmful; it is tolerated as the lesser of two evils—outlawing it would create a criminal black market—but it is not used as an "easy" source of revenues for public officials looking to avoid tax increases. In the United States, victimless crime has been associated with organized crime.

ORGANIZED CRIME

It is the time of Prohibition. At the Lexington Hotel, the president of the Chicago Crime Commission, Frank Loesch, has an appointment with the most powerful person in that city, a former saloon bouncer from Brooklyn named Alfonse Capone. After the meeting Loesch explains:

> I found him in an office-like room with a half dozen of his non-English-speaking guards standing with their hands on their guns.... I got down to business with Capone immediately. I was concerned about the election that was then about to be held for State's Attorney and a number of other important city and county offices.
>
> He asked me what I wanted, and I told him about my concern over the coming election. This arch criminal had the effrontery to tell me that he would give me a square deal if I did not ask too much of him. I then said to him: "Now look here, Capone, will you help me by keeping your damned cutthroats and hoodlums of the North Side from interfering with the polling booths?"
>
> "Sure," he said, "I'll give them the word." . . . It turned out to be the squarest and most successful election day in forty years. There was not one complaint, not one election fraud and not one threat of trouble all day. (Dobyns 1932: 2-3)

In the days before Prohibition (which lasted from 1920 to 1933), organized criminality centered primarily on vice—gambling and prostitution—and was closely tied to corrupt urban political machines. Prohibition resulted in a new form of organized criminality that spawned criminal syndicates and unleashed an unsurpassed level of criminal violence in the United States. Irish, Jewish, Italian, and, to a lesser extent, criminals from other ethnic groups, took advantage of Prohibition and used the money they made from the sale of illegal liquor to break into the middle and upper strata of society, just as earlier immigrants known as "robber barons" had done during the eighteenth and nineteenth centuries. When Prohibition was repealed, the more powerful of the criminal syndicates, which had been enriching themselves on bootleg whiskey, had to turn to other sources of income. The results are still with us: loansharking, labor and business racketeering, drug trafficking, extortion and the more traditional business of **organized crime**—gambling and prostitution. Some organized crime groups provide the

Before Prohibition, organized crime was closely tied to corrupt urban political machines, here satirized by cartoonist Thomas Nast.

THE POLITICAL PROBLEM.

THE LAW-MAKER AND LAW-BREAKER—ONE AND INSEPARABLE.

PART ONE   CRIME, CRIMINALS, AND CRIMINAL JUSTICE

The 1929 St. Valentine's Day Massacre ranks as one of the bloodiest episodes in the history of organized crime. The killings, which occurred in a garage on Chicago's north side, were the result of a gangland feud between Al Capone and George "Bugs" Moran. Police never solved the case.

"goods and services," while others merely use their private "police forces" to impose extortionate demands on illegitimate (and sometimes legitimate) entrepreneurs.

More has probably been written about organized crime than about any other type of crime, and books and motion pictures such as *The Godfather* reveal the public's fascination with the subject. Organized crime is often misunderstood and surrounded with myths, however. Adding to the problem is the difficulty of defining the phenomenon; even the federal Organized Crime Control Act of 1970 fails to define organized crime. This author (Abadinsky 1985) has described organized crime in terms of certain attributes:

1. *No ideology.* An organized crime group does not have political goals, nor is it motivated by ideological concerns. If involved in politics, the goal is to secure protection or immunity for its illegal activities.

2. *Hierarchy.* An organized crime group has three or more permanent positions of authority—ranks. The positions are continuous, and their authority does not depend on who happens to be occupying the position at any given time.

3. *Limited/Exclusive Membership.* An organized crime group has limitations on who is qualified to become a member. These may be based on ethnic background, kinship, race, criminal record, or other considerations. Those who meet basic qualifications need a sponsor, usually a ranking member, and must prove their qualification for membership by their behavior, such as a willingness to commit certain criminal acts, to follow orders, and to maintain secrets.

4. *Perpetuity.* An organized crime group constitutes an ongoing criminal conspiracy designed to persist through time, beyond the participation and lives of the current members.

5. *Specialization/Division of Labor.* An organized crime group will have certain functional positions filled by qualified members, such as *enforcer*, who, as the title implies, carries out difficult assignments involving the use of violence. The enforcer does not act independently; he receives his assignments directly or indirectly from the group's hierarchy, and he will employ members or trusted nonmember associates to carry out difficult executions.

6. *Monopoly.* An organized crime group strives for hegemony over a particular geographic area or a particular legitimate or illegitimate "industry," or both. Monopoly is secured and maintained by violence or the threat of violence, or by corrupt relationships with law enforcement officials, or both.

7. *Rules/Regulations.* An organized crime group, like most legitimate organizations, has a set of explicit rules and regulations by which members are required to abide. As opposed to most legitimate private organizations, organized crime enforces these rules by violence.

There are several groups in the United States that have been identified as having all or most of the attributes of organized crime:

1. Italian-American crime "families" (the Mafia),
2. outlaw motorcycle gangs such as Hells Angels,
3. black criminal gangs,
4. Latin-American crime "families,"
5. Asian criminal gangs, and
6. independent white criminal gangs.

Organized crime can be conceived of as one stage along a continuum dating back to the earliest days of the history of our republic. The precursors include early American adventurers who cheated and killed native Americans, and chartered pirates (privateers) who plundered the high seas. During the War of 1812 and later during the Civil War, profiteers accumulated fortunes by selling inferior, if not defective, goods to the North and the South, while soldiers and civilians suffered and died. The range wars in the West, the frauds, bribery, violence, and monopolistic practices of the "robber barons" are also part of the context in which we must understand modern forms of organized crime in the United States. (See, for example, Josephson 1962; Lloyd 1963; Myers 1936; O'Connor 1962; Swanberg 1959.)

Organized crime is difficult for law enforcement agencies to deal with effectively. Local police and sheriff's departments do not usually have the resources to devote to organized crime. Investigations in this area require highly trained personnel and extraordinary manpower deployments. The investigations are time-consuming and detract from the ability of local departments to respond to other pressing demands for service. Although most police and sheriff's departments of any substantial size have vice and drug enforcement units, extensive investigations and prosecutions of organized crime groups are usually on a federal level. (For a full discussion of organized crime, see Abadinsky 1985.)

"I'm very touched, fellows."

While some of the crimes discussed in this chapter are measured by official statistics, for example robbery and burglary, other crimes are omitted, for example, prostitution and corporate crime. Why? We will examine this question in chapter 3, as we attempt to answer the question, How much crime?

KEY TERMS

criminology
opportunistic criminal
situational criminal
violent personal crimes
domestic violence
occasional crime
fraud
employee crime

embezzlement
career criminals
political crime
corporate crime
professional criminals
victimless crime
consensual crime
organized crime

REVIEW QUESTIONS

1. What are the two kinds of characteristics that can be used to differentiate criminals?
2. What differentiates the occasional criminal from the career criminal?
3. What are the most prevalent forms of fraud?
4. Why is "political crime" difficult to define?
5. What test can be employed to differentiate political crime from conventional crime?
6. Why does corporate crime often go unprosecuted or unpunished?
7. What distinguishes a professional criminal from other criminals?
8. Why are professional criminals a serious law enforcement problem?
9. Why is the term "victimless crime" misleading?
10. Why is victimless crime a particularly difficult law enforcement problem?
11. What are the seven attributes of organized crime?

CHAPTER 3

How Much Crime? The Problems of Perception and Statistics

CRIME: A MATTER OF PERCEPTION

UNIFORM CRIME REPORTS
Problems with the UCR

NATIONAL CRIME SURVEY
Findings of the NCS
Problems with the NCS

HOW MUCH CRIME?

REVIEW QUESTIONS

Boxes

*Politics and Crime Statistics
Victimization Study*

Statistics don't lie! But they can be manipulated, distorted, and even suppressed. In the final analysis, statistics are only as valid as their interpretation. For instance, while it is simple to determine that an eight-ounce glass contains only four ounces of wine, how can we determine if it is *half full* or *half empty*?

CRIME: A MATTER OF PERCEPTION

Our perception of crime is mediated through newspapers and television—how many persons do you know who spend time studying crime statistics? What is the effect of media coverage of crime? The following scenario provides one example.

It had been a relatively uneventful week and the city's newspapers were having difficulty filling columns with exciting copy—the kind that helps to sell newspapers. As a result, routine

---

Some material in this chapter is adapted from publications of the Illinois Criminal Justice Information Authority.

crime stories, in ready abundance in any urban area, were moved from the back pages toward the front. As the news drought continued, crime-story headings grew bolder—"Assault Victim a Grandmother"—and newspaper sales increased. This triggered an increase in the number of crime stories, particularly those concerning crimes against the elderly, which seemed to generate a great deal of reader interest.

Television news programs began to pick up on the interest in crimes against the elderly, and stories about crimes committed against senior citizens became a regular feature on the evening news. Even after the drought of exciting national and local news ended, interest in crimes against the elderly remained quite high and the level of coverage remained unabated. There were feature stories and documentary specials. Public meetings were held to discuss ways of dealing with the upsurge in the victimization of senior citizens, and the news media gave these meetings extensive coverage.

It did not take long for public officials to take notice of the increase in crimes against the elderly. New legislation was enacted increasing penalties for crimes if the victim was over age sixty-five. Police agencies responded by forming special units to deal with crimes against the elderly, and federal funding was made available to deal with senior citizen victimization.

This scenario is not fiction; it occurred while the author was living in New York City. Because of that city's influence on the national media, particularly television, crime against senior citizens became a national issue. Ironically, this occurred at a time when crimes against the elderly were going down and had been declining for the past five years. At least that's what the statistics revealed. (See Fishman 1978 for research into this "crime wave." See Surette 1984 for a general discussion of the media's influence on criminal justice.)

If government is to respond to the problem of crime in a timely and appropriate manner, obviously it is necessary to know the answer to our question, How much crime? The amount of crime, however, can be affected by governmental decisions about law enforcement. For example, an increase in police officers to fight street crime will have the secondary result of an increase in crime statistics.

The amount of crime can also be influenced by what the government defines as criminal: for example, outlawing the private

The New York Times

FRIDAY, NOVEMBER 12, 1976

General News
Classified Advertising

L+ B1

A group of elderly Bronx residents on a bench in Poe Park. Fear of crime is driving many of the elderly out of the parks. "Everybody's scared, everybody's afraid," one resident commented.

Many Elderly in the Bronx Spend Their Lives in Terror of Crime

By JUDY KLEMESRUD

Clara Engelmann recently moved a bed into the foyer of her Bronx apartment. Every night, she crawls into it fully dressed. Her old black coat rests on a chair nearby, and she plans to grab it and run out the front door at the first sound of robbers jimmying her bedroom window.

They've done it three times before, and that's why she refuses to sleep in her bedroom.

"I don't know what I'd do if those Frankenstein monsters came in the front door at night," the 64-year-old woman said the other day, her head shaking with anger. "They did that once before, too, during the day, while I was away. They sawed out all the locks on the door. I don't know how they did it, the wood is like iron."

Mrs. Engelmann, who lives alone in a still ornate apartment building on the Grand Concourse, is one of 258,000 people older than 60 who live in the Bronx. Many of them have been victims of crime at least once, not to mention two or even three times.

And some of them are getting killed in the process. So far this year, 20 elderly persons have been murdered in the Bronx. Although

Continued on Page B6

A group of elderly people leaving the Mount Eden Center on Morris Avenue. Most of those who frequent the center prefer to travel in groups.

Clara Engelmann pointing to the front door of her Grand Concourse apartment. She sleeps in the foyer, with her coat nearby, to enable her to escape quickly in the event of a robbery.

For One Couple, Tarnished Golden Years

The Golden Years. It is a term that causes many elderly Bronx residents to smile sardonically or snort derisively. "You simply cannot enjoy life knowing that whenever you go out for a walk, someone may be following you," said Mae Cohen, who is 68 years old.

Mrs. Cohen, who lives with her 80-year-old husband, Samuel, in a $67-a-month walk-up on the Grand Concourse near 171st Street, suffered a broken arm two years ago when a young man pushed her down the sidewalk near her home. Strangely, he did not take her purse. Four months ago, Mr. Cohen was mugged on the second floor of the apartment building by two young men who escaped with $35.

The Cohens spend most of their daytime hours at a center for the elderly, where Mrs. Cohen loves to sing and dance. The couple used to spend additional hours sitting in the sun in a nearby park, but gave this up because youths began throwing bottles and stones at them.

Unlike many elderly Bronx residents whose children have virtually abandoned them, the Cohens have been invited by their son to live with him and his family in Plainview, L.I. But so far, the Cohens have refused.

They do, however, occasionally take the train to Plainview to visit their son and his family. They have to if they want to see their grandchildren because the son refuses to drive his family into the old neighborhood. The last time he did, someone stole the battery from his car.

"They were so frightened," Mrs. Cohen recalled.

Will the Cohens ever change their minds about leaving their crime-ridden Bronx neighborhood for the relative tranquility of Long Island?

"That's no life for us," Mrs. Cohen said firmly. "Our friends are around here and this is our life, and we sing and dance and keep active at the senior center. The center gives us a reason to exist. There is no center in Plainview, L.I., and if we moved there, it would be like sitting and waiting for death."

Media coverage has helped to make crime a national issue.

ownership of handguns except under certain circumstances. In New York, relatively few private citizens have the privilege of lawfully possessing a handgun. Thus, persons are arrested in New York for behavior—possessing a handgun—that would not constitute a crime in states such as North Carolina. When the Supreme Court overturned laws prohibiting abortion, it reduced the amount of crime, since medical doctors performing abortions were no longer considered criminals. The definition of a crime also determines the point at which private behavior becomes a public concern, for example, the point at which parental discipline becomes the crime of child abuse.

Finally, definition determines what is counted as a crime. For example, if a single burglar commits five burglaries in a particular year, we have a statistic to report: crime of burglary = 5. But, if twenty-nine major electric equipment manufacturers victimize millions of Americans for more than a decade, as in the case discussed in chapter 2, what statistic is reported? In fact, statistics on corporate crime are not collected by the government. Our definition of crime is influenced by perceptions; perceptions determine the crime data we collect; and crime data reinforce our perceptions. Prior to 1930 no state published statewide data on crime, and only one state published statistics on arrests—our response to crime was based solely on perceptions. Despite the advent of crime statistics, the response to crime remains based on perceptions, but these perceptions are now influenced by statistics.

UNIFORM CRIME REPORTS

Uniform Crime Reports (UCR) were begun as a voluntary program in 1930 by the International Association of Chiefs of Police. In that same year Congress assigned to the FBI responsibility for serving as a national clearinghouse for crime statistics. The FBI continues to produce the major UCR document, an annual report entitled *Crime in the United States*. More than 15,000 law enforcement agencies covering 97 percent of the U.S. population file UCR data. Most states require police agencies to submit crime data to a state agency that collects it for the UCR (and its own statistical purposes).

The report divides offenses into two major categories. **Part I**

> ## Politics and Crime Statistics
>
> **Crime is not only a serious social problem, it is an important political issue. Given the nature of crime statistics, this can lead to some unusual situations for politicians.**
>
> Running on a pledge to "do something about crime," the insurgent candidate for mayor swept past his opponent at the polls. Soon after being sworn in, the new mayor held a press conference to introduce his chief of police, a veteran police executive with a master's degree in public administration. Additional police officers were added to the force, and administrative changes effected by the new chief put more officers on the street. Police substations were established throughout the city to provide easier citizen access to police services. In-service training was upgraded and officers were professional and polite when dealing with civilians. A community-relations campaign and the increased police presence encouraged people to report crimes. The chief encouraged his officers to engage in aggressive patrolling; vehicle and pedestrian stops increased, and there was a corresponding increase in the number of arrests made by the police.
>
> The chief made special efforts in minority neighborhoods

offenses (also known as **index crimes**) are those that are most likely to be reported by victims or witnesses, that occur frequently, and that are serious by nature or as a result of their frequency of occurrence. Part I offenses are ranked in order of seriousness. There are four violent index crimes and four property index crimes. Index murder does not include attempted murder, but each of the other seven categories includes attempts.

    1. Criminal Homicide is the causing of the death of another person without legal justification or excuse. It includes:
- a. Murder and nonnegligent manslaughter (which means there is some mitigation, e.g., a "crime of passion"; it is not punishable by execution)

> where, under the previous administration, there had been numerous complaints about the behavior of the police, ranging from discourtesy and indifference to outright brutality. Improved community relations increased the number of crimes reported to the police in these neighborhoods; citizen confidence in the police had been restored.
>
> An article in a police journal highlighted the achievements of the chief, and the mayor was delighted with his choice. He smiled as he sat at his city hall desk reviewing the police budget for the next fiscal year. Suddenly an aide rushed in with the morning newspaper and the mayor stared at the startling headline, "City Crime Up 20 Percent!"
>
> **It is ironic that an improvement in policing can lead to a statistical increase in crime, and that the rate of crime can be reduced by poor police–community relations, a reduction in the number of officers on the street, poor police supervision, and discouraging citizen reports of crime by discourtesy or disinterest or by locating police stations in inaccessible places. What does all this add up to? Obviously, we must be skeptical of any conclusions based upon crime data, and we must challenge any self-serving statements by public officials based upon such data.**

    b. Manslaughter by negligence

2. Forcible Rape is sexual intercourse or attempted sexual intercourse with a female against her will by force or threat of force. It includes:
    a. Rape by force
    b. Attempted rape by force

3. Robbery is the unlawful taking or attempted taking of property that is in the immediate possession of another, by force or the threat of force, which includes:
    a. Using a firearm
    b. Using a knife or cutting instrument
    c. Using other dangerous instrument
    d. Strongarm robbery ("mugging")

4. Aggravated Assault is the unlawful intentional causing of serious bodily injury with or without a deadly weapon, or unlawful intentional attempting or threatening of serious injury or death with a deadly or dangerous weapon. This category includes attempted murder. It includes:

    a. Using a firearm
    b. Using a knife or cutting instrument
    c. Using other dangerous weapon
    d. Using hands, fist, feet, etc., causing aggravated injury

5. Burglary is the unlawful entry of any fixed structure, vehicle or vessel used for regular residence, industry or business, with or without force, with intent to commit a felony or larceny. It includes:

    a. Forcible entry
    b. Unlawful entry (no force)
    c. Attempted forcible entry

6. Larceny-Theft is the unlawful taking, carrying, leading, or riding away by stealth, of property, other than a motor vehicle, from the possession or constructive (that is, legal, rather than physical) possession of another, including attempts. It includes:

    a. Pocket picking
    b. Purse snatching
    c. Shoplifting
    d. Thefts from motor vehicles
    e. Theft of motor vehicle parts and accessories
    f. Theft of bicycles
    g. Theft from buildings
    h. Theft from coin-operated device or machine
    i. All other larceny

7. Motor-Vehicle Theft is the unlawful taking, or attempted taking, of a self-propelled road vehicle owned by another, with the intent to deprive the owner of it permanently or temporarily. Such vehicles include:

    a. Automobiles
    b. Trucks and buses
    c. Other motor vehicles

8. Arson is the burning or attempted burning of property with or without intent to defraud. (Arson was added to Part I of the UCR in 1979 by order of Congress, a gesture expressing concern over the apparent increase in arson.)

A single incident often involves more than one crime. For example, a robbery may include aggravated battery or a murder may also involve a rape or robbery. To standardize the counting of incidents, the UCR utilizes the **hierarchy rule**, according to which only the most serious crime committed in a single incident is counted. (An incident is a "single operation" in which all of the offenses occurred within the same time period and location.) For example, if in the course of a robbery the victim is killed trying to resist, only the murder is included in the index.

There are three exceptions to the hierarchy rule:

1. If an arson occurs in conjunction with an index crime, for example, murder, both offenses are counted.

2. In cases where several units of a complex, such as an apartment or office building, are burglarized, only one burglary per building is counted. However, when multiple motor vehicles are stolen in one operation, such as from a car dealership, one theft per vehicle is counted. In cases where a motor vehicle is stolen and items are taken from the vehicle, the motor vehicle theft, being the more serious crime, is counted.

3. The index counts one offense for each victim of a murder, rape, or aggravated assault. Thus, if three people are murdered in one incident, three index crimes are counted. If two persons are beaten and raped in the same incident, two rapes are counted. However, if more than one of these three crimes occurs in the same incident, and more than one person is victimized, only the most serious offense is counted. For example, if one person is murdered and another is raped in the same incident, only the murder is counted. For robbery, burglary, theft, and arson one offense is counted for each distinct incident. For example, if a store is robbed and money is taken from the cash register and from each of ten customers, only one robbery is counted.

A crime may become known to the police in several ways. It may be reported by the victim or by a citizen witness; it may be witnessed by the police; or it may be reported by an institution, such as a hospital notifying the police of a battered child. Once a crime comes to the attention of the police, several decisions must be made. The police must determine if a crime actually occurred and, if so, what specific crime was committed. The offense reported by the police is not necessarily the offense reported by the victim. For example, a victim flags down a police car, saying "I was robbed." However, the police determine that the crime actually involved someone entering the victim's unoccupied residence and stealing various items, with the victim discovering the ransacked home later. The police would count this offense as a burglary known to the police, rather than a robbery as the victim incorrectly reported.

It is not uncommon for citizens to report to the police what they believe to be a crime, only to discover later that no crime really occurred. For example, a person's lawnmower breaks and he decides to borrow his neighbor's. The neighbor is not at home, but the garage is unlocked. The man lets himself in and borrows the neighbor's mower. When the owner returns home and parks her car in the garage, she notices her mower is missing. She calls the police, who make a report. The next day the neighbor returns the mower. In this case, no crime actually occurred. The incident will be "unfounded."

In some situations, the decision to record an incident as unfounded may be subjective. For example:

1. The police respond to a burglar alarm at a factory warehouse and determine that the alarm had simply malfunctioned and that no burglary or attempted burglary had occurred.
2. Two patrons become intoxicated in a bar and begin to argue. The argument intensifies, and the pair exchange threats of violence. The manager of the bar calls the police to remove the men from the premises.

In the first incident, the police determined that no crime actually occurred. In the second incident, both men committed the crime of assault (threatened bodily harm). The police must determine if there was really any intent to carry out the threats, or if the men were simply being verbally abusive while drunk. In some jurisdictions, an assault known to the police might be reported. In others, no crime would be reported; the incident would be listed in police records as a "disturbance call."

Statistics on **Part II offenses** are based on the number of *arrests* recorded by law enforcement agencies rather than the complaints received by these agencies. Part II offenses do not meet the test of frequency of occurrence or seriousness, or they may be "victimless." They are as follows:

1. Simple assault
2. Forgery and counterfeiting

3. Fraud
4. Embezzlement
5. Buying, receiving, or possessing stolen property
6. Vandalism
7. Weapons (carrying, possessing, etc.)
8. Prostitution and commercialized sex
9. Sex offenses (other than forcible rape and prostitution)
10. Drug-abuse violations:
    a. Opiates (e.g., heroin) or cocaine
    b. Marijuana
    c. Synthetic or manufactured drugs
    d. Other dangerous nonnarcotic drugs
11. Gambling:
    a. Bookmaking
    b. Numbers and lottery
    c. All other gambling
12. Offenses against family and children
13. Driving under the influence of alcohol or drugs
14. Liquor law violations
15. Drunkenness
16. Disorderly conduct
17. Vagrancy
18. All other offenses (except traffic)
19. Suspicion (since this is not an offense, it is excluded from the total)
20. Curfew and loitering violations
21. Runaways (a juvenile "status offense" discussed in chapter 17)

There is one category of crime that is conspicuous by its absence: *corporate crime*—such as price-fixing, discharging hazardous waste, or producing unsafe products. There is some difference of opinion over the reason for this omission. These activities are difficult to detect or may only constitute a civil harm, not a crime. However, some persons argue that the government is not interested in crimes committed by the rich and powerful—the ruling economic and political elite.

The Uniform Crime Report program does not require reporting of offense data for Part II crimes, and they are not subject to the hierarchy rule. For example, if the police stopped someone for drunken driving and found drugs and a handgun in the car, three offenses would be counted. If an incident involves both

Part I and Part II crimes, the hierarchy rule applies to the index crimes only. For example, if an offender kidnaps someone at gunpoint, then robs and kills the victim, this incident would be counted as one murder (index crime), one kidnapping (Part II), and one possession of weapon–firearm (Part II). The index crime robbery would not be counted because of the hierarchy rule.

Before we examine the weaknesses of UCR statistics, it should be noted that two index crimes, motor vehicle theft and criminal homicide, have a high degree of data reliability. Motor vehicles are usually insured against theft, but an insurance company will not honor any theft claim unless a report has been filed with the police. This means that the vast majority of motor vehicle thefts are reported. This does not mean, however, that data on motor-vehicle theft present no UCR reporting problems. It is estimated that between 10 and 15 percent of reported vehicle thefts are fraudulent; they are "stolen" in collusion with the owner to defraud an insurance company. In a 1984 "sting" operation by the police and the FBI, a fake "chop shop" was set up in Brooklyn, New York. (A chop shop dismantles wrecks or stolen vehicles to sell salvageable parts.) In a six-month period the shop received 142 vehicles from owners who then reported their vehicles stolen to collect insurance money—and the shop turned away more business than it accepted (*Chicago Tribune*, December 18, 1984: 6).

Data on criminal homicides also have a high degree of reliability because every death in the United States requires a death certificate that states the cause of death, signed by a medical doctor. Suspected homicides (which include suicides) must be reported to the police and/or medical examiner or coroner. This is not to suggest that there are no problems with UCR data on criminal homicide. Investigations of medical examiner's offices have revealed numerous mistakes. For example, in one New York City case "it was discovered by accident that the severed head of an unidentified woman believed to have drowned actually contained a bullet" (Grunson 1983:E6). In 1985 *The New York Times* published four front-page articles (January 27, 28, 29, 30) on problems with the city's medical examiner's office, which was accused of producing misleading autopsy findings, many involving people who died while in police custody. The office was described as understaffed and using outmoded equipment, and it was generally regarded as unreliable by the law enforcement community. In 1985 Chicago detectives audited 800 death investigations of the Cook County medical examiner's office. As a result, six cases were reclassified as either murder or involuntary manslaughter; important evidence had been ignored by the medical examiner's office. (*Chicago Tribune*, February 11, 1985: 14). And, of course, the bodies of some murder victims—for instance, Jimmy Hoffa—are never found and thus do not appear in the murder category of the UCR index.

Problems with the UCR

There are many troubling aspects to UCR data, and it is important to emphasize that the UCR does not answer the question, How much crime? The statistics about index (or Part I) crimes are based on reports from a victim or witness who acts as a complainant, that is, who brings the crime to the attention of the police; in relatively few instances is the original complainant a police officer. This raises the specter of crimes that are not reported and thus not included in the UCR statistics. Surveys reveal a number of reasons why victims fail to report crimes to the police.

1. Rape victims often feel a sense of shame or degradation and wish to avoid discussing the crime with police officers. They may fear reprisals or view the matter as private, particularly if they knew their assailant—a family friend or even a relative, for example.

2. Some assault victims consider the matter to be private rather than criminal—an argument that turns into a fist fight, for example.

3. Victims of robbery, burglary, and larceny often feel that the crime is not worth reporting either because the amount lost was small or because they believe that the police are not in a position to do anything about it.

4. An unknown number of victims "take the law into their own hands" and rely on "private justice" rather than the criminal justice system.

Another problem with UCR data is that any change in reporting patterns can dramatically change the figures. For example, publicity and programs dealing with the crime of rape can increase the number of victims who report this crime to the police. But the increase in rape may only be statistical rather than actual.

A third problem with UCR data, which has been resolved, had to do with the census figures used to compute the **crime rate**. The rate of crime as reported by the UCR is the number of index crimes per 100,000 persons per year. The equation used is:

$$\frac{\text{number of reported crimes}}{\text{total United States population}} \times 100{,}000 = \text{crime rate}$$

From the mid-1930s until 1957 the FBI used census-year figures as the base U.S. population for determining the crime rate. However, a census is taken only once every ten years. The population increases steadily during each decade, but this fact was not reflected in the figures used by the FBI. The result was a "crime wave" that mysteriously ended at the end of every decade. The FBI now uses more relevant interim census estimates for the denominator in determining the crime rate.

A change in UCR definitions can also change the crime rate. For example, in 1973, Florida experienced a "crime wave" of larceny—a doubling of larceny cases known to the police. The cause was a change in the way the UCR recorded the offense. Until 1973, "theft" had been a larceny of over $50 and appeared in Part I, and "larceny" under $50 had appeared in Part II, which is not used for determining the crime rate. In 1973 the two categories were merged to form the "larceny-theft" category of Part I, raising Florida's index crime rate from 101,221 in 1972 to 234,263 in 1973 (Brantingham and Brantingham 1984).

Problems with UCR data can also result from changes in the way local law enforcement agencies record complaints of crime. In 1950, the New York City Police Department changed its crime-recording procedures; the previous system had vastly underreported crime. The result was a massive increase in the number of robberies, aggravated assaults, and burglaries. The underreporting of crime by police departments has been a perennial problem. For many years Chicago boasted of having one of the nation's lowest crime rates among big cities. Knowledgeable police officials realized that this was the result of a policy known as "killing crime." In 1982, Pam Zekman, an investigative reporter for the CBS-TV affiliate in Chicago, revealed that the police department had a policy of suppressing reports of crime by systematically "unfounding" them. As noted above, every police department has some "unfounded" complaints. For more than twenty years, however, Chicago had an extraordinary

The case of "subway vigilante" Bernhard Goetz (*left*) offers a well-publicized instance of an individual who executed his own form of private justice. On December 22, 1984, the thirty-seven-year-old electronics technician shot four youths who allegedly tried to rob him on the IRT subway train in Manhattan. Goetz claimed he only shot in self-defense; his case soon became a *cause célèbre*, generating considerable controversy over the right of people to defend themselves against criminals. One grand jury freed Goetz; a second indicted him on attempted-murder and assault charges. At this writing, Goetz was set to stand trial in the fall, 1986.

number of crimes listed as "unfounded"—fourteen times more than other city police departments.

Anne Schneider (1981: 39) summarizes problems with the UCR that led to the development of an alternate system to help answer the question, How much crime? She notes that these problems

> include the fact that official crime reports contain no record of the "dark figure of crime" resulting from victims who do not report the offenses. In addition, case studies of many police departments indicate that some proportion of the crimes that are reported by victims are not recorded as crime events. There is some documentation indicating that police departments may, at times, systematically "downclassify" crimes [for example, attempted rape may be reclassified as simple assault] in order to reduce the overall crime index, which includes only the more serious offenses.

NATIONAL CRIME SURVEY

The alternate system involves **victimization studies** and is known as the **National Crime Survey (NCS)**. Instead of waiting for victims to report crime (as the UCR does), the NCS seeks out crime victims (persons and commercial establishments), conducting interviews as does the census bureau. Indeed, it is the United States Bureau of the Census that conducts the victimization surveys for the Department of Justice (Bureau of Justice Statistics).

The NCS utilizes the **panel survey method** to collect data: a representative sample of households is drawn, and members of the households in the sample are interviewed seven times at six-month intervals; this is called a "panel" survey because the same people are interviewed repeatedly (each set of interviews is called a "wave"). Contact with a sample household is initially established by the personal visit of an interviewer from the Census Bureau who lists each household member and interviews all available respondents. The remaining interviews are conducted in person or by telephone. The NCS questionnaire (Form NCS-1) and crime incident report (Form NCS-2) are used to elicit information on the relevant crimes committed against the household as a whole (e.g., burglary) and against any of its members age

National Crime Survey Crime Categories

Sector and Type of Crime

<u>Personal sector</u>   (Total population age 12 and over)
- Crimes of violence
    - Rape
        - Completed rape
        - Attempted rape
    - Robbery
        - Robbery with injury
            - From serious assault
            - From minor assault
        - Robbery without injury
    - Assault
        - Aggravated assault
            - With injury
            - Attempted assault with weapon
        - Simple assault
            - With injury
            - Attempted assault without weapon
- Crimes of theft
    - Personal larceny with contact
        - Purse snatching
            - Completed purse snatching
            - Attempted purse snatching
        - Pocket picking
    - Personal larceny without contact

<u>Household sector</u>   (Total number of households)
- Burglary
    - Forcible entry
    - Unlawful entry without force
    - Attempted forcible entry
- Household larceny
    - Less than $50
    - $50 or more
    - Amount not available
    - Attempted larceny
- Motor vehicle theft
    - Completed theft
    - Attempted theft

twelve and over. In addition to basic screening questions such as the number of persons in the household over twelve years old and family income, there is a series of questions about crime. A sample victimization study (with slight modifications by the author) is included here.

Findings of the NCS

Victimization studies have been conducted by the Census Bureau since 1972. What information have they provided? The most interesting revelation has been the high number of crimes not reported to the police. In every category except one, motor vehicle theft, more than 50 percent of the crimes reported to the census bureau interviewers were not reported to the police.

The NCS uses households as the unit of analysis "because the entire household is affected when an individual is the victim of a crime; by the injury, the economic loss, the inconvenience, and the feeling of vulnerability." (Rand 1981: 2). The NCS has found that almost one-third of the households in the United States are touched by crime every year, mostly by larceny (theft).

The NCS has also made some interesting discoveries about the victims of crime:

- Men are more often victimized by personal crimes than women, except for the crime of rape (the NCS includes homosexual as well as heterosexual rape; the UCR only includes rape against females).
- In every category of crime, with one exception, the elderly have substantially lower victimization rates than do younger people. The exception is purse snatching and pocket picking, for which the rates for the elderly are about the same as for the rest of the population.
- Blacks are relatively more frequently victims of violence than whites.
- Black households are more likely to be victims of burglary than white households.
- Hispanics generally have higher rates of victimization for household burglary and larceny and for most crimes of violence than do non-Hispanics.
- Families with low incomes are more likely to be victims of burglary while, in general, the higher the income, the more

Victimization Study

The following questions refer only to the last six (6) months, between _____, 19_____ and _____, 19_____.

1. Did anyone break into or somehow illegally get into your apartment/home/garage or another building on your property?
   No_____ Yes_____ How many times?_____

2. Other than the incident(s) just mentioned, did you find a door jimmied, a lock forced, or any other signs of an attempted break in?
   No_____ Yes_____ How many times?_____

3. Was anything at all stolen that is kept outside your home, or happened to be left out, such as a bicycle, a garden hose, or lawn furniture? (Do not include any incidents already mentioned.)
   No_____ Yes_____ How many times?_____

4. Did anyone take something belonging to you or to any member of your household, from a place where you or they were temporarily staying, such as a friend's or relative's home, a hotel or motel, or a vacation home? (Do not include any incident already mentioned.)
   No_____ Yes_____ How many times?_____

5. Did anyone steal, try to steal, or use without your permission a motor vehicle (car, truck, motorcycle, etc.) owned by you or any other member of your household?
   No_____ Yes_____ How many times?_____

6. Did anyone steal or try to steal parts attached to any motor vehicle owned by you or any member of your household, such as battery, hubcaps, tape-deck, etc.?
   No_____ Yes_____ How many times?_____

7. Did you have your pocket picked/purse picked or snatched?

    No_____ Yes_____ How many times?_____

8. Did anyone take something else directly from you by using force, such as by a stickup, mugging or threat?

    No_____ Yes_____ How many times?_____

9. Did anyone try to rob you by using force or threatening to harm you? (Do not include any incidents already mentioned.)

    No_____ Yes_____ How many times?_____

10. Did anyone beat you up, attack you or hit you with something such as a rock or bottle? (Do not include any incident already mentioned.)

    No_____ Yes_____ How many times?_____

11. Were you knifed, shot at, or attacked with some other weapon by anyone at all? (Do not include any incident already mentioned.)

    No_____ Yes_____ How many times?_____

12. Did anyone threaten to beat you up or threaten you with a knife, gun, or some other weapon, not including telephone threats? (Do not include any incident already mentioned.)

    No_____ Yes_____ How many times?_____

13. Did anyone try to attack you in some other way? (Do not include any incident already mentioned.)

    No_____ Yes_____ How many times?_____

14. Did anyone steal things that belonged to you from inside any car or truck, such as packages or clothing? (Do not include any incident already mentioned.)

    No_____ Yes_____ How many times?_____

15. Was anything stolen from you while you were away from home, for instance at work, in a theater or restaurant, or while traveling? (Do not include any incident already mentioned.)

    No_____ Yes_____ How many times?_____

16. Other than any incidents you have already mentioned, was anything at all stolen from you?

    No_____ Yes_____ How many times?_____

17. Other than any incidents you have already mentioned, did you find any evidence that someone attempted to steal something that belonged to you?

    No_____ Yes_____ How many times?_____

18. Look over your responses to questions 1–17. Note any question to which you responded Yes __X__. If you notified the police about the incident(s), circle the question number (e.g., ③).

19. If there were questions to which you responded Yes __X__, and you did not notify the police about the incident(s), put the number of times you did not notify police next to the number of the question:

    (1) _____   (10) _____
    (2) _____   (11) _____
    (3) _____   (12) _____
    (4) _____   (13) _____
    (5) _____   (14) _____
    (6) _____   (15) _____
    (7) _____   (16) _____
    (8) _____   (17) _____
    (9) _____

20. Look at the answers to question 19. If the police were not notified, place a letter (a through l) next to the appropriate number in question 19 that best indicates why the police were not notified.

No Need to Call

(a) Object recovered or offender unsuccessful.
(b) Did not think it was important enough.
(c) Private or personal matter or took care of it myself.
(d) Reported to someone else.

Police Could Not Do Anything

(e) Didn't realize crime happened until later.
(f) Property difficult to recover due to lack of serial or I.D. number.
(g) Lack of proof, no way to find/identify offender.

Police Would Not Do Anything

(h) Police wouldn't think it was important enough, they wouldn't want to be bothered.
(i) Police would be inefficient, ineffective, insensitive (they'd arrive late, wouldn't pursue case properly, would harass/insult victim, etc.).

Some Other Reason

(j) Afraid of reprisal by offender or his family/friends.
(k) Did not want to take the time—too inconvenient.
(l) Don't know why it wasn't reported.

The actual NCS crime incident report would continue drawing data from a respondent by asking detailed questions about each crime that was reported—items such as type of weapon; any injuries; sex, race, and age of offender; and whether the offender was known to the victim.

likely a family is to be a victim of theft.
- Injury is more likely to occur when the offender is known to the victim than when the offender is a stranger.

Problems with the NCS

The first problem with the NCS is the large number of respondent households needed to find a statistically significant number of crimes in each of the eight categories used by the NCS. For example, it took a survey of about 10,000 households in Detroit to find 150 robbery victims. While a typical national survey (such as a Gallup poll) uses a sample of about 1,500 carefully chosen respondents, a victimization study needs to employ national samples as large as 60,000 households—a very expensive undertaking.

Wesley Skogan (1981: 4) notes that

> while crime is relatively infrequent in the general population, this is not the case among certain subgroups. Crime is spatially segregated. For example, in 1970 two-thirds of the reported robberies in the United States were concentrated in 32 cities which housed only 16 percent of the nation's population.... As a result, a relatively small portion of the population is exposed to extremely high levels of risk, especially from violent crime. People from those places contribute disproportionately to the total count of victims.

Of course, one does not have to be a criminologist to know how to locate high-crime areas in any city—just ask any cab driver.

Skogan (1981) notes the difficulty interviewers have in locating representative samples of certain subgroups that have the highest rates of victimization, such as persons in lower socioeconomic circumstances, young males, transients. Such persons tend to have unstable residential situations—they move about a great deal—making their use in panel research quite problematic.

There is also the general problem of panel attrition: over any three-and-a-half-year period, some respondents move, die, or refuse to be interviewed again. It is not uncommon to respond to a victimization by moving to another neighborhood. Researchers have found that the "more victimizations one reported, the higher the chance that he or she would move or refuse to be interviewed later" (Skogan 1981: 26).

Other methodological problems—although they are difficult

"I'm 76 years old. I was robbed and raped. By talking with New York Women Against Rape, I didn't have to face it alone."
Counseling is free and confidential.
(212) 877-8700

The shame that rape victims often feel may keep them from discussing the crime with the police or with loved ones. Studies conducted by the Census Bureau reveal that over 50 percent of all rapes go unreported.

to measure—have to do with the effect of an interviewer on the data received and recorded. The interviewer in a victimization survey must abstract the incidents from their social context for statistical purposes. Thus, while the interviewer may record an incident as a "crime," the respondent may not view it as such; violent disputes between family members, neighbors, and friends would be in this category. In part, this can account for the high level of nonreporting to the police found by the NCS. Moreover, interviewers interpret information differently, and some probe more vigorously, while others passively accept a "don't know" or other nonresponse. How they explain items in the survey to individuals who do not understand the questions also differs among interviewers. Skogan (1981: 28) points out, "The effects of interviewers can be quite substantial, especially when survey personnel have had comparatively little training and are only minimally supervised." Correcting this problem could add significantly to the costs of the NCS.

The third type of methodological problem has to do with the reliability of the respondents. Crime is so prevalent in the lives of some people that they are unable to disentangle one incident from another, and as Skogan (1981: 9) notes, "crimes can be recorded in victim surveys only if they are known as discrete events"—a series of events is not recorded. Other kinds of "misremembering" are poor recall and *telescoping,* or the tendency of respondents to "bring forward" crimes that actually occurred considerably earlier. Victims can respond to traumatic events by blocking them from memory, or, conversely, traumas may remain vivid as though they happened "only yesterday." This telescoping is one major reason for using the panel method. The same respondents are interviewed every six months and data is collected only on events that have occurred since the previous reference period and interview.

However, the panel method leads to another problem: *respondent fatigue.* The novelty of being interviewed may eventually wear off, causing respondents to suppress reports of victimization in order to speed up the interview. There is some speculation that persons more prone to experience such fatigue may also be more likely to be victimized by crime. If so, crime will be significantly underreported. On the other hand, "their ability to recall events could be enhanced by this unexpected continuing interest in their experiences on the part of Government" (Wesley 1981: 25), leading to a more accurate recording of incidents of crime.

Then, there is the problem of lying or simply not telling. There appears to be a correlation between lying or not telling and the relationship between the victim and the offender. Victims are more likely to provide accurate information about incidents when there is not a relationship between victim and offender. Skogan (1981: 16) speculates that

> persons who have been victimized by someone they know frequently may not think it is any of the interviewer's business. . . . Although these incidents . . . [may have been reported to] the police, the victim may not have been the party who called them; many crimes are reported to the police by friends, relatives, and bystanders, and the offended party may not wish to spread the story even further.

How Do UCR and NCS Compare?

	Uniform Crime Reports	**National Crime Survey**
Offenses measured:	Homicide Rape Robbery (personal and commercial) Assault (aggravated) Burglary (commercial and household) Larceny (commercial and household) Motor vehicle theft Arson	Rape Robbery (personal) Assault (aggravated and simple) Household burglary Larceny (personal and household) Motor vehicle theft
Scope:	Crimes reported to the police in most jurisdictions; considerable flexibility in developing small-area data	Crimes both reported and not reported to police; all data are for the nation as a whole; some data are available for a few large geographic areas
Collection method:	Police department reports to FBI	Survey interviews; periodically measures the total number of crimes committed by asking a national sample of 60,000 households representing 135,000 persons over the age of 12 about their experiences as victims of crime during a specified period
Kinds of information:	In addition to offense counts, provides information on crime clearances, persons arrested, persons charged, law enforcement officers killed and assaulted, and characteristics of homicide victims	Provides details about victims (such as age, race, sex, education, income, and whether the victim and offender were related to each other) and about crimes (such as time and place of occurrence, whether or not reported to police, use of weapons, occurrence of injury, and economic consequences)
Sponsor:	Department of Justice Federal Bureau of Investigation	Department of Justice Bureau of Justice Statistics

SOURCE: Zawitz, 1983: 6.

There is the problem of distinguishing the "do-ee" from the "do-er." Who was the perpetrator? Who was the victim? These questions can be a matter of perception and interpretation, and those involved may have conflicting answers to what is essentially a legal question: for example, when a verbal exchange following a minor traffic accident results in pushing and an exchange of blows. There are also those who view their own negligence as a factor in the incident—for example, leaving a key in the front door—and they may be less likely to report their experiences to an interviewer.

Finally, interviews may also increase interest and concern about crime, leading respondents to undertake protective measures such as better locks and guard dogs. This could mean that the surveys are underestimating the true level of victimization in the nation.

How much crime?

How can we respond intelligently and honestly to the central question of this chapter? There is obviously only one truthful answer: *No one knows*. This is not to say that crime statistics are meaningless or a waste of time and money. It simply means that we cannot answer this important question. Crime statistics—the UCR and NCS—can, however, offer valuable information about the question, Is crime increasing or decreasing?

Before entering into a discussion of this question, we must note the possibility of "vested interests." Quite simply, do the persons and agencies receiving, recording, and reporting crime data have an interest in the way the statistics turn out? Can there be some gain for "cooking the books"? It is clear that law enforcement agencies and those responsible for law enforcement operations are not disinterested (i.e., scientific) observers. Thus, the Uniform Crime Reporting system will always be suspect. The NCS, in spite of its methodological problems and limitations, has a greater likelihood of scientific objectivity—the Bureau of the Census has no stake in the outcome.

For many years, the UCR reported a continuing increase in the crime rate, while the NCS reported a continuing decline. This situation was ideal for some public officials. Those who were interested in arguing that crime was increasing could cite

A Chicago policeman frisks a suspect on a street corner in Chinatown in 1925.

UCR statistics as "proof." On the other hand, those who wished to argue that their policies had led to a decrease in crime could cite the statistics of the NCS. This situation came to an end in 1981; from 1981 to 1985, both the UCR and the NCS reported a decrease in the rate of crime. Public officials from President Ronald Reagan on down took credit for the decrease. Social scientists, who had been predicting a decrease in the crime rate for several years, were skeptical of these claims. They noted a direct relationship between age and criminality, and pointed out that the number of persons in the crime-prone age category (roughly 15 to 25) had been steadily decreasing. In any event, in 1985 the UCR reported an increase of 4 percent. In that same year, the NCS reported the lowest number of households affected by crime in a decade.

In this chapter, we have examined the deficiencies inherent in crime statistics, how they help to form our perceptions of crime and how that determines the resources society devotes to coping with the problem. In the next chapter, we will examine the fascinating and often conflicting theories that attempt to explain the cause of crime.

KEY TERMS

Uniform Crime Reports (UCR)
Part I offenses or **index crimes**
criminal homicide
forcible rape
robbery
aggravated assault
burglary
larceny-theft
motor-vehicle theft
arson
hierarchy rule
Part II offenses
crime rate
victimization studies
National Crime Survey (NCS)
panel survey method

3 ▪ HOW MUCH CRIME? PERCEPTION AND STATISTICS

REVIEW QUESTIONS

1. How does the news media influence our perception of crime?
2. What is the role of crime statistics in influencing our perception of crime?
3. How can crime statistics be influenced by the definition of a crime?
4. In what year did the United States first begin to develop a national system of crime reporting, the Uniform Crime Report (UCR)?
5. What is the difference between Part I and Part II offenses in the UCR?
6. What are the eight categories of crime in Part I of the UCR (index crimes)?
7. What major category of crime does not appear in the UCR?
8. What is the source of data for the UCR?
9. What two categories of crime in Part I of the UCR have the highest level of reliability, and why?
10. Why do crime victims fail to report crimes to the police?
11. How can a change in reporting patterns affect the UCR?
12. How can crime data be manipulated by law enforcement agencies?
13. What is the major difference between the UCR and the National Crime Survey (NCS)?
14. What agency conducts surveys for the NCS?
15. Why is it necessary to have very large samples for an NCS survey?
16. The NCS uses a panel method for collecting data. What is a panel method?
17. What is the unit of analysis used by the NCS?
18. What are the major problems and shortcomings of the NCS?
19. What is meant by "telescoping"?
20. What are the causes of panel attrition?
21. What changes in the population could account for a reduction in the crime rate?

CHAPTER 4

Why Crime? Theories of Causation

WHAT IS A THEORY?

THEORIES OF CRIME
Classical Theory
   Criticisms of the Classical Theory
Positivism
Biological Theory
   Criminal Man
   XYY Chromosome Theory
Psychological Theory
   Psychoanalytic Theory
   Behaviorism

Sociological Theory
   Anomie
   Cultural Transmission
   Differential Association
   Differential Opportunity
   Subcultural Theory
   Neutralization
   Delinquency and Drift
   Labeling
   Conflict Theory
   Functionalism

THE "MAGIC BULLET"

QUANTITATIVE RESEARCH
Survey Research
Experimental Design

QUALITATIVE RESEARCH
Case Study
Participant Observation

REVIEW QUESTIONS

Boxes

Smithkline Pleads Guilty
E.F. Hutton Pleads Guilty
General Electric Pleads Guilty
Sample Self-Report Instrument

Imagine, if you will, a "student tour of crime and justice," with the following scenario: the bus pulls into a depot where a large neon sign can be seen—"Crime Theories." The bright flashing lights and a line of chorus girls serve as a diversion, but it fails to stem passenger grumbling: "Who wants to stop here? How dull." "Let's get on with the trip." "Theory...how boring can you get!"

The tour guide has seen this reaction before and he moves quickly to deal with passenger discontent. "How many persons on this trip support President Reagan's policy on crime and criminals?" Some puzzled looks, a few whispers and shrugging shoulders. The tour guide continues. "In a speech before the National Sheriffs' Association in Hartford, Connecticut, President Ronald Reagan stated that crime "is the result of a conscious, willful, selfish choice made by some who consider themselves above the law" (June 20, 1984).

Now a number of passengers begin responding, defending and criticizing the statement, and finally a shouting match ensues.

"Stop!" our tour guide yells above the din. "How many persons on this bus recognize in the president's statement the classical theory referred to as eighteenth-century liberalism?" Mumbling, puzzled looks and the shrugging of shoulders: "Reagan a liberal?" "Classical theory?"

"Stay with me," the tour guide promises, "and you will see how theories of crime and policy for dealing with crime are intertwined—one dependent upon the other. Before we can proceed, however, can someone tell me what a theory is?"

WHAT IS A THEORY?

A **theory** helps us to explain events; it organizes events in the world so they can be placed in perspective; it explains the causes of past events and predicts when, where, and how future events will occur; and it offers "an intuitively pleasing sense of 'understanding' why and how events should occur" (Turner 1974: 2). According to Arnold Binder and Gilbert Geis (1983: 3), "A theory consists of a set of assumptions; concepts regarding events, situations, individuals, and groups; and propositions that describe the interrelationships among the various assumptions and concepts."

To persons not familiar with the methods of social science, a theory may seem synonymous with speculation—an "educated guess." While in the natural sciences, such as physics and chemistry, theory can often be subjected to rigorous laboratory testing and replication, social science is concerned with human behavior and testing is limited accordingly. We can, for example, subject a variety of substances to stress in order to test a theory about resiliency, but we cannot abuse a child to determine if abuse will lead to antisocial behavior in the adult. Nevertheless, to the social scientist theory is a basic building block indispensable for the advancement of human knowledge, and there are research methods that can be used to test social science theories; those used in the study of crime will be discussed later in this chapter. Because social science theories can rarely be proven or rejected with the same finality as theories in the natural sciences, there are often competing theories, as we shall soon see. It is important to note, however, that the theory one "buys" is linked to certain public policy stances; change the theoretical perspective, and new policy emerges.

Theories of Crime

Among those who study crime and criminal behavior, there is little agreement over its cause. In the first chapter we noted that the definition of crime can determine what is a crime and who is a criminal, and definitions—laws—are different depending on the time and the place.

Classical Theory

The earliest coherent approach to crime and criminal behavior grew out of the Enlightenment philosophy of the eighteenth century. This **classical theory of crime** has reemerged as an important doctrine in the 1970s and gained important adherents such as President Reagan.

Basic to classical thought is the concept of a *social contract* put forward by the French philosopher, Jean Jacques Rosseau (1712-1778). He refers to a mythical state of affairs wherein each person agrees to a pact whose basic stipulation is that conditions of law are the same for all—*all men are created equal* (as the Declaration of Independence says).

This notion of equality led to one of the central features of the classical theory of crime, *equality of punishment.* Punishment should be meted out without regard to station; all are equal and all shall suffer equally for equal offenses. The king who rapes a peasant shall be punished as would the peasant who raped a princess. A contemporary application of this concept would be that the company executive who knowingly causes death and injury by permitting the sale of defective products shall be punished as would any other murderer. The philosophy of Rousseau and the classical philosophers was revolutionary and, indeed, influenced both the American and French Revolutions. The concept of equality of punishment remains revolutionary, an unfulfilled vision about which President Reagan has made no speech.

Classical theory emerged in Europe as liberal reform in opposition to a reactionary system of justice in which punishments were often arbitrary and barbarous. Officials responsible for enforcing the law did so with little or no concern for the rights of a defendant. An Italian, Cesare Beccaria, was the first to set forth the principles of the classical theory of crime. Beccaria (actually Cesare Bonesana, Marchese de Beccaria, 1738-94), whose *Essay on Crimes and Punishment* was published in 1764, called for laws that were precise and matched to punishment intended to be applied equally to all classes of men. He argued that the law should stipulate a particular penalty for each crime, and judges should impose identical penalties for each occurrence of the same offense. This is the theoretical basis for the recent move from indeterminate to determinate sentencing, which will be discussed in chapter 13.

Basic to classical theory is a most controversial notion: *free will*. As stated by President Reagan, crime "is the result of a conscious, willful, selfish choice." In other words, every human being is endowed (by his or her creator) with the ability to choose "right" or "wrong." Those who choose "wrong"—crime—are making a conscious, willful, selfish choice (neither the devil nor poverty made 'em do it). According to classical theory, human beings tend toward hedonism—they are guided by the "pleasure principle"—and, thus, they must be deterred from committing antisocial, albeit pleasurable, acts by the specter of punishment. In sum, the tenets of the classical theory of crime and justice are the following:

1. All persons are created equal.
2. All persons have an equal stake in preventing crime.
3. Each person has the free will to do right or to do wrong.
4. People tend toward hedonism.
5. Punishment must be used to deter criminal behavior.
6. Punishment should be meted out fairly and with absolute equality.

Criticisms of the Classical Theory

Ian Taylor, Paul Walton, and Jock Young (1973) point out that classical theory is unrealistic insofar as it can be operational only in a society where wealth and property are equally distributed and where everyone has an equal stake in the system. For free will to be meaningful, each person must be equal to every other person with respect to being able to choose crime or to do otherwise. Of course, in the eighteenth century, as in our own time, the ability to "do otherwise" was linked to one's social and economic situation. Taylor, Walton, and Young (1973: 4) point out that "no real attention is given [by classicalists] to the fact that lack of property might make men more likely to commit crime; and no consideration is devoted to the possibility that the rewards held out by the system as rewards might be more easily available to those already in propertied (or otherwise privileged) positions." Common sense tells us that street crime is engaged in by persons from lower economic circumstances—do you know "rich kids" who snatch pocketbooks or commit burglary and robbery?

Classical theory is based on philosophy and law; it is concerned with crime, not the criminal. Criminal motivation, beyond that encompassed by a notion of hedonism, is given no consideration. This changed with the advent of the positivist revolution in criminology.

Positivism

Auguste Comte (1798-1857) advocated a science of society he referred to as **positivism**. Comte argued that the methods and logic of the natural sciences (the "scientific method") could be applied to the social sciences. In criminology this meant an examination of why people commit crimes. The answers explored from 1827 to 1876 were primarily social in nature as researchers during this period made use of national crime statistics being compiled and published in France. Early statisticians (such as Adolphe Quetelet and A.M. Guerry) examined the relationship between economic conditions and crime, and they found important correlations. Crime was ascribed to existing social and economic conditions, not free will. In 1876, however, criminology took a drastic turn toward biological explanations of crime.

Biological Theory

Early biological explanations of criminal behavior must be understood in their historical context, particularly the work of Charles Darwin (1809-1882) and his theory of organic evolution, and the work of Herbert Spencer (1820-1903), who coined the phrase "survival of the fittest" (often mistakenly attributed to Darwin). Stanislav Andreski (1971: 26) notes:

One biological theory of criminal behavior links high sugar levels to hyperactivity and aggression. During the 1979 trial of ex-policeman Dan White (*above*) for the murder of San Francisco Mayor George Moscone and Supervisor Harvey Milk (*right*), attorneys for White formulated the so-called Twinkie Defense—they claimed that White was adversely affected by consuming too much junk food before the murders. White, who sought revenge after being denied reappointment to the city's Board of Supervisors, was convicted of voluntary manslaughter by reason of diminished mental capacity. He served 6 years of a 7½-year sentence. On October 21, 1985, less than a year after his release from prison, White committed suicide.

81

Darwin's theory of natural selection supplied the conceptual ammunition for an ideology (later labelled as *social Darwinism* [italics added] which allayed the qualms of the rich about not helping the poor by telling them that the latter's sufferings were an inevitable price of progress which could occur only through the struggle for existence ending in the survival of the fittest and the elimination of the unfit.

Criminal Man

In 1876 Cesare Lombroso (1835-1909), a Venetian physician, published *L'Uomo Delinquente (Criminal Man)* in which he argued that the "secret" of criminality was Darwin's theory of **atavism.** According to Lombroso, atavistic man was a societal anomaly—a reversion to an earlier state in the evolutionary process. Lombroso claimed that **criminal man** was a throwback to earlier stages of evolution. Such persons could be recognized by certain physical stigmata—such as heavy jaws and prominent cheekbones—characteristic of a "Neanderthal." By the fifth edition of his book published in 1897, Lombroso, in the face of mounting criticism of his research (he examined only prison inmates), declared that the atavistic criminal type only accounted for a small part of the total criminal population. Lombroso also admitted to the possibility of environmental—social—factors as a basis for criminal behavior. This did not stop other researchers from continuing the search for "criminal man."

In the 1880s chromosomes were discovered, and theories of body type and intelligence became part of the eugenics movement (i.e., the attempt to improve the human species by eliminating undesirable genetic traits) which, as Philip Jenkins (1984: 136) notes, fell into disrepute because of its association with Nazism.

> Essentially what the Nazis did was to take the list of defectives, and add certain groups to it—notably Jews, Slavs, and Gypsies. They then did what some contemporary criminologists were already suggesting for criminals; they segregated, sterilized, and exterminated them.

Before discussing some recent biological theories of criminal behavior, it is important to note the implications of any theory that attributes criminality to variables over which an individual has no control—no free will. Such theories rely on the doctrine known as **determinism** (which has a theological parallel in "predestination") which leads to certain dilemmas. If criminal behavior is not a matter of conscious choice, but rather determined by physical or mental variables, how can a person be held accountable for that criminal behavior (*mens rea*)? What is a society to do if it is discovered that certain physical or mental traits increase the risk of criminal behavior? The specter of Adolph Hitler's *Mein Kampf* (1924) attaches to such beliefs, but the search goes on for "criminal man." Of course, criminal man is always a person who commits certain types of crime, and these do not include acts committed by the rich and powerful. It is difficult to escape problems of definition when discussing theories of criminality.

XYY Chromosome Theory

One of the most publicized theories of biological determinism was the **XYY chromosome theory** of the 1960s. The normal chromosome makeup for a female is XX, and for a male it is XY. In a relatively few cases males have an extra Y chromosome, an abnormality making them XYY. During the 1960s a number of studies revealed that a higher percentage of criminals had the extra Y chromosome than is normally found in the "noncriminal" population. It was also noted that these persons tended to be taller and more awkward than the general population. They often had acne skin conditions and scored low on IQ tests. Criminal man? Some in and out of science argued yes. Others were skeptical. The skeptics argued that the extra Y chromosome does not predict criminality; instead, they said, it predicts that a man with an extra Y chromosome who does commit a crime is more likely to be apprehended. The criminals who had been tested for the extra Y chromosome had all been arrested and convicted—and an excessively tall, awkward, young man with acne and a low IQ, if he commits a crime, is more likely to be arrested and convicted than someone who is smarter and less physically distinctive. Subsequent research refuted the earlier studies and revealed that persons with the extra Y chromosome are usually quite passive and are actually underrepresented in the criminal population.

Recent studies into links between biology and criminal behavior have found evidence that in some persons high levels of sugar or vitamin deficiencies lead to hyperactivity and aggression. Some violent behavior has also been linked to brain tumors and brain injuries, as well as to certain central nervous system disorders (Schmeck 1985).

Psychological Theory

Neither of the two major theoretical perspectives in psychology—psychoanalytic theory and behaviorism—are concerned with criminal behavior per se. Rather, psychology examines individual behavior, and sometimes, "abnormal" behavior involves criminality. Crime is a legal, not a scientific, construct; and, accordingly, psychological theories seek to explain human behavior, not *criminal* behavior.

Psychoanalytic Theory

This theoretical perspective was developed by Sigmund Freud (1856-1939), a Viennese physician who argued that psychosexual development and unconscious mental processes provide the keys to understanding human behavior. According to **psychoanalytic theory**, every human being from birth to about age five moves through three stages of psychosexual development. Linked to each stage is the formation of psychic mechanisms that control behavior. Memory of these stages of psychosexual development are routinely suppressed in the normal human being and can only be released by a process known as psychoanalysis (or sometimes by psychosis, or mental illness).

    1. *Oral Stage.* At birth the infant enters the oral stage. Until infants are about one-and-a-half years old, they are *asocial*—devoid of any sense of morality, without an appreciation of "right" and "wrong." The human organism is guided only by an *id*, a part of the psyche that demands immediate gratification of all desires.

    2. *Anal Stage.* Between the ages of one-and-a-half and three years, infants enter the anal stage. During this period humans are only partially socialized and often act in a destructive manner, breaking toys and injuring living organisms such as insects and small animals; they can also be a threat to infant siblings. At this stage the child develops an *ego*, a psychic mechanism that helps control id impulses. The ego is a human organism's contact with reality, and it inhibits behavior that will result in punishment or pain. In other words, behavior is controlled by the ego, not out of a sense of right and wrong—morality—but only out of concern for pain or punishment.

3. *Phallic Stage.* Finally, between the ages of three and five years, children enter the phallic stage, during which the psyche develops a *superego*. This conscience-like mechanism controls id impulses out of a sense of morality. In combination with the ego, it serves to restrain pleasure drives, whose source is the id.

According to psychoanalytic theory, abnormal behavior, including acts that are defined as criminal, is the result of a failure to adequately complete any of the three stages. Thus, for example, difficulty in completing the phallic stage can leave a person with a superego insufficient to control id impulses, which are antisocial. Such persons are guided only by the ego; they have no sense of morality and their behavior is controlled only by a desire to avoid punishment—they are referred to as *psychopaths* or *sociopaths*. Those who do not successfully complete the phallic stage may also develop an overbearing superego, one that demands punishment for improper thoughts—as opposed to improper behavior, which can be the cause of behavior that is self-punishing. For example, it can lead to the commission of crimes in such a clumsy manner as to insure apprehension and conviction. Problems in the anal stage of development are associated with sadistic behavior and aggression. Problems in the oral stage are associated with drug abuse and alcoholism (as well as smoking and obesity).

Behaviorism

The second major theoretical perspective in psychology is known as **behaviorism**, from which is derived **learning theory**. Learning theory is based on the premise that behavior is shaped by reward and punishment: behavior that is rewarded tends to be repeated; behavior that is punished or painful tends to be avoided. Rewards for particular behavior are referred to as *positive reinforcement*, punishment as *negative reinforcement*. The deliberate use of positive and negative reinforcement by behaviorists to alter behavior is called *operant conditioning* (although critics sometimes refer to it as "brainwashing"). It has been used in some prison systems as a method for gaining the cooperation of inmates.

In the United States, learning theory was popularized by B.F. Skinner, who contends that animal behavior, human and otherwise, is the result of learning responses to certain stimuli. Disturbed behavior, including that defined as criminal, is a matter of learning responses that are inappropriate (from the point of view of the definer). As in psychoanalytic theory, behaviorism makes no distinction between behavior in general and criminal behavior (which is a legal construct); both are based on the same principles of learning. Antisocial behavior is merely the result of learning directly from others (e.g., peers) or the failure to learn how to discriminate between lawful and unlawful norms, due to inappropriate reinforcement or inconsistent rewards for lawful behavior.

When conforming behavior is not adequately reinforced, or perhaps negatively reinforced, an individual can more easily be influenced by sources of positive reinforcement for antisocial behavior. On a simple level, crime may provide more rewards, financial and psychological (it can be exciting), than legitimate employment for certain individuals, for example, those without sufficient education or legitimate skills. The positive reinforcement (rewards) of criminal behavior can be offset by negative reinforcement (punishment) or by positive reinforcement of conforming behavior, such as the desire for "respectability." Some behaviorists maintain that the prevalence of certain types of crime among the lower classes is a result of faulty child-rearing practices. Many lower-class parents, they argue, fail to apply consistent moral principles in their children's socialization process, thus leaving them adrift and susceptible to the rewards for antisocial behavior readily available in areas of high crime and delinquency.

Sociological Theory

Sociology, like positivism, is a term coined by Auguste Comte. It is a discipline that examines social structures and social behavior, or that which is external to the individual—as opposed to the focus of psychology on the individual and the internal. Sociology has spawned a number of theoretical explanations for crime.

Anomie

This term, derived from the Greek word meaning "lack of law," was used by Emile Durkheim (1858-1917) to describe an abnormal social condition wherein the cohesion of the society is weakened by some crisis (for example, an economic depression) causing each individual to pursue his or her own solitary interests. Rapid industrialization and urbanization, for example, can lead to a breakdown of social controls as large numbers of people are suddenly thrown out of adjustment with their typical ways of life (Clinard 1964). The individual is left with a sense of "normlessness," or **anomie**, a feeling of being adrift without customary guideposts—social constraints on behavior. There is an accompanying growth of individualism as weakened social controls encourage a breakdown in discipline and allow unbridled appetites to run free. At some point in time, a readjustment restores social controls and moderation, but until then there is a lag during which high levels of deviance such as crime and suicide can be expected.

In 1938, Robert Merton "Americanized" the concept of anomie. He argued that no other society comes so close to considering economic success as an absolute value and that the pressure to succeed "tends to eliminate the effective social constraint over the means employed to this end. The 'end-justifies-the-means' doctrine becomes a guiding tenet for action when the cultural structure unduly exalts the end and the social organization unduly limits possible recourse to approved means" (p. 681). British sociologists Taylor, Walton and Young (1974: 93) made a similar observation several decades later: "The desire to make money without regard to the means in which one sets about doing it, is symptomatic of the malintegration at the heart of American society."

According to Merton (1964: 218) anomie results when people are confronted by the contradiction between goals and means and "become estranged from a society that promises them in principle what they are denied in reality [i.e., economic opportunity]." Despite numerous success stories—the poor boy from humble origins who becomes rich and famous—"we know that in this same society that proclaims the right, and even the duty, of lofty aspirations for all, men do not have equal access to the opportunity structure." This is particularly true of the disadvantaged segments of our population who fill our courts and prisons.

How do persons respond to anomie? Most simply scale down their aspirations and conform to conventional social norms. Some rebel, rejecting the conventional social structure and seek, instead, to establish a "new social order" through political action or by alternative lifestyles. Two other responses, retreatism and innovation, are of particular interest to criminologists. *Retreatism* means that all attempts to reach conventional social goals are abandoned in favor of a deviant adaptation—a "retreat" to alcohol and drug abuse. Time and energy are now expended to reach an attainable goal: getting "high." *Innovation* is a term used by Merton to describe the adoption of illegitimate means to gain success. When a person accepts societal goals of success but finds that access to legitimate means for becoming successful are limited, anomie results, and crime is a basically utilitarian adaptation to the dilemma.

Cultural Transmission

Some sociologists have sought to explain why crime is more prevalent in some parts of society than others. **Cultural transmission** of crime was one of the findings of the Chicago School of sociology (so called because its members were at the University of Chicago) and Clifford Shaw and Henry McKay (1972), whose findings were originally published in 1942. Their research in Chicago (and replicated in other cities) demonstrated that certain neighborhoods, or *ecological niches*, maintained high rates of delinquency although the ethnic makeup of the areas had changed a number of times. Shaw and McKay (1972: 175) found "that some members of each delinquent group had participated in offenses in the company of older boys, and so on, backward in time in an unbroken continuity as far as records were available." They concluded that "this contact means that the traditions of delinquency can be and are transmitted down through successive generations of boys, in much the same way that language and other forms of social norms are transmitted." They found that in certain identifiable neighborhoods, the community does not function effectively as a medium of social control, and as a result delinquency and crime are tolerated, if not accepted, through successive generations.

Differential Association

Proposed by Edwin Sutherland (1973), this theory, like cultural transmission, explains how criminal behavior is transmitted. According to Sutherland, criminal behavior is learned, and the principal part of learning criminal behavior occurs within intimate groups and is based on the intensity, frequency, and duration of the association. The individual learns, in addition to the techniques of committing crime, the drives, attitudes, and rationalizations that add up to a favorable predisposition to criminal behavior. Criminals and law-abiding citizens have the same goal: securing economic and personal status. **Differential association** helps to explain why some people choose criminal and others noncriminal methods to achieve that goal.

In sum, according to the theory of differential association, criminal behavior depends on the strength or intensity of criminal associations and is the result of an accumulative learning process. Thus, associating with criminals over a period of time increases the likelihood of becoming a criminal. The emphasis on crime as a *learning* process is similar to behaviorist views of criminal behavior (Akers and Burgess 1969).

Differential Opportunity

By integrating anomie with differential association, Richard Cloward and Lloyd Ohlin (1960) sought to explain how delinquent subcultures arise, develop various law-violating ways of life, and persist or change over time. They distinguished among three types of delinquent subculture that are a result of anomie and differential association:

1. *Criminal subculture:* gang activities devoted to money-making criminal pursuits, such as racketeering.
2. *Conflict subculture:* gang activities devoted to violence and destructive acting out as a way of gaining status; and
3. *Retreatist subculture:* activities in which drug abuse is the primary focus.

Cloward and Ohlin (1960: 106-7) note that:

> many lower-class adolescents experience desperation born of the certainty that their position in the economic structure is relatively fixed and immutable—a desperation made all the more poignant by their exposure to a cultural ideology in which failure to orient oneself upward is regarded as a moral defect and failure to become

Anomie results when people become estranged from a society that promises more than it delivers. One response is "retreatism," or withdrawal into alcohol and drug abuse.

mobile as proof of it.... Delinquent subcultures, we believe, represent specialized modes of adaptation to this problem of adjustment.

The criminal and conflict subcultures provide illegal avenues, while the retreatist "anticipates defeat and now seeks to escape from the burden of the future" (p. 107).

In their theory of **differential opportunity**, Cloward and Ohlin (1960: 145) point out that illegitimate means of success, like legitimate means, are not equally distributed throughout society: "Having decided that he 'can't make it legitimately,' he cannot simply choose among an array of illegitimate means, all equally available to him." This is an important insight: a career in professional or organized crime can be as difficult to attain as any lucrative career in the legitimate sphere of society. Most persons suffering from anomie cannot hope to achieve any significant level of success in crime without differential association, but "more youngsters are recruited into these patterns of differential associations than the adult criminal structure can possibly absorb. Since there is a surplus of contenders for these positions, criteria and mechanisms of selection must be evolved. Hence, a certain proportion of those who aspire may not be permitted to engage in the behavior for which they have prepared themselves" (1960: 148).

Subcultural Theory

Cloward and Ohlin described three types of delinquent subculture in 1960, and subsequently, many other sociologists explored subcultural theory. James Short (1968: 11) explains that "subcultures are patterns of values, norms, and behavior which have become traditional among certain groups. These groups may be of many types, including occupations and ethnic groups, social classes, occupants of 'closed institutions' [e.g., prisons, mental hospitals] and various age grades.... [They are] important frames of reference through which individuals and groups see the world and interpret it."

Albert Cohen (1965: 86) argues that in certain lower-class subcultures there is a negation of middle-class values, and this negation is a severe handicap. Cohen says that there are certain cultural characteristics that are necessary to achieve success in our society, and that middle-class children are more likely to have the following characteristics as a result of their upbringing:

- ambition
- a sense of individual responsibility
- skills for achievement
- ability to postpone gratification
- industry and thrift
- rational planning (e.g., budgeting time and money)
- cultivation of manners/politeness
- control of physical aggression
- respect for property
- a sense of "wholesome" recreation

Cohen states that class-linked differences "relegate to the bottom of the status pyramid those children belonging to the most disadvantaged classes, not by virtue of their class position as such but by virtue of their lack of requisite personal qualifications resulting from their class-linked handicaps" (p. 86). The affected youngsters lack the attributes listed above, and react in a manner that Cloward and Ohlin have referred to as the "conflict subculture."

According to Cohen (1965: 80) the delinquent ("conflict") subculture "takes its norms from the larger culture but turns them upside down." Thus, the subcultural delinquent's conduct is correct "by the standards of his subculture, precisely because it is wrong by the norms of the larger culture." His delinquent activities are totally non-utilitarian; "it is malicious, negativistic—'stealing for the hell of it'—and apart from considerations of gain and profit. . . ." The goal is status, not financial profit. According to Cohen, the rules of the wider society are not something merely to be evaded, they are to be flouted: there are elements of active spite, malice, contempt, ridicule, challenge, and defiance.

Walter Miller (1958) states that law-violating acts committed by members of adolescent street-corner groups in lower-class communities are not geared toward flouting conventional middle-class norms and that the delinquent subculture did not arise in reaction to the larger middle-class culture. Instead, the delinquent is adhering to norms of behavior as they are defined within his community. Lower-class culture is simply different than middle-class culture, and Miller identifies its focal concerns as:

1. *Trouble*—law-violating behavior
2. *Toughness*—physical prowess, daring
3. *Smartness*—ability to "con," shrewdness
4. *Excitement*—thrills, risk, danger
5. *Fate*—being lucky
6. *Autonomy*—independence from external restraint

Trouble often involves fighting or sexual adventures while drinking; troublesome behavior for women frequently means sexual involvement with disadvantageous consequences. Miller contends that a desire to avoid trouble is based less on a commitment to the laws or other norms of the larger social order than on a desire to avoid possible legal and other undesirable consequences. While trouble-producing behavior is a source of status, non-trouble-producing behavior is required in order to avoid legal and other complications; some lower-class youngsters resolve this conflict in a legitimate manner by joining the military or a law enforcement agency.

Miller (1958: 9) traces the emphasis on *toughness* to the significant proportion of lower-class males reared in female-dominated households and the resulting concern over homosexuality, which "runs like a persistent thread through lower-class culture." Gambling, which is also prevalent in lower-class culture, has its roots in the belief that "their lives are subject to a set of forces over which they have relatively little control" (p. 11). Miller states that expressions of autonomy commonly found in lower-class culture—such as "No one's going to push me around" and "I'm gonna tell him to take the job and shove it" often contrast with actual patterns of behavior; many lower-class persons actually desire a highly restrictive social environment (ranging from prison to the armed forces) with strong external controls over their behavior. Miller contends that for the lower-class person, "being controlled is equated with being cared for" (p. 13).

To summarize, Albert Cohen believes that the delinquent subculture is a reaction to middle-class standards in the form of acts that are grossly antisocial. Walter Miller, on the other hand, asserts that the lower-class culture is completely distinct from the larger middle-class culture. Trouble results from culture conflict; the standards of the middle-class are embodied in the legal codes, which means that the lower-class person, who acts according to different cultural standards, can easily become entangled in a web of officialdom.

The policies implemented in response to Cloward and Ohlin's work during the 1960s were part of President Lyndon Johnson's "War on Poverty." There was a substantial federal investment in opening up, or creating, legitimate opportunities for youngsters who were at risk—suffering from anomie. Equal opportunity laws were enacted and enforced, and anti-poverty programs were established throughout the United States. The policies that were eventually implemented in response to the Cohen and Miller theories were opposed by both theorists. Since class-linked behavior was viewed as relatively immutable, a "get tough" response by government seemed justified, and this approach continues into the 1980s. Cohen and Miller favored governmental efforts to provide greater educational and economic opportunity to ameliorate the deficiencies of the lower-class subculture; to enable lower-class persons to become middle-class.

Neutralization

Gresham Sykes and David Matza (1957) disagree with both Cohen and Miller: they maintain that the delinquent actually retains his belief in the legitimacy of official middle-class norms and they refer to a social-psychological mechanism—**neutralization**—that permits a delinquent to accept the social norms of the wider society and, at the same time, to violate them. They observe that "the juvenile delinquent would appear to be at least partially committed to the dominant social order in that he frequently exhibits guilt or shame when he violates its proscriptions, accords approval to certain conforming figures, and distinguishes between appropriate and inappropriate targets for his deviance" (p. 666). They conclude that "the delinquent represents not a radical opposition to law-abiding society but something like an apologetic failure, more sinned against than sinning in his own eyes" (p. 667).

By using various techniques of neutralization, the delinquent is able to avoid guilt feelings for his actions. He is able to do this by contending that moral and legal rules are merely qualified guidelines that do not apply to all times, places, persons, and conditions. The delinquent uses neutralization to deny *mens rea*, criminal intent—which must be present in order for penal sanctions to be imposed. The delinquent justifies his actions in a form that, while it is not valid to the larger society, is valid for him. Sykes and Matza (1957) present five types of neutralization:

1. *Denial of responsibility.* The delinquent rationalizes that the crime was not his fault and that he was, for example, simply a victim of circumstances.
2. *Denial of injury.* The delinquent claims not to have harmed anyone—nobody got hurt, it was just a prank, or the insurance company will cover it.
3. *Denial of the victim.* The delinquent claims the victim deserved it, because, for example, he's a "fag."
4. *Condemnation of the condemners.* The delinquent dwells on the weakness and motives of those in authority or judgment—the police and judges are corrupt, school officials hate kids.

5. *Appeal to higher loyalties.* The delinquent claims he had to do it for friends, family, or neighborhood.

Delinquency and Drift

Does the juvenile delinquent move on to become an adult criminal, or does he **drift** into being a law-abiding member of society as he matures? David Matza (1964) views the delinquent as drifting between criminal and conventional action, but behaving most of the time in a noncriminal manner and feeling ambivalent about his criminal behavior. Matza believes that juveniles are less alienated than adults and are not yet committed to an oppositional culture.

While Matza (1964: 158) does not contradict the idea of a delinquent subculture, he finds that the subculture is not a binding force on its members: "Loyalty is a basic issue in the subculture of delinquency partially because its adherents are so regularly disloyal. They regularly abandon the company at the age of remission for more conventional pursuits." The "age of remission" is a time when adolescent antisocial behavior is abandoned in favor of adult prosocial or conventional behavior. The crime-prone years for males are roughly fifteen to twenty-five, remission occurring after age twenty-five.

As noted in chapter 3, a decrease in the number of persons in this age category has been cited as a major factor in explaining the recent decline in the rate of crime as reported by the Uniform Crime Report and the National Crime Survey. Matza's theory also has another important policy implication: justice system intervention can stigmatize a juvenile, thereby blocking his entry into a conventional lifestyle as he matures into adulthood.

Labeling

Stigma, or **labeling**, sometimes referred to as the *societal reaction theory,* is the concern of a sociological perspective known as **symbolic interactionism**.

> Symbolic interactionists suggest that categories which individuals use to render the world meaningful, and even the experience of self, are structured by socially acquired definitions. They argue that individuals, in reaction to group rewards and sanctions, gradually inter-

nalize group expectations. These internalized social definitions allow people to evaluate their own behavior from the standpoint of the group and in doing so provide a lens through which to view oneself as a social object. (Quadagno and Antonio 1975: 33)

The focus is not on the behavior of the social actor, but on how the behavior or the person is viewed by others—by society. According to this perspective, an actor and his or her behavior are neither "good" nor "bad" in and of themselves. Their value is *imputed*, the result of social definition. For example, the ancient Hebrews viewed the cessation of work on the Sabbath as an act of great reverence; to the Romans, it indicated indolence on the part of the Hebrews.

The labeling perspective focuses not on the behavior of the actor but on the societal reaction to his or her behavior. Kai Erikson (1966: 6) states, "Deviance is not a property *inherent* in any particular kind of behavior; it is a property *conferred* upon that behavior by people who come into direct or indirect contact with it." The societal reaction labels, or stigmatizes, the actor, which results in a damaged self-image, deviant identity, and a host of negative social expectations. This process can be seen, for example, when an offender is described as a "former mental patient"—as if to say, "What can you expect?"

Furthermore, it is argued, a damaged self-image can become a self-fulfilling prophecy. Edwin Schur (1973: 124) notes that "once an individual has been branded as a wrongdoer, it becomes extremely difficult for him to shed that new identity." According to Edwin Lemert (1951: 76), the labeled deviant reorganizes his behavior in accordance with the societal reaction and "begins to employ his deviant behavior, or role based upon it, as a means of defense, attack, or adjustment to the overt and covert problems created by the consequent societal reaction to him." Lemert has termed this process *secondary deviance*.

Conflict Theory

This approach encompasses a wide spectrum of ideas, including those of Karl Marx (1818–1883) and Max Weber (1864–1920). What **conflict theories** share are the beliefs that society is better characterized by conflict than by consensus and that what is defined as crime is the result of laws determined by powerful

SMITHKLINE PLEADS GUILTY

In February 1985, one of America's largest drug manufacturers, the Smithkline Beckman Corporation, pleaded guilty to failing to notify the Food and Drug Administration about adverse reactions to a blood pressure drug, Selacryn. The drug has been linked to 36 deaths and more than 500 cases of liver and kidney damage. The company was fined $100,000 and three managers were sentenced to probation.

elite interests. Criminal law and patterns of law enforcement are seen as always serving the interests of the powerful and dominant classes. Otherwise, they argue, how could a burglary netting a few dollars be classified as a felony, while corporate officials who pad defense contracts with millions of dollars in overcharges are charged only with a civil "indiscretion." This issue was discussed in the first chapter's section on the definition of crime, which is a major issue for conflict theorists (see, for example, Schwendinger and Schwendinger 1981). They note that many of the most socially and personally damaging acts are dealt with as civil rather than criminal matters in the United States, for example, job discrimination, industrial safety violations, antipollution violations, and the manufacture of products with serious safety defects.

The conflict approach eschews theories that treat criminal behavior as a manifestation of individual pathology. Instead, crime is seen as a phenomenon generated by a capitalist system. Capitalism leads to a class system of inequities in wealth and power—in life chances—that cause alienation; an alienated segment of the underclass, those whose interests are not furthered by capitalism, react in ways defined as criminal. The legal apparatus, which has a monopoly over sanctions and the use of force, serves to control the alienated population and perpetuate domination by the ruling class. According to conflict theory, the

> # E.F. HUTTON PLEADS GUILTY
>
> In May 1985, the nation's fifth largest investment firm, E.F. Hutton, pleaded guilty to 2,000 counts of mail and wire fraud. The firm had systematically bilked four hundred banks by intentionally writing checks in excess of the funds it had on deposit in various banks—a two-year, $10-billion scheme. Although Attorney General Edwin Meese III announced, "We are as aggressive in the investigation and prosecution of so-called white-collar crime as narcotics and organized crime," the firm was merely fined, and not one person was imprisoned.

criminal justice system is a mechanism through which the self-interests of the ruling class are protected by functionaries in their employ. Their rule is given legitimacy by an ideology of democracy, free enterprise, and property rights, whose benefits accrue primarily to those who already have wealth and power. As Karl Marx pointed out, the ideas of the ruling class are always the ruling ideas.

Functionalism

While most of the theories explored above attempt to define the causes of crime in order to stop crime, **functionalism** provides a different perspective; it views crime as an indispensable aspect of society. According to Emile Durkheim (1966: 65-66):

> Crime is present not only in the majority of societies of one particular species but in all societies of all types. There is no society that is not confronted with the problem of criminality. Its form changes; the acts thus characterized are not the same everywhere; but, everywhere and always, there have been men who have behaved in such a way as to draw upon themselves penal repression.

Durkheim (1966: 67) states that "crime is normal because a society exempt from it is utterly impossible. . . . Assuming that

> # General Electric Pleads Guilty
>
> **In May 1985, General Electric pleaded guilty to defrauding the Air Force by filing 108 false claims for payment on a missile contract. GE is the nation's sixth ranking contractor for military equipment, with $4.4 billion awarded in 1984. A former company manager acknowledged his role in the scheme and implicated higher management. As a result of the guilty plea, General Electric was fined $1.04 million, and not one person was imprisoned.**

this condition could actually be realized, crime would not thereby disappear; it would only change its form, for the very cause which would thus dry up sources of criminality would immediately open new ones." This means that acts that had previously been only "impolite" or "in bad taste" would become "criminal." This is because crime is not only normal for a society, it is indispensable for a society to *function* (from whence we derive the term *functionalism*). In other words, every society requires social cohesion; collective sentiments in opposition to acts defined as "criminal" serve as a glue to hold that society together (as does a national flag and anthem)—they provide a sense of "us against them."

The "Magic Bullet"

If anything is apparent from the diversity of theories that attempt to explain crime and criminal behavior, it is that the subject is complex and defies the often simplistic remedies offered by public officials pandering after the votes of a fearful citizenry. That crime is but a symptom of wider social problems

Powell for the Raleigh News and Observer; ©1985, Los Angeles Times Syndicate

seems equally apparent, but this has not dampened the search for a "cure"—a "magic bullet."

Early attempts in this quest emphasized punishment. The forms of punishment we are willing to impose in the United States today seem quite tame compared to medieval practices such as stripping the flesh with hot combs or tearing a criminal apart on the rack. Even those punishments, however, appeared to be of no avail; it was alleged that pickpockets and other thieves favored public torture and executions because they provided large, enthralled crowds among which fellow criminals could ply their trade.

During the eighteenth century, religious reformers favored a Bible and isolation to instill penitence (from whence we derive the word *penitentiary*). Unfortunately, this often remedied criminal behavior by substituting insanity. In the late nineteenth and early twentieth centuries, medical and evolutionary science seemed to offer some answers: isolate and sterilize the "criminal type," and with the passage of time and evolution, we would be crime-free. Freudian psychology offered new insights into human behavior and a method for cure—psychoanalysis. Unfortunately, there is no record of any criminal being cured by undergoing psychoanalytic treatment. Behaviorists have often been quite successful in curing bed-wetting and a fear of heights—but not criminality. Social scientists, whose ideologies usually run from just plain liberal to fire-breathing Marxist, found the cause of crime in social arrangements. But, as Durkheim noted back in the nineteenth century, all human societies have had crime and criminals. What to do? Why not dig up Dr. Lombroso and start again!

There are many current efforts to find a "magic bullet" that share Cesare Lombroso's belief in "criminal man." However, he (the search is for criminal *man*) cannot be distinguished by an extra Y chromosome or any other biological anomaly. In fact, all we actually know about him is that he has a rather lengthy criminal history. He is reputed to be part of a small cadre of hard-core criminals who are responsible for most of the crime in the United States. A safer society can be had if we can simply identify and isolate (imprison) this hard-core—this is what many see as the "magic bullet." If crime is simply the evil committed by a few evil men, and if all we need to do is identify and isolate such persons, then we need not consider the possibility that crime is related to inequality, discrimination, and poverty. We need not explain why "criminal man" is always "lower-class man."

Unfortunately for the current proponents of a "magic bullet," criminal man has proven to be quite an elusive fellow. We have been able to identify him only after most, if not all, of his criminal career is already behind him. In other words, we have been able to identify a cohort of aging criminals who share two variables: they have extensive histories of unsuccessful crime, and they are from the lower class. The search continues as government grants generate interest in being able to predict who is likely to become criminal man, or rather the modern version of that doctrine, the hard-core or career criminal. The attempt to find definitive answers to the causes of crime and criminal behavior has generated a variety of quantitative and qualitative research techniques.

102

The ability to predict criminality has eluded social scientists in their search for a "magic bullet" to eliminate crime. The difficulty of predicting criminal behavior was made clear when Jack Henry Abbott (*far left*), a lifelong convict, was charged with murder after his release from prison in 1981. Abbott, a literary protégé of Norman Mailer (*left*), was paroled largely due to Mailer's efforts. He soon became a celebrity in his own right with the publication of his account of twenty-five years in prison, *In the Belly of the Beast*. Only a few weeks after his parole, however, Abbott was implicated in the fatal stabbing of a waiter on Manhattan's Lower East Side. Convicted of first-degree manslaughter, Abbott received a sentence of fifteen years to life in prison.

QUANTITATIVE RESEARCH

Research requires data, and quantitative research is based on data that are expressed numerically, as in the Uniform Crime Report and the National Crime Survey.

Survey Research

As noted in chapter 3, one way to accumulate data about crime is to interview people. As we saw, National Crime Survey data are the result of interviews conducted by Census Bureau employees using a questionnaire (in research language, a survey instrument). **Survey research** has been used to examine the attitudes of police officers toward issues such as gun control, and the attitude of the public toward the police. Another survey instrument for collecting quantitative data about crime is the **self-report study**. A sample of persons, usually a select group such as high school students, college students, or persons identified as delinquent or criminal are asked about their involvement in criminal activities. A typical self-report instrument guarantees anonymity and asks respondents to indicate the number of times they were involved in certain law-violative behaviors.

While the results of self-report studies have proven interesting, one is left with a nagging doubt about the veracity of answers provided by respondents. Adolescents often enjoy boasting about (real or imagined) misbehavior and seek to avoid being labeled as a "square" or a "nerd." Adult criminals may not be willing to share their criminal histories with social scientists. (Interestingly, self-report studies reveal that criminal behavior is quite common among youngsters of all economic classes. Middle-class youngsters report drug use, vandalism, and theft as often as their lower-class counterparts, who, however, are more likely to report involvement in acts of violence.)

Experimental Design

The most difficult form of research to accomplish in criminology is that which utilizes an **experimental design**, something that is quite routine in the natural sciences. Unlike experiments using

> ## Sample Self-Report Instrument
>
> 1. **Did you ever steal something worth less than $10.00?**
>   No_____ Yes_____ How many times?_____
>
> 2. **Did you ever steal something worth more than $10.00?**
>   No_____ Yes_____ How many times?_____
>
> 3. **Other than in self-defense, did you ever hit someone with your fist or feet?**
>   No_____ Yes_____ How many different persons?
>   _____
>
> 4. **Other than in self-defense, did you ever use a weapon (such as a firearm, knife, club, bottle) against someone?**
>   No_____ Yes_____ How many different persons?
>   _____

chemicals or laboratory rats, there are serious ethical questions involved in subjecting humans to "test variables." Typically, the researcher uses an *experimental group* and a *control group*, and the two (or more) groups must be quite similar. The experimental group is exposed to some type of test (*test variable*), while the control group remains untouched by the researchers. Following the test, both groups are compared to measure the effects, if any, of the experiment. One of the most interesting and important experimental studies in the field was the Kansas City Preventive Patrol Experiment. This study raised ethical issues, since it tested the effectiveness of police patrol by withdrawing such patrols from certain areas of the city. (This study will be discussed in greater detail in chapter 7.)

Less dramatic but nevertheless important experimental research was accomplished in Minneapolis by the Police Foundation from early 1981 to mid-1982. It resulted in a change in police policy, which in turn led to an increase in the number of recorded crimes. A group of Minneapolis police officers was instructed to use one of three strategies when responding to simple (misdemeanor) domestic assaults: (1) arrest the suspect, (2) send him from the scene of the assault for eight hours, or (3) give advice or mediate. Each officer's response to a particular domestic assault was predetermined by a lottery system. At the end of the experiment researchers had data on the three responses, and a follow-up study investigated whether there was further violence in each case. The findings were that "arrest was the most effective of three standard methods police use to reduce domestic violence. The other police methods—attempting to counsel both parties or sending assailants away from home for several hours—were found to be considerably less effective in deterring future violence in the cases examined" (Sherman and Berk 1984: 1). As a result of the experiment, Minneapolis (and other cities) changed its policy toward "wife-beaters" from avoiding an arrest to arresting the assailant.

QUALITATIVE RESEARCH

Qualitative research includes a variety of methods, but they all share one characteristic: they are not seeking numerical data.

Case Study

The **case study** involves the researcher in an in-depth examination of a single case (or sometimes a few cases), as opposed to the representative sample often used in quantitative research. A case study often involves extensive interviews with the subject of the study supplemented by material from criminal justice and social service records; or it may involve only the study of documents. The unit of analysis for a case study need not be a single individual; it can be concerned with other identifiable entities such as a family or a gang. Anton Blok (1975), for example, studied the Mafia of a Sicilian village using historical documents and interviews.

The clinical case study is often used in psychological research; clinical case studies provided the data for Sigmund Freud. Edwin Sutherland used the case study of a shoplifter (1972) and case studies of white-collar criminals (1949) in developing his theory of differential association. Case studies can be compared to identify common elements or contrasting aspects of certain criminal offenders or subcultural groups. For example, this author's case study of a jewel thief (Abadinsky 1983) provides a basis for comparison with other types of criminals in order to identify the variables that determine if a criminal is a "professional."

Participant Observation

Also known as the *field study*, **participant observation** involves the researcher in a relatively lengthy on-site investigation. It is a method often used in anthropology and it has produced important and fascinating research. For example, William F. Whyte (1961) studied street-corner society in Boston, and Francis Ianni and Elizabeth Reuss-Ianni (1972) studied an organized crime family in New York, using participant observation.

In the first four chapters we have seen how the policies and practices of criminal justice are determined by how society defines crime, by its laws, and by its perceptions of the frequency and causes of crime. The next chapter will be an overview of the American system of criminal justice.

KEY TERMS

theory
classical theory of crime
positivism
atavism
criminal man
determinism
XYY chromosome theory
psychoanalytic theory
behaviorism
learning theory
anomie
cultural transmission
differential association

differential opportunity
neutralization
drift
labeling
symbolic interactionism
conflict theories
functionalism
survey research
self-report study
experimental design
case study
participant observation

REVIEW QUESTIONS

1. What is a theory?
2. What are the essentials of the classical theory of crime?
3. What is positivism?
4. How did Charles Darwin influence some theories of crime?
5. What are the deficiencies of the so-called XYY theory of criminal behavior?
6. How does psychoanalytic theory explain criminal behavior?
7. How does learning theory/behaviorism explain criminal behavior?
8. How does Robert Merton's theory of anomie explain criminal behavior in the United States?
9. What is meant by the cultural transmission of criminal behavior?
10. How does differential association explain criminal behavior?
11. What are the three subcultures that, according to Cloward and Ohlin, result from a differential opportunity structure?
12. What are the characteristics of the lower-class delinquent subculture emphasized by Albert Cohen?

13. According to Walter Miller, what are the characteristics of the lower-class subculture that differ from the norms of middle-class society?
14. What do Gresham Sykes and David Matza mean by "neutralization"?
15. What does David Matza mean when he describes juvenile delinquents as in a state of "drift"?
16. What is labeling/societal reaction theory?
17. What is secondary deviance?
18. How do conflict theorists explain crime and criminal behavior?
20. How does functionalism view criminal behavior?
21. What is meant by survey research?
22. What is a self-report study in criminology?
23. What are the essentials of an experimental design in research?
24. What is the difference between quantitative and qualitative research?
25. What are two different units of analysis for a case study?
26. What is meant by participant observation?

CHAPTER 5

The System of Criminal Justice

THE PROBLEM OF GOVERNMENTAL COMPLEXITY
The Law and Jurisdiction
Law Enforcement and Jurisdiction

CRIME CONTROL VERSUS DUE PROCESS

DUE PROCESS OF LAW
The Right to Remain Silent
  Exceptions
The Right to Legal Counsel
The Right to Bail
The Right to a Jury Trial

The Right to Confront Witnesses
Double Jeopardy
The Exclusionary Rule
  Exceptions

THE CRIMINAL JUSTICE PROCESS
Preliminary Investigation
Arrest
Booking
Pretrial Hearings
Grand Jury
Plea Bargaining
Trial

Sentencing
Probation
Jail/Prison
Parole
Appeals

REVIEW QUESTIONS

Boxes

Cases of Mistaken Guilt
Miranda Warnings
Mapp v. Ohio
United States v. Leon
Crime Victims

We are about to enter the labyrinth that is criminal justice in the United States. The criminal justice "system" is actually a network of agencies at the local, state, and federal levels. Criminal justice in a democracy is made complex by the need to balance the goals of crime control with the protection of the rights of those accused of crime. This chapter will provide an overview of the criminal justice process from arrest to parole, paving the way to a more detailed examination of each step of the process in Part II.

THE PROBLEM OF GOVERNMENTAL COMPLEXITY

In 1788 a compromise between Southern agrarian interests and Northern commercial interests led to the United States Constitution, a relatively brief document consisting of a preamble and seven articles. Ten amendments, known as the Bill of Rights, were added in 1791. The Constitution provides for a **federal system** of government that is unique to the United States. Authority is divided between the central (federal) and state governments. At both levels, federal and state, power is further diffused; it is shared by three branches of government according to the principle of **separation of powers**. The three branches are:

1. executive (president, state governors),
2. legislative (Congress, state legislatures), and
3. judicial (Supreme Court and other federal courts, state court systems).

Authority is further shared within each state by governments at the municipal, county, and state levels.

LEVELS OF GOVERNMENT	BRANCHES OF GOVERNMENT
Federal	Executive
State	Legislative
County	Judicial
Municipal	

Why would men as intelligent as Alexander Hamilton, George Washington, John Jay, Benjamin Franklin, and James Madison, among others, leave us with such complexity? The answer: a distrust of democracy and a fear of tyranny. The efficiency that could have been accomplished by a unitary central system of government was sacrificed to insure liberty. An understanding of the American form of government allows us to respond to the question, Why doesn't the criminal justice system operate more efficiently? The answer: It's not supposed to! Efficiency would require a level of centralization of authority—for example, a national police force—that Americans have traditionally been unwilling to allow.

The Law and Jurisdiction

Under our republican form of government, laws are enacted by elected representatives at federal and state levels, while ordinances (local laws) are enacted at the county and municipal (city, town, village) levels. While some minor criminal violations may be based on ordinances, all serious crimes (misdemeanors and felonies) are based on federal or state criminal laws.

The United States Constitution reserves only two crimes for federal jurisdiction. Article I, Section 8, gives Congress the power to "provide for punishment of counterfeiting the securities and current coin of the United States" and "to define and punish piracies and felonies committed on the high seas, and offences against the law of nations." By virtue of the Tenth Amendment, "powers not delegated to the United States by the Constitution, nor prohibited by it to the States, are reserved to the States respectively, or to the people." Accordingly, the fifty states have the *reserved power* to enact laws in areas not exclusively assigned to the federal government by the Constitution or the Congress. Thus, the federal (United States) government and each state have their own code of criminal law and criminal justice system.

Violations of federal criminal laws are investigated by federal agencies such as the Federal Bureau of Investigation (FBI); violations of state criminal laws are investigated by local police and sheriff's departments and, at times, state-level law enforcement agencies such as the state police or state bureau of investigation. Any number of federal crimes—bank robbery and drug trafficking, for example—are also a violation of state criminal law. Which agency assumes jurisdiction—federal, state, or local—can depend on local custom, agreements between agencies or, simply, which agency arrests the perpetrator(s).

The **supremacy clause** of the Constitution, in Article VI, provides for federal law to be "supreme":

> This Constitution, and the laws of the United States which shall be made in pursuance thereof . . . shall be the supreme law of the land; and the judges in every state shall be bound thereby, any thing in the constitution or laws of any state to the contrary notwithstanding.

For issues not specifically reserved for the federal government, the states have *concurrent authority* to develop and enforce law; in such instances, however, state law must conform to the standards set down by Congress or the federal courts, because federal law is supreme.

For example, Title III of the 1968 Omnibus Crime Control and Safe Streets Act provides for the use of telephone wiretapping and electronic surveillance ("bugging") by federal agencies in accordance with certain rules and regulations (e.g., the requirement for court authorization). Congress had the right to enact this legislation because the U.S. Constitution empowers it to regulate interstate commerce, which includes interstate telephonic communications. States that enact legislation which conforms to the rules and regulations set forth in Title III are permitted to engage in "tapping" and "bugging."

Law Enforcement and Jurisdiction

Because government is fragmented, criminal justice agencies lack coordination. Most police agencies are on a municipal level; jails and prosecutors are usually on a county level; courts can be municipal, county, or state; and prisons and parole systems are part of state government. And there is a completely separate federal system of justice.

Each criminal justice agency is dependent on a different level of government for its funding. Municipal officials allocate funds for the police with little or no attention to the needs of the other parts of the system. Because of their primary role as protectors and their public visibility, the police receive proportionately more funding than other criminal justice agencies. Public officials often respond to a perceived increase in threats to public safety by increasing the number of police officers. The result is like a funnel, as the large number of police officers dump more cases into the criminal justice system than the smaller number of other personnel—judges, prosecutors, and public defenders—can handle.

CRIME CONTROL VERSUS DUE PROCESS

As if fragmented power were not enough to insure against tyranny, the founding fathers also saddled us with the concept of due process, which significantly hampers efforts at controlling crime. Herbert Packer (1968) describes this tension between liberty and efficiency in terms of two models of the criminal justice process. The first, the **crime control model**, "is based on the proposition that the repression of criminal conduct is by far the most important function to be performed by the criminal justice process" (1968: 158). In order to successfully repress

Collier's
THE NATIONAL WEEKLY

Pirate Treasure

VOL. XLVII NO. 26 — SEPTEMBER 16, 1911

Article I, section 8 of the Constitution reserves the crime of piracy (*left*) for federal jurisdiction. The Constitution also grants supreme authority to federal law in espionage cases. In October 1985 retired Navy communications expert John A. Walker, Jr. (*above*) pleaded guilty to charges that he spied for the Soviet Union and recruited three others in the operation. A federal judge sentenced Walker to two concurrent life terms in what many U.S. officials termed the most damaging spy case in decades.

criminal conduct, crime control requires a high level of *efficiency:* the ability of the system to apprehend, prosecute, and convict a large proportion of criminal offenders. However, the system must respond to a great number of cases with only limited resources. Consequently, efficiency demands that cases be handled speedily—with a minimum of formality and without challenges, which can be time-consuming. This efficiency is accomplished by the *presumption of guilt.* Packer (1968: 160) says, "The supposition is that the screening processes operated by the police and prosecutors are reliable indicators of probable guilt." After this screening, the system must move expeditiously to conviction and sentencing. The crime control model is characterized by a high level of confidence in the ability of the police and prosecutors to separate the guilty from the innocent.

This confidence conflicts with the assumption of the **due process model**, namely, that the criminal justice system is deficient. Packer (1968: 163) notes that this alternative model

> stresses the possibility of error. People are notoriously poor observers of disturbing events—the more emotion-arousing the context, the greater the possibility that recollection will be incorrect; confessions and admissions by persons in police custody may be induced by physical or psychological coercion so that the police end up hearing what the suspect thinks they want to hear rather than the truth; witnesses may be animated by a bias or interest that no one would trouble to discover except one specially charged with protecting the interests of the accused (as the police are not).

The due process model requires the system to slow down until it "resembles a factory that has to devote a substantial part of its input to quality control" (1968: 165). Due process confronts crime control and its need for efficiency and speed with an obstacle course of formalities, technicalities, and civil rights. As Packer notes (1968: 166): "Power is always subject to abuse—sometimes subtle, other times, as in the criminal justice process, open and ugly. Precisely because of its potency in subjecting the individual to the coercive power of the state, the criminal justice process must . . . be subjected to controls that prevent it from operating with maximal efficiency."

Arrest and prosecution disadvantage a defendant regardless of case outcome. The defendant may be incarcerated until the trial is completed; he or she will need to engage an attorney; and

In March 1985 New Hampshire housewife Cathleen Webb publicly announced that she had falsely accused a man of raping her seven years earlier in a Chicago suburb. At the time she claimed Gary Dotson—a man who resembled Webb's description—committed the crime; Dotson was convicted and sentenced to twenty-five to fifty years in prison. According to Webb, she was only able to recant her testimony after she had become a born-again Christian. But Cook County Circuit Court judge Richard Samuels, who presided over the rape trial, refused to overturn the verdict. Outraged Illinois citizens petitioned Governor James Thompson, who finally commuted his sentence, despite his belief in Dotson's guilt. After six years in prison, Dotson went free. The incident, which created national attention, made talk-show celebrities of Dotson and Webb, enabling them to sell their stories for a reported $350,000 to a TV production company. *Above*, the two appear on NBC's *Today* show. Despite all the publicity her recantation garnered, Webb maintained throughout that she was only trying to clear Dotson's name and record.

there is the shame and stigma associated with arrest and prosecution. Furthermore, innocent persons are sometimes found guilty, and the stories in the sidebar, "Cases of Mistaken Guilt," provide a few examples.

David Margolick (1984) provides an example of how an arrest can disadvantage a person found to be innocent: "A 62-year-old woman with no criminal record is charged with the sexual abuse of children. She spends the night in a cockroach-infested jail cell, hectored by prostitutes." The Bronx District Attorney had called a press conference to announce "grandma's" arrest, and "she is shown on television handcuffed and in tears as she fends off angry parents. Photographs and articles appear in the local newspapers." The grand jury found no reason to indict her, however. When the district attorney was asked about the case, he responded it is inevitable that from time to time innocent people find themselves embroiled in the criminal justice system.

An imperfect criminal justice system—and there is no such entity as a perfect system of justice—occasionally causes innocent persons to be imprisoned. More frequently, however, due process protections result in guilty persons going free. The relevant question is, What is the level of error that we, as a society, are willing to permit—and in which direction?

Due process of law

A defendant in a criminal case is automatically entitled to a host of legal protections that collectively are referred to as **due process.** As was noted at the beginning of the chapter, this was one of the ways the Founding Fathers sought to curb the abuse of government power. Before agreeing to ratify the Constitution, many states insisted that it be amended to include a Bill of Rights. Due process rights discussed below are those set forth in the Constitution's first ten amendments.

The Right to Remain Silent

The Fifth Amendment declares, "... nor shall [a person] be compelled in any criminal case to be a witness against himself"; this is known as the right against **self-incrimination.** Thus, defendants in criminal cases cannot be compelled to testify; they

Cases of Mistaken Guilt

Joseph M. Majczek was convicted for the murder of a Chicago police officer in 1932 and sentenced to ninety-nine years' imprisonment. He was released in 1945 after newspaper reporters discovered that the prosecutor had suppressed evidence that would have led to Majczek's acquittal. The story was dramatized in the motion picture *Call Northside 777*.

Isidore Zimmerman of Queens, New York, spent twenty-four years in prison for a murder that state officials have since conceded he did not commit. He was originally sentenced to execution, and in 1939 came within hours of being electrocuted in Sing Sing prison. In 1983 Zimmerman was awarded $1 million in compensation by the New York State Court of Claims (Shipp 1983).

Wilbur McDonald was sentenced to a term of 100 to 150 years in Illinois in 1970 for murder. After three years, one month, and six days, he was released; another man had confessed to the crime (M. Rich 1983).

William Bernard Jackson of Columbus, Ohio, was released from the maximum-security prison in Lucasville, Ohio, in 1982 after spending five years for two rapes he did not commit. A medical doctor who resembled Jackson, and who also had the same surname, confessed to the crimes (M. Rich 1983).

In 1985 Monty Hooper, who had spent ten months in a Fort Worth, Texas, jail awaiting trial on a charge of armed robbery, was released. The supermarket clerk who had identified him as the man who held her up identified him as the perpetrator of a subsequent robbery. But Hooper was already in jail as a result of his arrest for the first robbery (*New York Times*, March 22, 1985: 8).

On September 27, 1978, Charles Daniels was arrested for a vicious sexual attack on a two-year-old boy and the attempted murder of the child, who was hurled from a rooftop. Despite testimony from a number of witnesses who provided Daniels with an alibi, he was convicted and sentenced to a prison term of six to eighteen years. Sex offender are often at risk in prison, and Daniels was beaten and scalded with boiling water by inmates; he had to be kept in solitary confinement for four years. Seven years later, New York City officials acknowledged that he had been wrongfully imprisoned and in an out-of-court settlement agreed to pay him $600,000 (Raab 1985).

James Albert Tidewell of Rockford, Illinois, spent two years in prison for a robbery he did not commit. Tidewell was released from prison in 1982 after an appellate court discovered he had been erroneously convicted on the basis of perjured testimony (M. Rich 1983).

Ernest Holbrook, Jr., spent more than two years in prison for the rape and murder of a child. In 1984 the Wayne County (Ohio) prosecutor announced that another man had actually committed the crime (*New York Times*, April 16, 1984: 8).

Jerome Tyler spent three years in Illinois prisons for a rape and robbery he did not commit. In 1972 the Court of Claims provided him with compensation; he was awarded $600 (M. Rich 1983).

Nathaniel Carter of Queens, New York, was arrested in 1981 for murder and was subsequently convicted and sentenced to a term of twenty-five years to life. After twenty-eight months of imprisonment, Carter was released after someone else confessed to the murder—his estranged wife, who had been the chief witness against Carter at his trial (Shenon 1984). In 1986, Carter received an out-of-court settlement from the City of New York for $450,000. Ironically, his wife, Delissa, who has admitted to committing the murder, cannot be prosecuted; she had been given immunity from prosecution in return for testifying against her husband.

Lenell Geter, a black engineer whose life sentence for armed robbery in Texas drew national attention, was cleared of all charges against him on March 21, 1984. Mr. Geter had been convicted and imprisoned in 1982 (Applebome 1984).

In 1982 Mark Bowles, 21, of Annapolis, Maryland, was convicted of assault and battery in the rape of Kathryn Tucci. After serving almost fourteen months, Bowles was released from prison because Tucci admitted to a false accusation. She was subsequently sentenced to 1,000 hours of community work with a rape crisis center (*New York Times,* April 14, 1985: 12).

In 1986, after spending six years in prison, the life sentence of a twenty-six-year-old Brooklyn man was set aside. In a motion brought by the defense and supported by the district attorney, a New York Supreme Court judge declared that Robert McLaughlin had been wrongfully convicted of murder and robbery on the basis of a tainted identification by a witness (Buder 1986: 18).

cannot even be compelled to be sworn and take the witness stand. In other words, defendants cannot be forced to invoke their right to remain silent in front of a jury, since that could conceivably prejudice the jury members against them.

The case of *Miranda v. Arizona* (1966) extends this privilege to persons undergoing police interrogation. In the *Miranda* decision, the Supreme Court held that, if this privilege is not safeguarded at pretrial stages, people may forfeit their right to remain silent long before they ever see the inside of a courtroom—in a police station, for example. In its decision, the Court listed the safeguards that became binding on all law enforcement officers in the United States:

1. Prior to any questioning, suspects must be warned that: (*a*) they have the right to remain silent; (*b*) any statement they make can be used against them; (*c*) they have the right to have an attorney present at any questioning; and (*d*) if they cannot afford an attorney, one will be appointed without cost to be present at the questioning.

2. Any waiver by the suspect of the rights provided by *Miranda* must be made "knowingly and intelligently."

3. If the suspect "indicates in any manner" a desire for the presence of an attorney at any stage in the interrogation, the questioning must be immediately interrupted until a lawyer can be obtained.

4. If the suspect "indicates in any manner that he does not wish to be interrogated," the questioning will not begin or, if it has already commenced, it must be halted, even though the suspect may have already given incriminating information, until the suspect has consulted legal counsel and has consented to further questioning.

In 1981 the Supreme Court ruled that once a suspect requests a lawyer, the police are not allowed to interrogate the suspect in the absence of his or her attorney. In two 1986 cases, the police in Michigan obtained confessions after the defendants had requested counsel at their arraignments. In *Michigan v. Jackson* and *Michigan v. Bladel*, the Court ruled that the police cannot interrogate a defendant in the absence of counsel, if, at his arraignment, the defendant had asked that an attorney be appointed to represent him.

In a rare unanimous verdict, in 1986 the Court ruled that a defendant has a constitutional right to explain the circumstances surrounding his confession. In *Crane v. Kentucky,* a state court judge refused to allow a defendant in a murder trial to testify about the physical and psychological environment in which a confession had been obtained. The defendant was sixteen years of age at the time and had been arrested for the murder of a liquor store clerk. In court, in the absence of the jury, the defendant denied that he committed the crime and stated that the confession had been secured through the use of coercive methods. The trial judge ruled that the confession was valid and refused to allow the defendant to testify before the jury about the circumstances of the confession. The Supreme Court ruled that "confessions, even those that have been found to be voluntary, are not conclusive of guilt," and therefore, defendants have a right to challenge their "reliability and credibility" before a jury.

Exceptions

In 1984, in *New York v. Quarles* the Supreme Court, in a 5–4 decision, ruled that "overriding considerations of public safety" may justify questioning a suspect in custody without providing the warnings contained in *Miranda*. The **public safety exception** was the result of a woman's complaint to two New York City police officers that she had been raped and that the suspects had entered a nearby supermarket. The officers entered the store and apprehended, after a chase, one man who fit the description provided by the woman. He was handcuffed and found to be wearing an empty shoulder holster. One of the officers asked whether he had a gun. The suspect nodded toward a pile of boxes and said, "The gun is over there." The officer recovered a .38 caliber revolver. The defense moved to prevent the statement and the gun from being entered into evidence at the subsequent trial. Three New York courts agreed, noting that the suspect had not been given warnings as required by *Miranda*. The Supreme Court ruled that the unattended firearm represented a danger to public safety, and the gun and the statement were admitted into evidence.

MIRANDA WARNINGS

You have the right to remain silent. Anything you say can and will be used against you in a court of law.

You have the right to talk to a lawyer and have him present with you when you are being questioned. If you cannot afford to hire a lawyer, one will be appointed to represent you before any questioning, if you wish.

You can decide at any time to exercise these rights and not answer any questions or make any statements.

Do you understand each of these rights I have explained to you?

Having these rights in mind, do you wish to talk to us now?

In 1985, in *Oregon v. Elstad*, the Supreme Court, in a bitterly disputed 6–3 decision, again ruled in favor of the crime control position in a *Miranda* case. Pursuant to an arrest warrant, the police went to the home of an eighteen-year-old suspect and explained to him that they thought he was involved in a burglary. He responded, "Yes, I was there." An hour later at the police station, the officers informed the suspect of his *Miranda* rights. He indicated that he understood these rights and gave a full confession. On appeal the state conceded that the statement "I was there" was inadmissible. However, the Supreme Court, in overturning the Oregon high court, ruled that the second confession at the police station was valid, despite arguments that it was an extension of the original inadmissible confession and was thereby tainted.

In a 1986 decision, *Moran v. Burbine*, the Court ruled that a suspect's *Miranda* rights were not violated when the police misled his attorney. Brian Burbine had been arrested for the brutal murder of a woman in Providence, Rhode Island. An assistant public defender, who had been contacted by the suspect's sister, telephoned the police station where Burbine was being held and was told that there would be no questioning until the next day.

THE ONLY 'MIRANDA' ED MEESE EVER HEARD OF

The 1966 *Miranda* decision, which protects the rights of the accused, came under attack in the Reagan administration. Attorney General Edwin Meese, who called the decision "wrong," sought to limit its scope. "The thing is," said Meese, "you don't have many suspects who are innocent of a crime."

125

The suspect was not informed of the call. About an hour later, Burbine was advised of his rights and confessed to the murder. In a 6–3 decision, the Court stated that "events occurring outside of the presence of the suspect and entirely unknown to him surely can have no bearing on the capacity to comprehend and knowingly relinquish a constitutional right." Dissenters argued that the decision gives license to incommunicado interrogation.

It should be noted that the privilege against compulsory self-incrimination pertains only to evidence of a verbal or communicative nature; it is *not applicable when a suspect's body is the source of the evidence.* In *Schmerber v. California* (1966), the defendant had been involved in an automobile accident and was charged with intoxicated driving and arrested at the hospital where he was being treated for injuries. The police instructed a physician to take a blood sample from Schmerber, and this evidence was used to prove intoxication. The defendant claimed that taking and analyzing the blood sample violated his privilege against self-incrimination. The Supreme Court disagreed—the police had taken his blood, not his words.

The police can require a suspect to write or speak for identification, to stand, to assume a stance or pose, to walk, or to make a particular gesture. The police are also authorized to take fingerprints, photographs ("mug shots"), hair samples, breath specimens, fingernail scrapings, and objects concealed in body cavities. The police are also entitled to remove a suspect's clothing in order to search for concealed items such as stolen property and drugs. The suspect can be required to try on articles of clothing for size, and the police can inspect the suspect's body for identifying marks such as cuts, abrasions, bite marks, scars, and tattoos. The suspect can also be required to appear in a lineup for identification purposes. (In *United States v. Wade,* 1967, the Supreme Court ruled that a lineup after indictment requires the presence of legal counsel for the defendant.)

In 1985 the Supreme Court noted limitations in *Schmerber* when, in a 9–0 decision in *Winston v. Lee,* it ruled that the Constitution bars the forced removal of a bullet from the body of an armed robbery suspect. The suspect had been shot by his intended victim and was captured by police in Richmond, Virginia, twenty minutes later. The Court noted that drawing out a sample of blood was only a minor intrusion and thus constitutionally permissible. On the other hand, a compelled surgical intrusion, particularly one that is potentially life-threatening, is not permissible. (For an extensive discussion of the rules of criminal evidence, see Waltz 1983.)

The Right to Legal Counsel

The Sixth Amendment guarantees a criminal defendant "the Assistance of Counsel for his defence." In 1963 the Supreme Court ruled that states must provide counsel for all indigents in felony cases (*Gideon v. Wainwright*). In 1972 this was extended to misdemeanors where imprisonment might result (*Argersinger v. Hamlin*).

The Right to Bail

The Eighth Amendment states, "Excessive bail shall not be required, nor excessive fines imposed, nor cruel and unusual punishments inflicted." Although the Constitution prohibits "excessive" bail, the Supreme Court has ruled that every defendant is not constitutionally entitled to be released on bail. While **bail**, in theory, is designed to ensure the return of a defendant to stand trial, in practice a high bail is often imposed to detain the defendant and thereby preclude the commission of further crimes—a practice known as **preventive detention**. In 1987 the Supreme Court (*United States v. Salerno*) upheld the practice of denying bail to certain dangerous defendants.

The Right to a Jury Trial

The Sixth Amendment guarantees that "in all criminal prosecutions, the accused shall enjoy the right to a speedy and public trial, by an impartial jury." The Supreme Court has made a number of decisions further defining this right. It has defined who has the right to a jury trial. In *Duncan v. Louisiana* (1968) and *Baldwin v. New York* (1970), the Supreme Court ruled that the right to a jury trial only applies to crimes punishable by a term of imprisonment of six months or more. Some states, however, provide a jury trial for anyone accused of any criminal charges. The Court has also ruled on the size of juries. While most states and the federal government use twelve-member juries, in *Williams v. Florida* (1970), the Supreme Court upheld the use of a six-member jury in all but capital cases, but ruled against a five-member jury in *Ballew v. Georgia* (1978), even though the case only involved a misdemeanor. Finally, the Court has also ruled on the number of votes needed to reach a verdict. In most states jury decisions are required to be unanimous, or else a hung jury results. The Supreme Court in *Johnson v. Louisiana* (1972) and *Apodaca v. Oregon* (1972) ruled that verdicts as low as 9–3 and 10–2 are constitutional. In *Burch v. Louisiana* (1979), the Supreme Court ruled that if six jurors are used, the verdict must be unanimous.

The Right to Confront Witnesses

The Sixth Amendment provides for the defendant "to be informed of the nature and cause of the accusation; to be confronted with the witnesses against him; to have compulsory process [subpoena] for obtaining witnesses in his favor." Defense counsel can cross-examine all witnesses and attempt to impeach their testimony or credibility.

Double Jeopardy

The Fifth Amendment states, "... nor shall any person be subject for the same offence to be twice put in jeopardy of life or limb." This prohibition against **double jeopardy** means that a defendant found "not guilty" cannot be tried again for the same crime even if incontestable evidence is subsequently discovered that proves the defendant's guilt.

In 1985 the Supreme Court ruled in *Heath v. Alabama* that two states may prosecute a defendant for the same criminal act without violating the Fifth Amendment. Larry Gene Heath was sentenced in Alabama and Georgia for hiring two men to kidnap and kill his pregnant wife. She was kidnapped from their home in Alabama and shot to death in Georgia, which did not have the death penalty. In order to avoid a possible sentence of death, Heath pled guilty in Georgia. He was subsequently tried and convicted of the same charges in Alabama and sentenced to death. In a 7–2 decision, the Court stated that because each state is sovereign, the defendant had committed separate offenses against the law of each and, therefore, the convictions were an exception to the double jeopardy clause.

The Exclusionary Rule

The Fourth Amendment provides for "the right of the people to be secure in their persons, houses, papers and effects, against unreasonable searches and seizures, shall not be violated, and no Warrants shall issue, but upon probable cause, supported by Oath or affirmation, and particularly describing the place to be searched, and the persons or things to be seized." In the case of *Weeks v. United States* (1914), the Supreme Court established the **exclusionary rule** when it declared that evidence obtained in violation of the Fourth Amendment was not admissible in federal criminal cases.

In 1961 the Supreme Court extended the exclusionary rule to state criminal cases when it decided the case of *Mapp v. Ohio*. The Court recognized that this doctrine would sometimes have the effect, as Supreme Court Justice Benjamin Cardozo noted generations earlier, of permitting "the criminal . . . to go free because the constable has blundered." However, the Court also recognized the potential for a greater evil—unbridled police powers: "we can no longer permit it [the Due Process clause] to be revocable at the whim of any police officer who, in the name of law enforcement itself, chooses to suspend its enjoyment." Thus, if the police cannot make use of improperly secured evidence in court, they will be constrained from acting improperly.

Exceptions

Opponents of the exclusionary rule have argued for a good faith or **reasonable mistake exception** to the exclusionary rule so that evidence obtained in the *reasonable belief* that the search and seizure were consistent with the Fourth Amendment could be used in criminal cases. In the case of *United States v. Leon* (1984), the Supreme Court (in a 6–3 decision) agreed with this argument and ruled that when the police act on a defective warrant, the exclusionary rule need not apply.

MAPP V. OHIO

On May 23, 1957, three Cleveland police officers arrived at the home of Dollree Mapp and demanded admittance because they believed that a fugitive, as well as a large amount of illegal lottery paraphernalia, was being hidden in the house. After telephoning her lawyer, Mapp refused entry to the police. The officers conducted a surveillance, and three hours later, with additional officers, they forced their way into the house. Mapp and her attorney, who had arrived at the scene, demanded to see the search warrant. One of the officers held up a piece of paper. Mapp seized the paper and was arrested and handcuffed. The entire house was thoroughly searched, and police recovered obscene materials. No evidence that a search warrant had even been issued was presented at the subsequent trial. Despite this apparent violation of the Fourth Amendment, Mapp was convicted of possessing obscene materials.

On appeal the Supreme Court held that "the State, by admitting evidence unlawfully seized, served to encourage disobedience to the Federal Constitution which it is bound to uphold." The Court concluded, "The ignoble shortcut to conviction . . . tends to destroy the entire system of constitutional restraints on which the liberties of the people rest."

Some legal observers are troubled by the implications of the *Leon* decision. They argue that the reality of criminal justice in general, and the process of issuing warrants in particular, often belies theory. In theory, before a judge or magistrate issues a search warrant, he or she carefully scrutinizes police affidavits to determine if probable cause exists. In reality, the judge's or magistrate's review may often be quite perfunctory, and requests for search warrants are seldom denied. Critics of the *Leon* decision fear that the police might request search warrants even in the absence of probable cause, knowing that the fruits of the resulting search will be admissible in court.

United States v. Leon

Burbank, California, police officers were investigating Alberto Leon and others for cocaine and methaqualone trafficking. Based on information from a confidential informant of unproven reliability and on a lengthy investigation and extended surveillance, an application for a search warrant and supporting affidavit to search several automobiles and residences were prepared. The affidavit, which was based primarily on information from the informant, was subjected to review by several deputy district attorneys. Subsequently, a warrant was issued by a state superior court judge, and the ensuing search produced large quantities of drugs and other evidence.

Leon and the other defendants challenged the sufficiency of the search warrant and moved in district court to suppress the evidence seized pursuant to the warrant, which, they argued, was defective because it was based on insufficient evidence. The district court ruled that the affidavit was insufficient to establish probable cause since the reliability and credibility of the informant had not been established; the evidence was suppressed.

The case eventually reached the Supreme Court on appeal. The Court, in upholding the search, ruled that the exclusionary rule "is designed to deter police misconduct rather than punish the error of judges and magistrates" (who may issue defective search warrants). The Supreme Court, however, also noted circumstances when evidence might be excluded even where a judge has approved the search warrant:

1. where the officers "were dishonest or reckless in preparing their affidavit";
2. where the judge is not neutral and detached and instead serves merely as a rubber stamp for the police; and
3. where the officers "could not have harbored an objectively reasonable belief in the existence of probable cause."

Another exception to the exclusionary rule is the principle of **inevitable discovery** which the Supreme Court defined in the 1984 case of *Nix v. Williams*, which was a continuation of a famous case, *Brewer v. Williams*, decided in 1977. Robert Williams was suspected of killing a ten-year-old girl, and two hundred volunteers were combing the Des Moines, Iowa, area searching for her body. Although the police had promised the suspect's attorney that they would not question him, as they were driving Williams across the state, they asked him to think about the fact that "the parents of this little girl should be entitled to a Christian burial" for their daughter. His response was to lead the police to his victim's body. In the 1977 decision, the Court ruled 5–4 that the "Christian burial" speech had violated the suspect's constitutional rights by inducing him to incriminate himself outside of his lawyer's presence. The decision left open the possibility, however, that the evidence of the body's discovery could be used at a subsequent trial if the state could show that the body would have been discovered without the suspect's induced cooperation.

Williams was tried again, and the prosecution did not offer into evidence any incriminating statements of the defendant, nor did the state attempt to show that Williams had directed police to the body. The trial judge admitted the prosecution's evidence as to the condition of the body and related physical evidence on the grounds that the prosecution had shown that if Williams had not been improperly interrogated, the victim's body would nevertheless have been found by the search party; therefore, evidence resulting from the discovery of the body was admissible. In upholding Williams' conviction in 1984, the Supreme Court gave recognition to the principle of inevitable discovery.

In two 1986 cases, the Supreme Court ruled 5–4 that investigators do not need a warrant to conduct an aerial surveillance of a private area. In *California v. Ciraola*, Santa Clara police officers, based on an anonymous tip, flew over the backyard of a man alleged to be growing marijuana, and, using sophisticated equipment, took photographs from 1,000 feet. They used the photographs of the ten-foot-high plants to secure a search warrant. In a related case, *Dow Chemical Company v. United States*, investigators from the Environmental Protection Agency (EPA) took aerial photographs of a manufacturing complex. Before the photographs could be used by the EPA to prove violations of antipollution laws, Dow sued to bar their use. The Court stated that in these cases there was no reasonable expectation of privacy (the constitutional standard for the Fourth Amendment); areas around a home or business, even when fenced, are not protected against observations by an investigator "from a public vantage point where he has a right to be and which renders the activities clearly visible," even if visibility requires special equipment such as high-powered lenses.

Some opponents of the exclusionary rule have argued that the proper remedy for unconstitutional activity by police officers is a tort action, not suppression of the evidence. A 1986 decision by the Supreme Court appears to support that position. Previous Court decisions have held that judges and prosecutors have absolute immunity from liability as a result of actions taken in their official capacity. The Court has also determined that state and local governments have rather limited liability for the actions of their employees—it must be proven that the actions at issue represent official policy. A Rhode Island state police officer secured an arrest warrant on rather questionable grounds. The subjects of the arrest, a prominent couple from Narragansett, were accused of hosting a "marijuana party," but a grand jury refused to indict them and the charges were dropped. The Narragansett couple filed a $4-million lawsuit against the state, which was dismissed, and against the officer, which the Court ruled permissible. In *Malley v. Briggs,* the Court refused to extend liability protection to police officers, and its 7–2 decision suggested that forcing incompetent police officers to pay damages was a better remedy for violations of the Fourth Amendment than excluding evidence. Police representatives point out that this decision leaves the officer "holding the bag," and civil libertarians argue that police officers are not in a position to provide substantial monetary damages to potential victims of unconstitutional actions.

The impact of the exclusionary rule has been the subject of more rhetoric than research. One of the few research efforts (Burkhart et al. 1982: ii) found, however, that "of all felony cases rejected for prosecution in California in the years 1976–1979, 4.8 percent were rejected because of search and seizure problems. Almost three-quarters of these were drug cases. A study in Chicago (Tybor and Eissman 1986) revealed that judges exclude evidence for constitutional reasons in only 0.5 percent of violent crime cases; the figure for property crimes is 0.2 percent. As in California, most cases in which evidence was excluded involved drugs. It should also be noted that the rules of evidence vary somewhat from state to state. On the one hand, although state courts must apply constitutional *minimum* standards as interpreted by the Supreme Court, they can set a higher standard for evidence because they do not have to allow the exceptions to the exclusionary rule permitted by the Supreme Court. On the other hand, several states (e.g., Arizona and Colorado) have passed laws that recognize a "good faith" exception to the exclusionary rule, and in 1982, California voters approved a "truth-in-evidence" proposition, which requires state courts to construe the Fourth Amendment rights in the narrowest sense permitted by the Supreme Court.

CRIME CONTROL	**DUE PROCESS**
efficiency	liberty

The ongoing debate over the exclusionary rule shows us that the distance between crime control and due process can be conceived of as a zero-sum continuum; in other words, any action, such as new legislation or court decisions, that moves criminal justice toward one model does so at the expense of the other. For example, legislation or a court decision that allows an exception to the exclusionary rule may increase police efficiency, but it also lessens the ability of the courts to control police misconduct.

The Criminal Justice Process

In this chapter's introduction to the criminal justice system, we have looked at its overall structure—an often uncoordinated network of agencies at the various levels and branches of government—and at its goals—efficient crime control and protection of citizens' rights to due process. Now we will look at the criminal justice process, the series of stages through which a defendant moves, from investigation and arrest through prison and parole.

Preliminary Investigation

If an incident comes to the attention of the police (or other law enforcement agency) as a result of direct observation or a citizen report, the first step is to determine if a crime actually occurred. In the case of a citizen report, the incident simply may not have happened, or it may not have happened in the manner described; a mistake may have been made, or the witness/complainant was simply being vindictive. In other cases the observed or reported conduct may prove not to have constituted a crime under existing law.

If a crime is suspected or reported, the next investigatory step is to determine whether the available evidence is sufficient to establish **probable cause**, the minimum required to effect a lawful arrest. It consists of two interconnected variables:

1. information sufficient to cause a reasonable person to believe that a crime is being or has been committed; and
2. information sufficient to cause a reasonable person to believe that a specific person (the arrestee) is committing or has committed that crime.

If an officer observed the incident, the investigation consists of what he or she saw and heard, including the suspect's responses during interrogation and the results of a search of the suspect's person. An investigation based on a civilian complaint entails a visit to the crime scene and the collection and testing of any physical evidence found there. The suspect, if there is one, will be interviewed after being informed of his or her *Miranda* rights. The suspect's story, if he or she agrees to provide a statement, must be checked. The suspect may be subjected to surveillance, or "tailed," and a court order for electronic surveillance may also be requested, if this is permitted by state law.

Some investigations are made before a crime is committed and are based on information indicating that a criminal act is

Overview of the Criminal Justice Process

```
                    Crime
                      │                    ┌──────────────┐
                      │ Investigation      │   Juvenile   │
                      │              ┌────▶│   Justice    │
                      ▼              │     │    System    │
                    Arrest ──────────┘     └──────────────┘
                      │         Juveniles
                    Booking
                      │
                      ▼
              ┌───────────────────────┐
              │ Initial Court Appearance│
              │                       │ ────▶ Dismissal
              │  Preliminary Hearing  │
              │                       │
              │      Arraignment      │
              └───────────────────────┘
                      │
                      ▼
              Grand Jury/Information
                      │
                      ▼
                    Trial
                  Judge/Jury ─────────▶ Acquittal
                      │
                      ▼
                  Sentence ◀──── Guilty Plea
                   │    │
            ┌──────┘    └──────┐
            ▼                  ▼
          Fine              Probation
                      
                  Jail/Prison ────────▶ Parole
                      │
                      ▼
                   Release
```

being planned. Investigation of ongoing criminal conspiracies in drug trafficking and organized crime requires extensive use of informants, undercover operatives, and electronic surveillance.

Arrest

The most important product of an investigation is an arrest. *The Dictionary of Criminal Justice Data Terminology* (1981: 22) defines an **arrest** as "taking an adult or juvenile into physical custody by authority of law, for the purpose of charging the person with a criminal offense or a delinquent act or status offense." Reasonable force can be used, if necessary, to take suspects physically into custody and transport them to a holding facility, usually a police station equipped with cells, where they can be booked and a request that formal charges be instituted (usually by detectives or the prosecutor) can be prepared and submitted.

Occasionally, arrests are made pursuant to a court-issued **arrest warrant** (based on a showing of probable cause to a judge or magistrate). This procedure can be time-consuming and is employed when there is no pressing need for a speedy arrest and when the responsible officer wishes to have the legal protection of court authorization for the arrest. In most instances, however, an arrest will be made by an officer on the spot, without a warrant and only on probable cause.

At the time of the arrest (except for some minor offenses), the suspect will be searched and relieved of any weapons, contraband (e.g., drugs), and any evidentiary materials. The arresting officer will determine if the suspect is a minor, who according to law must be treated as a juvenile—for example, taken to a juvenile facility rather than an adult lock-up. In less serious cases, the arrestees are released after being given a summons or citation that requires them to appear in court on a fixed date. In some situations, the release from police custody may require the posting of bond.

Booking

Booking indicates the completion of an arrest. An administrative record of the arrest is made, identifying the person, place, time, and reason for the arrest, and it may involve fingerprinting and photographing. Whether fingerprinting occurs during booking depends upon the practice in a given jurisdiction, which may vary according to the type of offense (felony suspects are always fingerprinted) or the age of the person taken into custody (juveniles are usually not fingerprinted). In addition to helping

Cook County, Illinois, deputy sheriffs prepare to make an arrest.

identify the suspect, fingerprint checks reveal past arrests, convictions, and whether the suspect is wanted by any law enforcement agency.

After booking, the suspect will be allowed to use the telephone to alert family or friends or to secure legal counsel or bail. The suspect's personal property—such as watch, wallet—will be taken away and inventoried for later return. The suspect may be

When is a crime considered solved?

Law enforcement agencies measure solved cases by counting clearances; that is, the number of cases in which a known criminal offense has resulted in the arrest, citation, or summoning of a person in connection with the offense or in which a criminal offense has been "resolved" (location and identity of suspect known), but an arrest is not possible because of exceptional circumstances such as death of suspect or refusal of the victim to prosecute.

The interpretation of clearance statistics must be approached with caution. For example, a number of criminal offenses may be designated as cleared when a single offender has been apprehended for their commission. However, because the crimes may have involved the participation of multiple suspects, the term clearance may suggest that a criminal investigation has closed, when in fact it may be continued until the remaining suspects are apprehended. Additionally, a case may be cleared even though the suspect will not be processed for that offense or is later absolved of wrongdoing.

Most crimes are not cleared by arrest

	Reported crimes cleared by arrest
Murder	72%
Aggravated assault	58
Forcible rape	48
Robbery	24
Larceny-theft	19
Burglary	14
Motor vehicle theft	14
All UCR Index Crimes	19

SOURCE: Zawitz 1983: 52.

strip-searched and then assigned to a holding cell ("pen" or "tank") pending transportation to court.

Pretrial Hearings

Depending on what time of day the arrest occurred and whether it happened on a weekday, weekend, or holiday, the suspect may have to spend twenty-four hours or longer in detention before appearing in court. At the initial appearance, the official charges are read, the need for counsel considered, and bail may be set or reviewed if already set at a bond hearing. Unless the case is dismissed for lack of sufficient evidence, the suspect is now a defendant. At the first appearance, which may be only a **bond**

hearing, the primary, and perhaps the only, question is one of bail.

Bail is a monetary (or other valuable) security, which is put up by, or on behalf of, a criminal defendant to insure his or her return to court to stand trial. If the defendant fails to appear, bail is forfeited. The bail decision is a discretionary one on the part of the judge, who can set bail at a level that is impossible for the defendant to meet or order the defendant released on his or her own recognizance, which is simply a promise to return to court.

The prosecutor may play an important role in the bail decision by recommending, supporting, or objecting to a certain level of bail. The stage at which the prosecutor (usually a county official whose title may vary in different jurisdictions, e.g., district attorney, state's attorney) first becomes involved varies. In some jurisdictions, it occurs within twenty-four hours of an arrest and before the initial filing of charges against the suspect. In other jurisdictions, it occurs after initial filing by the police and within a few days of the arrest.

These pretrial hearings (which include bond hearings, initial appearances, preliminary hearings and/or arraignments) vary from jurisdiction to jurisdiction, but typically last only a few minutes. If the case is a misdemeanor, it may be adjudicated during these early stages of the judicial process by a plea of guilty or dismissal of the charges. Due to the large volume of cases entering the system, misdemeanor cases will usually be disposed of in a matter of minutes in a process referred to as "rough justice." There will be only minimal attention to due-process niceties, since decisions pertaining to the level of bail, to dismissal or acceptance of a guilty plea, and to sentencing are made with great rapidity. Defendants usually do not raise objections to such treatment since they are on the receiving end of the leniency that permeates this level of criminal justice—most defendants in misdemeanor cases are set free. An objection—that is, insistence on innocence and a demand for due process—slows down the system and the defendant may be remanded to the county jail to await his or her "day in court." It is ironic—a distortion of justice—that defendants who accept the charges against them may go free, while those who insist on their innocence may go to jail.

If the charge(s) constitutes a felony, the case is referred to a superior court (or the felony part of a unified court system, to be discussed in chapter 10). A preliminary, **probable cause hearing** will be held to determine if the arresting officer had sufficient evidence, or probable cause, to justify an arrest. The hearing is short, a mini-trial at which the prosecution may call witnesses and the defense may cross-examine them and call witnesses as well. The judge must determine if the defendant is to stand trial or if the case is to be dismissed for lack of evidence—no **prima facie case** (Latin for "on its face," meaning not requiring further evidence to establish credibility). The judge may also determine that there is insufficient evidence to support a felony charge but that there is probable cause for a misdemeanor proceeding.

Grand Jury

The Fifth Amendment of the Constitution provides that "no person shall be held to answer for a capital, or otherwise infamous crime, unless on presentment or indictment of a grand jury." However, the Supreme Court has not made the grand jury requirement applicable to the states through the due process clause of the Fourteenth Amendment. States east of the Mississippi River tend to use the grand jury, and prosecutors can bypass a probable cause hearing by presenting evidence directly to the grand jury. This enables the prosecution to avoid disclosing important aspects of the case so early in the process—grand jury hearings are secret.

The **grand jury** consists of twenty-three citizens who hear charges presented by the prosecution. The proceedings are *ex parte* (one-party)—witnesses and defendants are usually not allowed to be represented by counsel when appearing before a grand jury. The proceedings are also secret, and neither the public nor the news media may attend a grand jury session. Grand juries, because they hear only the prosecutor's version of the case, almost always return a **true bill**, or indict the defendant. A true bill brings the defendant to trial for a felony. A finding of no true bill causes the defendant to be released from custody or, if free on bail, to have the bail money returned. In states that do not routinely use the grand jury to bring charges, the prosecutor simply files an **information**, a concise statement charging the defendant with a felony crime(s); an information results in a probable cause hearing.

Plea Bargaining

Of the many cases that enter the criminal justice system as a result of an arrest by a police officer, few result in a jury trial—which is expensive and time-consuming. (Even fewer result in the defendant being sent to prison.) A few cases are dealt with by a **bench trial** in which the judge acts in place of the jury, but 85–95 percent of all criminal convictions are the result of **plea bargaining**. This widely practiced method of disposing of cases is often condemned in the popular media as a abuse of discretion resulting in lenient sentences for serious offenders. On the other hand, plea bargaining is also attacked for being unfair to defendants who must choose between waiving their constitutional right to a jury trial or running the risk of a substantially higher sentence if found guilty after a jury trial.

The essence of plea bargaining is an exchange: the defendant agrees to waive his or her due process rights and to insure the prosecution a positive case outcome by pleading guilty; the prosecution reciprocates by insuring that the defendant receives a lighter sentence than he or she might have received if prosecuted and convicted after a trial. The defense counsel often encourages the defendant to plead guilty (the reasons for this will be discussed in detail in chapter 12). The prosecutor not only has the discretionary power to determine the charges for which the defendant will be tried, but can decide whether to accept a plea in return for either reduced charges or a recommendation to the judge for some form of leniency.

Trial

The **trial** is an adversary proceeding in which both sides are represented by legal counsel (except in those rare situations when defendants insist on representing themselves). Each side can use the court's subpoena power to summon witnesses to give testimony and can introduce physical (known as criminalistic or forensic) evidence. Defendants can take the witness stand on their own behalf. If they prefer not to testify and thus not risk cross-examination by the prosecutor (which could cause a criminal record to be disclosed), defendants can maintain the Fifth Amendment privilege against self-incrimination, and the prosecutor is prohibited from commenting on this silence. Each side

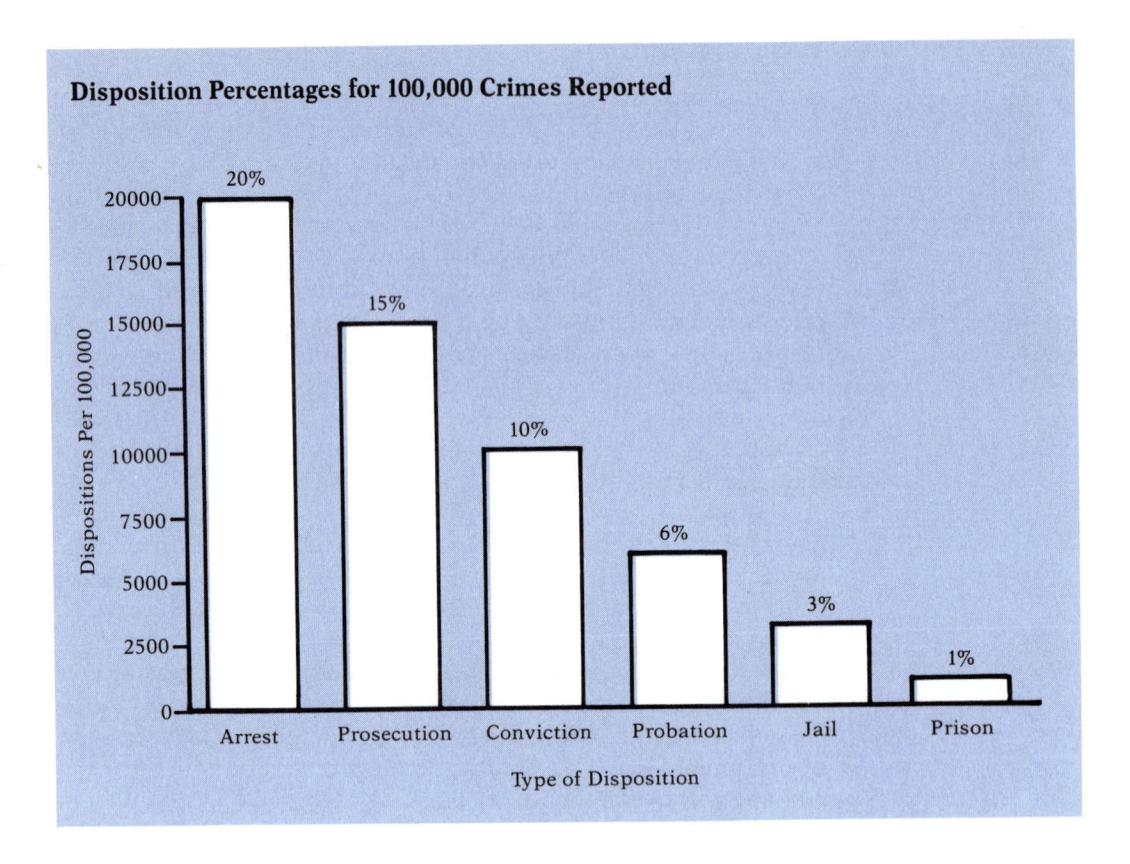

Disposition Percentages for 100,000 Crimes Reported

Type of Disposition	Percentage
Arrest	20%
Prosecution	15%
Conviction	10%
Probation	6%
Jail	3%
Prison	1%

has the right to cross-examine the other side's witnesses, and each side can make objections to the admission of each other's evidence. All of this is accomplished in accordance with established procedural guidelines and rules governing the admissibility of evidence (see, for example, Waltz 1983).

After each side has introduced all of its evidence to the jury (or judge in a bench trial), the judge instructs the jury on the principles of law applicable to the case. Every jury is told (charged) that the facts pointing to the accused's guilt must be established *beyond a reasonable doubt*, not just by a preponderance (greater weight) of the evidence (which is the standard in noncriminal cases). In most jurisdictions the jury's verdict must be unanimous—for guilt (conviction) or innocence (acquittal). A jury that cannot come to a unanimous verdict is a **hung jury**; the jurors are discharged and, if the prosecutor decides, the case is tried a second time before a different jury. If the jury finds the defendant not guilty, the case is dismissed. If the jury finds the defendant guilty of one or more of the charges, the case will proceed to the sentencing stage.

Sentencing

At this stage of the criminal justice process the judge may order a **presentence investigation report (psi).** (In most states the psi is optional; in some it is mandatory.) This report (an example appears in chapter 13), written by a probation officer, will inform the judge about the defendant: previous juvenile and adult criminal record, marital status, education, employment history, military record, physical and mental health, and so on. If requested by the judge, it may contain a sentencing recommendation. The psi is particularly important when the judge is considering a sentence of probation. It is unlikely that a judge would impose a sentence of probation when the probation department recommends against it.

Depending on the statutes of the particular jurisdiction, a sentencing judge can impose:

1. a fine, with or without some other punishment,
2. a suspended sentence,
3. probation, or
4. a jail or prison term.

After sentencing, the defendant is termed a "convict."

Probation

Traditionally, **probation** has been reserved for less serious first offenders. More recently, however, prison overcrowding has resulted in more serious offenders receiving sentences of probation. This sentence brings the convict under the supervision of a probation officer (PO). The probationer must abide by a set of probation regulations (an example appears in chapter 13); a violation of them can result in revocation proceedings and the probationer going to jail or prison. The PO provides counseling and otherwise assists the offender in efforts at employment, training, or education. Probation officers are often overwhelmed

CRIME VICTIMS

Victims are the primary reason for the criminal justice system, and each year more than six million victims of serious crimes are caught up in the justice system. A crime victim can be harmed psychologically, physically, and financially. "For some victims, the loss, burdens, and adjustments may merely be inconvenient; for others, the crime can be completely disabling; and for victims of homicide, the loss of life and costs to survivors defy measurement" (Forst and Hernon 1985: 2). Crime victims may suffer *secondary victimization* as a result of the need to be absent from employment for court appearances or because of subtle or overt intimidation by defendants. The victims of crime, however, have traditionally received very little attention from government. While the defendant, in battling the state, is entitled to a host of due process guarantees, the victim has no similar entitlements.

This situation began to change with the establishment of the Law Enforcement Assistance Administration (LEAA) in 1968. The LEAA encouraged research and the establishment of programs to deal with the needs of crime victims. This concern led to the development of a new field of study,

with too many cases, however, and their supervision may be perfunctory.

Jail/Prison

A judge may impose a sentence to be served in a jail (a county or municipal facility) for misdemeanors or in a prison for felony convictions. On entering jail or prison, the convict becomes an "inmate." Depending on the statutes, the sentence may be determinate (e.g., five years) or indeterminate (e.g., a minimum of two years, a maximum of eight years). Under an indeterminate sentencing system, a parole board determines the actual release

> *victimology*, and in 1976 the first issue of *Victimology: An International Journal* appeared. Persons interested in promoting services for crime victims established the National Organization of Victim Assistance (NOVA), and, in 1984, the Victims of Crime Act, which provides for the collecting of fines, penalties, and other assessments for victims from those convicted of federal crimes, was enacted.
>
> In order to successfully prosecute most criminal cases, a prosecutor is dependent upon the victim-complainant. Victims who are discouraged by the slow pace of justice, or who find the system confusing, may become reluctant or unwilling to continue cooperating with the state. In response, prosecutors have set up a variety of programs for crime victims. In some jurisdictions the victim is an integral part of the plea negotiation process. Some prosecutors have a special unit to assist victim-complainants with counseling or social service referrals. Many assign staff members to explain to the victim how the justice system operates and what to expect from it. Prosecutors and judges, sometimes as a result of crime-victim legislation, are cooperating in the use of restitution as a condition of probation. In addition, a number of states have established victim compensation programs which provide limited funds for some victims of crime.

date of the inmate. Inmates under both determinate and indeterminate sentences are eligible for **good time**, a certain number of days (usually ten to fifteen) each month, which are deducted from their sentence for "good behavior" in the institution. Inmates released on good time are often subjected to the supervision of a parole officer, as are those released on parole.

Parole

Inmates with indeterminate sentences usually become eligible for **parole** release when they complete the minimum sentence imposed by the judge. If the parole board releases the inmate before the maximum sentence is served, he or she comes under the supervision of a parole officer (the title varies from state to state); parole decisions and supervision are *state* functions. Like a probationer, a parolee (or an inmate released on good time) must abide by a set of regulations (an example appears in chapter 16). A violation of the regulations can result in parole revocation proceedings and the parolee being returned to prison to serve out the remainder of his or her sentence. Parole supervision is virtually identical to probation supervision; indeed, in some states the same agency supervises both probationers and parolees.

Appeals

The prosecution cannot **appeal** a verdict or judgment of acquittal; the defendant is free to appeal a guilty plea, however, in the hope of obtaining a reversal. He or she can ask a higher court to review the proceedings that culminated in conviction. The reviewing, or appellate, court, guided by written and oral arguments of counsel for both sides, will comb the trial record for legal mistakes. If the appellate court finds no legal errors, or concludes that such errors were "harmless" (did not prejudice the defendant), it will affirm the conviction. If the appellate court finds that one or more errors were prejudicial, it will *remand* the case—send it back to the trial court—for a new trial. If the appellate court finds that there was no basis whatsoever in law or in fact for the defendant's conviction, the case will be reversed unconditionally and the defendant will go free.

We have examined how crime is defined, the law, types of crimes and criminals, the limitations of crime statistics, theories explaining the cause of crime and, in this chapter, an overview of the criminal justice system. In Part II we will examine how society reacts to crime, beginning with policing.

KEY TERMS

federal system
separation of powers
supremacy clause
crime control model
due process model
due process
self-incrimination
public safety exception
bail
preventive detention
double jeopardy
exclusionary rule
reasonable mistake exception
inevitable discovery
probable cause
arrest
arrest warrant

booking
bond hearing
bail
probable cause hearing
prima facie case
true bill
information
bench trial
plea bargaining
trial
hung jury
presentence investigation report
probation
victimology
good time
parole
appeal

REVIEW QUESTIONS

1. Why does the U.S. Constitution provide for a government in which power is diffused?
2. What are the levels and branches of American government?
3. Why doesn't the American criminal justice system operate as efficiently as that of some other democracies?
4. Which criminal justice agency is funded out of proportion to the level of funding received by other agencies in criminal justice? Why?
5. What are the essential differences between the crime control model and the due process model of criminal justice?
6. What is due process?
7. What did the Supreme Court rule in the case of *Miranda v. Arizona*?

8. What is probable cause?
9. What is the significance of the decision in the case of *Mapp v. Ohio*?
10. Defendants cannot be forced to testify against themselves in a criminal trial. What evidence can a defendant be forced to provide?
11. What is meant by the exclusionary rule? What is its purpose?
12. What is the purpose of bail?
13. What is the purpose of a probable cause hearing?
14. What is meant by a *prima facie* case?
15. What is the grand jury?
16. What is a prosecutor's "information"?
17. What is a presentence investigation report?

Jack Levine, The Perpetrator

PART TWO

Reacting to Crime

6 The Police: History, Goals, and Organization
7 Police Operations
8 Issues in Policing
9 Federal Law Enforcement
10 Federal and State Courts
11 The Lawyers: Judge, Prosecutor, Defense Counsel
12 Plea Bargaining and Trials

CHAPTER 6

The Police: History, Goals, and Organization

STATE POLICE

SHERIFF

MUNICIPAL POLICE HISTORY

POLICE GOALS AND OBJECTIVES
The Dilemma of Law Versus Order

STYLES OF POLICING

POLICE ORGANIZATION

REVIEW QUESTIONS

Boxes
New Jersey State Police
The Boston Police Strike of 1919
Vollmer and Wilson: Pioneers in Police Administration
Organization of the Minneapolis Police Department

The agencies that share more than half of the total criminal justice budget are fragmented into approximately 20,000 state, county, and municipal law enforcement agencies employing more than half a million persons at a cost of more than $13 billion annually. Policing in this country is by tradition a local responsibility, and a single county may have dozens of police agencies. In Cook County, Illinois, for example, which includes the city of Chicago, there are 125 local police departments in addition to other agencies such as the State Police, the Secretary of State Police, the Sheriff's Police, the Park Preserve Police, the State University Police, the Railroad Police, and the Sanitary District Police. Before we examine the history and functions of the most familiar and numerous type of police—the municipal police—we will take a brief look at police forces at the state and county levels.

State Police

One of the earliest state police agencies still in existence is the Texas Rangers, which was created in 1835 to patrol the Mexican border. After the Civil War, the Rangers evolved into a regular state law enforcement agency. Following the lead of Texas, the Arizona Rangers was created in 1901 and the New Mexico Mounted Police in 1905, but they were primarily border patrol forces and remained in existence for only a few years.

Massachusetts had state constables as early as 1865, but the first *modern* state police force was created by Pennsylvania in 1905. The state police in Pennsylvania had a centralized and unified command, its officers were uniformed and chosen on the basis of ability, and the force had full police authority throughout the commonwealth. The state police in Pennsylvania was a response to labor unrest and strikes that were often beyond the ability (or the willingness) of local sheriffs and police agencies to deal with adequately. Thomas Reppetto (1978: 130) states, "the force was meant to crush disorders, whether industrial or otherwise, which arose in the foreigner-filled districts of the state." The Pennsylvania State Police was, in organization and management, a military body whose members—called troopers—resided in barracks.

Other industrial states followed the example of Pennsylvania, while in states with little or no union activity, there developed an alternative statewide agency referred to as the highway patrol. The activities of the highway patrol are limited mainly to matters involving vehicular traffic, and, with the decline of strikes and related violence, traffic control on major interstate arteries is now the major responsibility of both state police and highway patrol agencies. General police services such as routine patrol and responding to citizen requests for service are usually a function of municipal government.

Sheriff

The term "sheriff" derives from the title of the head man—*shire reeve*—of the county appointed by local nobles in medieval England to maintain order and settle disputes. Under the Norman king, William the Conqueror, who took power in England in

NEW JERSEY STATE POLICE

The New Jersey State Police, which was established in 1921, has a force of about 2,200 troopers (neighboring New York State has a force of about 3,600). There are five troops which are responsible for policing the state's major roadways and providing general police services for a number of municipalities and unincorporated areas. The state police also has responsibility for overseeing alcoholic beverage enforcement, the operations of Atlantic City gambling casinos, and the investigation of criminal activity at the state's licensed race tracks. The state police is responsible for maintaining the records of criminals received from all criminal justice agencies in the state, and the agency collects data for the Uniform Crime Report. The state police provides physical protection for the governor and the governor's family, the attorney general, and visiting dignitaries. State police officers also protect the state house complex and other important state offices.

The marine bureau provides a full range of services on

1066, the authority of the shire reeve was expanded, and he acted as a combination justice of the peace (a minor magistrate) and police officer. "Shire reeve" eventually evolved into "sheriff," an official who could muster a *posse comitatus*—the able-bodied men of the county who would assist the sheriff in carrying out his peace-keeping and law enforcement responsibilities. The English sheriff was also an officer of the court, acting as a bailiff by enforcing the orders of the judge, and he was also responsible for collecting taxes.

The office of sheriff was adapted to the American scene where it was made an elective county office, and services were usually limited to carrying out the orders of the court. The sheriff's salary was often dependent on fees for serving summonses, subpoenas, and writs and enforcing warrants. He also received payment for summoning juries and looking after prisoners in the county jail.

> the state's waterways, including law enforcement and rescue. There is also a helicopter patrol bureau whose six helicopters provide assistance with traffic, ground-related law enforcement, and medical evacuation services for all medical facilities in the state. The auto theft bureau provides assistance to other law-enforcement agencies, and the major crime unit assists local agencies investigating kidnappings and homicides. The arson unit initiates its own investigations of suspicious fires, and provides assistance to local police and fire departments in the investigation of arson. The unit also investigates all bombings and thefts of explosives in the state. The state police fugitive unit tracks persons wanted for the most serious offenses; these cases are submitted by state and local law enforcement agencies. The missing-persons unit coordinates investigations involving missing persons and unidentified bodies. In addition, there is an organized crime bureau, a narcotics bureau, and an intelligence bureau which provides crime analysis services to other state police units.
>
> **SOURCE:** Reports of the New Jersey State Police

In the expanding American West, the sheriff developed into a powerful elected official who often made use of the posse to accomplish his law enforcement responsibilities. The history of many of these sheriffs is shrouded in myth and exaggeration. Joe Frantz (1969: 131) notes that the Western "lawman was as closely associated with violence as the outlaw. The greatest gunfighters frequently played both sides of the law." James Butler ("Wild Bill") Hickok, for example, gained early notoriety as a civilian when he ambushed a former employee and the employee's 12-year-old son over a wage dispute; claiming self-defense, Hickok was acquitted. He worked for the Union Army during the Civil War, was known as a gambler and gunfighter, background that helped him to be commissioned a deputy U.S. marshal in Colorado. Hickok's exploits as a federal marshal led to his election as sheriff of Ellis County, Kansas, and he later gained further fame as a town marshal in Abilene, Kansas.

The exploits of gambler, gunfighter, and frontier scout "Wild Bill" Hickock are part of the folklore of the American West. Hickock, who served as a deputy U.S. Marshal in Colorado and sheriff of Ellis County, Kansas, gained notoriety before his career as a lawman when he killed three men in a quarrel in Rock Creek Station, Nebraska.

There are more than 3,000 counties in the United States, and most state constitutions provide for elected county sheriffs. The state of Alaska, however, does not have sheriffs, and in Hawaii, Rhode Island, the five counties that comprise New York City, Nassau County and Westchester County (New York), Dade County (Florida), and Denver County (Colorado), the sheriff is an appointed official. There are city sheriffs in Virginia; Baltimore and St. Louis have city and county sheriffs; and Louisiana has civil and criminal sheriffs.

The responsibilities of the modern sheriff can include:

1. serving civil processes such as subpoenas, garnishments, levies, and eviction notices;
2. providing security and bailiffs for court facilities;
3. operating county correctional institutions and jails;

4. preserving the peace and suppressing riots;
5. providing general police services in unincorporated areas, on county roads, or under contract with municipalities; and
6. collecting certain county taxes.

In the eastern United States, sheriffs tend to provide only limited services—usually serving civil processes and in some jurisdictions providing court security and operating county jails. In the southern and western United States, however, the sheriff is usually a powerful political figure who provides a full range of services. In the Midwest there is a mixture of limited-service and full-service sheriff's departments. Some counties (e.g., Suffolk County, New York, and Charleston County, South Carolina) have their own countywide police departments, and some have their own departments of correction, independent of the sheriff.

Because the sheriff is usually an elected official, he or she requires the support of an organized political party, which will expect to share in the patronage potential that the office may control, and political loyalty rather than competence has tended to be the basic qualification for deputy sheriffs. In the past, the election of a new sheriff often meant wholesale dismissals of deputy sheriffs. In more recent times, court decisions and civil service laws have done away with most of the blatant aspects of partisanship and patronage historically associated with the office of sheriff.

(For more information about the office of sheriff in the United States, contact the National Sheriffs' Association, 1450 Duke Street, Alexandria, VA 22314.)

Municipal Police History

Americans disapproved of the national police systems common on the European continent. They viewed a centralized and uniformed force as a threat to civil liberties and freedom, and they opted for locally controlled police forces "even when limited local resources meant that policing had to be reduced to a part-time activity," writes Donald Dilworth (1976: 1). "Within a few decades after independence, most large cities had developed full-time police forces, although this usually meant an odd assortment of watchmen, criers, bell ringers and fire marshalls supported by a patrol force that was loyal to the local political chief."

This fragmented system was inadequate, however, for coping with the crime and disorder of urban America. In this increasingly impersonal environment, traditional mechanisms of social control such as the family were often rendered impotent. Samuel Walker (1980: 59) sees the creation of a modern-style police as a result of the chaos in America's growing cities: "It was not simply a matter of periodic riots; urbanization brought new expectations about permissible levels of disorder." Eric Monkkonen (1981) argues, however, that the creation of a modern police force was a natural outgrowth of the increased bureaucratization and centralization that accompanied the expansion of municipal governmental services.

Whatever the reason, by the time of the Civil War, every major town in the United States had a modern-style municipal police force patterned after the London Metropolitan Police of Sir Robert Peel (from whence they get the nickname "bobbies"), which was established in 1829. American police forces borrowed the British strategy of round-the-clock, uniformed, preventive patrol and the quasi-military model of organization. Crime prevention became an important goal of the police; the night watch of earlier times had been a form of preventive patrol, but it was not a central police function. Now the entire city was to be continuously patroled by men who were neither soldiers nor civilians, and who were assigned specific territories. Until this innovation, "policemen" (actually troops) had been stationed at a central headquarters until they were summoned. Territorial patrol required decentralization—which suited the American apprehension about the abuse of power—and substations were established in each district, area, or precinct of major cities. Full-time, salaried police officers became another widespread innovation.

Modern policing in the United States can be traced back to 1844 when the New York state legislature established a unified paid force for New York City; until then there had been a day watch and a separate night watch. Within two decades, most large urban areas had established similar departments. New York City police officers were not uniformed until 1853, however; there was a great deal of resistance to uniformed police from the public as well as the officers themselves—most Americans saw uniforms as undemocratic and servantlike.

Examples of Quasi-Military Designations Used by Police Agencies

Chief
three or more stars

Colonel
gold eagle

Deputy Chief or Deputy Superintendent
two or more stars

Lieutenant Colonel
gold oak leaf

Inspector or Major
gold or silver oak leaf

Captain
two bars

Lieutenant
one bar

Sergeant
three stripes

STARTING ON NIGHT DUTY

THE PERILS OF STREET CROSSING

AN ARREST

In the United States, the modern-style municipal police force was patterned after the London Metropolitan Police, or "bobbies," which utilized round-the-clock, uniformed, preventive patrol and a quasi-military model of organization.

Uniformed police were accepted when it became clear that the uniform was important to one of the basic goals of the modern police force: crime prevention. Because of this goal, the role of the police had shifted from one of watchman and thief-catcher to that of controlling the "dangerous classes" of urban America. In order to impart fear into the hearts of would-be criminals, the police also gained new arrest powers; Eric Monkkonen

(1981: 42) points out that "although citizens could only arrest an offender after a crime had, in fact, been committed, the police could make an arrest if they thought a crime had been committed." The fearsomeness of the police was further enhanced by the routine carrying of firearms. In 1858, a New York City police officer shot a fleeing felon with a personal weapon. The case was presented to a grand jury, which failed to indict the officer. Subsequently, police officers in New York City began to arm themselves. A similar incident in Boston led to the arming of police officers in that city. "The practice spread, and by the early 1900s cities commonly issued revolvers to their police officers" (Matulia 1982: 1).

The role of the police was still ill-defined, and this, coupled with the lack of other specialized public agencies, led to police departments being "catchall health, welfare, and law enforcement agencies. . . . The police cleaned streets and inspected boilers in New York, distributed supplies to the poor in Baltimore, accommodated the homeless in Philadelphia, investigated vegetable markets in St. Louis, operated emergency ambulances in Boston, and attempted to curb crime in all these cities" (Fogelson 1977: 17).

While the British bobbies were a creation of Parliament and under the command of the Home Secretary, American police forces were controlled by local political organizations, which were often corrupt "machines." Policemen in New York, Chicago, Philadelphia, Kansas City, and elsewhere depended on political appointments for their jobs and promotions, and they had to be residents of the wards to which they were appointed and served (Richardson 1974). The captains of police districts or precincts were selected by ward bosses, and the captains hired, fired, and promoted officers under their command; there was little central command by either a police chief or board of police commissioners. Samuel Walker (1980: 61-62) points out that

> ignorance, poor health, or old age was no barrier to employment. An individual with the right connections could be hired despite the most obvious lack of qualifications. Recruits received no formal training. A new officer would be handed a copy of the police manual (if one could be found) containing the local ordinances and state laws, and sent out on patrol. There he would receive on the job training from experienced officers who, of course, also taught the ways of graft and evasion of duty.

VOL. XXXVI. No. 917. PUCK BUILDING, New York, October 3d, 1894. PRICE 10 CENTS.

Puck

In its earliest days, the local police force was little respected by the citizenry. Controlled by local political organizations, which were often corrupt, the police served primarily as overseers of the established criminal order, collecting "fees" for illegal licenses granted by the political machines.

THE POLICE VERSION OF IT.

"Let no guilty man (or woman) escape — widout dey put up de stuff!"

Not only was hiring based on patronage, but "most patrolmen who survived for any length of time quickly . . . learned that a patrolman placed his career in jeopardy more by alienating his captain than by disobeying his chief and more by defying his wardman, who regulated vice in the precinct, than by ignoring [his sergeant]" (Fogelson 1977: 25). The patrolman who offended the politicians of his precinct would be summarily transferred or even dismissed from the force.

Jonathan Rubinstein (1973: 372), in his study of the police in Philadelphia, found that "many police captains were actually little more than gambling and liquor commissioners whose primary responsibility was to enforce the illegal licenses which the political machines granted to favored operators. The police did not organize protection but carried out the orders established by the elected leaders of their city or state." In Minneapolis the police were actually placed in charge of criminal activities—in a supervisory, not a preventive, capacity. Lincoln Steffens (1957: 47) reported that in 1901 the mayor organized professional criminals and had them work "under police direction for the profit of his administration."

The problem of police corruption was compounded by the often brutal conduct of the police, especially toward those too powerless to complain effectively. Steffens, in his autobiography (1958: 207), recalled that during the 1890s in New York, he "saw the police bring in and kick out their bandaged, bloody prisoners, not only strikers and foreigners, but thieves too, and others of the miserable, friendless, troublesome poor." Citizens generally had little respect for the police, whom many viewed as political hacks. The police were subjected to frequent abuse by street gangs, and an arrest often required the officer to physically subdue the suspect. "A tradition of police brutality developed out of this reciprocal disrespect. Officers sought to gain with their billy clubs the deference to their authority that was not freely given," notes Samuel Walker (1980: 63), and he refers to police brutality as a form of "delegated vigilantism" tolerated by the "respectable" middle-class citizenry, who perceived a need to control the "dangerous classes."

Toward the end of the nineteenth century and the beginning of the twentieth, there were major practical and technological advances in policing. The health and social welfare responsibilities of the police were abandoned. Signal stations were placed throughout the city (first in Chicago, then Cincinnati), and offi-

The Boston Police Strike of 1919

At the turn of the century, the most professional of urban police departments was in Boston. Under the command of Commissioner Stephen O'Meara (1906-1918), the force operated with a minimum of corruption and brutality, and the Boston police were rigorous in their adherence to legal requirements. Unfortunately, the professionalism of the Boston police did not match their working conditions or salaries; they worked seven days per week, had to buy their own equipment, and were paid less than laborers. In 1919, the police of Boston went out on strike. The striking officers were permanently discharged. After citizen volunteers—mostly upper-class persons, many associated with Harvard University—proved unequal to the task of controlling increasing public disorder, Massachusetts Governor Calvin Coolidge sent in the state militia, which made him a national hero and eventually President of the United States (Russell 1975).

cers could check in for instructions or call for assistance (if they understood the Morse code—most didn't). The signal system was replaced by a new advance in communications, the telephone. Police officers could now call for assistance, and in the event of an arrest, a patrol wagon would be dispatched to transport prisoners. Prior to this system, police officers had to march prisoners through the streets to headquarters, often suffering the abuse of hostile crowds. A red light mounted atop the call box could alert an officer that he was wanted (it also alerted members of the public, who often crowded around to hear what was going on).

The next decades saw further technological advances that revolutionized policing; the automobile and the wireless two-way radio led to the gradual demise of foot patrol in most jurisdictions. The primary police response now focused on mobility and communications. The "cop on the beat" was no longer a

Sergeants' exam, Chicago, 1904.

familiar figure in many cities; the anonymous radio patrol car had replaced him. This had important implications for police-community relations, further distancing and estranging the police officer from the community being policed. Interestingly, recent advances in wireless communication—hand-held radios—have increased the viability of foot patrol, which is being used again on a limited basis to reduce the anonymity of the patrol car.

During the latter half of the nineteenth century, police chiefs were troubled by criminals who were taking advantage of the latest advance in transportation—trains—and the jurisdictional limitations of police agencies. There was an obvious need to track criminals beyond jurisdictional boundaries, but, without a national police force, no means to accomplish it. In 1871, a con-

6 ▪ THE POLICE: HISTORY, GOALS, AND ORGANIZATION

VOLLMER AND WILSON: PIONEERS IN POLICE ADMINISTRATION

In the small university town of Berkeley, California, August Vollmer (1876-1955) was elected town marshal in 1905, and in 1909 was appointed chief of police. He established the first police training school in America, using faculty from nearby universities. Vollmer himself became a full professor of police administration at the University of California (although he only had a grade-school education). He saw police officers "as social workers dealing with a range of societal problems which manifested themselves in crime and disorder. In his view, policemen should become college-educated professionals akin to doctors or lawyers" (Reppetto 1978: 243). Advances in policing that he accomplished in Berkeley, however, had only a limited influence on other police departments. Vollmer's protégé in Berkeley, Orlando W. Wilson, became dean of the School of Criminology at the University of California and eventually superintendent of police for Chicago (1960-1967). Wilson's publications on police administration have exerted a great deal of influence on policing.

vention was held in St. Louis with 112 police executives from twenty-one states to deal with this problem; however, no organized effort resulted from this meeting. In 1892, the police chiefs of Chicago and Omaha organized another convention of police chief executives, which was held in Chicago the following year. Out of this convention emerged the National Chiefs of Police Union, which in 1902 became the **International Association of Chiefs of Police (IACP)** The IACP provided impetus and support for an independent, "professional police" (Dilworth 1976), and in the early decades of the twentieth century there developed formal police training schools.

By the turn of the century, reformers were becoming successful in removing the police from the control of corrupt political machines through election and civil service reform, and the centralization of police organization enabled police chiefs to exert greater control over their forces. Eric Monkkonen (1981: 153) notes, however, that successful police reform was not matched on the personnel level; police officers were among the least educated persons in society, and there was strong opposition from the rank and file to increasing the educational requirements of police officers:

> The police remained steadfastly working class and resistant to upgrading, partly because of their job culture, which was almost a half-century old by 1900. In fact, in the 1980s this culture still keeps advanced positions limited to former rank and file officers, thus insuring a police administration responsive to rank and file demands.

POLICE GOALS AND OBJECTIVES

The police are the major representatives of the legal system in their transactions with the public, and they constitute the most visible symbol of governmental authority. The police have four primary goals:

1. *The control of crime.* This is operationalized by preventive patrol, investigating criminal activity and identifying offenders, effecting arrests, participating in court proceedings, and providing information about criminal activity and crime prevention to the public.

2. *The protection of life and property.* This is operationalized by guarding public and private property, ensuring and facilitating the safe movement of persons and vehicles, aiding persons who are in danger of physical harm, for example, those trapped in a building with a gas leak, and aiding persons in need of care, such as accident victims, children, and the mentally ill.

3. *The maintenance of peace and order.* This is operationalized by crowd control activities, preventing disorderly conduct, and resolving conflicts between persons that have the potential for disturbing the peace.

4. *The safeguarding of constitutional rights.* This is operationalized by the police presence at parades, public demonstrations and similar activities, and by protecting places of worship and worshipers.

To approximate these goals a police department will adopt one or a combination of two basic models of policing (Wilson 1975): (*a*) the community service model and (*b*) the crime attack model. The **community service model** stresses the assignment of a team of officers and supervisors to patrol a small area, often on foot, and thereby learn about the neighborhood. The assumption is that familiarity with the community and the needs of its residents will result in better follow-through on citizen requests for service and in better cooperation of citizens, which is so essential in matters of crime control. The **crime attack model** is based on the assumption that police officers should be deployed as close as possible, not to citizens, but to the scene of potential crimes. Accomplishing this requires a highly mobile force that can apprehend criminals in the act by detecting or responding quickly to reports of a crime in progress.

Within each of these models there is a mixture of two basic strategies: reactive and proactive. **Reactive policing** means awaiting calls for service; it is the basic strategy used by fire departments. This strategy is dependent upon crime victims or witnesses reporting to the police. **Proactive policing** means police officers go out on the streets "looking for trouble." Proactive policing uses both uniformed patrol officers and plainclothes personnel who may assume disguises, which is the only viable strategy for dealing with "victimless crime" such as drug and gambling violations.

The Dilemma of Law Versus Order

Whatever the models or strategies, there remains a fundamental conflict in policing, which Jerome Skolnick (1975) refers to as the "dilemma of law and order." Instead of the usual cliché, Skolnick is referring to *law* that restrains police efforts at maintaining *order*. Although the police are required to maintain order, in a democratic society they must do so under the rule of law. Whatever goals and objectives we assign the police, we insist that they be achieved in conformity to law, and this is no small task. As Elmer Johnson (1969: 2) points out, police "observance of individual rights is essential to making democracy a reality in a mass society, but achievement of this ideal is made particularly difficult by demands that the police also be efficient in protecting the community against criminals and the disorder attending social unrest."

This conflict between crime control and due process (discussed in chapter 5) places the police in an unenviable position: they must strive to achieve goals and objectives, such as the prevention of crime and the apprehension of criminals, that are rendered impossible to achieve in a democratic society. The failure to recognize and accept the anomaly of policing in a democratic society can lead to the "Dirty Harry" syndrome. An editorial in *The New York Times* (May 3, 1985: 26) responding to a police brutality scandal in that city noted that "a public outraged over crime demands more aggressive law enforcement. But then some officers become overly aggressive, creating new outrage over citizen abuse."

Styles of policing

James Q. Wilson (1976) in his classic work, *Varieties of Police Behavior*, delineated three styles of policing to compare the ways that police departments maintain order and respond to less serious violations of law. (Within each style the police treat serious violations—felonies—in a serious manner.)

1. *The Watchman.* In this type of department, the primary concern is for order maintenance, and the police will ignore common minor violations involving juveniles, traffic offenses, domestic disputes, and, to a lesser degree, vice offenses. Police interventions are kept to a minimum. In general, the seriousness of an offense is judged not by what the law says, but by the immediate circumstances and the persons involved; police officers in watchman-style departments exercise a great deal of discretion, avoiding formal arrests and often rendering informal "street justice." This style of policing is usually found in working-class or "blue collar" communities.

2. *The Legalistic.* In this type of department, the officer is expected to be a strict enforcer of the law—*all of the law*. Differences among neighborhoods and communities, among racial, ethnic, and economic groups do not change enforcement, and there is a high rate of arrests and traffic citations. This style of policing often occurs in the aftermath of a scandal in a watchman-type department that results in the hiring of a "reform" police chief executive.

3. *The Service.* In this type of department, the police take all requests for service seriously, be they for law enforcement or order maintenance. There is a high rate of police intervention, but the number of arrests is considerably less than for legalistic-style departments. Arrests and traffic citations are often avoided through counseling, or warning minor offenders (some departments issue written warnings for traffic violations), or by referring them to social service agencies. Departments exhibiting this style of policing are usually found in more affluent suburban areas.

> ## ORGANIZATION OF THE MINNEAPOLIS POLICE DEPARTMENT
>
> **Chief**
> The Office of the Chief coordinates the collective effort of the Department and maintains the professional integrity of department members. For this purpose, the Internal Affairs section is located within the Office of the Chief and reports directly to him. The main responsibility of Internal Affairs is to investigate complaints, both from citizens and those internally derived against officers relating to personal misconduct or to imprudent performance of duty.
>
> **Patrol**
> Approximately 58 percent of departmental resources are devoted to the Patrol Bureau. It performs such comprehensive police services as control of crime, resolution of citizen conflict, regulation of traffic, and the provision of miscellaneous emergency services. The Patrol Bureau is the heart and center of departmental operations. Its importance and size can be best understood in the context of the two main tactics which police employ to achieve their objectives. The first is a reactive tactic; that is, where the police re-

POLICE ORGANIZATION

More than 90 percent of all municipalities with a population of 2,500 or more have their own general service police forces; there are more than 11,000 general service municipal police departments in the United States (Zawitz 1983). As we would expect, the larger the population, the more sworn officers in a police department. Thus, New York City has the largest police force, about 23,000 sworn officers and 5,000 civilians. Second is the city of Chicago with about 12,000 sworn officers and 2,000 civil-

spond to the scene of an incident at the request of a citizen. The second tactic is proactive; that is, where police, on their own initiative, undertake some activity designed to accomplish police department objectives. Examples of proactive tactics include surveillance of possible criminal activity, gathering of crime-related intelligence, and patrol designed to intercept criminal activity. Since in democratic societies, custom, legal standards guiding police operations, and resource constraints limit police initiative, the principal tactic used by the police is the reactive one. The vast proportion of incidents which police handle come to its attention through citizen calls for assistance. The Patrol Bureau is particularly organized to react to such requests.

Investigation
The Investigation Bureau is primarily responsible for investigating cases not cleared by the Patrol Bureau, for gathering information about possible organized crime activity in Minneapolis, and for obtaining additional evidence about the crimes of persons arrested in order to assist in their prosecution. The Service Bureau provides varied technical and logistical support to these operations.

SOURCE: Minneapolis Police Department publications

ians. Los Angeles, however, with a population larger than Chicago, has a little more than half as many officers as the Windy City. Research indicates that police strength is related to population density; "as the number of residents per square mile increases, there is likely to be an increase in the number of police per capita" (Zawitz 1983: 49).

Police departmental strength in various cities is often compared on the basis of the ratio between the number of sworn officers and the size of the population; approximately 80 percent of all counties have between one and three officers per one thousand residents (Zawitz 1983). The police-citizen ratio can some-

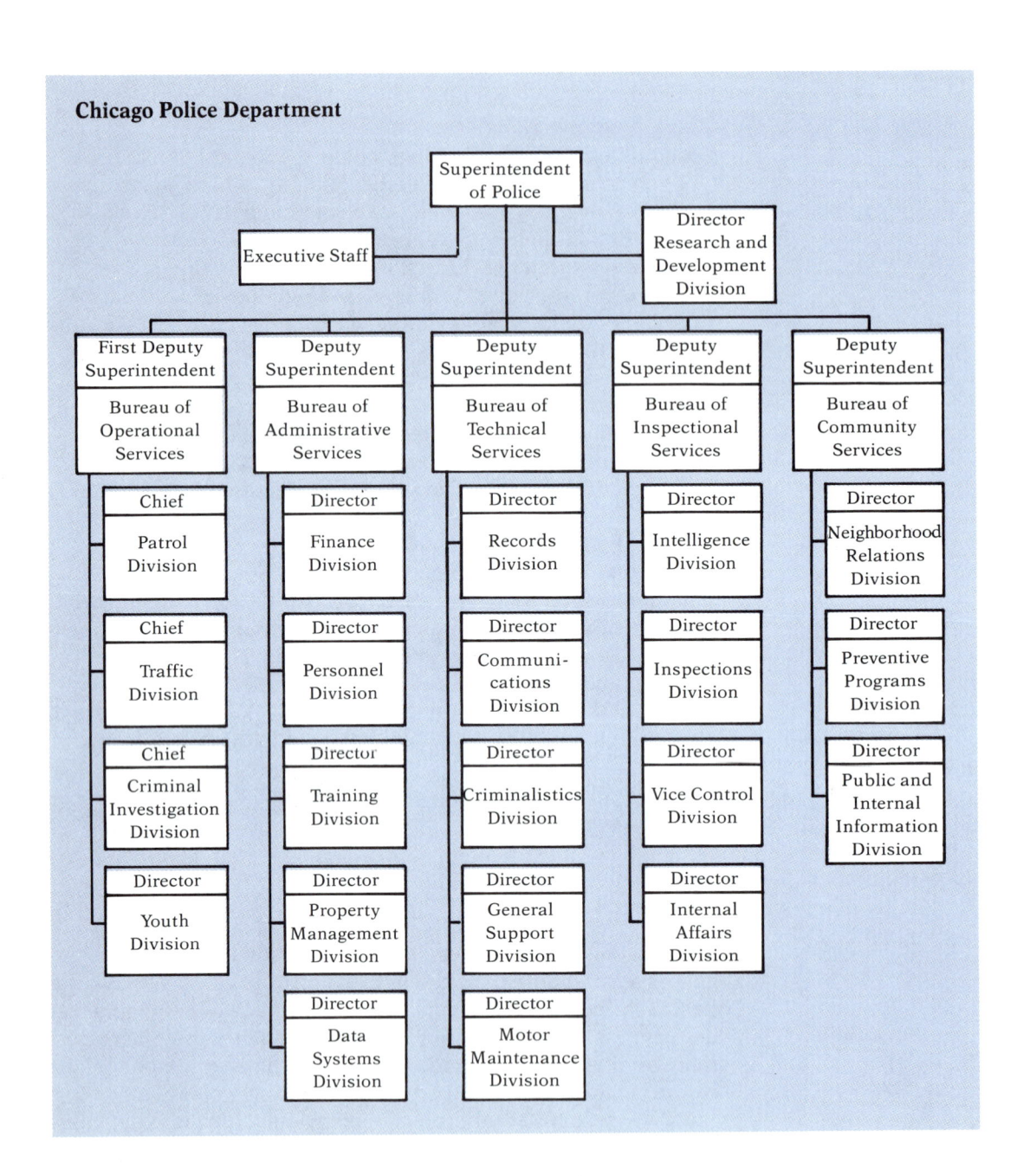

Chicago Police Department

- Superintendent of Police
  - Executive Staff
  - Director, Research and Development Division
  - First Deputy Superintendent — Bureau of Operational Services
    - Chief, Patrol Division
    - Chief, Traffic Division
    - Chief, Criminal Investigation Division
    - Director, Youth Division
  - Deputy Superintendent — Bureau of Administrative Services
    - Director, Finance Division
    - Director, Personnel Division
    - Director, Training Division
    - Director, Property Management Division
    - Director, Data Systems Division
  - Deputy Superintendent — Bureau of Technical Services
    - Director, Records Division
    - Director, Communications Division
    - Director, Criminalistics Division
    - Director, General Support Division
    - Director, Motor Maintenance Division
  - Deputy Superintendent — Bureau of Inspectional Services
    - Director, Intelligence Division
    - Director, Inspections Division
    - Director, Vice Control Division
    - Director, Internal Affairs Division
  - Deputy Superintendent — Bureau of Community Services
    - Director, Neighborhood Relations Division
    - Director, Preventive Programs Division
    - Director, Public and Internal Information Division

Los Angeles Police Department

- Police Commission
  - Chief of Police
    - Administrative Commander
    - Administrative Commander Inspection
    - Administrative Commander Press Releases
    - Commission Services
    - Office of Administrative Services
      - Liaison
      - Personnel & Training
      - Planning & Fiscal
        - Planning & Research
        - Fiscal Operations
      - Automated Information
      - Communications
      - Technical Services
        - Records & ID
        - Supply
        - Jail
        - Property
        - Motor Transportation
        - Scientific Investigation
    - Office of Operations
      - Assistant to Director
      - Operations — Central Bureau
      - Operations — South Bureau
      - Operations — Headquarters Bureau
        - Uniformed Services
          - Air Support
          - Metropolitan
          - Traffic
          - Tactical Planning
        - Detective Services (7 Divisions)
      - Operations — West Bureau
      - Operations — Valley Bureau
    - Office of Special Services
      - Bureau of Special Investigation
        - Narcotics Administrative Vice
        - Labor Relations
        - Public Affairs
      - Internal Affairs
      - Organized Crime
      - Public Disorder Intelligence

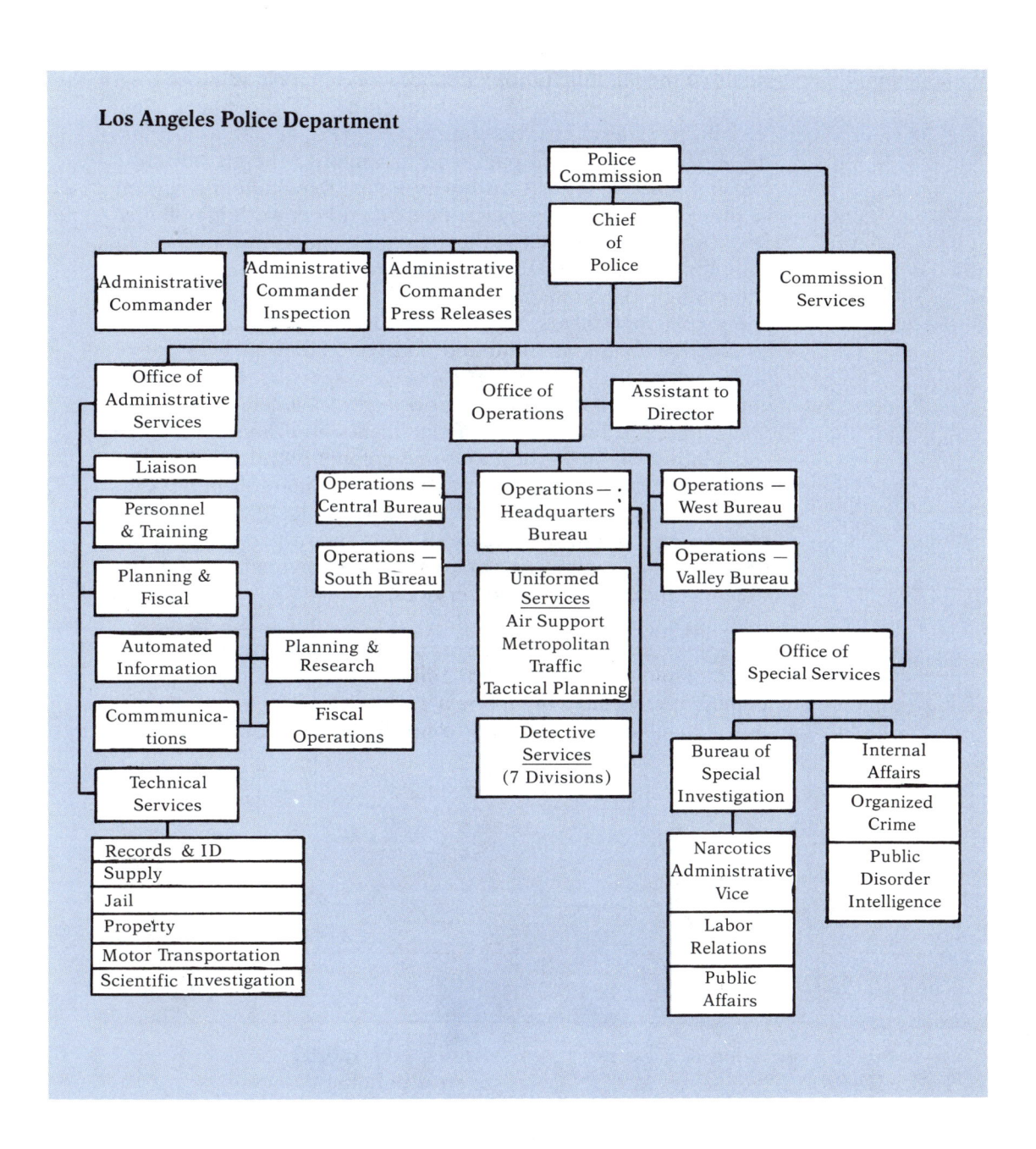

175

times be misleading, however, since some cities have more than one police department. For example, in 1986 the city of New York had a general citywide force, the NYPD, as well as a Housing Authority Police Department assigned to the city's public housing units, a Transit Authority Police Department assigned to the city's mass transit facilities, and a Port Authority Police Department, which has authority over airports and tunnels in New York and New Jersey. Chicago, on the other hand, has only one municipal police force.

Police departments are highly bureaucratic organizations with strict chains of command and fixed titles such as patrol officer, sergeant, lieutenant, captain, inspector, deputy chief, chief of police or superintendent or commissioner. (Some state police forces, a few sheriff's departments and municipal agencies also use the titles of major and colonel.) While each police department has a unique structure, as the diagrams of the Chicago and Los Angeles police departments indicate, most departments assign about 60 percent of their sworn personnel to patrol, and the remaining 40 percent are divided among the various other divisions and services.

In this chapter we have examined the history of policing, the goals of policing, and the dilemma inherent in policing in a democratic society. In the next chapter we will examine how police departments function to fulfill the goals that have been set for them.

KEY TERMS

International Association of Chiefs of Police (IACP)
community service model

crime attack model
reactive policing
proactive policing

REVIEW QUESTIONS

1. What is the major responsibility of state police forces today?
2. Which was the first state to establish a modern state police force? What was the primary reason for its creation?
3. What are the various responsibilities of a county sheriff's department?
4. What was the major strategy American municipal police forces borrowed during the middle of the nineteenth century from the Metropolitan Police of London?
5. What was the major difference between the nineteenth-century British and American police forces?
6. What incidents led to police officers carrying firearms?
7. Why was the decentralized nature of police organization at the turn of the century linked to corrupt political machines?
8. Why was police brutality around the turn of the century generally tolerated by middle-class citizenry?
9. What is the fundamental conflict inherent in policing in a democratic society, which Jerome Skolnick refers to as the "dilemma of law and order"?
10. What are the four primary goals of the police?
11. What are the differences between the community service model and the crime attack model of policing?
12. What is meant by:
    (a) proactive policing?
    (b) reactive policing?
13. What are the differences among the watchman, legalistic, and service styles of policing?
14. What variable can explain varying ratios of police officers to population in different cities?
15. What aspect of policing utilizes more than half of the sworn personnel?

CHAPTER 7

Police Operations

PATROL
Calls for Service
Preventive Patrol
Officer-Initiated Activities
Administrative Tasks

SPECIALIZED PATROL
Uniformed Tactical Patrol
Decoy Operations
Stakeouts
Covert Surveillance

INVESTIGATION
Proactive Investigation
Reactive Investigation

TRAFFIC
Sobriety Checkpoints

INTERNAL AFFAIRS

SPECIAL WEAPONS AND TACTICS (SWAT) TEAMS

POLICE AUXILIARIES

OTHER SPECIALIZED BUREAUS AND UNITS

REVIEW QUESTIONS

Boxes
Decoy
Street Crime Unit

Operationalizing police goals and objectives is the responsibility of two major components of any police department, patrol and investigation, and a number of more specialized units.

PATROL

William Gay, Theodore Schell, and Steven Schack (1977: 2) define the goals of patrol as "crime prevention and deterrence, the apprehension of criminals, the provision of non-crime related services, the provision of a sense of community security and satisfaction with the police, and the recovery of stolen property."

These goals can best be met if the police are clearly visible in the community, and this visibility is accomplished by the deployment of uniformed officers.

Gay and his colleagues (1977: 3-6) have divided routine patrol activity into four basic functional categories: calls for service, preventive patrol, officer-initiated activities, and administrative tasks.

Calls for Service

These account for about 25 percent of patrol time. The general use of two-way radios has made the call for service an important aspect of patrol operations. Much of the officer's patrol time only serves to insure the availability of a quick response to requests for service. Stanley Vanagunas and James F. Elliott (1980: 110) describe routine patrol activity as a "'working poise' for servicing incoming calls from the citizenry." Indeed, the call for service takes precedence over most other patrol activities, and police chief executives have devoted a great deal of energy and resources to reduce response time on the assumption that "the faster the response to a crime report, the more likely that patrol officers would apprehend an offender at or near the scene" (*Efficient Use of Police Resources* 1984: 2).

However, a three-year study conducted in Kansas City, Missouri, and subsequently replicated in Jacksonville (Florida), San Diego (California), Peoria (Illinois), and Rochester (New York), revealed that:

- more than 86 percent of all calls for service were placed more than five minutes after the incident occurred—the time period considered critical for making an on-the-scene arrest;
- on-the-scene arrests that could be attributed to a fast police response time were made in less than 3 percent of reported serious crimes; and
- a fast police response may be unnecessary in three out of every four reported serious crimes because it is too late to apprehend a perpetrator at the scene. Moreover, responding to emergency situations usually involves the use of excessive speed, increasing the potential for accidents and injury to both police officers and civilians. Motor vehicle accidents are the primary cause of police job-related injuries and deaths.

Because of this research on response to calls for service, police departments have developed **differential police response strategies**—or strategies to prioritize calls for service. For example, while a call indicating a serious "crime-in-progress" would receive immediate response, the discovery of a burglary by a resident returning home from work would receive a delayed response (unless the burglars were still at the scene). Certain crimes such as auto theft may be dealt with by taking a report over the telephone. Many calls for service are only requests for information, or they may reveal a person in need of a referral to a social service agency; such calls can be handled without dispatching a patrol vehicle. Because police agencies operate 24 hours every day of the week, while many public and private agencies have limited hours of operation, the police are often called upon for a host of non-crime-related services.

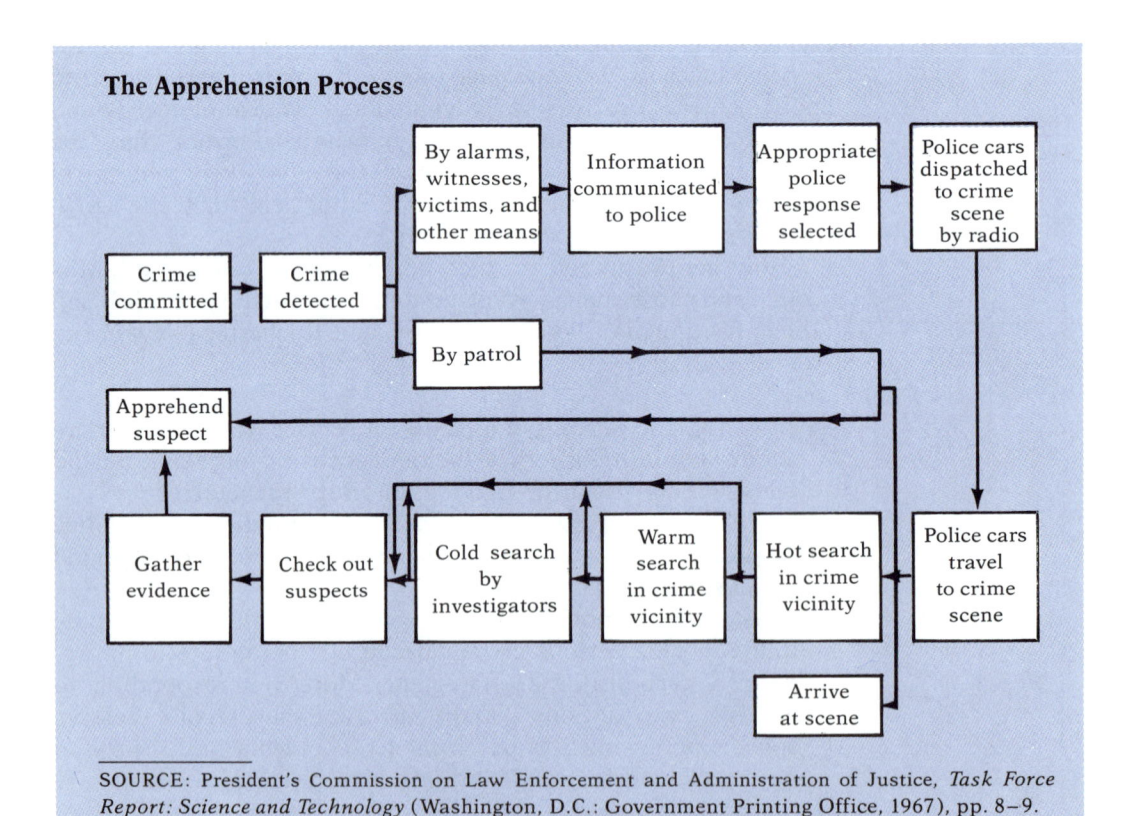

The Apprehension Process

Crime committed → Crime detected → (By alarms, witnesses, victims, and other means) → Information communicated to police → Appropriate police response selected → Police cars dispatched to crime scene by radio → Police cars travel to crime scene → Arrive at scene → Hot search in crime vicinity → Warm search in crime vicinity → Cold search by investigators → Check out suspects → Gather evidence → Apprehend suspect

(Crime detected → By patrol → Apprehend suspect)

SOURCE: President's Commission on Law Enforcement and Administration of Justice, *Task Force Report: Science and Technology* (Washington, D.C.: Government Printing Office, 1967), pp. 8–9.

Preventive Patrol

This approach to crime control accounts for about 40 percent of patrol time and is based on the assumption that the deployment of highly visible police vehicles will prevent and deter criminal activity. When officers are not otherwise involved—answering calls for service, for example—they are considered to be engaged in **preventive patrol,** which means quasi-random movement through their assigned sectors or beats. Highly visible police officers in uniform and marked police vehicles, however, also provide an "early warning system" for persons engaged, or preparing to engage, in criminal acts; that they will ultimately deter such persons is, at best, a dubious proposition.

From October 1972 until September 1973, an attempt was made to test this proposition in Kansas City, Missouri. The **Kansas City Study** was the result of a grant from the Washington-

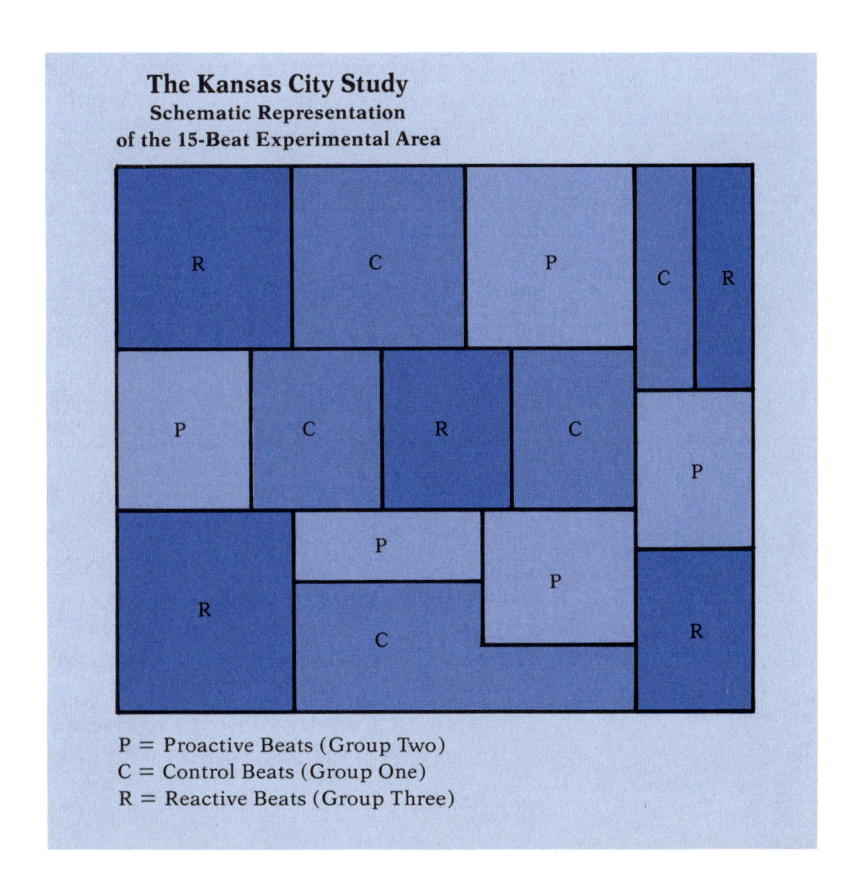

The Kansas City Study
Schematic Representation
of the 15-Beat Experimental Area

P = Proactive Beats (Group Two)
C = Control Beats (Group One)
R = Reactive Beats (Group Three)

based Police Foundation to the Kansas City police department. It involved an experimental model with fifteen police beats that were matched according to characteristics such as the rate of crime, the socioeconomic status of residents, and the number of calls for service. The fifteen beats were divided into three groups: Group One (control beats) received the normal level of police patrol; Group Two (proactive beats) received two to three times the normal level of police patrol; and Group Three (reactive beats) had its preventive patrol eliminated entirely—police officers would enter these five beats only in response to calls for service. "Noncommitted" time, when the five patrol cars that would have normally been assigned to the five reactive beats were not responding to calls, was spent patrolling the boundaries of the reactive beats or patrolling in adjacent proactive beats. Despite some flaws in the research design and implementation, the results of the study were startling: after one year, no differences were found in rates of reported crime, rates of victimization, levels of citizen fear of crime, or the degree of citizen satisfaction with the police. Indeed, there tended to be a higher level of fear of crime in the districts receiving intensified patrol services; apparently the sight of more police cars led to a perception of increased crime (Kelling et al. 1974).

Officer-Initiated Activities

These account for about 15 percent of patrol time. In preventive patrol, the mere presence of police vehicles and officers is supposed to act as a deterrent to criminal behavior. During the course of routine patrol, however, officers are expected to carefully observe their surroundings in order to spot suspicious or illegal activities, which can sometimes lead to an arrest. In most instances, officer-initiated activity involves community relations or crime prevention activities such as pedestrian and vehicle stops and checking residential and commercial buildings. "If, for example, an officer observes a suspicious action or an order maintenance problem, his/her presence or field interrogation may be sufficient to prevent or deter a criminal act" (Gay et al. 1977: 6).

Jonathan Rubinstein (1973: 134) notes that police officers usually restrict their daytime patrol work to the main streets of

Police officers in Brooklyn, N.Y., make arrests after discovering firearms in a car stopped for a routine traffic check.

the district and do not venture into the small side streets and alleys where there are very few people about. At night, however, officer-initiated activity increases as they begin to work the back streets and alleys, checking doorways and windows with the help of powerful spotlights that are operated from inside the patrol car. If something appears suspicious, the officer leaves the car for a "hand-check." Officers are expected to be on the alert for persons and vehicles that look out of place and for doors or windows that look like they have been tampered with. Officers are also responsible for enforcing motor vehicle laws and parking regulations during their patrol shift.

Administrative Tasks

These account for about 20 percent of patrol time and include maintaining patrol cars, transporting prisoners, writing reports, running departmental errands, and appearing in court.

Specialized Patrol

The strategy of dividing the city into districts or precincts and further subdividing them into beats to be subjected to routine patrol by uniformed officers on foot or in marked vehicles limits the ability of the police to approximate their goals. Law enforcement is hampered by the very visibility that, at least in theory, is supposed to deter crime. Specialization allows a police department to deploy officers in a manner that more directly responds to particular problems of law enforcement—to be in close proximity to crime.

In order to improve the crime-fighting capabilities of patrol officers, police departments have utilized the strategy of specialized patrol, which has been defined as "the activities of officers who are relieved of the responsibility for handling routine calls for service in order to concentrate on specific crime problems" (Schack 1977: 1). The four most common tactics employed in specialized patrol operations are uniformed tactical patrol, decoy operations, physical and electronic stakeouts, and covert surveillance.

Uniformed Tactical Patrol

Uniformed tactical patrol (UTP) combines preventive patrol and officer-initiated activities, with the difference that officers are relieved of routine patrol responsibilities, such as handling calls for service or parking violations, in order to concentrate on proactive crime control. UTP is often used to saturate a particular area that is experiencing a serious crime problem with additional officers. Officers are encouraged to be aggressive, to make numerous pedestrian and vehicle stops in an effort to establish high visibility in the area and increase the likelihood of encountering offenders. These **field interrogations** "serve to generate information about the activities of probable suspects and, more importantly for deterrence, they make the suspects aware that the police know of their presence in a given area, regard them as suspicious, and are watching them closely" (Schack 1977: 84-85).

Aggressive patrolling by UTP officers is controversial—individuals may resent being stopped and questioned by the police, particularly in low-income, high-crime areas. There is often a very thin line between harassment and legitimate enforcement tactics, a line that the citizens involved may not be able to distinguish. Stephen Schack and his colleagues (1977) report, however, that a study in San Diego revealed that field interrogations suppressed crime without doing irreparable harm to police-community relations. There is another concern with UTP: *displacement*. Is the decrease in crime simply a function of its being displaced from one area to another or from one time period to another? The results of research on this issue are inconclusive.

Decoy Operations

The probability of a uniformed police officer being at the scene of crime while that crime is in progress is extremely low. **Decoy operations** are designed to increase this probability by having officers pose as likely victims. A San Francisco police sergeant states:

> The underlying theory . . . is that the type of criminal that is responsible for most violent street crime is an opportunist. The criminal walks the streets looking for a victim that is weaker than himself, looking for an opportunity to make a "score" without any danger to himself, or any danger of apprehension. The decoy program is intended to respond to this type of criminal. (Edelman 1979: 54)

A variety of index crimes are seen as natural targets of decoy operations: street robbery/mugging, purse-snatching, rape, and theft from vehicles. Although the primary purpose is to catch criminals in the act, decoy operations can also deter crime; if would-be criminals know that the police are using decoys, they have to decide whether the crime is worth the risk that the prospective victim is a police officer.

The basic tactics of a decoy operation involve a specialized patrol unit whose members assume a variety of disguises. One officer will play the likely victim, disguised as a vulnerable citizen—an elderly woman or a taxicab driver, for example—while other members of the unit remain inconspicuous but in visual or radio contact with the "victim." When a "hit" occurs, the backup officers move in to apprehend the perpetrator.

Decoy operations have been used successfully by the New York Police Department (NYPD), and its tactics have often set the standard for other police agencies (Halper and Ku, n.d.). The *Street Crime Unit* (SCU) of the NYPD is made up of volunteers, experienced police officers from high-crime precincts who are

Decoy

Amid the noise and jostle of a sidewalk society, a derelict, clutching a bottle-shaped paper bag beneath his rumpled coat, weaves his way along Seattle's Skid Road in the Pioneer Square District. It is the first week of the month, and a tan window envelope, carelessly prominent in his coat pocket, reveals some of the state-provided funds with which he has begun his night on the town. Mumbling to himself, the decrepit old man staggers into the doorway of a boarded-up hotel, and pulling up his collar around his face, curls up in the corner to sleep off his apparent inebriation. Farther down the street, a husky youth, whose faded bluejeans and boots identify him as possibly a longshoreman or itinerant cowboy, balances himself on a pair of wooden crutches. His bandaged head and abrasion scabs attest to a recent fight of which he was not necessarily the victor. A torn pay envelope, readily accessible for his evening's enjoyment, protrudes from his jacket pocket.

Still another young man walks slowly through the district, mentally recording the details of his surroundings. Glancing into the doorway, he notes the sleeping man and

aggressive, curious, and especially "street smart." They receive specific training in decoy operations and tactics. SCU squads are normally assigned to areas of the city with a high rate of reported crimes that are susceptible to decoy operations. Consideration is also given to the requests of precinct commanders who may have particular crime problems in their precincts. For example, SCU personnel have been deployed in areas housing large numbers of Hasidic Jews, whose distinctive mode of dress has caused them to become targets of some street criminals.

The ability of decoy officers to successfully disguise themselves has also caused some serious problems—they have been mistaken for perpetrators by other (non-SCU) officers. To deal with this potentially dangerous situation, SCU officers wear headbands or apparel of a particular color, which changes peri-

> the tempting welfare envelope. The old man appears to sleep soundly in his convenient doorway, oblivious to his surroundings. The youth hesitates only momentarily, then leans over and takes the envelope from the man's pocket. Upon opening the envelope, he notices it contains only two $1 bills. As the youth searches through the old man's remaining pockets for more money, two men emerge from the shadows, arrest him, and take him into custody.
>
> Only minutes after emerging onto the street, the young man on crutches is approached by a large man who, shouting epithets, knocks him to the ground and snatches his pay envelope, paws brusquely through his clothing for still more money, and threatens to beat him further unless he relinquishes all valuables. Two apparent idlers in the vicinity step from an alleyway and intervene, brace the assailant against the wall, handcuff him, and take him away to jail.... The "cripple" and the "derelict" and their two-man back-up teams are members of the "Decoy Squad" of the Seattle Police Department.
>
> SOURCE: Thomas C. Martin, "Seattle Police Department's 'Decoy Squad,'" *FBI Law Enforcement Bulletin* (February 1978: 17).

odically and about which other police units are informed at roll call. However, off-duty officers and those from other agencies—such as federal agents or state law enforcement officers—may not be aware of the "color of the day."

Another problem with decoy operations is the question of "entrapment," and there have been instances in which clergy and other "respectable" citizens have been arrested despite their claim of seeking to aid—not to victimize—the decoy officer. While decoy operations often result in a high number of "quality" arrests—those that can be successfully prosecuted—the tactic is quite expensive. Many officers have to be deployed for considerable periods of time in order to accomplish the arrest of a single perpetrator. In addition to the lengthy waiting times, court appearances are often required of every member of the

> ## Street Crime Unit
>
> **My office in the state division of parole building adjoined the high-crime Times Square area of Manhattan, and going to lunch required walking down 42nd Street. It was noontime on a pleasant spring day when I observed a young man wearing jeans and sneakers being chased by an older man wearing a suit and tie who was yelling "Robber! He robbed me!" As the suspect glanced over his shoulder to see his pursuer, I grabbed his arm and shoved him against a wall. Before I could do or say anything, a dishevelled man wearing an earring and a headband appeared at my side—brandishing a revolver. I recall a combination of panic and adrenalin as I pulled out my .38 and turned quickly to save my life. "I'm a cop!" he yelled. I am not sure who was more frightened, the SCU officer, this author, or the suspect who hadn't moved from the wall.**

unit who was involved in the arrest, thus tying up a number of highly skilled and aggressive police officers and keeping them from other crime-fighting activities.

Stakeouts

Many crimes occur indoors, that is, in places not subject to routine police patrol, which is usually limited to public space such as streets and alleys. If police receive a "tip" or have other reasons to suspect that a crime is likely to occur at a particular location, they will sometimes "stake out" this target in anticipation of the crime. There are two basic types of stakeout, physical and electronic.

Physical stakeouts involve the covert placement of officers in and about the site of an anticipated robbery or burglary. Typically, stakeout teams use officers who are adept with firearms; they are usually heavily armed—with shotguns, magnum re-

7 ▪ POLICE OPERATIONS 189

NBC found a huge hit in "Miami Vice," its prime-time TV drama of two undercover cops, which first aired in the fall of 1984. In one episode, Sonny Crockett (Don Johnson, *left*) and Ricardo Tubbs (Philip Michael Thomas) discuss a porno king's possible connections to the FBI.

volvers, and rifles—and wear bulletproof vests. Physical stakeouts require an extraordinary expenditure of manpower hours; "hits" are relatively infrequent, but when they occur there is a high probability of violence, death, and injury, mostly to perpetrators, but sometimes innocent civilians and police officers. For these reasons, physical stakeouts are rarely used, usually only when a tip about an impending burglary or robbery is received.

Electronic stakeouts utilize a variety of electronic alarm systems to notify the police of a crime in progress. These may be passive devices that are tripped by a burglar or mechanisms that are activated by employees of the victimized establishment—bank tellers, for example. The police may install temporary wireless alarms at high-risk sites. These devices may be monitored by special mobile police teams or by district or headquarters personnel.

In many areas the police are reluctant or unwilling to respond to signals from passive alarm devices because of the high number of them that are false alarms. As a result, alarm systems are often monitored by private security personnel who may notify the police or send armed employees to the alarm site. To solve the problem of police responding to false alarms, the Pasadena (California) city council enacted an ordinance requiring the licensing of alarm systems, the Burglary and Robbery Alarm Permit Ordinance. Before anyone can legally operate an alarm in Pasadena, a permit must be obtained from the city. The system must conform to certain performance guidelines, and an excessive amount of false alarms results in the cancelling of the permit. Police Chief Robert McGowan (1978: 4) reports that "officers responding to alarms [in Pasadena] can expect that they will meet head-to-head with a suspect, that all of their skills will be tested, and that their alertness must be at peak efficiency.... And because response times have steadily decreased since the statute's implementation, apprehension at crime scenes has gone up 21 percent over the same period."

Hidden cameras and video recorders can be used alone or in conjunction with alarm systems. These enable law enforcement authorities to better identify criminals and may serve as a deterrent to crime. These devices are most often used by banks or other financial institutions.

Covert Surveillance

Covert surveillance can be used against virtually any type of index crime. There are two types: suspect surveillance and area surveillance.

Suspect surveillance can be used when the police are able to identify an active offender but cannot determine his or her targets in advance and do not have enough evidence to warrant prosecution. It is difficult to conduct a successful surveillance because suspects are usually aware of the possibility of being watched, and the officers have to be quite skilled in surveillance techniques—"tailing" on foot and in vehicles. This writer has been involved in many surveillance situations and can testify to how difficult, and often boring, this task can be. Obviously, suspect surveillance is quite expensive and is used only when the suspect represents a serious danger to the public, is a professional criminal, or is associated with organized crime. Suspect surveillance can be handicapped by the jurisdictional limitations of municipal police agencies; criminals are highly mobile, and professional criminals often travel interstate to reach targets.

Area surveillance can be used when there are no suspects or too many suspects for personal surveillance, when decoys would be inappropriate, or when there are too many potential targets to warrant physical or electronic stakeouts. It is used in response to a rash of burglaries, commercial robberies, or auto thefts in a particular area. Stephen Schack and his colleagues (1977: 105-6) concisely describe area surveillance:

> This tactic simply involves the covert patrol of a particular area and the observation of suspicious or unusual activities and occurrences which might indicate the likelihood of a crime occurrence. Suspicious individuals are not stopped, but are watched until they either commit an offense or the officers' suspicions are removed.

The method used is known as "blend and observe," and officers often dress as civilians and conduct surveillances from rooftops, garbage trucks, taxicabs, or telephone poles, disguised as repairmen. In certain tightly knit neighborhoods and in those with units of active organized criminals, however, area surveillance cannot be used with any degree of success. For example, in several areas of Brooklyn, where this writer worked, people in the street or sitting in front of their homes, on their porches, or at their windows would notice any strangers in their midst. If this was an organized crime stronghold, word would be sent by phone or messenger to whoever was interested in the information that strangers were about.

Investigation

Police personnel whose primary function is criminal investigation account for about 13 percent of the total number of sworn officers on a municipal force. Their titles vary—investigators, detectives, plainclothes officers—and some are involved in proactive policing, others in reactive policing.

Proactive Investigation

Certain victimless crimes do not normally come to the attention of the police. Covert activity and criminal informants are used in **proactive investigation** by vice squads enforcing gambling and prostitution statutes and by narcotics bureaus dealing with violations of controlled-substance laws. Some departments also have units specializing in organized crime that use these tactics.

Effective enforcement action against these victimless crimes requires a great deal of covert police activity, including what James Q. Wilson (1978: 22) refers to as *instigation*, "a legally neutral term referring to a law enforcement officer who, by assuming the role of a criminal, provides an opportunity to commit a consensual crime for a person who is ready, willing, and seeking an opportunity to do so."

Effective enforcement also requires the use of criminal informants. The **criminal informant** (as opposed to the civic-minded citizen informant) must be active in the criminal "underworld" to be effective. In return for his or her cooperation, the informant expects a reward, usually an unofficial "license" to continue plying an illicit occupation or leniency in a pending prosecution. Sometimes an investigator will pay informants with cash or drugs. As a result of undercover work or working with informants, the proactive investigator often spends a great deal of time consorting with criminals in a criminal environment. He or she may tread a narrow line between legal and illegal activities, and the possibility of compromise and corruption is always present. Wilson (1978: 59) points out that the narcotics investigator "can easily agree to overlook offenses known to him but to no one else or to participate in illegal transactions (buying and selling drugs) for his own rather than for the organization's advantage." Corruption has been a perennial problem in vice enforcement and, in more recent years, drug enforcement. (This problem will be discussed in the next chapter.)

Law enforcement against prostitution usually involves a police officer who acts the role of a "john" (customer). Police officers may also impersonate prostitutes in order to arrest johns for patronizing a prostitute. Gambling enforcement usually requires the use of undercover officers or informants who disclose the existence of a gambling operation. This information is used to secure a search warrant, and a raid is conducted.

Drug enforcement is sometimes referred to as "buy and bust." The standard tactic is to have an informant introduce an undercover officer to a seller. The officer usually makes at least two buys that are observed by other officers who maintain a surveillance of the transaction site. Days or even weeks after the buys are made, the seller is arrested, and the surveillance officers serve as witnesses to avoid "blowing the cover" of the undercover officer and the "snitch." In other cases, information from informants and/or undercover officers is used to secure a search warrant, and a drug raid is conducted. When a large wholesale drug buy is arranged, a "controlled buy" situation is put into operation. Since there is usually a large amount of cash to be exchanged for the drugs, the possibility of a "ripoff," a robbery instead of a "buy," must be considered in the elaborate planning necessary for a successful operation. Heavily armed officers maintain a visual and/or audio surveillance, often using hidden microphones and video cameras; immediately after the buy is completed, arrests are made.

Reactive Investigation

Most police investigative work involves responding to citizen complaints. This type of investigation is referred to as **reactive investigation.** These reactive or detective units may be organized on a decentralized basis, with each detective a generalist responsible for investigating all types of crime committed in a specific geographic area, or investigative units may operate out of a central headquarters. Some police departments have both decentralized and centralized investigative units, the latter usually being specialized, such as homicide and sex crimes units.

"Traditionally, the criminal investigator—popularly the detective—has been thought of as embodying the essence of law enforcement: solving crimes by shrewd deduction, scientific in-

194 PART TWO REACTING TO CRIME

Pop culture has lent detectives their own mystique.

quiry, and artful surmise," notes James Q. Wilson (1978: 17). The work of the detective has been shrouded in glamour and mystique by books, movies, and television. The reality of detective work, however, usually has little in common with its media representations. Herman Goldstein (1977: 56), a former ranking official with the Chicago Police Department, states, "A considerable amount of detective work is actually undertaken on a hit-or-miss basis; and . . . the capacity of detectives to solve crimes is greatly exaggerated."

The reactive investigative process begins when a patrol officer responds to the scene of a crime. He or she is responsible for assisting the victim, securing the crime scene, conducting a preliminary investigation, determining the location of any witnesses, and deciding if evidence technicians are required. The patrol officer is usually expected to return to patrol ("back in service") as quickly as possible, so the preliminary investigation usually involves only basic information, which is turned over to the investigative division.

The patrol officer's preliminary report is screened, usually by a superior officer in the investigative division, and distributed to the investigative unit that covers the type of crime or geographic area where the crime occurred. Within each unit a case is assigned on the basis of geography, current caseload size, or the investigator's area of specialization. The detective will then informally assign the case a priority on an intuitive basis according to three possibilities (Greenberg and Wasserman 1979):

1. Suspect has been identified, witnesses remain to be interviewed, or there are strong leads (e.g., license plate number of perpetrator's car).
2. Case is serious enough to warrant attention even in the absence of concrete leads. The victim may be re-interviewed, or the crime scene may be searched again for evidence, or new witnesses sought.
3. Case is routine, and there are no obvious leads. It may be checked against other cases in the files, but little action will be taken unless new evidence is discovered.

After a suspect is in custody, the investigator will interview him or her and may arrange for a lineup if the suspect has been seen by the victim and/or witnesses. Finally, the investigator will also testify in court if the case goes to trial.

Bernard Greenberg and his colleagues (1977) note that unless the responding patrol officer gathers relevant information at the crime scene, if the offender is not immediately apprehended, the chances of the case being solved at the detective level are minimal. Indeed, a great deal of research evidence indicates that investigators account for only a small portion of arrests for serious crimes. Of those cases actually solved, most are the result of a victim or witness supplying a positive identification of the suspect. In response to this research, some police departments have instituted the MCI program.

Managing criminal investigations (MCI) is the result of a report published by the Rand Corporation (Greenwood, Chaiken, and Petersilla 1975) that concluded that the patrol officer is the key figure in solving most crimes. The report noted that more than half of all serious crimes reported to the police receive no more than superficial attention from investigators. The report also pointed out that investigators actually spend more time on paperwork than on the task of identifying perpetrators. It was recommended that the role of the patrol officer be increased, and the Rand researchers suggested the use of a managerial system that graded cases according to their solvability. Several *solvability factors*—Is there a witness? Is a suspect named or known? Can a suspect vehicle be identified?—are each given a numerical weight, and the total weight of all solvability factors—the score—determines what will happen to a case. Cases receiving a low score—little or no evidence to work with—would be inactivated immediately, conserving investigative resources for cases that are more likely to be solved by investigative efforts.

Under an MCI program the responding patrol officer is responsible for a great deal of follow-up activity that heretofore had been reserved for detectives:

1. locating and interviewing the victim and witnesses;
2. detecting physical evidence such as fingerprints and toolmarks;
3. preparing an initial investigative report that will serve as a guide for investigators, with sufficient documentation to determine if the case should be assigned for continued investigation or immediately suspended for lack of evidence. In some programs the patrol officer may also make a recommendation that the case be inactivated or continued (Greenberg and Wasserman 1979).

TRAFFIC

Traffic control and enforcement are part of the larger police responsibility for protecting lives and property. Motor vehicle accidents cost more than $40 billion annually in wages lost, property damages, medical expenses, and insurance administration costs; they take the lives of more than 40,000 people, and another 1,500,000 suffer disabling injuries. About two-thirds of all motor vehicle accidents in the United States are attributable to driving offenses such as speeding, improper turns, and tailgating, often in conjunction with driving while intoxicated.

The traffic control function is part of the responsibility of the patrol division, although in larger departments there is often a traffic bureau that concentrates on specific problems such as speeding and accident investigation. In some departments it may include a motorcycle unit; others have done away with the routine use of motorcycles for traffic enforcement because of the dangers involved. The police respond to the scene of traffic accidents to protect life and property from further harm, to provide emergency assistance, to assist in the removal of disabled vehicles, to insure the smooth flow of traffic, and to compile an accurate report of the incident in order to help establish civil liability. The police are also responsible for the enforcement of driver and motor vehicle licensing and safety laws.

In most jurisdictions the police have the discretion to issue a citation for moving violations or to effect an arrest of the violator. Arrests usually occur for serious violations such as driving while intoxicated (DWI, or DUI—driving under the influence), reckless driving, or leaving the scene of an accident. Some jurisdictions allow the police to issue written warnings for certain minor violations such as a defective light. Persons with out-of-state licenses may be taken directly to court for the posting of bond (to insure their return to stand trial). A number of states have reciprocal agreements, however, whereby each will enforce the other's citations; this can avoid the need for taking a traffic violator into custody and the posting of bond.

Traffic enforcement is one aspect of policing that can easily be subjected to measurement, and police activity can directly affect the statistics. Creating or adding personnel to a specialized traffic enforcement unit or the setting of "norms" (usually a euphemism for ticket quotas) can increase the number of traffic citations; while this can increase government revenues, its impact on accident rates has been questioned (see Lundman 1979). In many jurisdictions, various levels of government share in the proceeds of the revenue generated as a result of police traffic enforcement activities, and the police themselves may also benefit. For example, in North Carolina some of the revenue from traffic fines is paid into the police retirement system.

Life without a driver's license?

Think about it before you drink and drive.

Sobriety Checkpoints

Alcohol is a factor in at least half of all fatal motor vehicle crashes, and the increasing concern with intoxicated driving—which causes twice as many deaths annually as murder—has led to the use of *sobriety checkpoints* in many jurisdictions. Jerome Campane, Jr. (1984: 24) describes a DWI roadblock/checkpoint:

> Officers conducting a roadblock may stop all traffic or some numerically objective number, like every fifth vehicle. After a vehicle is directed to the side of the road, an officer may request to see an operator's license and vehicle registration and may ask several questions to observe the driver's demeanor. If the officer detects the signs of inebriation, the motorist may be directed to move the vehicle to a secondary area, step out, and submit to a roadside sobriety coordination or breathalyzer test. The failure to pass either test constitutes sufficient probable cause for arrest.

Henry Rockel (1984: 38) explains why this tactic developed:

> Unfortunately, at the time most drunk driving violations occur (between 8 P.M. and 4 A.M.) there is a need for police patrols to respond to a variety of other types of police service calls. The magnitude of the drunk driving problem is such that normal patrols, even when bolstered by selective traffic enforcement teams, are not enough to adequately address the problem.
> The potential drunk driver perceives little risk of detection and apprehension. Even if he encounters a police unit while driving, he frequently believes the officer will not detect any erratic driving that would result in being stopped.

Thus, the deterrence value of a sobriety checkpoint is based on the potential intoxicated driver's perception of a substantially increased risk of detection.

There have been legal problems with the sobriety checkpoint. Campane (1984: 25) notes that "the Fourth Amendment requires that all searches and seizures be reasonable. It is now beyond dispute that stopping a motor vehicle and detaining its occupants constitutes a seizure, even though the detention is brief and limited in scope." In *Delaware v. Prouse* (1979), the Supreme Court ruled that in the absence of "articulable and reasonable suspicion that a motorist is unlicensed or the automobile is not registered, or that either the vehicle or an occupant is otherwise subject to seizure for violation of law, stopping an automobile and detaining the driver in order to check his driver's license and registration of the automobile are unreasonable under the Fourth Amendment." The Court recommended that states develop constitutionally sound guidelines for spot checks, and the police officer should not have unrestrained discretion. Christopher Gontarz (1984: 177) summarizes guidelines that have been established by a series of court decisions:

1. The location of the roadblock must be based on an analytical analysis of accident reports.
2. The roadblock should be approved and implemented by a police executive, and there should be written policy detailing roadblock operations in order to limit police officer discretion.
3. The roadblock location should be well lighted; there should be ample room to provide for the safety of vehicles pulled over; officers should be in uniform, and marked police cars should be visible to the approaching motorists.
4. An announcement should be made as to the time and geographical areas where the roadblocks will be utilized. Exact locations do not have to be disclosed.
5. The police may stop all cars—a "100 percent roadblock"—or a systematically determined sample—for instance, every fifth car—may be used.

Internal Affairs

Quis custodiet ipses custodes? "Who polices the police?" In most departments it is **IA, internal affairs,** a unit of police officers who investigate the activities of their fellow officers. Kevin Krajick (1980a: 7) states that the earliest IA units were established during the late 1950s and early 1960s to investigate allegations of corruption in big-city police departments, and then "during the social upheavals of the middle and late 1960s . . . citizens, especially members of minority groups, became more and more prone to question the behavior of the police. They demanded not only corruption investigations, but review of the day-to-day street activities of police, especially regarding the use of force."

In small departments, those with a dozen or less sworn officers, the police chief usually conducts internal investigations. Slightly larger departments usually have an inspector who reports directly to the chief. Departments serving a population of 100,000 or more usually have a full-time internal affairs unit. In addition to corruption, IA officers investigate citizen complaints about brutality, charges that officers were discourteous or used ethnic or racial slurs, or conducted illegal searches and seizures.

In some departments, IA investigations are limited to cases of corruption, and other agencies will investigate citizen complaints. In Chicago, for example, civilian investigators in the Office of Professional Standards investigate complaints of unnecessary force. In recent years, the FBI has also become increasingly active in the investigation of police corruption cases that are violations of the federal Racketeer and Corrupt Organizations (RICO) section of the Organized Crime Control Act of 1970.

IA is feared and often hated by rank-and-file police (who often refer to IA officers as "shoo-flies"). On the other hand, IA units have often been criticized by civilian groups for not vigorously pursuing police misconduct. In some cities this criticism, especially by minority groups, led to the creation of civilian review boards (see chapter 8).

The most aggressive IA unit is the NYPD's Internal Affairs Division, whose controversial tactics—such as integrity tests—were initiated in the aftermath of the disclosures of Frank Serpico (portrayed in the movie by Al Pacino), resulting in an investigation by the Knapp Commission. The integrity tests come in many forms (Krajick 1980a: 13):

> Money or valuables may be left in an illegally parked, unlocked car to test the honesty of police tow truck drivers. Internal affairs officers may pose as drunks; they create a disturbance and get arrested to see if officers will roll [rob] them for the money they are carrying. IAD has created phony gambling operations to see if neighborhood police will demand protection money. Agents have posed as heroin dealers to see if officers turn in all of the evidence when they make an arrest.

SPECIAL WEAPONS AND TACTICS (SWAT) TEAMS

The **SWAT team** is a product of the late 1960s and early 1970s, when a great deal of funding from the federal government was available to local police agencies. A perceived increase in sniper and hostage situations led to the creation of these units, whose officers often wear military-style camouflage gear and are armed with high-powered rifles, shotguns, and 9mm submachine guns. A typical SWAT team consists of seven officers (Williams 1984): a team leader who coordinates unit operations, a fire team leader who directs the activity of the entry-fire team, two fire team officers, two sniper team officers, and one officer cross-trained in the use of gas, sniping, assault, negotiating, and any other needed specialties. Except in large cities, these officers are usually assigned to regular police units and are mobilized as a SWAT team only for training or in response to an emergency.

P.K. Williams (1984: 32) summarizes SWAT team tactics:

1. The situation to which the team is responding is evaluated at the scene.
2. SWAT officers scout inside the perimeter.
3. Contact is established with the aggressor(s).
4. The team negotiator initiates negotiations while the team is deployed.
5. Negotiations are continued as long as they are productive.
6. If negotiations break down, an attack is contemplated as attempts to re-establish productive negotiations are pursued.
7. The fire team is deployed for attack.
8. An attack is accomplished as swiftly as possible.

Although the NYPD, America's largest municipal police department, has no SWAT unit, since 1930 it has had the comparable Emergency Service Unit (ESU). This is a unit of about 250 officers, most of whose time is spent on rescue—not shooting—missions (Mancini 1983: 22). An ESU volunteer recruit

> is schooled in a staggering syllabus of skills. He is trained as a marksman so he can play a key role when an armed perpetrator takes cover or a terrorist takes hostages. Then he is taught the psychology of barricaded criminals so he can avoid using his marksmanship talents. He is certified as an emergency medical technician and can administer cardiopulmonary resuscitation and oxygen to victims of coronaries, respiratory ailments, smoke inhalation and asphyxiation. He's versed in the art of extrication and rescues people trapped in not only elevators but also vehicles, heavy machinery and cave-ins. He knows how to secure dangerous cornices and scaffolds, repair downed electrical wires and poles . . . and navigate an armored personnel carrier for rescuing people pinned down by gunfire.

Sergeant John Casey, a twenty-three-year veteran of the ESU, says, "It's 90 percent boredom and 10 percent sheer terror" (Rimer 1985: 14). The sergeant is a two-time winner of the Police Medal of Valor who nearly lost an eye when a man he was trying to prevent from setting fire to an oil-saturated kitchen floor stabbed him in the head. Sergeant William Manor, a thirty-year veteran of the ESU, works with only one lung; the other was removed after he was stabbed in an attempt to disarm a mental patient on a weekend pass.

POLICE AUXILIARIES

The inadequacy of manpower in policing is a perennial problem. The cost of employing full-time police officers is quite high, and

In the late 1960s and early 1970s an increase in sniper and hostage situations led to the creation of Special Weapons and Tactics (SWAT) units. *Below,* SWAT team members lead a teenaged boy to safety following a hostage taking in Newport, Ky. The thirty-hour siege ended when a police sniper fatally shot Dennis Lucas, twenty, who had demanded $50,000 and plane tickets to Europe. Another teenager held was also released unharmed.

there can never be "enough" police officers, given the goals of policing (discussed in the previous chapter). Personnel shortages may be ongoing or seasonal, depending on the jurisdiction. For example, resort communities often face an influx of vacationers and tourists during the summer or during the winter skiing months, which can more than double the normal size of the population. In response to this annual influx, some communities employ "summertime cops." Cape May County, New Jersey, has ten departments that hire summer police officers, most of whom are students of criminal justice programs (Donohue 1982: 3): "Highly motivated students seeking internships or work exper-

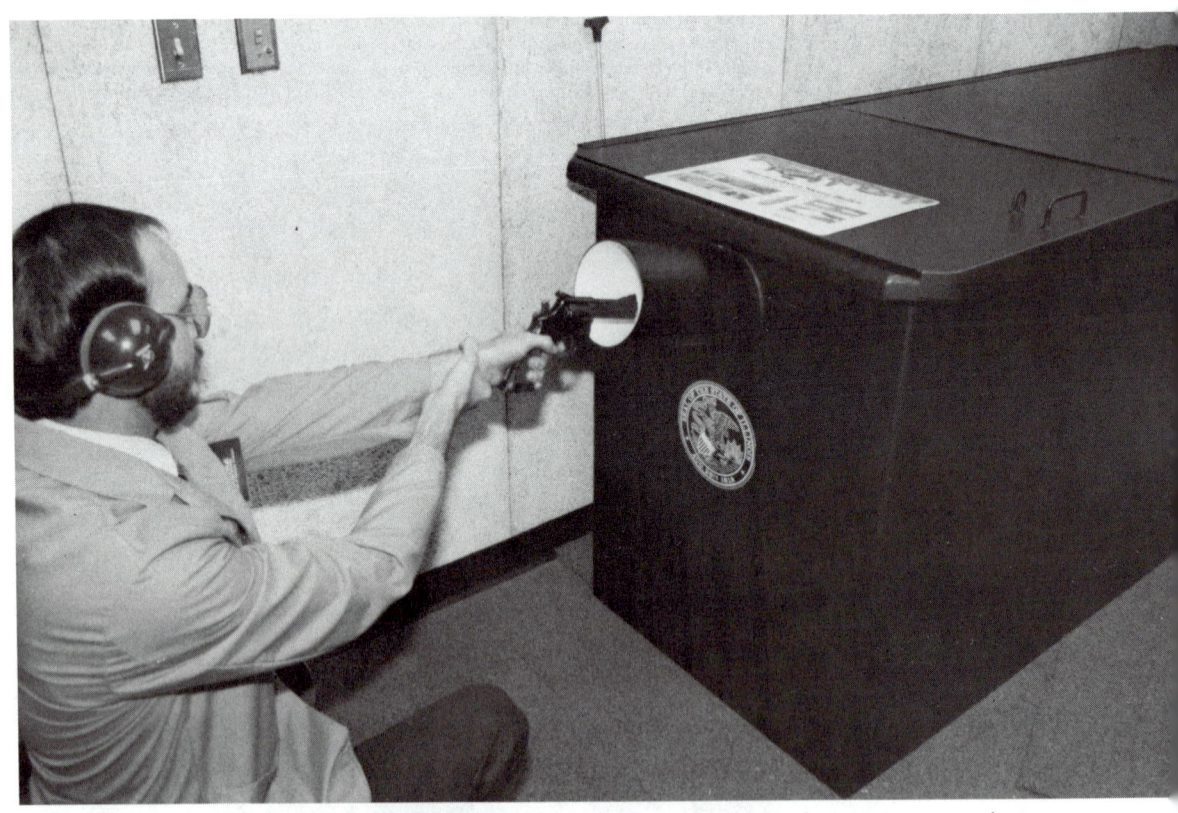

Two Illinois State Police technicians examine evidence taken from a crime scene. *Above*, a ballistics expert fires a weapon into a water tank. The water prevents any distortion of the bullet so that its markings can be compared with one found at the site of a crime. *Right*, a technician pours plaster of Paris into a mold to make a cast of a footprint left at the scene of a burglary.

ience abound. Accustomed to the learning environment, they possess a basic understanding of the American system of criminal justice." Candidates for these positions are carefully screened, and those accepted are subjected to an intensive forty-hour training program. The summertime officers are fully sworn and carry firearms.

Police agencies in other communities employ part-time officers throughout the year. These men and women, sometimes referred to as reserve or auxiliary officers, are either unpaid volunteers or paid less than full-time officers. In Illinois and North Carolina, they are sworn officers who carry firearms. In

Arizona, the highway patrol has used unpaid reserve officers for more than thirty years. These troopers are fully certified state law enforcement officers. L. I. Deitch and L. N. Thompson (1985: 60) write that "the only distinguishing element of their uniform is the word 'Reserve' written on the badge. The public sees reserve officers as Highway Patrol officers, which, by statute and training, they are. Reserves issue traffic citations, effect felony or misdemeanor arrests, investigate accidents and perform all the functions of a full-time officer." In some cities, such as New York (which has more than 8000), auxiliary officers are unpaid volunteers who, although they wear police-type uniforms and carry nightsticks, are civilians with no police powers, and they do not carry firearms. They usually patrol their own communities, acting as a deterrent force and providing the police with extra ears and eyes.

Other Specialized Bureaus and Units

There are a number of other units or bureaus that a police department may establish, usually depending on its size and how various problems of policing are perceived by the police chief executive. A *juvenile bureau* deals with a variety of law enforcement and social service matters involving young persons and their families. A *police-community relations* (PCR) unit develops programs for fostering a better relationship between the police and the policed—an outgrowth of the turbulence of the 1960s, particularly between white police officers and minority residents of urban areas. PCR units are often involved in efforts at crime prevention; these include providing speakers for community groups, lectures on crime control, the formation of "citizen watch" groups, and programs for marking valuable property. Other functional units or bureaus include personnel, training, research, and planning, operating under a variety of titles, as we saw in chapter 6 in the diagrams of the Chicago and Los Angeles police departments.

As we have seen in this chapter, specialization in policing is an attempt to better fulfill the goals set for the police. In the next chapter, we will examine some specific issues in policing.

KEY TERMS

differential police response strategies
preventive patrol
Kansas City Study
Uniformed tactical patrol (UTP)
field interrogations
decoy operations
physical stakeouts
electronic stakeouts

suspect surveillance
area surveillance
proactive investigation
criminal informant
reactive investigation
managing criminal investigations (MCI)
internal affairs (IA)
SWAT team

REVIEW QUESTIONS

1. What are the purposes of police patrol?
2. What are the four functional categories of routine police patrol?
3. Why is a speedy response to a citizen request for police services usually unnecessary?
4. What was the purpose of the Kansas City Study? What were its findings?
5. What are the various styles of policing?
6. Describe the four most common tactics employed in specialized patrol operations.
7. What is the potential problem in the police use of criminal informants?
8. What are the responsibilities of a patrol officer in a reactive investigation?
9. What is the managing criminal investigations (MCI) program?
10. Provide three examples of solvability factors.
11. What is the responsibility of the police with respect to motor vehicle and traffic control?
12. What is the purpose of a sobriety checkpoint, and what are the legal questions such checkpoints raise?
13. What is the purpose of an internal affairs bureau?
14. Why do police departments use seasonal or part-time officers?

CHAPTER 8

Issues in Policing

LIMITATIONS OF POLICING
Structural Limitations
Resource Limitations
Legal Limitations

POLICE DISCRETION

CONTROLLING THE POLICE
Police Alienation,
  Authoritarianism,
  and Solidarity

POLICE DEVIANCE
Corruption
Brutality
Deadly Force
  Common Law Statutes
  Modified Common Law
  Model Penal Code

PROFESSIONALISM

POLICE UNIONISM

AFFIRMATIVE ACTION

PRIVATE SECURITY

LEGAL ISSUES
Search and Seizure

REVIEW QUESTIONS

Boxes

Homicide
Patterns of Police Corruption
Terry v. Ohio

In chapter 6 we noted the ambivalence with which Americans tend to view the police: while there is recognition of the need for social control and order, there also exists a strong sense of individualism and concern for freedom. The history of policing has reflected this conflict, and a varied public continues to demand *both* vigorous law enforcement and leniency; the police are expected both to "get tough" and to respect civil liberties. Adding to the dilemma inherent in policing a democratic America are the goals society has set out for the police to accomplish: to control crime, to protect life and property, to maintain peace and order, and to safeguard constitutional rights. The ability of the police even to approximate these goals is severely constrained by limitations of structure, resources, and law.

LIMITATIONS OF POLICING

The very serious limitations of policing cannot be overcome by dedication, professionalism, and plain hard work—it is a "no-win" situation. The frustration and cynicism of police officers must be understood in terms of their ambivalent role and the limitations of policing in a democratic society.

Structural Limitations

Of the eight index crimes we looked at in chapter 3, several are not readily amenable to preventive police activity; homicide, rape, arson, and larceny-theft often occur in places not routinely subjected to police scrutiny—inside dwellings and business establishments. Thus, even increases in police efficiency or personnel will not prevent many kinds of crime, ranging from shoplifting to murder. In addition, the police have no control over other actors and agencies in the criminal justice system whose actions affect policing: prosecutors, judges, and parole boards.

Homicide

"The number of homicides experienced by any city attests to the value its citizens place on human life. However, since the majority of murders normally occur behind closed doors—by people who are related, friends, neighbors, or otherwise acquainted—police officers are restricted in their ability to prevent this crime."—Fred Rice, Superintendent of Police, Chicago.

SOURCE: Wood 1986.

Resource Limitations

How many police officers are enough? A cop on every corner is obviously an unrealistic goal. Police officers typically work in eight-hour shifts, five days a week. There are police officers at work all 168 hours of each week. Each officer, however, works an average of forty hours a week, and from that must be subtracted training time, vacation time, sick leave, court time, and so on. This adds up to the need for about five officers for each officer actually on duty at any given time. Thus, increasing the total number of sworn officers in a general service police department by x actually requires hiring $5x$ officers, an obviously expensive proposition. Since police resources are always limited, or inelastic, resources allocated for one particular activity, such as decoy operations or school security, reduces the number of officers available for other police activities, such as traffic control or vice enforcement.

Charles Silverman (1978: 201) notes, however, "there is no observable correlation between the number of police a community has and either the number of crimes that are committed or the proportion of those crimes that are solved." David Greenberg, Ronald Kessler, and Colin Loftin (1983: 385) conducted research into the relationship between the number of police officers and the rates of crime in 269 American cities and found "no evidence that police employment reduces violent or property crime." The number of police officers a community has, however, is related to "quality of life" matters that are not easily quantifiable. These include control of a variety of public nuisances such as rowdiness, panhandling, street prostitution, drug sales, and parking and motor vehicle violations.

Legal Limitations

In chapter 5 we reviewed the due process rights that protect citizens from the power of government; these protections, to the extent that they actually protect, limit the ability of the police to achieve their goals. The *Miranda* decision, the *Mapp* decision, and the exclusionary rule limit the ability of the police to control crime and to protect the community.

In short, the police are expected to achieve the impossible: to resolve social problems over which they have no control, burdened by structural limitations, inadequate resources, and legal restrictions. In practice, the police respond to unrealistic expectations and the realities of policing by the exercise of discretion.

POLICE DISCRETION

Discretion refers to "a situation in which an employee of a criminal justice agency, within the scope of his/her duties, has the lawful authority to choose between two alternatives" (Abadinsky 1984: 3). Each police officer decides when and how to enforce the law, conserving police resources for those situations most in need of police action.

Why is this a problem? In 1776 the Declaration of Independence proclaimed that "all men are created equal," and the Fourteenth Amendment to the Constitution guarantees "equal protection of the laws." The exercise of discretion by a police officer (or any other agent of government), however, leads to *unequal justice*, to persons in similar situations being treated differently.

What is the nature of discretionary decision making by police officers? At the command level, the police chief executive determines how the police force is to be deployed: the number of officers assigned to each division and to special units, the number of officers on each shift, the number of officers in each area or precinct, the size of patrol beats, the ratio of supervisors to line staff, and so on. In order to gain public and political support for the department, the chief may allocate personnel on the basis of citizen demands rather than efficiency, further limiting the effectiveness of the police in controlling crime. The chief may be pressured into "cracking down" in response to a particular community crime problem. Such crackdowns can lead to excessive—improper, if not illegal—activities on the part of officers responding to the chief's exhortations. While a crackdown is usually a response to community outrage, the excesses that can result further alienate the police from the community—another "no-win" situation.

Discretionary powers are guided by two principles:

1. *The more serious the offense, the less discretion possible, and vice versa.* Thus, a police officer having probable cause to arrest a suspect for robbery cannot exercise discretion and issue a summons or reprimand; an arrest must be made. On the other hand,

A Chicago police officer hands out a parking ticket, 1934.

a violation of laws against public drinking will often result in a reprimand and warning, not an arrest. In certain categories of offense, however—for example, "domestic conflicts" and drug violations—discretion is often exercised even when the offense is serious. A felony, such as an assault on a spouse, even with injuries, is often treated differently than a similar situation between strangers would be. Or a drug offender may be used as an "informant," in exchange for immunity from arrest or prosecution.

2. *The exercise of discretion must meet the fairness test.* The police exercise discretion in determining which vehicles to stop or which pedestrians to question. If the decision is to be "proper," it must advance the goals of the officer's agency, for example, to protect the community. A discretionary decision should not be based on personal considerations such as convenience or prejudice. For example, an arrest should not be avoided because the officer is about to go off duty, and blacks should not be arrested for crimes that are ignored when committed by whites, and vice versa.

The specter of discrimination is raised when discretionary decisions by a police officer are based on age, gender, race, or ethnicity. The reality of policing, however, often leads a police officer to use an unofficial "probability table." The officer, because of experience, education, or simple prejudice, is more likely to stop and question a young black male, all other things being equal, than, for example, an older white woman. Where common sense and good policing end and discrimination and prejudice begin is not easy to discern. Discriminatory use of discretion can also occur when the police downgrade the seriousness of an offense based on victim characteristics. Black-on-black crime, or white-on-black crime, for example, may not receive the same response that a black-on-white offense would. Such discriminatory enforcement, of course, places blacks at greater risk of being the victims of crime.

While every police officer is sworn to enforce *all* the law, this is neither possible nor expected. Many statutes are symbolic; for example, laws prohibiting adultery or other consensual and noncommercial sexual practices are merely an expression of society's disapproval; they are not meant to be enforced. While all states have laws prohibiting gambling that is not licensed by the government (e.g., betting on horse races), police officers seldom arrest persons playing cards in their own homes even if this violates gambling statutes. Laws against noncommercial gambling are simply not supposed to be enforced. (The only illegal gambling this author has done for the past two decades—poker—has been with law enforcement officers in several states.) The decision to arrest in nonfelony cases is frequently based on the *attitude test*. All other variables being equal, an offender is more likely to be arrested if he or she fails to show proper respect and deference to a police officer or "gives some lip."

Although the police are uniformed, carry firearms, salute superiors, and share the same titles of rank, the discretionary activities of police officers differ dramatically from their military counterparts. Police officers are typically not under the direct supervision of a superior officer, so their actions are free of immediate supervisory control. This contrasts markedly with the situation of a private in the infantry who is usually under the direct observation of a corporal or sergeant. The police also differ from most other public and private agencies in the relationship between rank or position and the amount of discretion exercised. Normally, the higher the rank, the greater the discretionary power. In policing, however, the most important discretionary decisions, including those of life and death, are made by patrol officers—the lowest-ranking persons on a police force—and the patrol officer makes these decisions without direct supervisory controls. The difficulties encountered by police chief executives in controlling the exercise of discretion by their officers is part of a wider problem of controlling the police.

CONTROLLING THE POLICE

How is the behavior of a police officer controlled? Most police officers work in uniform, which includes a shield or star with a number and a name plate; they drive marked vehicles whose identifying numbers are easily observed. These forms of identification serve to control police behavior because they prevent the officer from acting anonymously; they make it easier for civilians to record the officer's identity and for police supervisors and inspection personnel to observe the patrol officer's actions. Thus, while increasing the number of plainclothes officers could improve crime control, it could create additional problems of police control.

Police Alienation, Authoritarianism, and Solidarity

Adding to the difficulties involved in controlling the behavior of the police are the intertwined problems of alienation, authoritarianism, and solidarity.

Arthur Niederhoffer (1969: 9), a former New York City police officer and sociologist, states that

> in contrast to their English counterparts, the police in America have never been acclaimed as models for middle-class scions, and they are acutely aware of this. The police feel that they deserve respect from the public. But the upper class looks down on them; the middle class seems to ignore them, as if they were part of the urban scenery; the lower class fears them.

The result is the police officer's perception of the public as an enemy, and this "binds the policeman's group to isolation and secrecy," which is reinforced by the secrecy and suspicion that are part of their job. William Westley (1970: 49) also points out that in spite of the police officer's role as a protector of the public, "he usually meets only those he is protecting [the public] from, and for him *they* have no love." The responsible public, on the other hand, often views the police as ineffectual, brutal, corrupt, and ignorant. In short, the American police officer is often alienated from the society he or she is paid to police.

Policing has been viewed as an occupation that tends to breed **authoritarianism**—a social-psychological term referring to a preoccupation with conventional values, a dislike of minority groups, an inflexibility toward social change, an exaggerated concern with masculinity, a distrust of education and "eggheads," and political conservatism. The authoritarian personality type has been seen as characteristic of the working class (Niederhoffer 1969). Traditionally, entry into policing required at most only a high school education, and most police officers come from the ranks of the working class, whose members have limited education. To such persons, police employment promises job security and a salary level often not available elsewhere. Wayne B. Hanewicz (1978: 166) states that the personality style described above "appears to dominate in the police population, and the subculture which develops around these personalities 'is remarkably constant despite variations in size and organization of police departments.'" There is debate about whether the reason is that working-class authoritarians tend to enter policing, or that police officers tend to become authoritarian because of their job experience. In either case, the relatively recent stress on education for police officers—some departments require college education for entry or promotion, others encourage their officers to attend college—can be seen as an effort to offset these traits by either attracting middle-class (i.e., college-educated) candidates or modifying the attitudes of police officers by exposing them to higher education and the middle-class environment of college.

Authoritarian attitudes and alienation have led to a solidarity—an "us" versus "them" outlook—that has traditionally insulated the police from outside scrutiny. Police officers have placed a greater emphasis on loyalty to each other than even to their sworn responsibilities under law. Thus, Officer Frank Serpico of the NYPD was viewed as a pariah by other police officers. Writes Peter Maas (1974: 22-23), "He had broken an unwritten code that in effect put policemen above the law, that said a cop could not turn in other cops." As proof of this code, one need only note the continued presence of corruption and the absence of other "Serpicos." Chicago journalist William Brashler (1977: xi) notes, for example, "Chicago's police scandals have had no Serpicos, no unblemished police officers willing to supply golden information against fellow cops for federal prosecutors."

Societal ambivalence toward the police and their marginal social status has led to a form of "solidarity" among police, or a "police subculture," that makes control over the police quite difficult. It has also made it difficult to integrate civilian specialists into police departments, as crime analysts, for example. Police officers are reluctant to deal with civilian personnel, to interact and share information, with the same level of confidence that they have for fellow sworn officers.

POLICE DEVIANCE

Tom Barker and Robert Wells (1982: 9) refer to police occupational deviance as "violations of criminal laws, departmental rules and regulations, and ethical police standards, which occur during the course of occupational activity and are related to employment as a police officer." Such deviance can be related to furthering organizational goals—by disregarding the require-

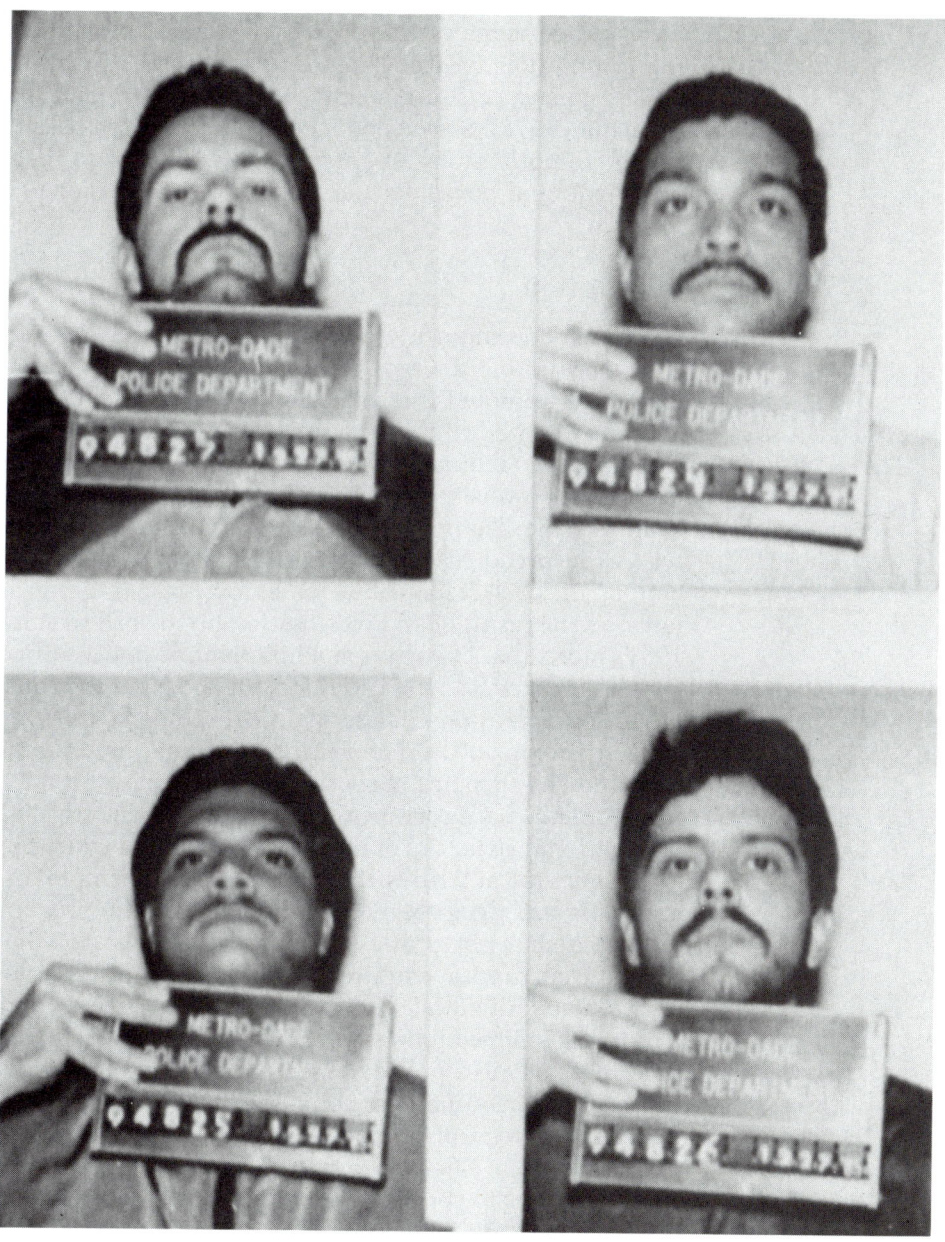

In 1985, an investigation into police corruption in Miami brought forth eleven arrests of policemen for crimes ranging from robbery to cocaine possession. On December 27, three officers (*at top right and bottom*) were charged with the murder of three suspected drug dealers; a fourth (*at top left*) was included in additional charges of racketeering, armed cocaine trafficking, and aggravated battery.

ments of due process, for example. The pressure on the police to meet public demands for order and crime control gives rise to the temptation to use "short cuts," such as "roughing up" or harassing suspects, a deviant means to attain legitimate goals (Sherman 1978). Serious police deviance is often based on purely selfish motivations, or **corruption**, which is "an illegal use of organizational power for personal gain" (Sherman 1978: 30).

Corruption

In certain communities, police corruption may be encouraged by a public tolerance of vice activities such as gambling. In chapter 6 we noted that historically the problem of police corruption was tied to the corruption of urban political organizations—the "machines." Even after the demise of most political machines, however, police corruption has continued. In 1972, for example, the Knapp Commission found that police corruption was widespread in New York City, particularly among plainclothes officers responsible for enforcing gambling and drug laws. As the result of an investigation by the FBI which began in 1981, more than two dozen Philadelphia police officers were convicted of federal violations for taking bribes to protect illegal gambling operations. These included the department's second-highest-ranking officer, four inspectors, and three captains. Law enforcement agencies in southern Florida have been experiencing problems with corruption related to cocaine trafficking. The occupational structure of the police provides a wider opportunity for corrupt activities than other types of employment, and gambling and drug enforcement (since they are proactive), provide greater opportunities than other forms of policing.

Police corruption can involve "scores," one-time transactions between an individual officer and a civilian, such as a bribe from a motorist stopped for speeding. Or it can involve "pads," bribes paid regularly to a police officer. Officers not personally receiving bribe money may cooperate passively by failing to report instances of corruption about which they have knowledge. Police corruption can also involve officers taking advantage of their positions to commit predatory crimes such as pilfering, or even burglary and robbery. In New York City, for example, it was not unusual for police officers to rob drug sellers instead of arresting them. In one 1985 incident, several city of Miami po-

PATTERNS OF POLICE CORRUPTION

1. *Corruption of Authority.* Officer receives free meals, services or discounts, and liquor not authorized by the department.
2. *Kickbacks.* Officer receives money, goods, or services for referring business to towing companies, ambulances, lawyers, etc.
3. *Opportunistic Thefts.* Thefts from arrestees, victims, burglary scenes, and unprotected property.
4. *Shakedowns.* Officers extort money or other valuables or services (e.g., sex) from traffic offenders or criminals caught in the commission of an offense.
5. *Protection of Illegal Activities.* Protection money accepted by police officers from vice operators or legitimate businesses operating illegally.
6. *Traffic Fix.* "Taking up" or disposing of traffic citations for money or other forms of material reward.
7. *Misdemeanor Fix.* Quashing of misdemeanor court proceedings (by failing to show up in court, for example) for some material reward or gain.
8. *Felony Fix.* "Fixing" felony cases (for example, by altering evidence or testimony) for money or other forms of material gain.
9. *Direct Criminal Activities.* Officers engage in serious felonies such as burglary, robbery, and larcenies.
10. *Internal Payoffs.* The sale of days off, holidays, work assignments, etc., from one officer to another.

SOURCE: Barker and Wells 1982: 10.

---

lice officers were charged with stealing 900 pounds of cocaine from drug dealers, who they failed to arrest.

Lawrence Sherman (1978: 4) distinguishes between two types of police corruption: (1) *organizations in which deviance occurs,* that is, the individual "rotten apples" in every police department

In 1971 Frank Serpico (*above, right*) testified before the Knapp Commission, which investigated police corruption in New York City. Serpico, then a police detective, helped expose widespread graft, pay-offs, and cover-ups; his fight later became the subject of a best-selling book and movie. *At left* is his attorney, Ramsey Clark.

who make "scores," and (2) *deviant organizations*, that is, police departments in which corruption is so systematic that criminals can purchase immunity from arrest. A deviant police organization may have a political base; it may be the result of domination by political leaders who have "captured" the department; or it may be the result of privileged local politicians who have the power to control the police in their districts. The deviant organization may also be based on the strategic positions of corrupt police district commanders without ties to elected officials.

Sherman notes that dealing with police corruption requires that a chief have extensive information on what the officers are doing, but this is extremely difficult to obtain. As noted above, police officers typically work alone or in pairs scattered throughout a municipality. Random acts of corruption are not predictable and, therefore, difficult to control; systematic corruption, on the other hand, is predictable and more easily subjected to investigative techniques such as physical and electronic surveillance and the use of informants. Monitoring personnel by surreptitious means is, however, "generally distasteful in a society valuing privacy and always opposed by the officers subjected to them" (1978: xviii). Moreover, systematic corruption is that engaged in by a deviant organization, and, by definition, "such departments approve of corruption and do not seek to punish it, except in excessive instances that threaten to draw public attention to police corruption in general" (1978: 45). Accordingly, the investigation of systematic corruption usually requires the efforts of an outside agency such as the FBI.

Brutality

The excessive use of force—**police brutality**—has been a long-standing problem for most police departments. Just where the legitimate use of force ends and brutality begins is not always clear. Police officers are authorized to use force, but the amount of force that is appropriate varies with the circumstances and cannot be determined in advance. In addition, statutes concerning the use of force employ terms such as "reasonably believes," which are difficult to define or measure. Illinois law (chapter 38: 7-5), for example, states that a law enforcement officer

> need not retreat or desist from efforts to make a lawful arrest because of resistance or threatened resistance to the arrest. He is justified in the use of any force which he reasonably believes to be necessary to effect the arrest and of any force which he reasonably believes necessary to defend himself or another from bodily harm while making the arrest. However, he is justified in using force likely to cause death or great bodily harm only when he reasonably believes that such force is necessary to prevent death or great bodily harm to himself or such other person, or when he reasonably believes both that (1) such force is necessary to prevent the arrest from being defeated by resistance or escape; and (2) the person to be arrested has committed or attempted a forcible felony or is attempting to escape by use of a deadly weapon, or otherwise indicates that he will endanger human life or inflict great bodily harm unless arrested without delay.

Jennifer Hunt (1985) states that the restraint taught in the police academy is routinely undermined by peer support, if not outright encouragement, for using force. She provides an example: A rookie police officer found out from the television news that she was the subject of a brutality suit. The young officer was horrified, and it was with great reluctance that she went to work and faced her peers. Hunt (1985: 319) reports, "In fact, male colleagues greeted her with a standing ovation and commented, 'You can use our urinal now.'" As a result of her eighteen months of participant observation research in a major urban police department, Hunt (1985: 321) argues, "For a street cop, it is often a graver error to use too little force and develop a 'shaky' reputation than it is to use too much force and be told to calm down."

While police brutality is, by definition, a crime, a prosecutor's office is seldom interested in such cases unless corruption or a killing is involved; discipline is usually left to the police department. Police investigations of the use of excessive force by police officers have often been criticized, particularly by minority groups whose members have been subjected to such treatment. In some jurisdictions this has led to the establishment of **civilian review boards** or other civilian agencies for investigating complaints against the police.

Civilian review boards are bitterly opposed by police officers, who argue against civilian "intrusion" into police matters, and proposals for them have been defeated in many large cities, such as Baltimore and Los Angeles. A particularly bitter struggle took place in New York City when Mayor John V. Lindsay, a liberal Republican, established a civilian review board by executive order in 1966. The board had seven members, four civilians and three police officials. An extensive campaign to abolish the board was initiated by the Patrolmen's Benevolent Association (PBA), a police union representing the city's patrol officers, and it was assisted by conservative political groups. The PBA was successful in forcing a referendum on a proposition designed to abolish the board; the proposition was approved by an overwhelming majority of voters, who apparently saw the board as impairing the ability of the police to deal with criminals.

No matter who investigates complaints against the police, however, establishing the existence of brutality resulting from an arrest is quite problematic. Paul Chevigny (1969) notes that police abuses often stem from the traditions of police work and expectations. The police expect deference to, or at least acceptance of, their authority; and untoward behavior, ranging from a show of disrespect to outright resistance, usually brings a strong physical reaction. Peter Scharf and Arnold Binder (1983: 135) suggest "a community education program informing citizens about police expectations and about typical police responses to citizen threats ... [so] that citizens might communicate with police officers to avoid violent confrontations."

Deadly Force

The use of **deadly force**—firearms—by the police, even when it does not constitute "misconduct," is quite controversial. James Q. Wilson states (1980: 16), "No aspect of policing elicits more passionate concern or more divided opinions than the use of deadly force."

Lawrence Sherman and Robert Langworthy (1982) point out that precise data on the number of homicides by the police is not available; they argue that the national incidence of police homi-

Charges of police brutality were rampant during the riots of the 1968 Democratic National Convention in Chicago. Police wielded clubs, tear gas, and mace in battles with thousands of anti–Vietnam War protesters.

cide is significantly underreported and that the statistics are so poor that they cannot be used to compare police homicide rates from one city to another. Official statistics report that the average number of police homicides is 240 a year; unofficial estimates double that figure.

The solutions are as controversial as the statistics. James Fyfe (1979) reports that guidelines issued by the NYPD in 1972, which stressed "the value of life" and declared that police revolvers are "for personal protection against persons feloniously attacking an officer or others at close range," significantly reduced police homicides in New York without any increase in injuries to police officers. Peter Scharf and Arnold Binder (1983: 178) state, however, that "many shooting policy statements . . . are not designed for human beings. Humans differ in relative capacities, strengths, weaknesses, and so forth, and the best of us are limited in which [sic] we can do under stress in a rapid time frame. In short, these policies may be asking the human beings who become police officers to perform at unrealistic levels."

Kenneth Matulia (1982: 15-20) notes that police departments have generally adhered to one of three alternative standards governing police use of deadly force: common law, modified common law, or the model penal code.

Common Law Statutes

Deadly force is authorized when an officer has probable cause that a felony has been committed and the suspect either flees from or resists arrest. This is the **fleeing felon rule**, which developed in medieval England, at a time when many crimes, even those against property, were punishable by execution. Lawrence Sherman (1982) refers to the fleeing felon rule as an anachronism that often has constituted "execution without trial" for crimes that are not punishable by execution. Matulia (1982) notes that the states that adhered to the common-law fleeing felon rule appeared to exhibit the highest rate of justifiable homicide.

Modified Common Law

Deadly force may be used to effect the arrest of a person who is using a weapon to escape, who is a clear danger to others, or who has committed a "dangerous or atrocious" felony (usually meaning murder, arson, kidnap, aggravated assault, mayhem, rape, extortion, residential burglary or robbery).

Model Penal Code

Deadly force by a peace officer or a civilian assisting a peace officer is authorized to effect an arrest when a felony involving the use or threatened use of deadly force has occurred or when the officer believes there is a substantial risk that the person to be arrested will cause death or serious harm if apprehension is delayed. Deadly force can also be used to prevent the escape of a prisoner from detention, jail, or prison or to prevent the commission of a crime that places innocent persons at risk of death or serious bodily harm. It can also be used to suppress a riot or mutiny after sufficient warning has been issued.

In 1985, however, the Supreme Court invalidated the fleeing felon rule that was employed in about half the states. In *Tennessee v. Garner*, it ruled 6–3 that the Constitution prohibits a police officer from using deadly force against fleeing suspects who are neither armed nor dangerous. The case involved an unarmed fifteen-year-old boy in Memphis who, in 1974, was shot in the back of the head by a police officer as he began to climb over a fence. The officer was investigating a report of a prowler and had ordered the youngster to halt. The court decision noted that the police office did not believe the suspect to be armed but was convinced that if he made it over the fence, he would elude capture. The officer was acting under the authority of a Tennessee law that was declared unconstitutional. The Court ruled,

> The use of deadly force to prevent the escape of all felony suspects, whatever the circumstances, is constitutionally unreasonable. It is not better that all felony suspects die than that they escape. Where the suspect poses no immediate threat to the officer and no threat to others, the harm resulting from failing to apprehend him does not justify the use of deadly force to do so.

The guidelines that the Court set out for the use of deadly force are essentially those of the model penal code listed above.

Professionalism

In response to the various criticisms of the police and policing, Arthur Niederhoffer (1969: 3) recounts that a small but articulate elite composed of superior officers who were college graduates "acknowledged that allegations of inefficiency, corruption, and brutality were sometimes justified, and they set in operation a plan to put their house in order, a plan that can be described in one word—professionalism." While there is no generally accepted definition of police professionalism, Niederhoffer (1969: 19) has compiled the general attributes of a profession (e.g., law and medicine):

1. High standards of admission
2. A special body of knowledge and theory
3. Altruism and dedication to the service ideal
4. A lengthy period of training for candidates
5. A code of ethics
6. Licensing of members
7. Autonomous control
8. Pride of the members in their profession
9. Publicly recognized status and prestige

The move toward professionalization has been a "mixed bag." In some jurisdictions, *standards of admission* now include an associate or bachelor's degree. Most large urban police departments, however, still only require a high school education, and virtually all supervisory ranks are filled by those who have entered the particular department at the patrol officer level. While a *special body of knowledge and theory* has been growing, most police officers have not been exposed to it, nor is it a particular requirement for entry or advancement. The attribute of *altruism and dedication to the service ideal* is not firmly established in policing (and it is questionable whether it has been in other professions either), and the rise of police unionism and militancy (which will be discussed shortly) has mitigated against such abstractions.

Training has certainly improved if measured by the amount of time and resources expended to accomplish it. Each state now has a **POST (Peace Officer Standards and Training) commission**, which is responsible for establishing minimum levels of training for local law enforcement officers. An officer not meeting the criteria established by the POST commission is ineligible to practice as a police officer within the state. But the minimum levels of training are scarcely comparable to the lengthy periods of education and training required of professionals in law, medicine, and other disciplines. There is a *code of ethics*, however, that can match that of any profession.

Some states require a comprehensive written examination that must be successfully completed by all newly hired police officers as a condition to receiving their certification to practice within the state. More than a dozen states have established licensing commissions that have the authority to issue and revoke

---

Law Enforcement Code of Ethics

AS A LAW ENFORCEMENT OFFICER my fundamental duty is to serve mankind; to safeguard lives and property; to protect the innocent against deception, the weak against oppression or intimidation, and the peaceful against violence or disorder; and to respect the Constitutional rights of all men to liberty, equality and justice.

I WILL keep my private life unsullied as an example to all; maintain courageous calm in the face of danger, scorn, or ridicule; develop self-restraint; and be constantly mindful of the welfare of others. Honest in thought and deed in both my personal and official life, I will be exemplary in obeying the laws of the land and the regulations of my department. Whatever I see or hear of a confidential nature or that is confided to me in my official capacity will be kept secret unless revelation is necessary in the performance of my duty.

I WILL never act officiously or permit personal feelings, prejudices. animosities or friendships to influence my decisions. With no compromise for crime and with relentless prosecution of criminals, I will enforce the law courteously and appropriately without fear or favor, malice or ill will, never employing unnecessary force or violence and never accepting gratuities.

I RECOGNIZE the badge of my office as a symbol of public faith, and I accept it as a public trust to be held so long as I am true to the ethics of the police service. I will constantly strive to achieve these objectives and ideals, dedicating myself before God to my chosen profession...law enforcement.

licenses to practice policing within the state. Typically, in these states a local police chief or sheriff can set standards higher than the licensing commission requires, but they may only employ persons licensed, or eligible to be licensed, by the commission.

The most questionable aspect of professionalism for the police is *autonomy*, such as that enjoyed by a medical doctor or lawyer, since it actually runs counter to many decades of police reform. Historically, a decentralized, more autonomous police force meant control by often corrupt ward bosses. Under such circumstances, greater centralization and control of police activities was reform. This meant greater bureaucratic control over police officers, but professionalism is judged, in part, on the degree of freedom from bureaucratic control. On the other hand, police officers exude *pride in their profession*, and this is reinforced by numerous magazines published for police officers. With respect to *publicly recognized status and prestige*—the jury is still out on this one.

As part of the trend toward professionalization, in 1979 four law enforcement associations (International Association of Chiefs of Police, National Organization of Black Law Enforcement Executives, National Sheriffs' Association, and Police Executive Research Forum) formed the **Commission on Accreditation for Law Enforcement Agencies, Inc.**, to develop a set of law enforcement standards and administer a voluntary accreditation process. The accreditation process involves the submission of documents and an on-site visit to the agency by commission assessors. The assessors, each a specialist in one or more aspects of law enforcement, evaluate the agency against the almost one thousand standards promulgated by the commission. About 60 percent of these standards are mandatory, meaning that there must be compliance with those applicable to the agency in order to be considered for accreditation. The first agency to receive accreditation from the commission was the Mt. Dora (Florida) Police Department in 1984. (For further information write to Commission on Accreditation for Law Enforcement Agencies, Inc., 4242B Chain Bridge Road, Fairfax, VA 22030.)

Professional standards of this kind do not reflect the values of all police officers, and Elizabeth Reuss-Ianni (1983: 212) notes the existence of "two cultures" in large, modern police departments: *management cops*, who represent a form of police professionalism, and the more traditional *street cops*.

> Now there are two cultures which confront each other in the department: a street cop culture of the good old days, working class in origin and temperament whose members see themselves as career cops; opposed to this is a management cop culture, more middle class, whose members' education and mobility have made them eligible for jobs totally outside of policing, which makes them less dependent on, and less loyal to, the street cop culture.

The management cops even have their own organization: the American Academy for Professional Law Enforcement (AAPLE), housed at the John Jay College of Criminal Justice in New York City.

Police unionism

Should police officers be permitted to join unions? What if the union insists on the right to strike? At the beginning of chapter 6 we noted that the police in Boston went out on strike in 1918; they were responding to poor wages and working conditions and the dismissal of the police union leadership. Looting and rioting ensued, and eight persons were killed and at least fifty others injured as a result of the strike. The attitude of the American public toward that strike can best be summed up by a statement in a speech made by President Woodrow Wilson (Russell 1975: 170):

> I want to say this, that a strike of the policemen of a great city, leaving that city at the mercy of thugs, is a crime against civilization.
> In my judgment the obligation of a policeman is as sacred and direct as the obligation of a soldier. He is a public employee, and the whole honor of the community is in his hands. He has no right to prefer any private advantage to the public safety.

The Boston police strike was a failure for police unionism; all of the striking officers were dismissed and never rehired. While police officers have often been members of local police associations, these groups were quite passive, and police unionism remained relatively dormant until the 1960s. In that era the activities of civil rights and antiwar groups appeared to moti-

Boston police responded to poor wages, working conditions, and the dismissal of union leadership by going out on strike in 1919. Squads of cavalry and infantry (*above*) were stationed throughout the city to maintain order following riots that killed eight people.

vate police officers to engage in militant collective action. During the late 1960s and 1970s there were police labor actions—the "rule-book slowdown," the "ticket blitz," the "blue flu"—and work stoppages in a number of American cities and one in Montreal, Canada. Except in Montreal, police strikes did not result in any discernable upsurge in criminal activity; superior officers and detectives usually remained on duty, and they were sometimes assisted by sheriff's deputies and state police officers.

A number of local and national unions began competing for police membership, the largest and oldest being the **Fraternal**

Order of Police (FOP), founded in 1915. Other national organizations include the International Union of Police Associations (IUPA), an affiliate of the AFL-CIO founded in 1978 as an umbrella group for local police associations; the National Association of Police Organizations (NAPO), an umbrella group independent of the AFL-CIO; and the International Brotherhood of Police Officers, an affiliate of the Service Employees International Union, AFL-CIO. There are also locals affiliated with the International Brotherhood of Teamsters as well as a host of local unaffiliated police associations such as the Patrolmen's Benevolent Association representing police officers in New York City. In response to effective political action by police groups, states began moving from a position that prohibited police officers from even joining a labor union to providing for some type of collective bargaining.

The competition between various unions for the right to represent police officers continues. So do important issues surrounding the collective bargaining rights of police officers. In their negotiations with management, nonpublic employee unions are free to use the strike as a bargaining tool; they can withhold their labor and thereby inflict damage on an employer. Public employees in general, and public safety employees in particular, are prohibited by law from striking. Thus, they lack the most effective bargaining instrument. There are obvious contradictions when officers sworn to enforce the law threaten to, or actually, violate the law by striking, and this issue dominates the question of police of unionization. Alternatives to the strike have been legislated in some jurisdictions in the form of binding arbitration; a mutually agreed-upon third party hears from both sides and renders a decision to which each side is bound.

Collective bargaining also involves working conditions, for example, using single-officer patrol cars. Collective bargaining can be used by the union to limit what have traditionally been the prerogatives of management. For example, police unions have attempted to negotiate the firearms police officers should be allowed to carry—.38 revolvers, .357 magnums, or automatics. In order to guarantee fairness for their members, police unions have fought to maintain three equally distributed shifts, despite the fact that crime and calls for service are not equally distributed throughout the twenty-four-hour day. A basic issue

LAW ENFORCEMENT DIVISION
TEAMSTERS UNION
Affiliated with the I. B. of T., C., W. and H. of A.
APPLICATION AND AUTHORIZATION

We Serve . . . and Protect

I want to become a member of the Teamsters. I authorize this Union to represent me as my sole and exclusive bargaining agent with my employer.

Date_____

Name of Employer_____ (Please Print) District_____

Name of Applicant_____ (Please Print) Star No._____

Address_____ (Please Print) Phone No._____

City and State_____ Zip Code_____

Payroll No._____ Signature_____ (Please Do Not Print)

For Information Call 242-3215 and 666-5772
Only the Union has access to this confidential information.

NO DUES UNTIL CONTRACT

The International Brotherhood of Teamsters is one of many local and national unions that compete for police membership.

remains: Which conditions of employment should be subjected to collective bargaining, and which should remain part of the prerogatives of management?

AFFIRMATIVE ACTION

Police ranks have historically been filled by the working class—the white male working class. During the past two decades efforts at correcting this imbalance have been instituted by the United States Department of Justice, which has brought suit against dozens of police departments for discriminating against women, blacks, and Hispanics. Civil rights organizations have succeeded in getting state and municipal governments to implement affirmative action programs designed to increase minority and female representation on police departments. These efforts have included the active recruitment of women and minority-group candidates, and in some cases the use of quota systems for hiring and promoting female and minority officers.

Intertwined with the issue of affirmative action and equal opportunity is the question of job-related examinations. Black and Hispanic groups have argued that written examinations used as the basis for hiring and promoting police officers are biased against them. Many police departments have hired outside testing firms to develop unbiased examinations—tests that would withstand court scrutiny—and in many cases these efforts have failed. In some cities, quota systems for hiring and promoting officers have been instituted as part of out-of-court settlements or consent orders arising out of legal action brought by the Justice Department or individual litigants.

Physical requirements for police officers, such as weight and height requirements, have often discriminated against women and Hispanics. When police departments are unable to prove that their physical requirements are reasonably related to the job of a police officer, they must be discarded. For the most part, such artificial barriers to police employment have been abandoned by police departments.

Private security

There were privately employed police officers in the United States before there were public police forces, and some private security agencies, such as the Pinkertons, have a history that dates back to before the Civil War. Today there are more than one million persons employed as private security officers and far more money is expended on private security efforts than is spent for federal, state, and local law enforcement (Cunningham and Taylor 1984). Interestingly, about 36,000 private security officers work for a branch of government—for example, the U.S. Department of Defense (Tolchin 1985). While the number of personnel working for police and sheriff's departments has remained about the same, the number of private security officers has grown by about 50 percent during the last decade. William Cunningham and Todd Taylor (1984) state that private security can be separated into three components:

1. *Physical security.* Protecting people and property, protecting the integrity of a facility (e.g., keeping those without tickets from entering a concert or sporting event), and maintaining order.
2. *Information security.* Protecting against the unauthorized use of customer lists, marketing plans, computer programs, research and development.
3. *Personnel security.* Protection of workers, executive protection (e.g., against terrorists who might target corporate executives), and conducting background investigations of prospective employees.

There are two basic methods used for providing private security: *proprietary security* involves the hiring of employees by the principal; *contractual security* involves renting the services of security firms such as alarm, armored car, or security guard services.

The discretion exercised by private security personnel may exceed that of public law enforcement officers: since they are not *sworn* to enforce the law, all actions are optional.

> Private security managers who were surveyed indicate that they generally report Uniform Crime Report index crimes—largely "ordinary crime"—to a law enforcement agency. Incidents of employee theft, insurance fraud, industrial espionage, commercial bribery, and computer crime tend *not* to be reported. These incidents are frequently resolved by direct contact with a prosecutor or through other "private justice" procedures within the victimized organization.

Private security officers are generally not restricted by the constitutional limitations and court decisions which restrain the activities of police officers. For example, they need not inform a suspect of his or her *Miranda* rights, and the exclusionary rule applies only to those in the employ, or who are acting on behalf, of government.

Two of the most serious problems in private security are the limited training required for private security employment and the questionable backgrounds of some private security personnel. Such personnel are usually not subjected to the same extensive background checks employed by police departments. Many are persons who have been unable to secure employment with public law enforcement agencies, and the low pay for most private security positions tends to attract persons of limited ability or commitment to public safety.

A number of persons employed as private security officers are themselves sworn police officers or sheriff's deputies: there are an estimated 150,000 police officers who work off-duty as regular employees of private security (Cunningham and Taylor 1984), and such employment is problematic. To whom is such an officer responsible—his primary employer (the government) or his secondary employer (the private firm)? Who is liable for the actions of the officer? Should there be restrictions on the types of situations in which a sworn officer can work? For example, they are usually prohibited from working in establishments having liquor licenses, but what about a theater that shows pornographic movies, or other situations that may tend to discredit the police or sheriff's department? Can the officer wear his official uniform and firearm while working for a private employer, and must he report a crime that the secondary employer does not want reported?

States have been licensing private security personnel and requiring minimum levels of training, particularly for those who are permitted to carry firearms. The growth of private security has also led to the establishment of courses, and sometimes entire degree programs, in security management at colleges and universities.

Legal issues

In chapter 5 we looked at two legal decisions, *Miranda* and *Mapp*, that affected policing in the United States. Let us look at some other important cases affecting the police.

Search and Seizure

In order for police search and seizure activities (which includes arrest) to be in conformity with the Fourth Amendment, there must be probable cause, except in certain exigent (or emergency) circumstances, according to *Stacey v. Emery* (1878). Probable cause is the minimum level of evidence required for an arrest

> # TERRY V. OHIO
>
> **A veteran Cleveland detective observed John Terry and two other individuals acting in a suspicious manner outside of a store; the officer concluded that they were planning to execute a robbery. He approached the three individuals, identified himself, and asked for their names. After receiving a mumbled response, the officer spun Terry around so that he faced the others and patted down the outside of his clothing. This led to the discovery of a pistol, and the officer then patted down the other two men; a second pistol was discovered. In upholding the conviction of Terry and his companion for carrying concealed weapons, the Supreme Court ruled "that there must be a narrowly drawn authority to permit a reasonable search for weapons for the protection of the police officer, where he has reason to believe that he is dealing with an armed and dangerous individual, regardless of whether he has probable cause to arrest the individual for a crime." In this case the Court distinguished a *pat-down* (for weapons) from a *search* (for such items as drugs), which would not be authorized under the *Terry* decision.**

without a warrant or to secure an arrest or search warrant. However, the Supreme Court, in *Terry v. Ohio* (1968), has ruled that an officer is permitted to stop and frisk persons for weapons even in the absence of probable cause.

In 1983, the Supreme Court extended the *Terry* decision with *Michigan v. Long* to include **protective searches** of the passenger area of a car without a warrant even if the suspect is outside the car. The ruling came as the result of a Michigan case in which the police stopped a car for speeding, observed a knife on the floor of the driver's side, and removed the driver from the car. The driver was not arrested, but the police conducted a search and found a pouch of marijuana in the passenger compartment. In a 6–3 decision, the Supreme Court overturned a Michigan court decision that had ruled the marijuana inadmissible as evidence.

In *California v. Carney* (1985), the court extended *Terry* further by upholding the search of a motor home without a warrant. The decision concerned a motor home that was parked in a downtown San Diego parking lot with its curtains drawn. The vehicle was placed under surveillance by the police after they were informed that it was being used as a base for distributing drugs. After an hour the police entered the vehicle without a warrant and found a quantity of marijuana. In a 6–3 decision, the Court noted that while a motor home had "some if not many of the attributes of a home," it more closely resembled a motor vehicle. Chief Justice Warren E. Burger, who wrote the decision, stated that it was limited to motor homes that could be driven away by simply turning on the ignition key; it did not include motor homes parked at fixed locations and connected to utility lines.

There are a number of emergency circumstances that justify a warrantless search by the police:

1. when officers respond to an emergency situation in which lives may be at risk—for example, entering an apartment from which smoke is billowing;
2. when officers observe a crime in progress;
3. when there is a likelihood that contraband will be destroyed or removed or a suspect will otherwise escape;
4. when officers are in "hot pursuit" of suspects;
5. when officers are searching a vehicle and there is probable cause to believe that it contains contraband and that the vehicle may be moved before a warrant can be secured;
6. when officers inventory private property to protect the police against claims for lost property, or for protecting the owner's property while it is in police custody, or to protect the police or the public from potential danger;
7. when there is abandoned property, such as items left behind in a hotel room after it is vacated, or garbage set out for collection; and
8. when the person in control of the premises voluntarily consents to a search.

It should be noted that the Fourth Amendment protects people, not places, meaning it protects a person's *reasonable expectation of privacy* against government intrusion. Thus, privacy is

Some emergency situations may justify a warrantless search by police.

protected in public telephone booths (*Katz v. United States*, 1967), a union office (*Mancusi v. DeForte*, 1968), or even areas of a store open to the general public (*Lo-Ji Sales Inc. v. New York*, 1979). In *Katz* the Court ruled: "What a person knowingly exposes to the public, even in his own home or office is not a subject of Fourth Amendment protection. But what he seeks to preserve as private [such as a telephone conversation], even in an area accessible to the public may be constitutionally protected." This gave rise to the **plain view doctrine**, whereby conduct or objects in "plain view" are not protected by the Fourth Amendment, such as a firearm on the seat of an automobile that is observed by a police officer using a flashlight, or a loud conversation by occupants of a motel room who have left the door ajar.

The court has ruled that a person who is legally arrested may be searched without a warrant, and there does not have to be any indication that the arrested person possesses a weapon, contraband, or other evidence (see, for example, *Chimel v. California*, 1969). This can include a brief strip search, conducted without abuse and in a professional manner for visual inspection of body surfaces or to detect hidden evidence or objects that could be dangerous. Even body cavity searches are permitted subsequent to an arrest if there is a clear indication that contraband is present in the cavity. Articles carried by the arrestee—such as a handbag or luggage—may be searched. A search accompanying a lawful arrest may be made of areas within the arrestee's immediate control; for example, the area under a mattress in a room where a defendant was taken to get a shirt. In 1982 the Supreme Court ruled that closed containers found in an automobile whose occupant is the subject of a lawful arrest may be searched without a warrant (*United States v. Ross*); and in 1985 (*United States v. Johns*) the Court ruled 7–2 that a warrantless search of these closed containers can be delayed for as long as three days.

In this chapter we examined the limitations of policing in a democratic society, particularly the dilemma between crime control and due process. Many of the problems inherent in policing—the police subculture, alienation, brutality—can be explained, at least in part, by this dilemma. We examined the stress on professionalism as a response to these problems, and the use of discretion as a response to the limitations of policing.

KEY TERMS

discretion
authoritarianism
corruption
police brutality
civilian review boards
deadly force
fleeing felon rule

POST (Peace Officer Standards and Training) commission
Commission on Accreditation for Law Enforcement Agencies, Inc.
Fraternal Order of Police
protective searches
plain view doctrine

REVIEW QUESTIONS

1. What are the two parts of the ambivalence with which Americans tend to view the police?
2. What are the restrictions that prevent the police from achieving their goals?
3. What are police "quality of life" activities?
4. What is meant by police discretion?
5. Why is police discretion a problem?
6. What are the discretionary powers of a police chief?
7. What are the principles that guide the exercise of discretion?
8. Why are many statutes symbolic?
9. What is meant by the police subculture?
10. Why is it difficult to control the behavior of patrol officers?
11. How is police behavior subjected to control?
12. What is meant by authoritarianism in this chapter?
13. Why are police officers often alienated from society?

14. What are the negative effects of police solidarity?
15. What are the two most serious forms of police misbehavior?
16. Why is police corruption a continuing problem?
17. What is the common law standard with respect to police use of deadly force? What did the Supreme Court rule with respect to this standard?
18. What are the nine attributes of professionalism?
19. What improvements have moved the police closer to professionalism?
20. Which of the nine attributes of professionalism is most questionable for the police and why?
21. Why is the issue for unionism more complex for police than for nonpolice employees?
22. Under what circumstances can the police conduct a warrantless search?
23. What authority did the *Terry* decision give the police?
24. What is meant by the statement, "The Fourth Amendment protects people, not places"?
25. What is the plain view doctrine?

CHAPTER 9

Federal Law Enforcement

UNITED STATES MARSHALS SERVICE

SECRET SERVICE

BUREAU OF ALCOHOL, TOBACCO AND FIREARMS

IMMIGRATION AND NATURALIZATION SERVICE

CUSTOMS SERVICE

GENERAL SERVICES ADMINISTRATION

INTERNAL REVENUE SERVICE

POSTAL INSPECTION SERVICE

DRUG ENFORCEMENT ADMINISTRATION

FEDERAL BUREAU OF INVESTIGATION

COAST GUARD

MILITARY LAW ENFORCEMENT AGENCIES

OFFICES OF INSPECTOR GENERAL

MISCELLANEOUS AGENCIES

INTERPOL

REVIEW QUESTIONS

Policing in the United States is fragmented into thousands of departments, one for virtually every incorporated jurisdiction—village, town, city. There is no national police force such as those of Canada, Great Britain, France, Italy, West Germany and other democratic countries. Because the police are the most visible agents of government and Americans distrust government in general and the federal government in particular, there has never been any serious consideration of a federal police force. Over the decades, necessity led to the creation of a variety of individual federal enforcement agencies in an unplanned and uncoordinated manner. Thus, while they all have the same nominal boss, the president of the United States, federal law enforcement agencies are fragmented. The lack of a unified law enforcement effort on the national level has led to the creation of special "task forces" that bring together agents from various federal (and sometimes state and local) agencies to deal with national problems such as organized crime. The task force, however, is the exception; federal law enforcement agencies operate autonomously and each jealously guards its jurisdictional mandates. In some cases, both local and federal enforcement agencies have jurisdiction—for example, over crimes such as bank robbery or drug trafficking. In other cases, only federal agencies have jurisdiction, as in instances of counterfeiting and espionage.

In general, federal law enforcement agencies perform investigative and enforcement functions of a highly specialized nature. As a result, the personnel requirements for federal law enforcement agencies are generally higher than those for most state and local agencies. While most police agencies require only a high school education, federal agencies such as the FBI, DEA, Secret Service, and IRS require at least a four-year college degree, and often a graduate degree or relevant experience.

UNITED STATES MARSHALS SERVICE

The Marshals Service is the oldest federal enforcement agency; as a result of the Judiciary Act of September 24, 1789, President George Washington appointed the first thirteen marshals; the first marshal, Isaac Huger of South Carolina, was appointed on September 26th. The marshals appointed by Washington carried on the tradition of the English sheriff; they attended to the federal courts in their district and executed all lawful precepts issued under the authority of the government of the United States. A marshal was appointed to each new federal judicial district created in the course of the westward expansion of the United States. The U.S. marshal played a significant role in the Wild West, where he was often the only real symbol of law and order. As the Oklahoma territory was being settled, for instance, sixty-five U.S. Marshals were killed within five years (*Then . . . and Now*, n.d.). The activities of marshals such as Wyatt Earp and Bat Masterson have become part of the legend of the American frontier.

U.S. marshals have been used as an alternative to military intervention during civil disturbances, rioting, and mob violence. The first instance of such use was in the Whiskey Rebellion of 1794. They participated in the maintaining of order during the Pullman Strike of 1894 and the Homestead Riot of 1892. In more recent times marshals have enforced federal judicial

U.S. Marshals were used to maintain order during the Homestead Riot (1892). After workers struck the Carnegie Steel Company in Homestead, Pennsylvania, marshals helped halt an armed battle between the strikers and 300 Pinkerton detectives hired to protect the plant. The strike, which was called off after almost five months, led to a serious weakening of unionism in the steel industry until the 1930s.

orders regarding school integration and have protected federal property during anti-Vietnam War demonstrations in Washington, and in 1973 they policed disorders at Wounded Knee, South Dakota.

Today, there are ninety-four marshals, one in each U.S. judicial district, and they supervise more than 1,500 deputy U.S. marshals. The U.S. marshals are presidential appointees; deputy U.S. marshals, once selected and appointed by individual marshals on the basis of political patronage, are now employed under the competitive merit system. While they were originally "officers of the court," marshals have been called upon to perform a variety of tasks for many federal departments, including Justice, State, Treasury, and Interior. Since 1870 the marshals have increasingly "come under the control and coordination of the Department of Justice. This process culminated in the official establishment of the United States Marshals Service in 1969, and the attainment of full Bureau status in 1974" (*Then . . . and Now*, n.d.: 7), making them a distinct agency within the Justice Department.

> Deputy U.S. Marshals perform a variety of duties primarily law enforcement in nature. Deputies are charged with primary responsibility for providing security to the Federal courts, insuring the personal safety of judges, jurors, and attorneys, as well as the physical security of court buildings and facilities. They remove disorderly spectators from court premises and in some cases repel attempted attacks by intruders during Federal judicial proceedings. During crucial court cases, Deputies conduct surveys of Federal court buildings to determine the adequacy of security, and, where necessary, recommend the use of fixed and mobile security units. Specially trained Deputies furnish 24-hour protection to Federal judges and their immediate families when threats, whether real or apparent, are made as a result of decisions rendered by the court. (*Criminal Justice Careers Guidebook* 1982: 56)

U.S. marshals are responsible for the custody of federal prisoners from the time of arrest to their sentencing or their release from confinement, and they provide transportation for federal prisoners between court and prison facilities. Marshals serve civil writs issued by federal courts, which can include seizing and disposing of property and they are responsible for the custody and control of property, money, and evidence confiscated under federal law.

The Marshals Service has primary responsibility for investigating violations of certain federal fugitive statutes such as violations of federal bail, probation, parole, or escaping from a federal prison. The service's special program known as FIST (Fugitive Investigative Strike Team) has been responsible for the apprehension of thousands of persons wanted on state charges who have also violated federal UFAP (Unlawful Flight to Avoid Prosecution) and UFAC (Unlawful Flight to Avoid Confinement) laws. Each FIST team consists of marshals and local enforcement personnel who can be deputized as special U.S. marshals, permitting them to operate across jurisdictions and even into neighboring states. The Marshals Service subsidizes the expense of team operations (about $800 per apprehension, not including the salaries of the marshals) while local enforcement personnel provide knowledge of their areas and sources of information for apprehending the fugitives. In one eight-week sweep in 1984, FIST officers netted 3,309 persons wanted in eight eastern states. This highly publicized operation used a variety of techniques for "flushing out" fugitives. For example, officers in one case "sent word that fugitives had a package waiting at the 'Brooklyn Bridge Delivery Service.' When they came to claim it, they were handcuffed" (*U.S. News & World Report*, December 3, 1984: 64).

The Special Operations Group performs specialized law enforcement tasks in emergency situations that have a national impact such as terrorist activity, major civil disturbances, riots, and situations involving mob violence. Under the Organized Crime Control Act of 1970, the Marshals Service is responsible for providing protection to state and federal witnesses who testify for the government in cases involving organized crime. The protection of these witnesses and members of their families, whose lives may be jeopardized by court testimony, can extend from the initial court appearance, through the completion of the trial and subsequent relocation of the witness and his or her family. This aspect of the Marshals Service's responsibilities has been quite controversial. (For a further discussion of this issue, see Abadinsky 1985.)

(For further information, contact Office of Public Affairs, U.S. Marshals Service, Department of Justice, One Tysons Corner Center, McLean, VA 22102; telephone 703-285-1131.)

Secret Service

The Secret Service was created by Congress in 1865 as a bureau of the Department of the Treasury to deal with counterfeiting as well as the forgery of government checks, bonds, and securities. During the period that followed the Civil War, about one-third of the currency in circulation was believed to be counterfeit. Philip Melanson (1984) notes that during each of its first four years of operation, the Secret Service arrested more than two hundred counterfeiters. Since it was the only general law enforcement agency in the federal system, the responsibilities of the service were soon expanded to deal with smuggling, piracy, mail robbery, and land fraud. The service was also called upon to investigate the post-Civil War activities of the Ku Klux Klan, and over a three-year period, agents arrested hundreds of Klansmen. During the Spanish-American War and the First World War, the Secret Service served as an intelligence and anti-espionage agency. The intelligence and anti-espionage responsibilities were eventually taken over by the Federal Bureau of Investigation and the Central Intelligence Agency (CIA). The agency continues to be responsible for combatting counterfeiting, and in 1984 the Secret Service was empowered to investigate long-distance phone call fraud against telephone companies.

As a result of the assassination of President William McKinley in 1901, the third president to be assassinated in thirty-seven years, the Secret Service was given the responsibility of protecting the president. Prior to the Secret Service, presidents rarely had protection, and sometimes they had to protect themselves. Legislation authorizing presidential protection was enacted in 1907, but it was not until 1951, after the attempted assassination of President Harry S Truman, that Congress granted the Secret Service permanent protection authority. The executive protection responsibilities of the service have been expanded to include the vice president, the immediate families of the president and the vice president, the president-elect and the vice president-elect and their immediate families, former presidents and their wives and children (until age sixteen), major presidential and vice presidential candidates, and visiting heads of foreign governments.

The Secret Service's protective measures are basically the

In 1907 Congress granted authority to protect the president to the Secret Service. *Above,* President Gerald Ford is almost completely surrounded by Secret Service agents while skiing in Vail, Colorado.

same for all these individuals. Security arrangements are planned, organized, and implemented well in advance of the person's arrival. Advance agents work with the special agent in charge of the district field office. Specific plans depend on such variables as the identity and number of persons to be protected; time, location, and length of visit; and itinerary and methods of transportation. Advance arrangements include the creating of security perimeters, inspecting the area, and determining the personnel and equipment needed. These arrangements may include the deployment of police patrols on the streets parallel, adjacent, or with access to the travel route, and helicopters above it; if the route is on or near waterways, Coast Guard and police patrol craft may also be used. The advance team will brief personnel, assign them to duty posts, and select sites to be used in the event of an emergency, for example, hospitals and evacuation routes.

The Intelligence Division of the Secret Service collects and evaluates essential information for use by agents responsible for protective activities. Agents assigned to intelligence gather a great deal of their information from state and local law enforcement agencies, in addition to federal agencies such as the FBI and the CIA. The Intelligence Division collects information about individuals who advocate the violent overthrow of the government, about persons or groups who make direct threats against or display intent to harm anyone under Secret Service protection, about persons with a history of violent behavior, grudges, or strong grievances against public officials; and about persons or groups who advocate interference with or harm to public officials. Information about persons or groups that criticize or oppose government policies or public officials in a lawful manner are beyond the scope of interest of the Secret Service.

The Uniformed Division of the Secret Service is responsible for protecting the president and other officials while they are in their official residence:

> The Secret Service Uniformed Division was begun in 1922. In September of that year, the Congress of the United States, at the urging of the President, authorized the creation of a uniformed security unit to be known as the White House Police Force, working under the supervision of the President's military aide. In 1930, supervision was transferred to the Director of the Secret Service. This force was given the responsibility of protecting the President and his family when in residence at the White House, and for maintaining security for the Executive Mansion and grounds in the District of Columbia; or any buildings in which the White House offices are located. In 1970, the name of this police force was changed to the Executive Protection Service. Its staff was increased and it was given the added responsibility of maintaining security at the foreign diplomatic missions located in the Washington, D.C., metropolitan area. In November 1977, President Carter signed into law a bill which changed the name of the Executive Protective Service to the present title of U.S. Secret Service Uniformed Division. (*Criminal Justice Careers Guidebook* 1982: 62)

(For further information, contact Office of Public Affairs, United States Secret Service, Department of the Treasury, 1800 G Street NW, Washington, D.C. 20223; telephone 202-535-5708.)

Bureau of Alcohol, Tobacco and Firearms

The Bureau of Alcohol, Tobacco and Firearms (ATF) dates back to 1791 when Alexander Hamilton, then Secretary of the Treasury, inspired the Whiskey Rebellion of 1794 by placing a tax on spirits. The tax was abandoned in 1802, but was reintroduced to help finance Union efforts during the Civil War. As part of these efforts, the commissioner of Internal Revenue hired three persons to investigate the illegal manufacture of distilled spirits—bootlegging and moonshining. During the Prohibition era, 1920–1933, this handful of agents evolved into the Prohibition Bureau, which became a notorious source for political patronage, employing agents who were untrained and often corrupt. In addition, they ran up a record of being killed (by 1923 thirty had been murdered) and of killing hundreds of civilians, often innocent women and children (Sinclair 1962).

With the repeal of Prohibition in 1933, the agency became known as the Alcohol Tax Unit, and as recently as 1962, 90 percent of the bureau's resources were committed to investigating moonshining, primarily in the southeastern United States (Werner 1985). With the disappearance of moonshining in recent decades, these efforts represent only a small portion of the agency's resources. Today, the bureau regulates the liquor and tobacco industries, accounting for about $10 billion annually in liquor and tobacco taxes. ATF agents are empowered to seize and destroy contraband and illegal liquor production facilities, and they are responsible for combatting contraband cigarette smuggling and the bootlegging of untaxed tobacco products (*Criminal Justice Careers Guidebook* 1982).

In 1942, ATF was given jurisdiction over federal firearms statutes. Under the Gun Control Act of 1968, the agency licenses 250,000 firearms dealers. In 1970, ATF gained jurisdiction over arson and explosives. As a result of these bills, today the ATF enforces federal laws concerning the sale, transfer, manufacture, import, and possession of firearms and explosives. This has led the agency into investigations of outlaw motorcycle gangs and drug traffickers who have been involved in illegal sales of firearms. The bureau is also responsible for the inspection of records and inventories of licensed firearms and explosives distributors to insure compliance with federal law and uncover any indications of unlawful activities. It also investigates a variety of cases involving the illegal transport across state lines of firearms and explosives. The agency is particularly concerned with the use of explosives by terrorist groups and organized crime.

The Anti-Arson Act of 1982 increased the bureau's jurisdiction over arson. (The FBI has jurisdiction in arson or bombings occurring at federal buildings or other institutions that receive federal funds, and in incidents that fit the Department of Justice's definition of terrorism; this can overlap with the jurisdiction of the ATF.) ATF's four National Response Teams (NRT) investigate cases of arson and bombings in conjunction with state and local agencies. Each is composed of ten special agents, a forensic chemist, and an explosives specialist. The teams are equipped with sophisticated, state-of-the-art equipment, including ATF explosives response vehicles (Sanders 1981).

In 1972, the Department of the Treasury transferred ATF out of the Internal Revenue Service and gave it bureau status. ATF currently enjoys a reputation of being a highly professional law enforcement agency—so professional, in fact, that the Reagan administration attempted to abolish it because it had raised the ire of the National Rifle Association. Congress, however, refused to go along with the administration.

(For further information, contact the Director, Bureau of Alcohol, Tobacco and Firearms, Department of the Treasury, 1200 Pennsylvania Avenue NW, Washington, D.C. 20226; telephone 202-566-7777.)

IMMIGRATION AND NATURALIZATION SERVICE

The Immigration and Naturalization Service (INS) was created by an act of Congress on March 3, 1891. INS is responsible for administering immigration and naturalization laws relating to the admission, exclusion, deportation, and naturalization of aliens. These laws are enforced by uniformed Border Patrol agents and plainclothes criminal investigators, who are responsible for investigating alleged or suspected violations of federal immigration and naturalization laws (*Federal Register* 1984).

The Border Patrol is responsible for preventing the illegal entry of aliens into the United States.

The INS has primary responsibility for the detection and prevention of the illegal entry or smuggling of aliens into the United States; its agents and investigators take into custody and arrange for the deportation of those persons living illegally in this country. Border Patrol agents are responsible for patrolling more than 8,000 miles of land and coastal areas that constitute the international boundaries of the continental United States, often uninhabited areas of rugged mountains, canyons, and deserts. Using sophisticated electronic sensing devices, pursuit vehicles, airplanes, helicopters, and patrol boats, the Border Patrol attempts to stem the tide of illegal aliens entering this country. They make more than one million apprehensions yearly at the southern border.

Roaming groups of bandits often prey upon illegal aliens making their way into the United States. The Border Crime Prevention Unit (BCPU) was formed in 1984 by the Border Patrol and the San Diego Police Department to deal with this growing problem along the border with Mexico. Shotgun-carrying Border Patrol agents and police officers in teams of ten to twelve in four-wheel-drive vehicles go into the border zone each night (Allen-Baley 1984).

The Border Patrol is quite visible at official border crossings, where they stop vehicles and determine the citizenship of the occupants. They also inquire into the immigration status of farm and ranch employees, particularly in states bordering Mexico. Agents inspect and search trains, buses and other motor vehicles, aircraft, ships, and passenger and cargo terminals to locate illegal aliens. This work often results in Border Patrol agents uncovering drug smuggling operations (*Criminal Justice Careers Guidebook* 1982).

(For further information, contact Office of Information, Immigration and Naturalization Service, Department of Justice, 425 I Street NW, Washington, D.C. 20536; telephone 202-633-4316.)

Customs Service

The fifth act of the First United States Congress, on July 31, 1789, established customs districts and authorized customs officers to collect duties on a variety of imports. The Bureau of Customs was established as a separate agency in the Treasury Department on March 3, 1927, and, effective August 1, 1973, was redesignated the United States Customs Service (*Federal Register* 1984). Customs inspectors examine cargoes and baggage, articles worn or carried by individuals, and vessels, vehicles, and aircraft entering or leaving the United States.

> When carriers such as ships, aircraft or motor transport enter U.S. borders, Customs Inspectors are authorized to go aboard to inspect, search and determine the exact nature of the cargo. Cargo manifests and baggage declarations are reviewed, cargo containers examined, and unloading activities overseen to prevent smuggling, fraud, or cargo thefts. Customs Inspectors may weigh and measure imported merchandise to make certain that customs, neutrality, and commerce laws are followed. For example, in order to protect U.S. distributors of certain trademarked, imported merchandise, restrictions are placed on the amounts that may be brought into the

country. Inspectors are also responsible for the examination of crew and passenger lists, health clearances, store lists, ships' documents, and for issuing required permits. They seal holds of ships and compartments containing sea stores used by crew members as a means of preventing the illegal sale or smuggling of dutiable merchandise into the United States. In certain cases, where wrongdoing is suspected, they conduct body searches.

Customs Inspectors often question suspicious-looking individuals to clarify irregularities related to customs laws, and to explain customs procedures and laws to tourists or others unfamiliar with them. When the situation warrants, Inspectors search suspected individuals and seize contraband and undeclared merchandise. (*Criminal Justice Careers Guidebook* 1982: 53-54; edited)

Special agents of the Customs Service are responsible for carrying out investigations involving smuggling, currency violations, criminal fraud against the revenue system, and major cargo thefts. Their targets include professional and amateur criminals—ranging from international criminal syndicates to importers undervaluing goods to avoid duties or taxes to tourists giving false information on baggage declarations.

Customs Patrol Officers (CPOs) are a uniformed branch of the Customs Service who work at official border crossings, airports, and seaports, in addition to borders, secluded coastlines, and desert areas. Their primary targets are individuals illegally transporting smuggled merchandise and contraband such as drugs, jewelry, weapons, plants and food products from areas of the world infested with pests and diseases.

In addition to being concerned with items being imported (or smuggled) into this country, the Customs Service is responsible for the enforcement of export laws, such as the one that requires a disclosure whenever $10,000 or more in currency or negotiable financial instruments is to leave the country; this is an effort to deal with the "money laundering" activities frequently used by drug traffickers. Military items and certain technical products require export licenses to prevent violations of neutrality laws or to keep advanced scientific technologies from being used or copied by other countries.

(For further information, contact Public Affairs Office, U.S. Customs Service, Department of the Treasury, 1301 Constitution Avenue NW, Washington, D.C. 20229; telephone 202-566-5286.)

GENERAL SERVICES ADMINISTRATION

The General Services Administration (GSA) is an independent agency established by Congress in 1949 to manage government property, procure and distribute supplies, and stockpile strategic materials. Among its responsibilities is the enforcement of laws and regulations that pertain to the protection of life and property under the control of the GSA. To this end the GSA employs Federal Protective Officers who patrol on foot and in vehicles, parking areas, loading platforms, building interiors, and public entrances of facilities under GSA control for evidence of trespass or hazardous conditions. Officers are also assigned to fixed posts or control desks where they are responsible for monitoring automated security and fire-protection systems and dispatching personnel and equipment in cases of emergency. Officers assigned to entrance-control posts examine credentials of those desiring entrance to federal facilities under GSA control (*Criminal Justice Careers Guidebook* 1982).

(For further information, contact Office of Federal Protective Services Management, General Services Administration, Eighteenth and F Streets NW, Washington, D.C. 20405; telephone 202-655-4000.)

INTERNAL REVENUE SERVICE

The Office of the Commissioner of Internal Revenue was established by an act of Congress on July 1, 1862. The Internal Revenue Service (IRS) "is responsible for administering and enforcing the internal revenue laws and related statutes, except those relating to alcohol, tobacco, firearms and explosives. The IRS mission is to encourage and achieve the highest possible degree of voluntary compliance with the tax laws and regulations" (*Federal Register* 1984: 433-34). When voluntary compliance is not achieved, a case may become the responsibility of the special agents of the Criminal Investigation Division (CID).

CID investigations center primarily on income, employment, and excise taxes. If special agents determine that a criminal violation has occurred, they set out to determine the true taxable income of the subject by interviews and extensive reviews of financial records. Agents are skilled at detecting tax frauds and uncovering unreported income or hidden assets. If taxpayer records have been withheld, destroyed, or altered, the agents reconstruct the subject's financial record by locating alternative sources of information. This is accomplished by examining bank records, cancelled checks, brokerage accounts, property transactions, and purchases—in short, compiling a financial biography of the subject's lifestyle. IRS special agents target organized crime figures and major drug traffickers for special attention. As a result of IRS investigations, many crime figures have been convicted of tax evasion.

(For further information, contact Internal Revenue Service, Criminal Investigation Division, Department of the Treasury, 1111 Constitution Avenue NW, Washington, D.C. 20224; telephone 202-566-5000.)

Postal inspection service

Protection of the U.S. Mail is the responsibility of the second oldest federal law enforcement unit still in existence, the Postal Inspection Service. The service has three major responsibilities:

1. *Criminal Investigation.* Postal inspectors investigate illegal acts committed against the Postal Service and its property and personnel, such as the burglary or robbery of postal facilities, thefts from private (house) or U.S. Postal Service mailboxes, and embezzlement by postal employees. They also investigate cases of fraud involving the use of the mails, such as land, charity, chain letter, and advance-fee schemes. Use of the mails to transport controlled substances (drugs) is a special target of the service. Postal inspectors also deal with incidents involving the sending of bombs or incendiary devices, the illegal transport of firearms, and extortion attempts using the mails.

2. *Audit Investigations.* Postal inspectors conduct in-house audits in order to evaluate operations and identify problems within the postal system. They determine whether the Postal Service is operating in conformity with applicable laws and regulations and in the best interests of the public. They determine whether

postal revenues are being adequately protected and economically used.

3. *Security and Administrative Functions.* Postal inspectors conduct personnel investigations and evaluate the fire, safety, and security systems being used in postal facilities.

The mail fraud unit of the Postal Inspection Service has been involved in the investigation of significant criminal cases in the financial district of New York's Wall Street. Financial crimes that make use of the mails come under the unit's jurisdiction and they have been working an increasing number of "insider trading" cases. These involve the violation of laws against using inside information in the purchase of securities. They also investigate "boiler room" operations—high pressure telephone sales of worthless securities—which use the mails to receive payments. Members of the unit are trained in accounting and securities transactions and use the basic tools of police investigation—informers, search warrants, and electronic surveillance. (Postal inspectors are usually chosen from the ranks of postal employees.) Many of their cases result from reports of irregular trading activities and are worked jointly with the Securities and Exchange Commission (Lubasch 1986).

(For further information, contact Chief Postal Inspector, 475 L'Enfant Plaza West SW, Washington, D.C. 20260; telephone 202-245-4000.)

Drug enforcement administration

At the Hague Conference in 1912, the United States became a signatory to an international agreement designed to control trafficking in certain drugs, particularly heroin. Because the Constitution contained nothing specific to deal with drug trafficking, Congress used its taxing authority and passed the Harrison Narcotics Act in 1914. Since the law was ostensibly a tax matter, responsibility for drug law enforcement was placed in the Treasury Department's Bureau of Internal Revenue. With the advent of prohibition, drug enforcement went into the Treasury Department's new Prohibition Bureau. In 1930, Congress established the Federal Bureau of Narcotics (FBN). In 1968, the FBN was taken out of the Treasury Department, merged with the Bureau of Drug Abuse Control (which had been in the Department of Health, Education, and Welfare), and placed in the Department of Justice as the Bureau of Narcotics and Dangerous Drugs (BNDD). In 1973, Congress created the Drug Enforcement Administration (DEA).

The agents and the methods used in drug law enforcement have always been controversial. Drug enforcement is a difficult and often "dirty" business. Because the offense in question is "victimless," law enforcement must be proactive. This requires agents to act out the role of criminals—"undercover" work—and to associate with drug traffickers and criminal informants. Agents become enmeshed in a shadowy world of drugs and money, a great deal of money. Drug transactions are known only to the participants, and an agent participating in them can easily divert money or drugs for his or her own purposes. The history of drug law enforcement has been filled with transactions made for personal, rather than public, advantage.

DEA is responsible for enforcing federal statutes dealing with narcotics (e.g., heroin) and dangerous drugs (e.g., cocaine) by investigating alleged or suspected *major* drug traffickers. (Low-level dealers are usually left to local enforcement agencies.) Supervisors assign cases to special agents working alone or in teams. The agents review and analyze all of the data the agency has on file and make preliminary plans for conduct of the investigation. Additional facts and evidence are obtained by interviewing, "observing, and interrogating witnesses, suspects, and informants with knowledge of the case. In many instances, agents carefully examine and evaluate financial and inventory records or other sources of information to verify facts previously obtained or to uncover new evidence indicating criminal activities" (*Criminal Justice Careers Guidebook* 1982: 68).

The DEA is also responsible for regulating the legal trade in controlled substances such as morphine, methadone, and barbiturates. Special agents conduct accountability investigations of drug wholesalers, suppliers, and manufacturers. DEA establishes import, export, and manufacturing quotas for various dangerous drugs, and registers all authorized handlers of such substances. Special agents inspect the records and facilities of major drug manufacturers and distributors, and investigate instances where drugs have been illegally diverted from legitimate sources. DEA special agents are also stationed in other countries, where their mission is to gain cooperation in efforts against drug trafficking. Agents share information and expertise with officials from other nations in their efforts against international drug traffickers.

(For further information, contact Drug Enforcement Administration, Department of Justice, 1405 I Street NW, Washington, D.C. 20537; telephone 202-633-1000.)

FEDERAL BUREAU OF INVESTIGATION

The FBI is the best known federal law enforcement agency. Its origins date back to the establishment of the Department of Justice in 1870. Until 1908, the department used private detectives from the Pinkerton Agency or men borrowed from the Secret Service. In that year, President Theodore Roosevelt directed the Attorney General to develop an investigative unit within the Justice Department; it was named the Bureau of Investigation. In 1935, Congress renamed it the Federal Bureau of Investigation.

Originally, bureau activities were restricted to the investigation of crimes against the United States. It had no authority to investigate the activities of political groups or even foreign agents. In 1916, with war raging in Europe, the bureau was authorized to undertake investigations as directed by the Attorney General or the Secretary of State. The Espionage Act of 1917 provided a further legal basis for the bureau to investigate "radical" political activity, subversion, and espionage. The bureau was active in rounding up men believed to be avoiding military service during the First World War.

After the First World War, at the direction of Attorney General A. Mitchell Palmer, the bureau was involved in a great deal of anti-radical activity, conducting raids and arresting thousands of people in what became known as the Red Scare of 1919. These "Palmer Raids" were the subject of a congressional investigation and were strongly defended by the bureau's assistant director, John Edgar Hoover, who was appointed director of the FBI in 1924 and remained at its head until his death in 1972.

Over the years prior to the Second World War, the bureau was given additional responsibilities: interstate transportation of stolen motor vehicles, kidnapping, bank robbery, and interstate

Pinkerton's National Detective Agency.

FOUNDED BY ALLAN PINKERTON, 1850.

ROBT. A PINKERTON, New York,
WM. A. PINKERTON, Chicago,
} Principals.

GEO. D. BANGS, General Manager, New York.
ALLAN PINKERTON, Assistant General Manager, New York

JOHN CORNISH, Manager, Eastern Division, New York.
EDWARD S. GAYLOR, Manager, Middle Division, Chicago.
JAMES McPARLAND, Manager, Western Division, Denver.

Attorneys:—GUTHRIE, CRAVATH & HENDERSON,
New York

TELEPHONE CONNECTION.

OFFICES.
DENVER, OPERA HOUSE BLOCK.
JOHN C. FRASER, Resident Sup't.
NEW YORK, 57 BROADWAY.
BOSTON, 30 COURT STREET.
MONTREAL, MERCHANTS BANK BUILDING.
BUFFALO, FIDELITY BUILDING.
PHILADELPHIA, 441 CHESTNUT STREET.
PITTSBURGH, SECOND NAT'L BANK BLDG
CLEVELAND, GARFIELD BUILDING.
CHICAGO, 201 FIFTH AVENUE.
ST. PAUL, ERNST BUILDING.
ST. LOUIS, WAINWRIGHT BUILDING.
KANSAS CITY, 622 MAIN STREET.
OMAHA, NEW YORK LIFE BUILDING.
PORTLAND, ORE. MARQUAM BLOCK.
SEATTLE, ARCADE BUILDING.
SPOKANE, PEYTON BUILDING.
LOS ANGELES, BRYSON BUILDING.
SAN FRANCISCO, CROCKER BUILDING.

REPRESENTING THE AMERICAN BANKERS' ASSOCIATION.

$2,000.00 REWARD.

CIRCULAR No. 3.

DENVER, Colo., November 14th, 1904.

THE FIRST NATIONAL BANK OF WINNEMUCCA, Nevada, a member of THE AMERICAN BANKERS' ASSOCIATION, was robbed of **$32,640** at the noon hour, September 19th, 1900, by three men who entered the bank and "held up" the cashier and four other persons. Two of the robbers carried revolvers and a third a Winchester rifle. They compelled the five persons to go into the inner office of the bank while the robbery was committed.

At least **$31,000** was in **$20** gold coin ; **$1,200** in **$5** and **$10** gold coin ; the balance in currency, including one $50 bill.

Since the issuance of circular No. 1, dated Denver, Colo., May 15th, 1901, and circular No. 2, dated Denver, Colo., February 3rd, 1902, it has been positively determined that two of the men who committed this robbery were :

1. **GEORGE PARKER**, alias "**BUTCH**" **CASSIDY**, alias **GEORGE CASSIDY**, alias **INGERFIELD**.

2. **HARRY LONGBAUGH**, alias "**KID**" **LONGBAUGH**, alias **HARRY ALONZO**, alias "**THE SUNDANCE KID.**"

PARKER and LONGBAUGH are members of the HARVEY LOGAN alias "KID" CURRY band of bank and train (express) "hold up" robbers.

For the arrest, detention and surrender to an authorized officer of the State of Nevada of each or any one of the men who robbed the FIRST NATIONAL BANK OF WINNEMUCCA, the following reward is offered by THE FIRST NATIONAL BANK OF WINNEMUCCA :

$1,000 FOR EACH ROBBER. ALSO **25** PER CENT., IN PROPORTIONATE SHARES, ON ALL MONEY RECOVERED.

Persons furnishing information leading to the arrest of either or all of the robbers will be entitled to share in the reward.

Until 1909 the Department of Justice hired private detectives from the Pinkerton Agency. In 1904 the agency set a $2,000 reward for the detention of outlaws George Parker and Harry Longbaugh, also known as "Butch Cassidy and the Sundance Kid."

Below appear the photographs, descriptions and histories of GEORGE PARKER, alias "BUTCH" CASSIDY, alias GEORGE CASSIDY, alias INGERFIELD and HARRY LONGBAUGH alias HARRY ALONZO.

GEORGE PARKER.
First photograph taken July 15, 1894.

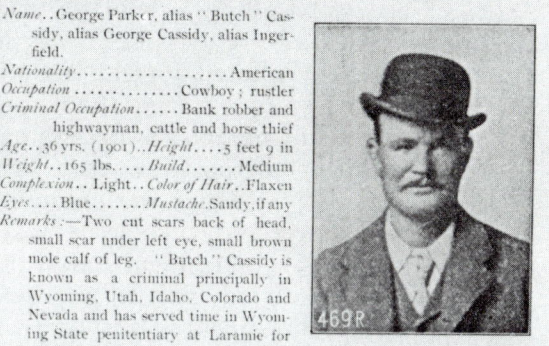

GEORGE PARKER.
Last photograph taken Nov. 21, 1900.

Name..George Parker, alias "Butch" Cassidy, alias George Cassidy, alias Ingerfield.
Nationality.....................American
Occupation..............Cowboy; rustler
Criminal Occupation......Bank robber and highwayman, cattle and horse thief
Age..36 yrs. (1901)..Height....5 feet 9 in
Weight..165 lbs.....Build.......Medium
Complexion..Light..Color of Hair..Flaxen
Eyes....Blue.......Mustache.Sandy, if any
Remarks:—Two cut scars back of head, small scar under left eye, small brown mole calf of leg. "Butch" Cassidy is known as a criminal principally in Wyoming, Utah, Idaho, Colorado and Nevada and has served time in Wyoming State penitentiary at Laramie for grand Larceny, but was pardoned January 19th, 1896.

HARRY LONGBAUGH.
Photograph taken Nov. 21, 1900.

Name.........Harry Longbaugh, alias "Kid" Longbaugh, alias Harry Alonzo alias Frank Jones, alias Frank Boyd, alias the "Sundance Kid."
Nationality........Swedish-American..Occupation............Cowboy; rustler
Criminal Occupation.........Highwayman, bank burglar, cattle and horse thief
Age...........35 years................Height..........................5 feet 10 in
Weight......165 to 175 lbs.............Build.........................Good
Eyes......Blue or gray..............Complexion...................Medium
Mustache or Beard.................(if any), natural color brown, reddish tinge
Features......Grecian type............Nose....................Rather long
Color of Hair.........Natural color brown, may be dyed; combs it pompadour
IS BOW-LEGGED AND HIS FEET FAR APART.
Remarks:—Harry Longbaugh served 18 months in jail at Sundance, Cook Co., Wyoming, when a boy, for horse stealing. In December, 1892, Harry Longbaugh, Bill Madden and Henry Bass "held up" a Great Northern train at Malta, Montana. Bass and Madden were tried for this crime, convicted and sentenced to 10 and 14 years respectively; Longbaugh escaped and since has been a fugitive. June 28, 1897, under the name of Frank Jones, Longbaugh participated with Harvey Logan, alias Curry, Tom Day and Walter Putney, in the Belle Fourche, South Dakota, bank robbery. All were arrested, but Longbaugh and Harvey Logan escaped from jail at Deadwood, October 31, the same year. Longbaugh has not since been arrested.

☞ Officers are warned to have sufficient assistance and be fully armed, when attempting to arrest either of these outlaws, as they are always heavily armed, and will make a determined resistance before submitting to arrest, not hesitating to kill, if necessary.

☞ This circular cancels circulars No. 1 and 2, issued by us from Denver, Colo., May 15th, 1901 and February 3rd, 1902, respectively.

IN CASE OF AN ARREST immediately notify PINKERTON'S NATIONAL DETECTIVE AGENCY at the nearest of the above listed offices.

Or

JOHN C. FRAZER,
Resident Sup't., DENVER, COLO.

Pinkerton's National Detective Agency,
Opera House Block, Denver, Colo.

fugitives. In 1932, the FBI laboratory was established and a national fingerprint identification service was inaugurated. In 1935, the FBI National Academy was established and became a national training school for selected local police officers. In 1936, at the request of President Franklin Roosevelt, the FBI began to collect information on domestic Communists and extremist groups. During the war this activity was intensified as part of the bureau's efforts against subversion and espionage.

During the postwar years, FBI resources were expanded in dealing with domestic Communism, and the problem of organized crime and racketeering was left unattended. This changed in 1961 when President John F. Kennedy appointed his brother Robert Kennedy as Attorney General. In addition to becoming involved in efforts against organized crime, the FBI, reluctantly at first, became more involved in investigating federal civil rights violations that were occurring frequently in the South. During this era and into the 1970s, the FBI also investigated the civil rights movement and later the antiwar movement, sometimes using methods that were at best questionable, and often illegal, such as unauthorized bugging and wiretapping and "black bag jobs" (burglaries). The targets of this activity included the Reverend Martin Luther King, Jr., and the leaders of the anti-Vietnam War movement. During the late 1970s and early 1980s a number of reforms were instituted in an attempt to prevent such abuses (Morgan 1982).

The FBI has responsibility for the investigation of over two hundred different types of cases. Special agents enforce federal laws dealing with kidnapping, bank robbery, thefts of government property, organized criminal activities, espionage, sabotage, civil rights violations, and white-collar crimes. When a case assignment is received, special agents, working alone or in teams, review and analyze all of the available data and plan the details of the investigation. They gather facts and evidence through interviews, observations and surveillance, and interrogation of suspects, informants, and witnesses. Agents examine and evaluate any available records in order to uncover evidence or to discover information that will confirm evidence already obtained. Under some circumstances, agents assume other identities and work undercover (as in the Abscam case). The FBI also makes extensive use of court-authorized electronic surveillance—bugging and wiretapping.

In addition to its investigative activities, the FBI assists law enforcement agencies at the federal, state, and local levels with a

9 ▪ FEDERAL LAW ENFORCEMENT   263

variety of supportive services. Bureau personnel assist local agencies through the FBI's extensive files of fingerprints, nicknames of criminals, firearms, document examinations, typewriter faces, heelprints, tire treads, paper watermarks, and automotive paint samples, among a number of subject areas. The FBI has the world's largest forensic laboratory, which provides microscopic and chemical analyses, spectography, and cryptography. The FBI National Academy provides additional

A technician examines bomb components in the explosives unit of the FBI laboratory—the largest in the world.

training for some members of enforcement agencies throughout the United States.

(For further information, contact Federal Bureau of Investigation, Department of Justice, Ninth Street and Pennsylvania Avenue NW, Washington, D.C. 20535; telephone 202-324-3000.)

Coast Guard

The Coast Guard, in the Department of Transportation, is responsible for saving life and property on the high seas. It has also been responsible for maritime law enforcement since 1790, when its predecessor, the Revenue Cutter Service, was established to combat smuggling. The law enforcement role of the Coast Guard is contained in Title 14 of the United States Code: to "make inquiries, examinations, inspections, searches, seizures, and arrests upon the high seas and waters over which the United States has jurisdiction, for the prevention, detection, and suppression of violations of laws of the United States." The Coast Guard is particularly active in combatting the use of vessels to smuggle drugs and in enforcing safety and pollution regulations applicable to commercial and pleasure vessels, as well as the 200-mile fishery conservation statute. Coast Guard personnel are federal law enforcement officers who, at sea, do not have to establish probable cause prior to boarding a vessel; they are authorized to act upon a "reasonable suspicion" (Gracey 1985).

Military law enforcement agencies

In addition to the Military Police (MP), each branch of the military has an investigative arm, and their functions and services are quite similar. The U.S. Army's Criminal Investigation Command (often referred to as CID, because it was originally named Criminal Investigation Division) deals with crimes committed by military personnel as well as civilians who sell drugs to military personnel or are involved in larceny of military property. CID special agents do not have authority over civilians, however, unless the person commits a crime on a federal reservation—for example, a military base—or unless a direct link to the Army can be established. When dealing with civilians, the CID usually seeks cooperation with local police agencies. If a crime is committed by a civilian on an Army post, it can be investigated by the CID or the FBI. CID agents also provide protective services to the Secretary of Defense and the Secretary of the Army and assist the Secret Service in special circumstances (Brighton 1983).

The U.S. Naval Investigative Service (NIS) has the exclusive responsibility for investigating felony crimes and provides counterintelligence support for the U.S. Navy and Marine Corps. NIS special agents investigate all felonies committed by or against Department of Navy personnel or property. Such investigations involve violations of the Uniform Code of Military Justice or federal and state criminal statutes applicable to military reservations. The NIS also investigates and arrests military personnel for felony offenses committed off military bases. NIS agents may arrest civilians in connection with certain federal violations. The service provides protective services for cabinet members and other dignitaries visiting Navy installations or traveling on Navy ships, planes, or other vehicles. The NIS has approximately nine hundred special agents, both civilian and military personnel; they operate out of more than 150 offices throughout the world, as well as on assignments afloat in support of the Navy's aircraft carriers and battleships.

> NIS also provides assistance in the conduct of joint interviews or interrogations of military suspects, victims or witnesses; locating military personnel around the world; and reviewing service records of current and former military personnel who are criminal suspects, or who are seeking employment in law enforcement. In the area of joint operations, NIS has willingly provided manpower and funds for narcotics investigations and undercover store front "sting" operations. (Pascoe 1985: 36)

The U.S. Air Force Office of Special Investigations (OSI) employs about 1,900 special agents, both civilian and military personnel. The agency is responsible for investigating crimes against Air Force personnel and property, crimes committed by Air Force personnel, and offenses committed on Air Force reservations. OSI is also involved in counterintelligence activities for the Air Force and provides protective services for Department of Defense officials, the Secretary of the Air Force, generals, and dignitaries visiting Air Force installations or using Air Force transportation.

Offices of Inspector General

Concern about fraud against government programs led Congress to enact the Inspector General Act of 1978, which established separate Offices of Inspector General in a number of federal agencies. For example, in the Department of Education, criminal investigations are carried out by eleven geographically dispersed offices employing about fifty special agents. They are responsible for personnel security, the protection of classified information, and the investigation of wrongdoing involving funds of the Department of Education. Most criminal investigations conducted by the special agents involve embezzlement of department funds entrusted to both public and private educational institutions, kickbacks to bank officials with respect to student loans, the filing of false statements, mail fraud, and conspiracy (Sinai and Dahl 1985).

Another federal department that has an Office of Inspector General is the Department of Defense (established by an act of Congress in 1982). Here the criminal investigators for the Inspector General are responsible for protecting resources for a department that employs 6.3 million persons and spends over $600 million each day; it has 5,500 properties located in the United States and twenty-one other countries. The department uses 6,000 criminal investigators who are assigned either to the military or directly to the Inspector General ("The Department of Defense Hotline" 1985).

Miscellaneous agencies

In addition to the law enforcement agencies we have already discussed in this chapter, there are a variety of other investigative and enforcement personnel employed by the federal government. Park Rangers are responsible for law enforcement, fire control, and search and rescue in the 30 million acres that comprise the national park system of the Department of Interior's National Park Service (Hart 1977). The Department of the Interior also employs Wildlife Law Enforcement Agents in its U.S. Fish and Wildlife Service. Among their responsibilities, these agents investigate persons illegally trafficking in government-

Park rangers are responsible for law enforcement, fire control, and search and rescue throughout the 30 million acres of the National Park System. *Above*, a ranger assists a volunteer building an igloo at 11,000 feet on Alaska's Mount McKinley.

protected birds of prey such as falcons, which can fetch prices of $50,000 to $100,000 apiece in Saudi Arabia. The Department of Agriculture, the Department of Labor, the Department of Health and Welfare, and the Department of State also employ a variety of investigative and enforcement personnel.

INTERPOL

The International Criminal Police Organization, known by its radio designation as INTERPOL, assists federal agencies with investigative activities that transcend international boundaries. INTERPOL was the brainchild of the Police Commissioner of Vienna, Johann Schober. In 1923 he organized a conference of police officials from twenty countries to promote mutual assistance and cooperation between their various law enforcement entities. As a result, a headquarters with a small staff was established in Vienna. In conjunction with the League of Nations, which was established in the wake of World War I, INTERPOL became active in dealing with the problem of counterfeiting that was rampant in the years following the war. Membership increased, and legislation in 1938 authorized the Attorney General, who in turn authorized J. Edgar Hoover, to accept membership in INTERPOL on behalf of the United States. The following year Austria was annexed to Nazi Germany. INTERPOL was moved to Berlin, where the Gestapo used its resources to help capture fleeing Jews. Police agencies of other nations began to realize that the Germans were only interested in their own political enemies, and Hoover ordered all connections severed. INTERPOL fell silent until the end of the Second World War.

In 1946 INTERPOL was reorganized, the United States resumed its membership, and Hoover was elected a vice-president of the organization. There was a stormy relationship between the director of the FBI and the leaders of INTERPOL, and in 1950 the FBI withdrew from participation. The Treasury Department, anxious to maintain international contacts to help with its enforcement responsibilities in drug, currency, and customs violations, continued an informal liaison with INTERPOL. In 1958 the Attorney General officially assigned the Treasury Department to represent the United States to INTERPOL. Until 1968, however, "INTERPOL meant very little to the United States law enforcement community and was virtually unknown"

(Fooner 1985: 19). In that year, Iran announced that it was going to end its ban on opium production; at the same time, there appeared to be an epidemic of drug use in the United States. A National Central Bureau (NCB) was quickly activated in Washington, and by 1970 the NCB was handling about 300 cases a year.

In the mid-1970s a turf battle ensued between Treasury and Justice; the Attorney General, after decades of neglect, decided that he wanted INTERPOL back, and Treasury resisted. In 1977 an agreement—a memorandum of understanding—was effected between the two departments; they would share the responsibility of representing the U.S. to INTERPOL and operating the NCB. The memorandum was subsequently amended, and in 1981 the INTERPOL-USNCB became an agency within the Department of Justice.

By 1986 there were 138 INTERPOL members, although some countries were inactive. A country merely announces its intention to join in order to become a member. Most communist countries are not members and, although no member can be expelled, South Africa was allowed to resign. In each member country there is an NCB that acts as a point of contact and coordination with the General Secretariat located in the Paris suburb of St. Cloud. INTERPOL has a headquarters staff of 250, about 60 of whom are law enforcement officers from about 40 different countries ("TVI Interview" 1985). There is a large communications facility which links 72 member countries into a radio network; other nations use telex or cable facilities. INTERPOL is under the day-to-day direction of a secretary general; it is a coordinating body and has no agents or investigators of its own.

Article 3 of the INTERPOL constitution prohibits involvement in activities of investigations of a racial, military, religious, or political character. This has presented a problem when dealing with crimes committed by terrorists. As we noted in chapter 1, "One man's terrorist is another man's freedom fighter." This has made difficult the utilization of INTERPOL against persons whose behavior, while it violates the law of one or more nations, is political in nature. With the rise in terrorist acts, however, INTERPOL members have adopted resolutions that encourage full cooperation among INTERPOL members as far as their national laws permit, and another resolution provides guidelines and parameters for interpreting Article 3 and removes the political ramifications from crimes which are committed against innocent victims or property outside the area of conflict.

About 12,000 requests for assistance from federal, state, and local law enforcement agencies are received by the USNCB in Washington each year. They are checked and coded by technical staff and entered into the INTERPOL Case Tracking System (ICTS), a computer-controlled index of persons, organizations, and other crime information items. The ICTS conducts automatic searches of new entries, retrieving those that correlate with international crime. The requests are forwarded to senior staff members who serve as INTERPOL case investigators, usually veteran agents from a federal agency whose experience includes work with foreign police forces. Each investigator is on loan from his or her principal agency.

As Michael Foner (1985: 6) notes, the types of requests for investigative assistance received by the USCNB range "from murder, robbery, narcotics violations, illicit firearms traffic, and large frauds, to counterfeiting, stolen works of art, bank swindles, and locating fugitives for arrest and extradition. The bureau also receives investigative requests for criminal histories, license checks, and other ID verifications. Sometimes locations of persons lost or missing in a foreign country are requested."

Since the Second World War, INTERPOL has distributed information concerning stolen works of art to the international law enforcement community. The General Secretariat issues about 250 new notices to member nations in monthly and annual circulars that contain descriptions and pictures of stolen art objects such as paintings, sculptures, books, coins, furniture, and archeological items. Urgent messages are transmitted whenever a member nation believes that the artwork may be in transit from their country to another country. The Financial and Economic Crime Unit at the headquarters in St. Cloud facilitates the exchange of information stemming from credit card fraud, airline ticket counterfeiting, computer crime, off-shore banking, commodity futures, and money-laundering schemes. The monitoring of this type of activity can sometimes lead to the identification of suspects involved in drug trafficking or organized crime who had previously escaped detection.

We have completed our examination of the law enforcement response to crime and criminals. Now we will examine the next stage of the criminal justice system, the courts and their key actors.

REVIEW QUESTIONS

1. Why doesn't the United States have a federal police force?
2. Why is federal law enforcement fragmented?
3. What is the oldest federal law enforcement agency, and what are its responsibilities?
4. What are the current responsibilities of the Secret Service?
5. Why did the Reagan administration attempt to disband the Bureau of Alcohol, Tobacco and Firearms?
6. What are the responsibilities of the Immigration and Naturalization Service?
7. What are the responsibilities of Federal Protective Officers of the General Services Administration?
8. How do special agents for the Internal Revenue Service detect hidden or unreported income and assets?
9. What are the responsibilities of the Postal Inspection Service?
10. Why are the law enforcement methods of the Drug Enforcement Administration so controversial?
11. What are some of the major responsibilities of the Federal Bureau of Investigation?
12. What are the responsibilities of the Coast Guard?
13. What are the responsibilities of military law enforcement agencies, and how do they differ from those of other federal law enforcement agencies?
14. What are the responsibilities of an Office of Inspector General?
15. What is INTERPOL and how does it operate?

CHAPTER 10

Federal and State Courts

U.S. DISTRICT COURTS AND MAGISTRATES

U.S. COURT OF APPEALS

U.S. SUPREME COURT

THE STATE COURTS: EARLY HISTORY

THE STRUCTURE OF STATE COURTS

LOWER COURT/COURT OF LIMITED JURISDICTION

SUPERIOR COURT/COURT OF GENERAL JURISDICTION

INTERMEDIATE COURT OF APPEALS/APPELLATE JURISDICTION

COURT OF APPEALS/COURT OF LAST RESORT

THE APPELLATE PROCESS

ADMINISTERING THE COURTS

COURT REFORM

REVIEW QUESTIONS

We are now at the courthouse steps. The large grey columns provide only a slight hint of the archaic nature of the transactions occurring within. At the top of the pediment stands a female figure with flowing robes. In one hand a sword, in the other the scales of justice, and over her eyes a blindfold. She is the visual representation of the classical concept of justice embodied in our most precious historical documents: *equality before the law*. In this chapter, we will examine the federal and state court systems, cornerstones of America's unique system of federalism.

The Articles of Confederation, which governed these United States until 1787, did not provide for federal courts; the national government relied on state courts. In that year delegates to the Constitutional Convention debated the merits of federal versus state power—Northern federalists arguing for a strong central government against Southern supporters of states' rights. Only a compromise permitted adoption of the Constitution, and it did not contain details of a federal court system. Instead, Article III provided that "the judicial Power of the United States shall be vested in one Supreme Court, and in such inferior Courts as the Congress may from time to time ordain and establish." As Mary Ann Harrell and Burnett Anderson (1982: 9-10) note, "Without any argument at all, the delegates accepted the proposal for a Supreme Court. They agreed on the kinds of cases courts of the United States should try; when they disagreed over details for the lower courts, they left the matter up to the new Congress."

The Federalists succeeded in passing the Judiciary Act of 1789, which created circuit and district courts. These were primarily trial courts with appeals going to the Supreme Court. The authority and personnel of these new federal courts were limited, however, and the Federalists' attempts to establish a strong national court system were stymied by the Democratic Republicans (who later became the Democrats) led by Thomas Jefferson. The Civil War temporarily broke the power of the Southern Democrats, and between 1867 and 1925 legislation was enacted that strengthened considerably the authority of federal courts. Since 1925 the structure and jurisdiction of the federal courts have remained basically the same (Glick 1983).

While the Constitution provides for only *federal* courts, the Tenth Amendment states, "The powers not delegated to the United States by the Constitution, nor prohibited by it to the States, are reserved to the States respectively, or to the people." Thus, each state is free to establish its own court system, and the result is a dual system of justice in the United States. First, we will examine the federal judicial system.

U.S. DISTRICT COURTS AND MAGISTRATES

There is a U.S. District Court in each of the ninety-four federal judicial districts (eighty-nine within the fifty states, one for the District of Columbia, and four for the U.S. territories); each state has at least one (districts do not cross state lines), and heavily populated states such as New York, California, and Texas have as many as four. There are about 600 district court judges, and the number of judges assigned to each district varies with the size of the population, the largest being the Southern District of New York, located in Manhattan, which has twenty-seven.

District courts are **courts of general jurisdiction,** meaning they are trial courts with authority to handle all prosecutions for

The Federal Judiciary

```
                    Supreme Court of the United States
                                   |
   ┌──────────────┬────────────────┼─────────────────────┐
Court of      U.S. Courts of    Court of Customs and   Customs
Claims         Appeals          Patent Appeals          Court
              (12 Circuits)
   |               |                                      |
Administrative  U.S. District Courts   U.S. District Courts
Quasi-Judicial  (with federal and      (with federal
Agencies        local jurisdiction)    jurisdiction only)    Appeals from
(Tax Court,     Canal Zone             89 Districts in       state courts in
Federal Trade   Guam                   50 states             50 states, from
Commission,     Virgin Islands         1 in Puerto Rico      the Supreme
National Labor  Mariana Islands        1 in District of      Court of Puerto
Relations                              Columbia              Rico, and from
Board, etc.)                                                 the District of
                            |                                Columbia Court
                    U.S. Magistrates                         of Appeals
```

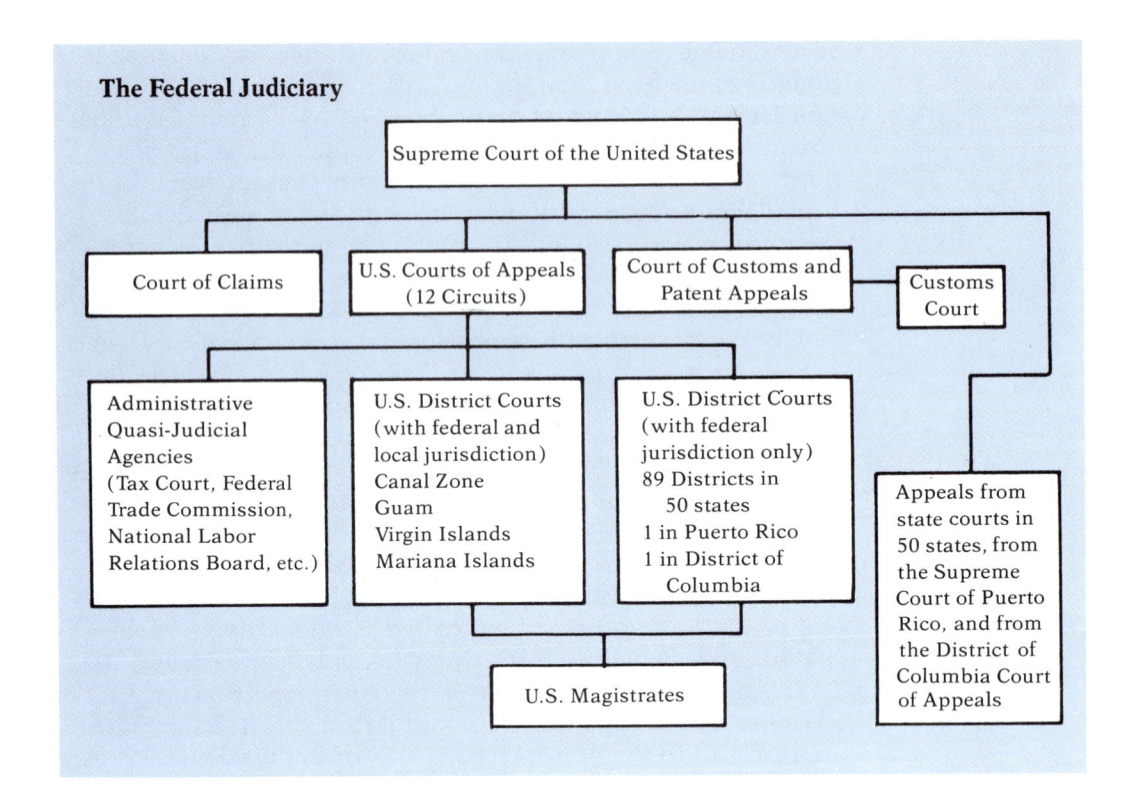

violations of federal law, although this usually means felonies and civil cases where the amount in dispute exceeds $10,000. Since most crimes are violations of state law, in any given year the district courts dispose of less than 15 percent of all felony prosecutions (there are relatively few federal misdemeanors) initiated in the United States. The district courts in three states—California, Illinois, and New York—process more criminal cases than the rest of the federal judiciary in any one year.

In addition to dealing with criminal and civil cases, district courts serve an appellate function in matters relating to certain writs of habeas corpus. In such cases, a person convicted of a crime in state court files a petition claiming the conviction was a violation of the U.S. Constitution. (This will be discussed in chapter 15.)

Under certain circumstances a special three-judge district court may be convened. Such panels include two district court judges and one judge of the circuit court. The special courts were

The Twelve Federal Judicial Circuits

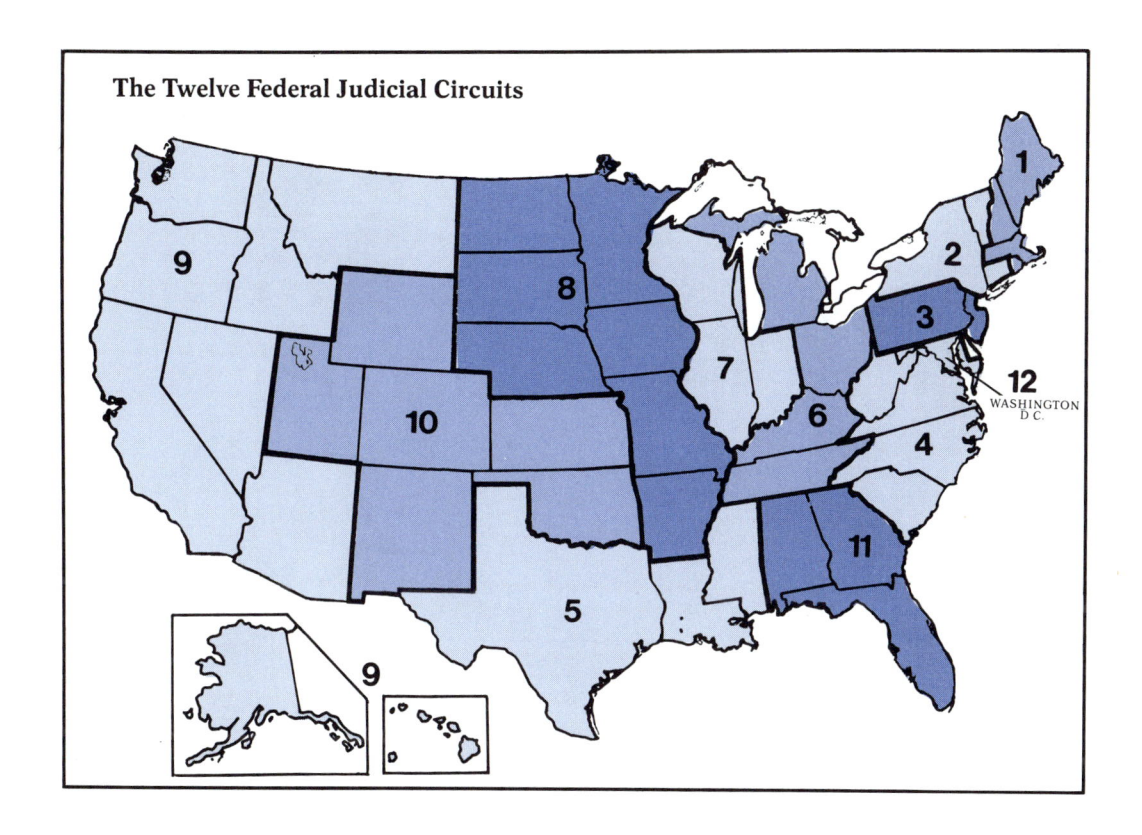

first established in 1903 to consider requests for injunctions against orders of the Interstate Commerce Commission (a federal regulatory agency). In 1910, the authority of these special courts were expanded to include cases in which the validity of a state law was being challenged. Their authority was again increased in 1913 for requests for injunctions against state administrative actions, and in 1937 for requests for injunctions against federal statutes. In 1976, Congress voted to limit the use of the special three-judge tribunal to congressional and legislative apportionment cases, and issues involving the Voting Rights Act of 1965 and the Civil Rights Act of 1964. Appeals from the decision of a special district court ruling go directly to the Supreme Court.

All federal judges are appointed to lifetime terms by the president with the advice and consent of the Senate; lifetime tenure helps to insulate judges from political pressures and popular sentiment. In practice, the senior senator of the president's po-

The concept of equality before the law is often represented by a blindfolded female figure in flowing robes—in one hand a sword, in the other the scales of justice.

litical party from the state in which a vacancy exists often controls the appointment. At a minimum, the senator can veto the appointment through a device known as "senatorial courtesy." The quality of judges selected for the federal bench through this process, however, is reputed by most lawyers to be quite high; federal judges tend to exhibit greater resistance to improper pressures and a higher degree of legal competence than do many of their state court counterparts who are elected to office. (The issue of judicial selection will be discussed in the next chapter.)

In dealing with criminal cases, district courts are assisted by U.S. magistrates, lawyers who are appointed by the district court judges for terms of eight years (part-time magistrates serve four-year terms). Magistrates are empowered to issue search warrants, conduct preliminary stages of felony cases such as the setting of bail, and to adjudicate misdemeanor cases when the defendant waives the right to a jury trail. On appeal, decisions of a magistrate are reviewed by district court judges.

U.S. COURT OF APPEALS

An **appellate court** is not a trial court; it considers only cases on appeal that have already been tried by a lower court. The U.S. Court of Appeals was created by Congress in 1891 as the Circuit Court of Appeals (judges "rode the circuit" to hold court) in order to relieve the Supreme Court of the growing number of cases being appealed. The country is divided into eleven circuits, each of which embraces several states, and a twelfth circuit serves the District of Columbia. The second circuit, for example, covers New York, New Jersey, and Connecticut. Each court has at least four judges, and a circuit with a great deal of litigation will have more than twenty appellate judges. The chief judge of each circuit (the most senior judge in terms of service in the circuit who is under seventy years of age) has supervisory responsibilities for the circuit. Court-of-appeals cases are usually considered by panels of three judges, selected at random, although occasionally, very important cases will be heard by the full court of the circuit (referred to as an *en banc*, "on the bench"); if that is not feasible, the panel will consist of as many of the judges of the circuit as possible.

Judges of the court of appeals (appellate courts have no juries) review issues of law that have been applied by district court judges in civil and criminal trials and by judges in a number of quasi-judicial tribunals such as the Federal Trade Commission and the Federal Communications Commission. The appellate court also has the power to deal with certain legal issues that arise during the course of pending litigation—*interlocutory appeals*. Appellate courts provide a forum for the review of rulings and judgments of district courts; they do not try new cases, but rather determine whether or not the decisions of a district court are correct.

Every criminal defendant is entitled to a review of the district court proceedings against him or her by the circuit court covering the district. Appeals are usually expensive and quite time-consuming, however, and a criminal defendant is not constitutionally entitled to court-appointed free legal counsel for the purpose of appealing his or her conviction. Appellate courts usually provide long written reasons on which they base their decisions. The reversal of a case by the appellate court is usually considered a "slap" at the trial judge; the courts of appeals reverse about 10 percent of the cases that they review.

Each circuit is assigned a Supreme Court justice, with the two most senior Supreme Court justices assigned to two circuits. This is a holdover from an earlier era, before the appeals courts were established as separate intermediate-level courts. At that time, during recesses of the Supreme Court, justices would literally "ride the circuit" and sit as circuit judges. On occasion, Supreme Court justices are asked to act on emergency petitions from their circuits when the Supreme Court is not in session. These petitions often involve cases of capital punishment. The Courts of Appeals must consider all cases brought to them. Appeals from a decision of the Circuit Court go to the Supreme Court, which has discretion over the cases it hears.

U.S. SUPREME COURT

America's system of government with its three equal branches is quite unique, and at the pinnacle of the judicial branch is a most unique institution, the Supreme Court. While the president (executive branch) and the Congress (legislative branch) must be more or less responsive to the concerns of the voting public, the judicial branch can remain aloof, not at all dependent upon the whims of the electorate, and it can even render the acts and decisions of the other branches null and void, or **unconstitutional.** As the least democratic institution of our government, the Supreme Court can protect the rights and interests of persons who may be quite weak—who do not represent a significant bloc of votes or source of funds—or who may be quite unpopular, such as the mentally ill, the mentally retarded, prison inmates, welfare recipients, juveniles, disenfranchised minority groups, and persons in police custody.

It began as a court of little consequence; only three judges were present in New York (the temporary capital city) when the

10 ▪ FEDERAL AND STATE COURTS

Chief Justice John Marshall (1755–1835) helped formulate the basic principles of constitutional law. With *Marbury v. Madison* (1803), the Supreme Court defined the doctrine of judicial review, in which federal and state acts may be declared unconstitutional.

Supreme Court convened for the first time in 1790.* The Supreme Court was required by law to have two sessions per year, so it began its first term with a crowded courtroom and an empty docket. For the first three years of its existence, it had almost no business at all. The Judiciary Act of 1789 required the justices to travel twice a year to distant parts of the country to preside over circuit courts and hear appeals. The justices complained about their long journeys, sometimes lasting nineteen hours a day, on a stagecoach, and the first chief justice, John Jay, threatened to resign if Congress did not change the law. In 1793, Congress relented; there would only be one circuit trip a year.

---

*Much of the historical material in this section is based upon Harrell and Anderson 1982.

The Supreme Court emerged into a controversial and powerful body with the appointment of John Marshall as chief justice in 1801 by a Federalist lame-duck president, John Adams. Marshall (1755-1835), a Virginian and, like George Washington, a Federalist, formulated the basic principles of what became known as **constitutional law,** and in the case of **Marbury v. Madison** established the power of the Supreme Court to declare an act of Congress unconstitutional. Although this was not the first time the court had reviewed a federal law—in 1796 it had upheld a federal statute as valid—*Marbury* clearly established the Supreme Court's role as the final interpreter of the Constitution. However, while the president commands an army and Congress controls the budget of the executive branch and can impeach the president, the Supreme Court must depend on its prestige, the power of public opinion, Congress and, in the end, the executive branch to carry out its decisions. Thus, for example, although the Supreme Court ruled in 1954 that segregation of public schools was unconstitutional (*Brown v. the Board of Education,*) it had no ability to force a high school in Little Rock, Arkansas, to admit black students in 1957. In the face of opposition by the state of Arkansas, only the president of the United States, Dwight D. Eisenhower, could (and did, albeit reluctantly) send federal troops to enforce the orders of the federal district court pursuant to the *Brown* decision.

As the highest court in the federal system, the Supreme Court is the **court of last resort.** The deliberations of the eight associate justices are presided over by the chief justice—all of whom are appointed for life by the president with the advice and consent of the Senate. (It should be noted that the Constitution does not require that members of the Supreme Court be lawyers.) Unlike the Court of Appeals, the Supreme Court decides which cases it will hear; each case requires a **writ of *certiorari***—an agreement to place the case on the Court's calendar by a minimum of four justices. *Certiorari* is granted in less than 10 percent of the cases appealed to the Supreme Court; the remaining petitions are simply denied any hearing. A citizen or lawyer who proclaims "I'll take this case to the U.S. Supreme Court" is either ignorant of how the Court operates, or is simply engaging in a rhetorical exercise. A petition for review will be granted only if the case raises unique and consequential issues involving interpretations of the Constitution or federal statutes and treaties.

Appellate courts in general, and the Supreme Court in par-

In 1957 President Eisenhower sent federal troops to Little Rock, Arkansas, to enforce the Supreme Court's ruling declaring segregation of public schools unconstitutional.

ticular, are expected to adhere to precedent, or the rule of **stare decisis**, literally, to stand by that which was already decided. Although this rule is not inviolable, the Supreme Court is constrained by its own prior decisions: "our judicial system demands that [*stare decisis*] be overturned only on a showing of good cause" (Gifis 1975: 198). The Supreme Court has developed several rules governing its review of cases:

1. Cases must not be presented in a friendly, nonadversarial proceeding (to get an advisory opinion, for example); the dispute must be a real one.
2. The Court will not anticipate a question of constitutional law in advance of the necessity for deciding it.
3. The Court will not formulate a rule of constitutional law broader than is required by the precise facts to which it is to be applied.
4. If a case can be decided either on constitutional grounds or on the grounds of statutory construction or general law, the Court will decide on only the latter.
5. The Court will not decide the validity of a statute upon the

complaint of a person who fails to show that he or she is injured by its operation.
6. The Court will not pass upon the constitutionality of a statute at the request of a person who has benefited from it.
7. Whenever possible, the Court will avoid making a determination of the validity of an act of Congress.

In hearing a case, all nine justices always sit together in a rather small but impressive chamber of the Supreme Court building across the street from the Capitol. Decisions of the Supreme Court are usually lengthy documents written with the help of law clerks (who do much of the research). A decision requires agreement of a majority of the justices, but each is free to add his or her own reasons or to dissent from the majority opinion. At times, a justice may ask to be excused from hearing a case because of a possible conflict of interest, for example, a case involving a corporation that the justice represented as an attorney.

THE STATE COURTS: EARLY HISTORY

From the founding of the first permanent English colony in North America (Jamestown, Virginia, in 1607) until the Revolutionary War, the English legal system underwent significant changes, and each group of colonists brought with them knowledge of the English legal system as it existed at the time of their departure from the mother country. Thus, each colony—whether Massachusetts in 1620 or Georgia in 1733—set up its legal system based on a different version of the one they had experienced in England, and some ignored their English roots in favor of the Bible. "This meant," Lawrence Friedman (1973: 16) notes, "that the colonies began their careers at different points in the process of legal development." There were other differences between the various colonies, later to become states; for example, Massachusetts based its law on the Bible, while the Southern colonies tended to base their codes on English common law. While colonial law was subordinate to English law, it was often not clear which acts of Parliament and which court decisions were binding on Americans. Throughout the colonial period, Americans borrowed as much English law and judicial practice

JUSTICE IN NEW YORK.

CLERK OF COURT—"*How say you, Prisoner—are you guilty or not guilty?*"
PRISONER—"*Now you've got me. Ye see, Jedge, I've bin layin' nineteen months in the Tombs, waitin' trial, an' I raily forgit the circumstances of the case.*"

---

as they wanted or were forced to adopt. Even after the Revolution, English law continued to be imported as needed. In any event, the primitive nature of the early colonies often made necessity, not tradition, the basis for law and judicial practice. As settlers moved further west, given the difficulties of communication, they tended to become even further distanced from English roots. As a result, no two state court systems are exactly alike.

The early colonies were actually "companies"; that is, they

were corporate entities chartered by the Crown. As such, there was no separation of powers between legislative, executive, and judicial authority; as Lawrence Friedman (1973: 33) notes, "The same people made laws, enforced them, decided cases, and ran the colony." Over time, the increased complexity of colonial life resulted in the establishment of a variety of courts. "Conditions between the time of settlement and Independence were worlds apart; the legal needs of a small settlement run by its clergymen, clinging precariously to the coast of an unknown continent, were fundamentally different from the needs of a bustling commercial state" (Friedman 1973: 29). Branches of government continued to be mixed, however, and it was not unusual for a governor to serve as chief judge of a court of appeals, nor for legislators to serve as justices of a state supreme court, nor for mayors to be empowered as magistrates. There are some remnants of this past in municipalities where the mayor retains the power to serve as a magistrate.

With independence and the subsequent ratification of the United States Constitution, a division of responsibility and hierarchy of function evolved as states began to pattern their system after that of the federal government. A separate judicial branch emerged, and state constitutions began to distinguish between trial courts and courts with appellate jurisdiction. While the court system of each state generally resembled that of the others, each state had a distinct history and no two court systems were, or are, exactly alike. Court reform has occurred in some states, but not yet in others—as we shall see later in this chapter—another reason for differences in state court systems.

THE STRUCTURE OF STATE COURTS

States present a confusing system of courts with names that only add to the confusion. The only way out of this dilemma is to present a generic portrait, a *model court system* that approximates the court system of every state but is not exactly like that of any state. Here we see a diagram of the generic model, and later in the chapter we will see some of the ways that model varies from state to state in diagrams of the court systems of New York, Texas, and Illinois.

Model State Court System

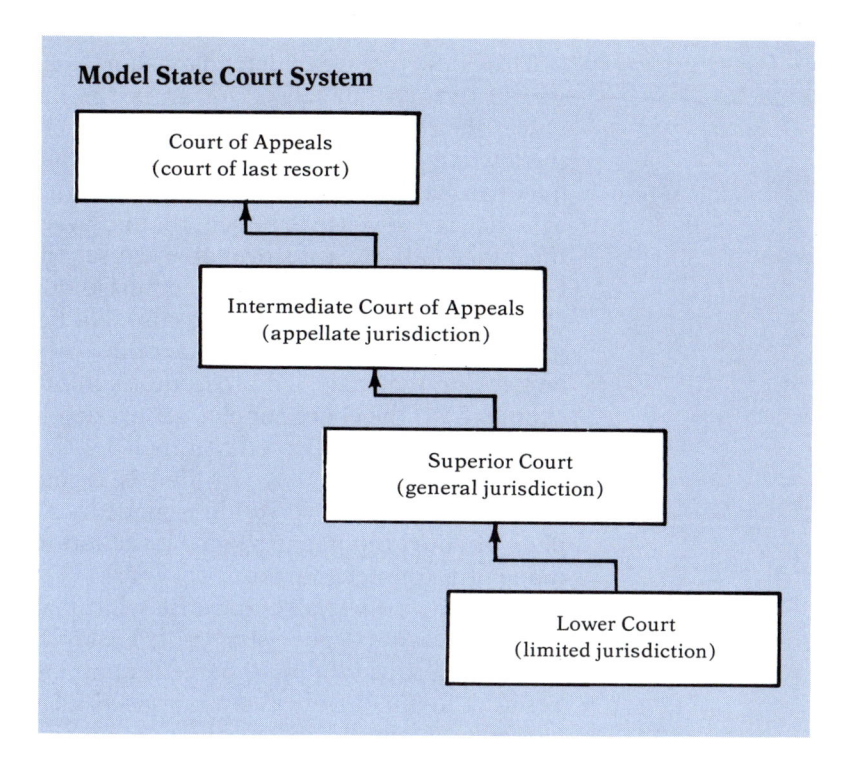

- Court of Appeals (court of last resort)
- Intermediate Court of Appeals (appellate jurisdiction)
- Superior Court (general jurisdiction)
- Lower Court (limited jurisdiction)

Lower Court/Court of Limited Jurisdiction

At the bottom of our model state system is the lower court or the court of limited jurisdiction (sometimes referred to as magistrate court, city or county court, and in some rural areas as justice of the peace court), although some states, such as Illinois, do not have a lower court. (In Illinois and other states with a **unified court system**, misdemeanor cases are handled in the misdemeanor division of the superior court.) In some states, judges (magistrates or justices of the peace) sitting in lower court need not be attorneys. In addition to having authority over civil cases in which the dispute does not involve a sum in excess of some maximum amount—for example, $5,000—the lower court has authority to try misdemeanors, traffic offenses, sometimes juvenile cases, and in many jurisdictions, the lower court is the entry level for felony cases.

This court receives a defendant shortly after an arrest (usually within twenty-four hours) for an initial appearance, which involves the reading of charges and setting of bail. In felony cases, the lower court may arrange for counsel and conduct a preliminary (probable cause) hearing to determine if there is sufficient evidence for the case to be sent (bound over) to superior court. If the judge fails to find probable cause, the case is dismissed. Since this is a court of limited jurisdiction, if the charge or charges constitute a felony, the case will be moved to the grand jury (in states that use this body) or directly to superior court to be tried on the basis of a prosecutor's information (discussed in chapter 5). If the charge or charges are an offense or misdemeanor, the case is adjudicated at this level. The lower court is not necessarily a **court of record**; that is, a court where a verbatim (word-for-word) transcription is made by a high speed stenographer, or court reporter (in some jurisdictions a tape recording is made of the proceedings).

The lower courts also dispense what many observers refer to as *rough justice* (Robertson 1974; Feeley 1979). Because of the heavy caseloads (about 90 percent of all criminal cases are disposed of at this level), there is a need for speed (justice is dispensed very rapidly, in a matter of minutes). Anything that tends to delay case processing is avoided. In minor cases, defendants may be lined up before the bench, or in the aisles, and given a rendering of their rights en masse. Under such circumstances there is obviously very little attention paid to individualized justice and due process. These "niceties" serve to slow down the pace of case processing, and defendants who insist on their rights may be viewed as disruptive. Being disruptive entails costs; the defendant is likely to receive a higher bail or a more severe sentence than is the norm.

John Robertson (1974) argues that rather than serving as a vehicle for seeking truth or resolving conflict, the lower court serves simply as a system of sentencing. On the other hand, the typical case adjudicated in lower court receives rather lenient treatment, a factor for gaining the acquiescence of defendants, few of whom are represented by counsel. For a defendant who is unable to raise the price of bail, a request for counsel may require a continuance and, thus, a return to the county jail to await another court appearance. A plea of guilty, however, may bring a suspended sentence and immediate freedom. Such circumstances obviously provide a great incentive to cooperate and not slow down the system.

Superior Court/Court of General Jurisdiction

A superior court has *general jurisdiction*, meaning that it can try any type of case—offense, misdemeanor, or felony—although this court usually handles only felony cases. The civil division of the superior court will deal with domestic, probate, and divorce cases, as well as disputes involving sums above a certain minimum, for example, $5,000. Most cases entering superior court have been transferred from a lower court directly or via the grand jury. The superior court may also hear appeals from the lower court.

A superior court is a court of record, which means that a transcript is made of the proceedings, which will serve as the data necessary for any subsequent appellate review of a trial (to be discussed below).

As noted above, the superior court receives only a small percentage of the cases entering the criminal justice system. As a result, there is a welcome absence of the hectic pace and noise usually encountered in the lower court. Because of the seriousness of the charges—most cases are felonies—there is usually scrupulous concern for due process lest the case be overturned on appeal. The criminal trials usually portrayed in motion pictures and on television are modeled on superior court trials.

Intermediate Court of Appeals/Appellate Jurisdiction

About half of the states have an intermediate court of appeals, or justices (appellate judges) who sit in panels of three to hear cases appealed from superior court. These courts are called "intermediate" because on the judicial organizational chart they are situated between the superior court and the state's highest court. Historically, this court is the result of an effort by the state legislature to ease the workload of the court of last resort. H. Ted Rubin (1984) states that this purpose has not been accomplished, because more appellate courts seem to encourage more appeals.

Usually there is only one intermediate court of appeals reviewing cases from throughout the state, but in a few populous states there are several divisions of the intermediate appellate court that each cover separate multiple-county districts; Illinois, for example, has five appellate district courts employing thirty-four judges. As opposed to a single-district appellate court located in the state capital, multiple district appellate courts are located throughout the state, making them more accessible. Rubin (1984) notes a major disadvantage of such a system: the decision of one district court of appeals is not binding on the judges in another district.

COURT OF APPEALS/COURT OF LAST RESORT

In states not having an intermediate court of appeals, an appeal goes directly from the superior court to the court of last resort. In states having an intermediate appellate court, however, the highest court's appellate jurisdiction is often discretionary. In other words, except in cases involving capital punishment, this court (like the United States Supreme Court) can decide which cases it will hear. They are likely to be those thought to raise especially important legal questions not previously resolved by the court. This generally involves less than half of the cases brought to the high court's attention.

A court of last resort is usually located in the state capital, although its judges may from time to time sit in other cities in the state for the sake of convenience. For example, in Illinois the court of last resort (called the Supreme Court) is located in the capital, Springfield, but occasionally it sits in Chicago. A court of last resort usually has between five and nine judges, often referred to as "justices." Ordinarily, they do not divide themselves into panels, but rather sit as a group. Lawyers who appear before the state's highest court know in advance that they will be confronted by the full court, and the justices will pepper them with questions about the case. The only avenue of appeal from a decision of a state court of last resort is the U.S. Supreme Court; as noted earlier, the Supreme Court grants *certiorari* in only a fraction of the cases that are appealed.

THE APPELLATE PROCESS

The experienced prosecutor or defense attorney realizes that even if the defendant is convicted in a trial court, an appeal to an appellate court is always a real possibility. The losing lawyer representing the defendant will try to demonstrate to an appellate court that prejudicial errors occurred in the trial court; the prosecutor must be prepared to show that this is not true. Thus, a prosecutor must be mindful of the possibility of an error that could result in an appellate order for a new trial. (Prosecutors are ordinarily not free to appeal in an effort to obtain a new trial since this would place the defendant in double jeopardy, which is prohibited by the Fifth Amendment.)

Trial lawyers—prosecutor or defense—must not only seek to win their cases in the trial (superior) court, but they must do everything they can to generate a record of the trial that will convince an appellate court that justice did or did not prevail. Attorneys must be careful to create a complete and accurate record of the trial because an appellate court can neither speculate about what occurred at the trial nor take on faith an attorney's uncorroborated description of events in the trial court. An appellate court can only act on the formal record of the trial that has been officially transmitted to it by the clerk of the superior court. That record, assembled and bound into one or more volumes after the trial is over, consists of papers in the case, such as the grand jury indictment or any written motions that may have been filed. The record will also contain a "Report of the Proceedings," the verbatim transcript of any on-the-record in-court trial proceedings recorded by the court reporter. There may also be a transcript of any on-the-record pretrial or out-of-court hearings and conferences. Attached to the back of the trial transcript or included in the final volumes of a lengthy record will be the documentary exhibits received in evidence at the trial. Bulky exhibits such as firearms will be tagged for identification and maintained separately from the typed record.

In general, the decision of a trial court judge has no significance beyond the parties immediately affected. It is usually given orally at the conclusion of the trial and is then made into a written order for the judge's signature. If the trial judge renders a written opinion, it is not binding on other judges and is seldom

The Appellate Process

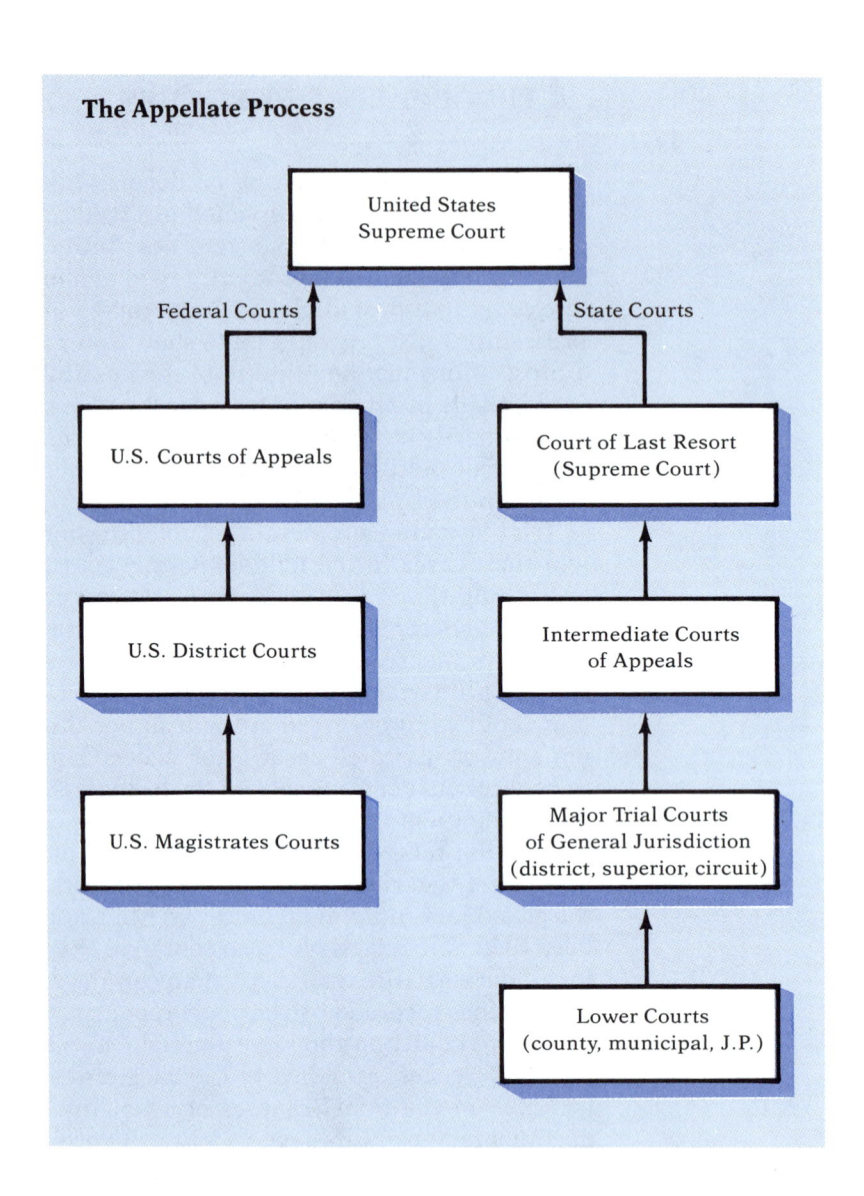

```
                    United States
                    Supreme Court
                         ↑
      Federal Courts ────┴──── State Courts

  U.S. Courts of Appeals      Court of Last Resort
            ↑                    (Supreme Court)
                                      ↑
    U.S. District Courts       Intermediate Courts
            ↑                      of Appeals
                                      ↑
  U.S. Magistrates Courts      Major Trial Courts
                               of General Jurisdiction
                              (district, superior, circuit)
                                      ↑
                                 Lower Courts
                              (county, municipal, J.P.)
```

Organization of the New York State Courts — 1985

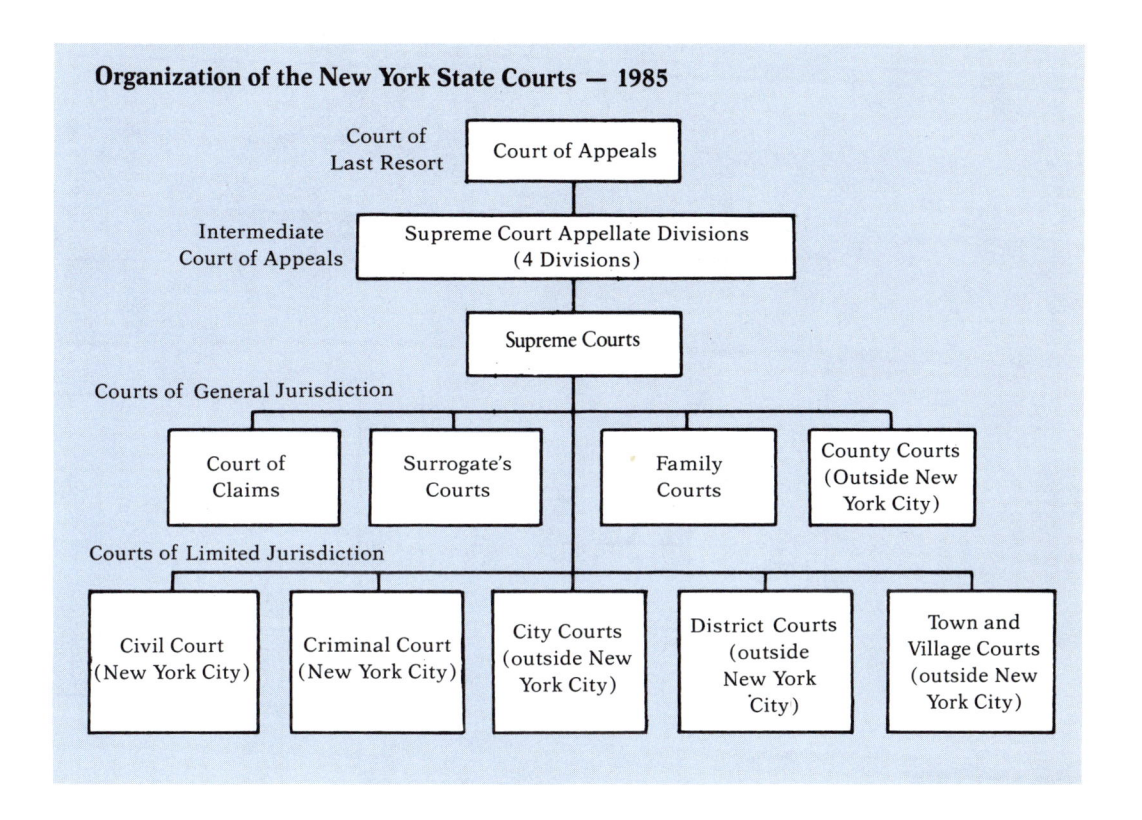

- Court of Last Resort: **Court of Appeals**
- Intermediate Court of Appeals: **Supreme Court Appellate Divisions (4 Divisions)**
- **Supreme Courts**
- Courts of General Jurisdiction: Court of Claims | Surrogate's Courts | Family Courts | County Courts (Outside New York City)
- Courts of Limited Jurisdiction: Civil Court (New York City) | Criminal Court (New York City) | City Courts (outside New York City) | District Courts (outside New York City) | Town and Village Courts (outside New York City)

published for inclusion in a law library. An appellate court decision, on the other hand

> is binding upon all trial courts in that [district or] state. It is "precedent." Legal precedent is necessary to give stability to a legal system. Otherwise a state supreme court might speak one day, a trial court judge a week later could ignore the decision and reach his own, and judges, lawyers, and the general and litigating public would have no standard from which to understand the meaning of the law. (Rubin 1984: 143)

As we noted in the first chapter, appellate court decisions are published in books called reports or reporters. For example, the *National Reporter System* includes the decisions of all state intermediate courts of appeal, all state courts of last resort, and federal courts, including the U.S. Supreme Court.

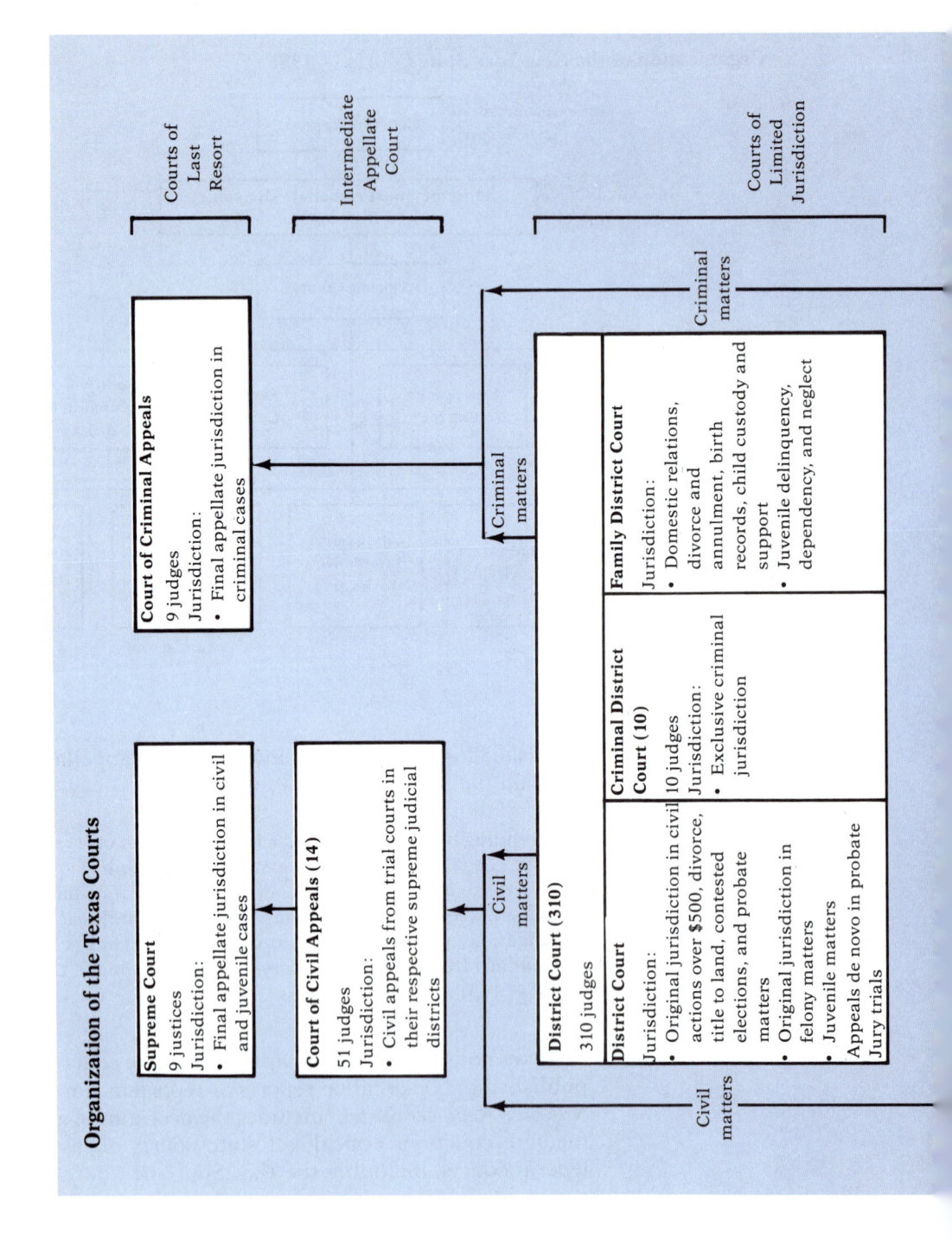

Organization of the Texas Courts

Courts of Last Resort

Supreme Court
9 justices
Jurisdiction:
- Final appellate jurisdiction in civil and juvenile cases

Court of Criminal Appeals
9 judges
Jurisdiction:
- Final appellate jurisdiction in criminal cases

Intermediate Appellate Court

Court of Civil Appeals (14)
51 judges
Jurisdiction:
- Civil appeals from trial courts in their respective supreme judicial districts

Courts of Limited Jurisdiction

District Court (310)
310 judges

District Court
Jurisdiction:
- Original jurisdiction in civil actions over $500, divorce, title to land, contested elections, and probate matters
- Original jurisdiction in felony matters
- Juvenile matters
- Appeals de novo in probate
- Jury trials

Criminal District Court (10)
10 judges
Jurisdiction:
- Exclusive criminal jurisdiction

Family District Court
Jurisdiction:
- Domestic relations, divorce and annulment, birth records, child custody and support
- Juvenile delinquency, dependency, and neglect

Civil matters / *Criminal matters*

County Court (260)
360 judges

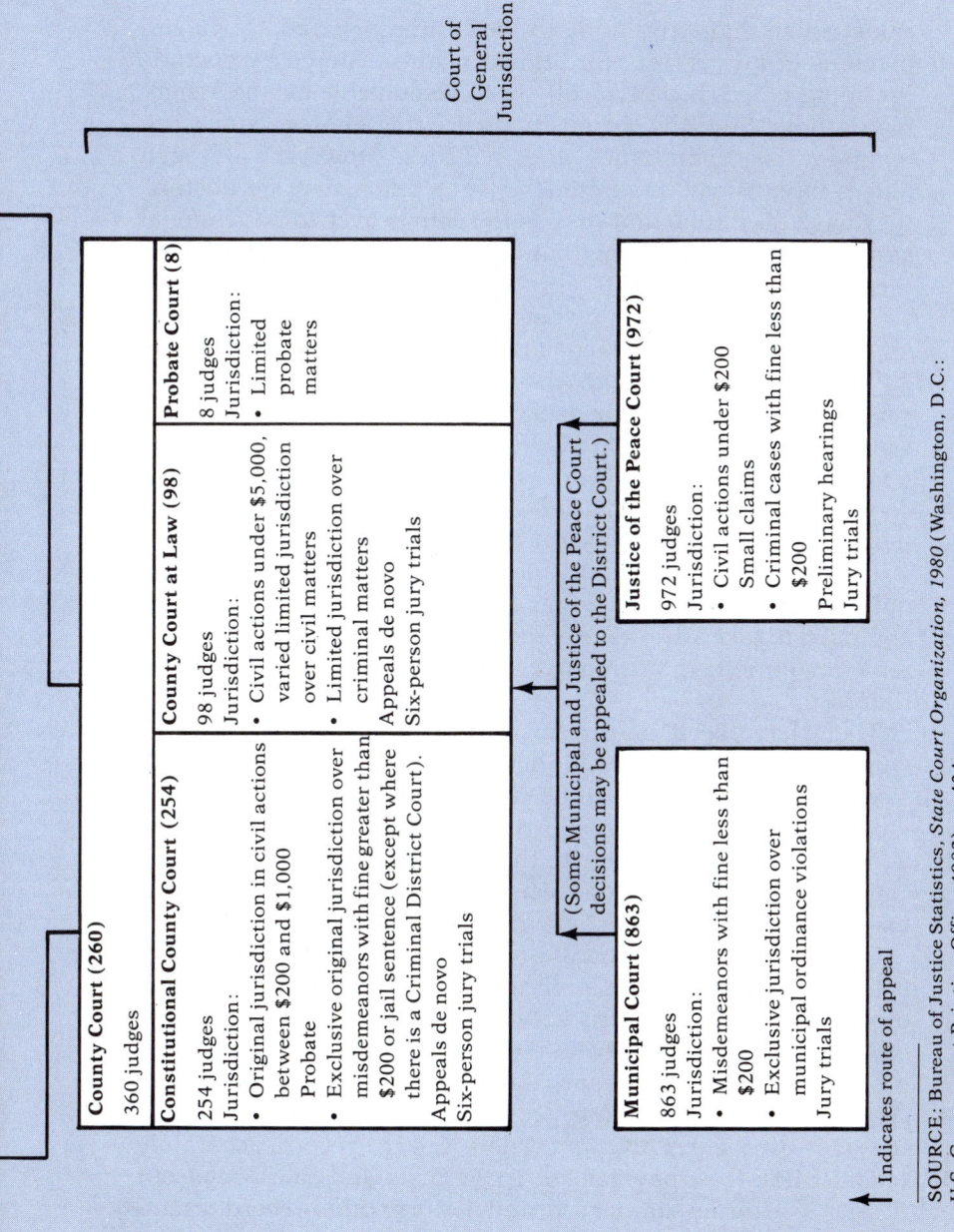

Constitutional County Court (254)	**County Court at Law (98)**	**Probate Court (8)**
254 judges Jurisdiction: • Original jurisdiction in civil actions between $200 and $1,000 Probate • Exclusive original jurisdiction over misdemeanors with fine greater than $200 or jail sentence (except where there is a Criminal District Court). Appeals de novo Six-person jury trials	98 judges Jurisdiction: • Civil actions under $5,000, varied limited jurisdiction over civil matters • Limited jurisdiction over criminal matters Appeals de novo Six-person jury trials	8 judges Jurisdiction: • Limited probate matters

} Court of General Jurisdiction

Municipal Court (863)
863 judges
Jurisdiction:
• Misdemeanors with fine less than $200
• Exclusive jurisdiction over municipal ordinance violations
Jury trials

Justice of the Peace Court (972)
972 judges
Jurisdiction:
• Civil actions under $200
Small claims
• Criminal cases with fine less than $200
Preliminary hearings
Jury trials

(Some Municipal and Justice of the Peace Court decisions may be appealed to the District Court.)

← Indicates route of appeal

SOURCE: Bureau of Justice Statistics, *State Court Organization, 1980* (Washington, D.C.: U.S. Government Printing Office, 1982), p. 434.

Administering the Courts

State courts have traditionally been administered by judges, much as hospitals were traditionally administered by doctors. Presiding judges have typically been responsible for the assigning of judges and the various housekeeping chores required to maintain court buildings and facilities. However, although judges have no more administrative acumen than do doctors, they have been reluctant to turn the courts over to professional administrators, something that has become the norm for hospitals.

The courts suffer from serious maladies; they have traditionally been a center for partisan politics and patronage. While police departments have generally adopted civil service or merit systems for selecting personnel, the courts in general have continued to operate outside of such systems. Because personnel tended to be chosen on the basis of political loyalty rather than competence, technological advances have been slow to enter most court systems. The sight of a clerk's office bulging with written records, filed and misfiled, on shelves and in cabinets is quite fresh in this author's memory. Few court employees were equipped to take advantage of the management information systems revolution; the computer remained a mystery for a long time.

There have been improvements, however. While politics is still part of the courthouse milieu, in many jurisdictions professional administrators have been brought in to handle the various nonlegal tasks required in any courthouse from the buying and changing of lightbulbs to the assigning of court personnel. One of the most difficult aspects of the judicial administrative task is the management of the criminal calendar.

The maintaining of records and the setting of court calendars is the province of the clerk of the court—a very important public official who in some jurisdictions (e.g., Illinois) is elected to office. Rubin (1984: 219) notes "it is no easy task for clerks, particularly in medium- and high-volume courts, to open a record on each new case filing, get the records to the right judge at the right time, enter all court orders into the record, accurately record filing fees, payment of court costs and fines, send out notices to attorneys or parties, and perform other record-oriented functions."

Rubin notes (1984: 212) that "effective criminal calendar

management involves the coordinated scheduling of judges, their clerks, certified shorthand reporters, bailiffs, jurors, prosecutors and defense counsel, jailers, victims, witnesses and expert witnesses [e.g., forensic scientists] and police witnesses, the defendant, and a courtroom."

Court reform

Because federal trial courts do not suffer from the caseload pressures encountered in state trial courts, reform has been focused primarily on state systems. Changes designed to improve state court operations encompass a variety of proposals, the most important being merit selection of judges (which will be discussed in the next chapter), unified courts, and central (statewide) administration (which includes state funding and the use of professional administrators).

Court unification involves the consolidation of the many lower and superior courts into a single or unified court system. This is the system that exists in Illinois (see diagrams of Illinois and Cook County court systems) where the circuit court of each county tries all cases—civil, criminal, and juvenile, misdemeanor and felony. Judges in this system are equal and interchangeable; they receive the same salary and enjoy the same powers and prestige and each judge can preside over any type of case that enters a trial court. In court systems that distinguish between lower courts and superior courts, where the prestige and salaries are different, lower court judges will usually aspire to the higher (superior) bench, and the lower court becomes a training ground and "poor cousin" to the superior court.

Central court administration involves a hierarchical system that combines all administrative responsibility in a single office, usually that of the chief justice of the state court of last resort, or a state court administrator appointed by the chief justice. The central administration will be responsible for the promulgation of rules, assignment of judges, designation of presiding judges of trial courts, disciplining and removing judges for violations of rules or incompetence, and preparing budgets for legislative action. Central administration is designed to provide uniformity and efficiency throughout a state court system and can add such benefits as technical assistance, training, and research.

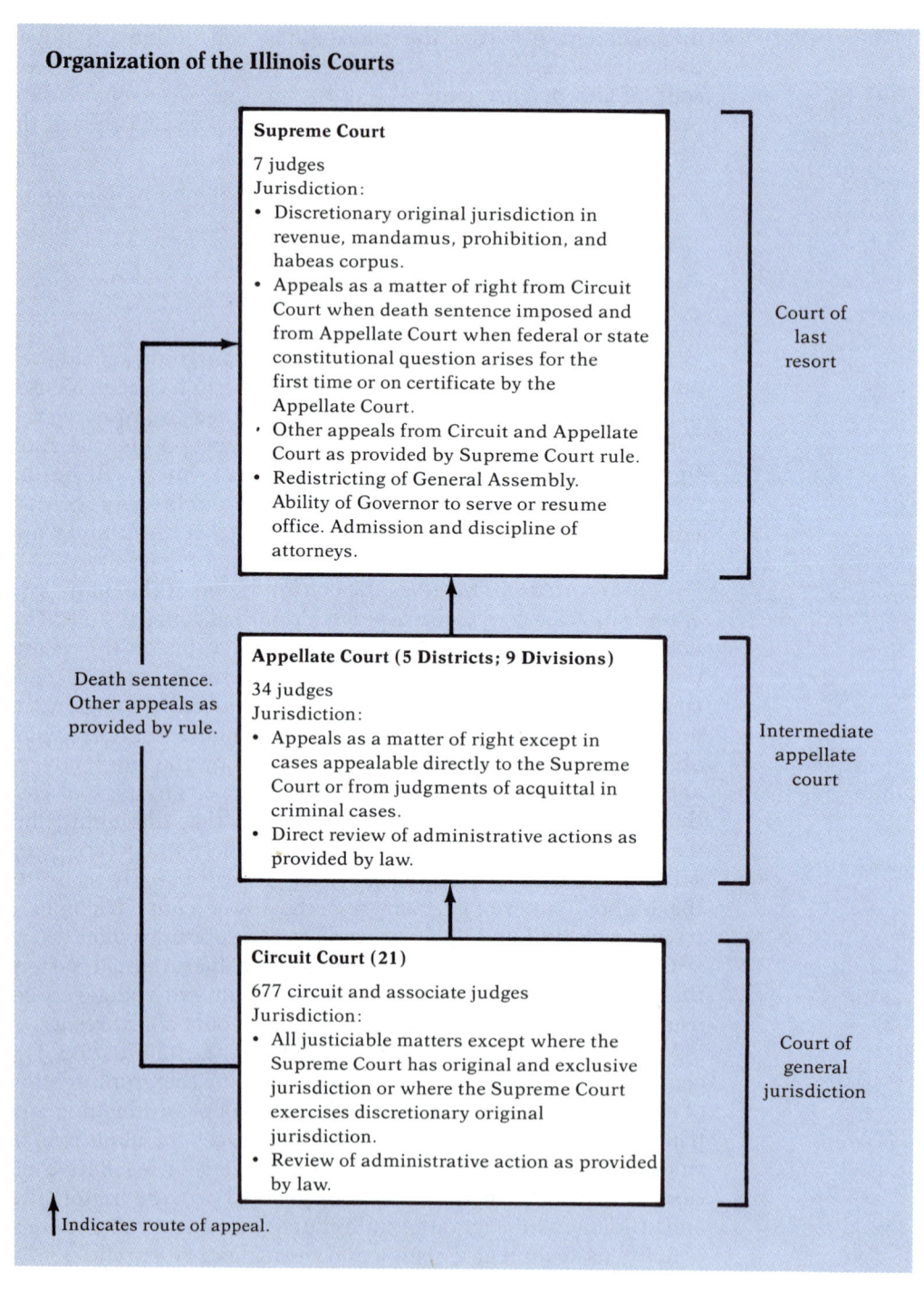

Organization of the Illinois Courts

Supreme Court

7 judges
Jurisdiction:
- Discretionary original jurisdiction in revenue, mandamus, prohibition, and habeas corpus.
- Appeals as a matter of right from Circuit Court when death sentence imposed and from Appellate Court when federal or state constitutional question arises for the first time or on certificate by the Appellate Court.
- Other appeals from Circuit and Appellate Court as provided by Supreme Court rule.
- Redistricting of General Assembly. Ability of Governor to serve or resume office. Admission and discipline of attorneys.

Court of last resort

Appellate Court (5 Districts; 9 Divisions)

34 judges
Jurisdiction:
- Appeals as a matter of right except in cases appealable directly to the Supreme Court or from judgments of acquittal in criminal cases.
- Direct review of administrative actions as provided by law.

Death sentence. Other appeals as provided by rule.

Intermediate appellate court

Circuit Court (21)

677 circuit and associate judges
Jurisdiction:
- All justiciable matters except where the Supreme Court has original and exclusive jurisdiction or where the Supreme Court exercises discretionary original jurisdiction.
- Review of administrative action as provided by law.

Court of general jurisdiction

↑ Indicates route of appeal.

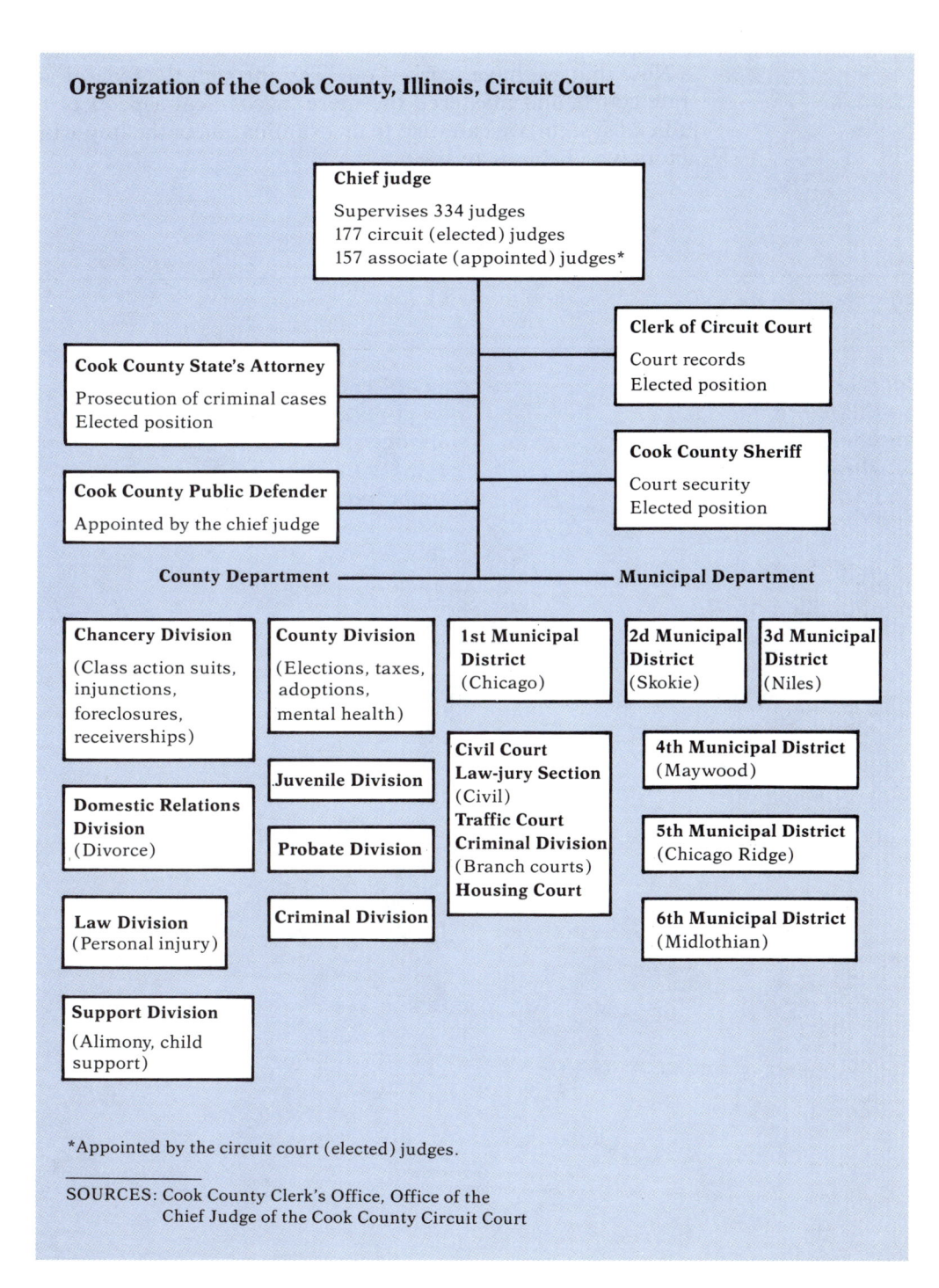

Organization of the Cook County, Illinois, Circuit Court

Chief judge
Supervises 334 judges
177 circuit (elected) judges
157 associate (appointed) judges*

Clerk of Circuit Court
Court records
Elected position

Cook County State's Attorney
Prosecution of criminal cases
Elected position

Cook County Sheriff
Court security
Elected position

Cook County Public Defender
Appointed by the chief judge

County Department — **Municipal Department**

Chancery Division
(Class action suits, injunctions, foreclosures, receiverships)

County Division
(Elections, taxes, adoptions, mental health)

1st Municipal District (Chicago)

2d Municipal District (Skokie)

3d Municipal District (Niles)

Domestic Relations Division (Divorce)

Juvenile Division

Civil Court
Law-jury Section (Civil)
Traffic Court
Criminal Division (Branch courts)
Housing Court

4th Municipal District (Maywood)

Probate Division

5th Municipal District (Chicago Ridge)

Law Division (Personal injury)

Criminal Division

6th Municipal District (Midlothian)

Support Division
(Alimony, child support)

*Appointed by the circuit court (elected) judges.

SOURCES: Cook County Clerk's Office, Office of the Chief Judge of the Cook County Circuit Court

297

Now that we have worked our way through the federal and state courts and mastered the more mechanical aspects of the judicial system, we can turn to an examination of the important actors who bring it to life.

KEY TERMS

courts of general jurisdiction
appellate court
unconstitutional
constitutional law
Marbury v. Madison

court of last resort
writ of *certiorari*
stare decisis
unified court system
court of record

REVIEW QUESTIONS

1. Why is there a dual system of justice in the United States?
2. What does the Constitution provide for with respect to a federal court system?
3. Who can exercise an unofficial veto over the appointment of a federal district court judge?
4. What are the functions of a U.S. magistrate?
5. Who appoints U.S. magistrates?
6. What are the functions of the U.S. Court of Appeals?
7. What is a *writ of certiorari*?
8. What is the basis for a *grant of certiorari* by the Supreme Court?
9. What is the legal precept of *stare decisis*?
10. Why was there no separation of powers in early American colonies?
11. Why is each state court system different from the others?
12. What is meant by a "court of record"?
13. Why have the lower courts been described as dispensing "rough justice"?
14. What is meant by a "court of general jurisdiction"?
15. What was the original purpose of an intermediate court of appeals?
16. What is the advantage and what is the disadvantage of a system of multiple-district appellate courts?
17. Why can't a prosecutor appeal a case that he or she loses?
18. What are the major functions of the court clerk?
19. What are three important proposals for court reform?

CHAPTER 11

The Lawyers: Judge, Prosecutor, Defense Counsel

LEGAL EDUCATION
Langdell and Twentieth-
 Century Legal Education
Legal Education Today

THE LEGAL PROFESSION
National Law Firms
Stratum IV Lawyers

THE JUDGE: ROLES AND RESPONSIBILITIES

SELECTING JUDGES
Executive Appointment
Partisan Election
Nonpartisan Election
Merit/Missouri Plan

PROSECUTORS
Horizontal Prosecution
Vertical Prosecution
Mixed Prosecution

DEFENSE COUNSEL
Private Defense Counsel
Public Defender
Assigned Counsel
Attorney Competency

REVIEW QUESTIONS

In this chapter we will examine the three key actors in the judicial segment of the criminal justice system, all of whom are lawyers. Judges, prosecutors, and defense attorneys share a common education—law school—and, often, a common employment and political background. Thus, it is not unusual to find judges and defense attorneys who at one time were employed as prosecutors, and they will all usually be part of the dominant city or county political organization. In order to better understand the role of the judge, prosecutor, and defense counsel in criminal justice, we must first examine legal education and the legal profession. The values and perceptions of the latter are based on the former—legal education is the basis of a profession that provides the foundation for criminal justice in the United States.

LEGAL EDUCATION

Only a small number of attorneys in the American colonies were trained in England, and some aspiring American lawyers traveled to England to attend the Inns of Court (law schools) in London. Most Americans, however, including such notables as Thomas Jefferson and Abraham Lincoln, gained a legal education through the system of *clerkship*—serving as an apprentice to an established attorney. The law clerk studied the classics of English law as set down by Sir Edward Coke (1551–1634) and Sir William Blackstone (1723–1780), jurists who championed common law over statutory law. "The common law of England evolved from spontaneously observed rules and practices, shaped and formalised by decisions made by judges pronouncing the law in relation to the particular facts before them" (Central Office of Information 1976: 4). "The cementing factor in this process is the principle of *stare decisis*, the legal rule that past precedents determine the outcome of contemporary legal disputes" (Sigler 1968: 12). Statutory law, on the other hand, is enacted by legislative bodies without the restraint of precedent.

In America, an aspiring lawyer read the statutes, copied legal documents and watched his tutor practice law. The first law schools evolved out of this system as some attorneys found the teaching of law more rewarding than the practice of law. The earliest law office/school was established in Litchfield, Connecticut, in 1784; the pressure of competition forced it to cease operations in 1833.

The university law school began to develop at the same time as the clerkship system and the "Litchfield" type school. A chair of law was established at William and Mary College in Virginia as early as 1779, and other schools—the University of Virginia, the University of Pennsylvania, and the University of Maryland—established law professorships by the early part of the nineteenth century. The first university law school was established at Harvard University and began operations in 1817. At Harvard the study of law required three years of undergraduate education and led to the awarding of an LL.B. The school stressed the common law, a pattern that was followed by other university law schools (Friedman 1973). In the two decades before the Civil War, however, interest in a university-based legal education dwindled, and Harvard shortened its curriculum to eighteen months (Seligman 1978).

In 1850 there were fifteen law schools in twelve states, and no law schools in the remaining nineteen states. On the eve of the Civil War, there were only twenty-one law schools in the entire United States. The postwar decades, however, experienced a dramatic growth in formal legal education. There were thirty-one law schools by 1870 and sixty-one by 1890; by 1900, thirty-three states had law schools, and only thirteen small or sparsely populated states had to import formally educated lawyers from other states. Lawrence Friedman (1973: 527) notes that during this period:

> The relationship of law school to university was a far cry from what it became in the twentieth century. The usual law degree, the LL.B., was certainly not a postgraduate degree. It was not standard for law schools to require *any* prior college work. The more pretentious law schools tightened their entrance requirements toward the end of the century; none required a full college education. Many "university" law schools merely coexisted with their parent institutions, to which they were rather loosely connected. They were not an organic part of the general world of scholarship.

Langdell and Twentieth-Century Legal Education

Just as his illustrious namesake had transformed the map of the world, Christopher Columbus Langdell (1826–1906) revolutionized legal education and, indirectly, the legal profession in the United States. Langdell was described as a genius while a student at Harvard, but his entry into trial practice was less than sensational. As a result, he apparently retreated into legal research, and his ability in this area led to a law-firm partnership. In 1870, he was appointed to the newly created position of dean of the Harvard University School of Law—a position he held for twenty-five years, during which time, as Friedman (1973: 530) notes, he turned the school "upside down." First he raised standards for admission; an applicant who did not have a college degree had to pass an entrance exam. The prospective student had to exhibit mastery of Latin or French and was tested on the classic legal reference, Blackstone's *Commentaries*. Despite strong opposition from faculty and students, Langdell instituted written final examinations for each of the required courses in the two-year curriculum. By 1876, the school was encouraging students to pursue a three-year course of study, and in 1899 this

Christopher Columbus Langdell (1826–1906), dean of Harvard University Law School, revolutionized legal education in the United States.

became a formal requirement. Langdell's most controversial and revolutionary change, however, concerned the way the law was taught.

Langdell introduced the **case method**; textbooks were abandoned in favor of casebooks containing appellate court decisions. By reading and analyzing the opinions of appellate judges, the law student learns how to spot similar issues in factually different situations and gains an understanding of judicial thinking. Absent from the curriculum was any discussion of statutes, and Langdell's casebooks were devoid of explanatory notes or comments; there was nothing to aid the student. Classroom lectures often bewildered students as every possible legal principle was extracted from each case. Martin Mayer (1969: 86) refers to Langdell's approach as the *Socratic method*: "By presenting several cases with substantially different facts all resolved by judges on the basis of a similar *ratio decidendi* (reason for the decision), Langdell would force the aspiring lawyer to see what was and was not legally relevant."

By the end of Langdell's first year as dean, the number of students had declined significantly, and in 1872 nearby Boston University opened a law school for students who were not happy with the innovations at Harvard. Contrary to the expectations of his critics, however, Langdell's case method began to gain adherents. Joel Seligman writes (1978: 41), "Enrollment increased. Gradually, the advantages of Langdell's technique became appreciated. By teaching students law from court decisions, an original source, Langdell taught students legal reasoning more effectively than did the textbook professors." Enrollments soared and standards were raised; law at Harvard became a graduate program requiring three years of study. Harvard became the model for other university law schools and the use of the case method spread rapidly; many schools hired Harvard professors and law graduates to help them convert to the new system of teaching law. By 1910 there were 124 law schools using the case method (Mayer 1969). What started as innovation at Harvard led to a revolution and eventually became the norm for legal education in the United States.

Langdell viewed the study of law as a science, and as such politically neutral. Consequently, he "purged from the curriculum whatever touched directly on economic and political questions, whatever was argued, voted on, fought over. He brought into the classroom a worship of common law and of the best common law judges. Legislation [statutory law] he disdained; illogical decisions he despised. All this he cloaked with the mantle of science" (Friedman 1973: 535). The preoccupation with judicial decisions and opinions of the past meant that this legal science would be distinctly conservative. The lawyer qua scientist was to be rigorously educated to serve clients without regard to political beliefs or issues. But who could afford the price of such talented scientists, who had an undergraduate college degree and three years of intensive graduate education? It was apparent that the Harvards of America were preparing lawyers to serve corporate America.

During the same period of time that university law schools and the case method were blooming, an alternate type of school developed in response to the desire of working-class Americans to become lawyers. Friedman (1973) notes that a law school actually required very little capital to open, and in response to market conditions, the local law school, often a night law school, began to proliferate. Night-school students worked during the day and attended classes in the evenings. Some university law schools offered both day and night classes. Education at a local law school was usually quite practical and consisted primarily of the study of local practice and statutes, offerings that were eschewed by Langdell and the case-method university law schools. The graduates of these law schools—immigrants and the sons of immigrants, Irish, Polish, Jewish, and Italian lawyers—served their local communities and filled the ranks of political organizations in the urban areas of America.

Legal Education Today

This history led to a stratification of legal education in the United States which reflects the stratification in the legal profession. Less than twenty schools are consistently referred to as comprising the most prestigious law schools in the United States. It is largely irrelevant whether these schools actually provide a "superior" education; the fact is they are perceived by those who employ law school graduates, particularly national law firms, corporations, and investment banks, as being superior—in this case, perception creates its own reality. Most are private institutions that are part of equally prestigious universities—Chicago, Columbia, Cornell, Duke, Harvard, New York, Northwestern, Stanford, Yale—but several state universities are also prominent—University of California at Berkeley and at Los Angeles, Michigan, Virginia, University of Texas at San Antonio. Some include the Universities of Illinois, Minnesota, North Carolina, Washington, and Wisconsin among the ranks of elite law schools. There is a certain amount of homogeneity across elite schools, since their faculty are generally graduates of elite law schools.

At the middle of the stratification system are law schools that are part of other state or private universities, a number of which are church-affiliated, such as Notre Dame, St. John's, and Loy-

Stratification of Legal Education

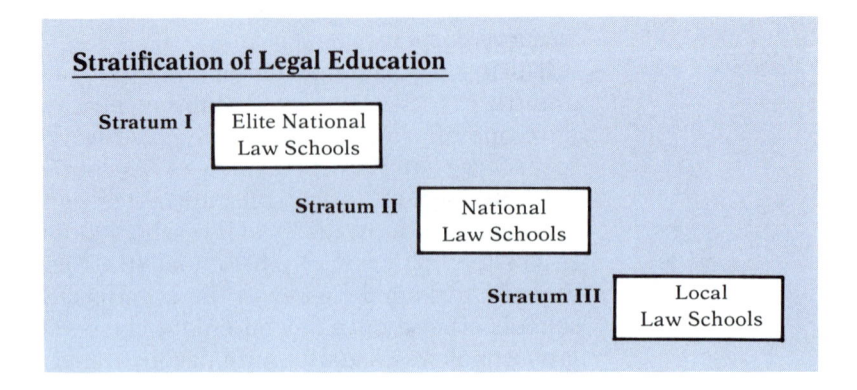

- Stratum I: Elite National Law Schools
- Stratum II: National Law Schools
- Stratum III: Local Law Schools

ola. Top graduates of these institutions, particularly those who have served on law review, may be found in national law firms. At the bottom of the stratification system are law schools which are not part of a larger university, commuter schools which tend to educate local students for a local practice. Graduates of these schools are overrepresented in the ranks of solo practitioners and local government agencies.

THE LEGAL PROFESSION

"The first thing we do, let's kill all the lawyers," a sentiment expressed in William Shakespeare's *King Henry VI, Part II*, which does not fall far from the feelings of many early American colonists. Lawyers were banned in Massachusetts and Connecticut, and the Fundamental Constitutions of the Carolinas declared that it was "a base and vile thing to plead for money or reward." Friedman (1973) notes, however, that if lawyers were an "evil," they became a necessary evil as life in the colonies became more secure and more complex; lawyers flourished amidst animosity. The importance of lawyers by the time of the Revolution is highlighted by the fact that twenty-one of the fifty-six signers of the Declaration of Independence, and thirty-one of the fifty-five delegates to the Constitutional Convention were lawyers (Friedman 1973).

Each colony set its own standards for admission to the bar, which usually involved a long period of apprenticeship. In some areas lawyers formed guilds (bar associations) in an attempt to restrict the entry of new practitioners by holding down the number of apprentices. While there were a variety of bar associations by the early part of the nineteenth century, these groups were not very effective and they failed to exert any real control over who was admitted to the practice of law. Standards were quite lax in most states, and not at all uniform from state to state; government regulation of occupations was quite weak. The American population grew dramatically, and an open-ended bar attracted ambitious, if not talented, persons; by 1850 there were more than 20,000 lawyers in the United States and more than 100,000 by 1900. After 1870, bar associations became vigorous in their fight to limit entry into the practice of law, primarily by way of raising standards. The bar association movement to limit entry coincided with the appointment of Langdell at Harvard and the rise of the case method in legal education—"the two movements went hand in glove" (Friedman 1973: 536). The case method served to define law as a distinct and scientific discipline that required extensive education and training; there was now justification for a monopoly of practice.

For the most part, bar associations represented a distinct part of the legal profession—exclusively white, male, mostly Protestant, and devoid of the immigrant class. This was epitomized by the forming of the American Bar Association (ABA) in 1878 as a "gentlemen's club." As bar associations became more effective, standards for practice were raised. By 1890 nearly half of the states required some minimum preparation for practice, and after 1890 more and more states began requiring minimum levels of education.

At the same time, the legal profession was becoming more and more stratified. Before the Civil War the most prominent lawyers made their reputations in courtrooms and often went into politics—they were great litigators and orators. By the close of the nineteenth century, while most lawyers still went to court, "the Wall Street lawyer, who perhaps never spoke to a judge except socially, made more money and had more prestige than any other lawyer" (Friedman 1973: 549).

The substantial requirements for admittance to the practice of law separated the lawyer from the layman. Restrictions on who could practice law had the effect of creating a "priestly class" whose benedictions could be purchased by those with the necessary fees. Stratification of legal education provided the impetus for a stratified legal profession. Most graduates of elite national law schools went into corporate practice; graduates from local law schools went into local practice.

Stratification was given important impetus by the advent of the **Cravath system.** In 1906 Paul D. Cravath (1861–1940) became the head of an old Wall Street law firm. Cravath, Swaine and Moore, which became the model for other elite national law firms, continues to represent corporate interests (Stewart 1984). Cravath recruited associates right out of law school, thus avoiding experienced lawyers who had developed "bad habits," the ideal candidate being a Phi Beta Kappa and law review editor from Harvard, Columbia, or Yale. "The Cravath system set up an internship for new recruits which was designed to supplement Ivy League law school study with a kind of practical postgraduate induction into corporate lawyering" (Smigel 1964: 88). The system continues today, and each new associate is assigned to work with various partners for rigorous training and responsibility is increased in accord with increasing competency. Training under the Cravath system requires many years, after which the associate usually becomes a partner or leaves the firm: "up or out." There are heavy odds against an associate becoming a partner and, thus, leaving a firm that uses the Cravath system for another firm or position does not carry the slightest suggestion of stigma.

National Law Firms

National law firms in general, and elite law firms in particular, recruit graduates with good grades from the elite law schools, and the top graduates of university law schools. Traditionally, qualifications included lineage—the "right social background"—which had the effect of keeping out many Catholics and Jews, and virtually all blacks, and women, few of whom graduated from prestigious law schools. This has changed with the times, although the law firms representing "blue-chip" corporations remain about 95 percent white (Margolick 1983b). One of the recruitment tools used by these firms is a summer internship, which employs hundreds of senior year students from Ivy League law schools who are paid more than $800 per week. In 1986 the starting salary for a Cravath, Swaine and Moore associate was $65,000. Partners receive no salary, but share in the profits of the firm. "From their plush offices high in

Stratification of the Legal Profession

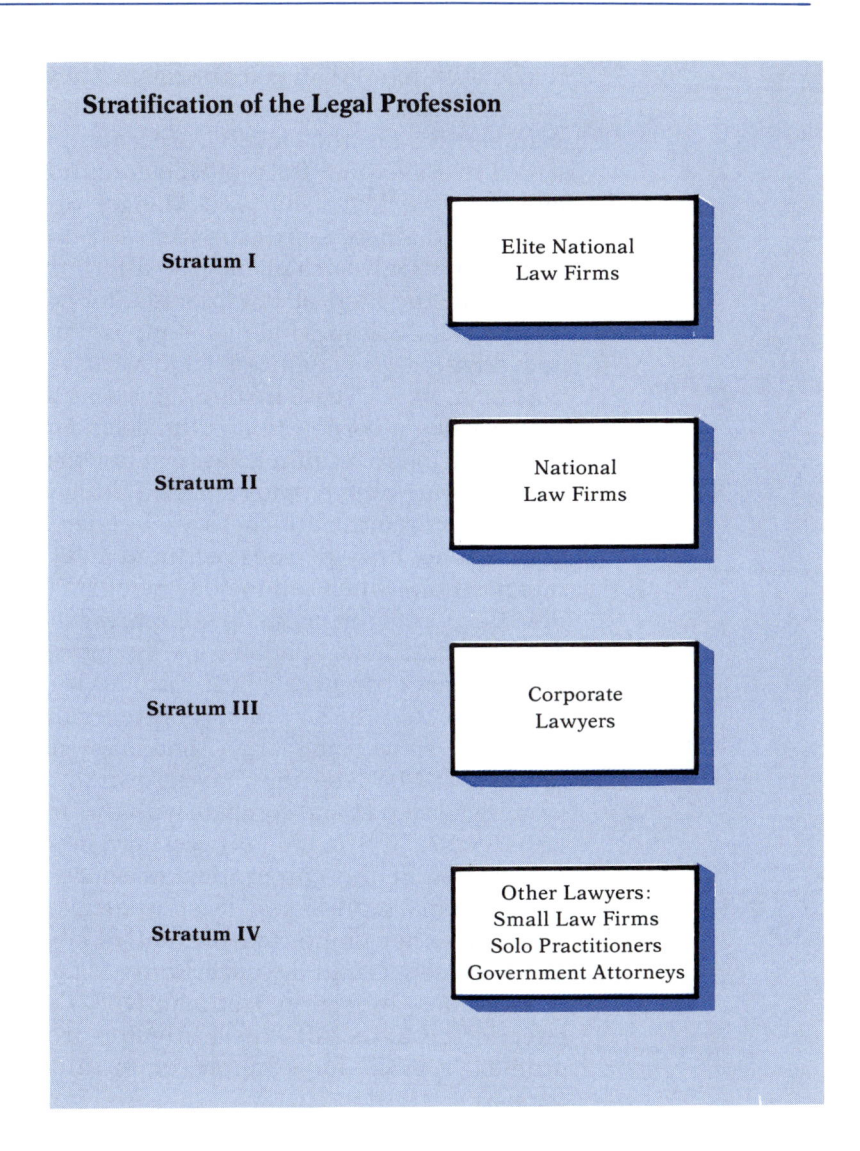

Stratum I	Elite National Law Firms
Stratum II	National Law Firms
Stratum III	Corporate Lawyers
Stratum IV	Other Lawyers: Small Law Firms, Solo Practitioners, Government Attorneys

skyscrapers in the nation's financial centers," says James Stewart (1984: 14), "these lawyers survey the rest of the profession with at least a touch of arrogance and disdain."

The oldest elite firm, Cravath, Swaine and Moore, was founded in 1819; the youngest is Debevoise and Plimpton of New York, founded in 1931. There are about ten elite national law firms, and about fifty national law firms. Each has more than 200 lawyers, the largest being the Chicago firm of Baker and Mackenzie with more than 600 attorneys. They represent the corporate elite, firms found on the *Fortune* magazine "500" list; for example, Exxon, the richest corporation in America, is represented by Baker and Botts of Houston; General Motors is represented by Well, Gotshal and Manges of New York; Cravath, Swaine and Moore represents IBM. As James Stewart (1984: 14) points out, "Only such clients can afford the elite corporate law firms and the kind of law practice for which the firms pride themselves—one in which no stone is left unturned, no matter how seemingly insignificant, and with virtually no regard for time or money." These firms do not deal with criminal matters except when a corporation is the defendant.

In addition to retaining national law firms as *outside counsel*, the corporate elite employ salaried attorneys as *in-house counsel*. These corporate attorneys are frequently "drop-outs" from a national law firm, persons recruited away for a salaried corporate position, which can include being an officer of the corporation. Corporate attorneys do not represent their employer; rather, they provide legal advice for the myriad of routine matters that are part of corporate business activity. Paul Hoffman (1982) points out that the size of corporate legal staffs has grown significantly, some being larger than many national law firms. He says (1982: 28), "Now they have grown so big that they can train their own lawyers and compete with the firms in recruiting from law schools." If litigation is necessary, however, outside counsel will represent the corporation in court. Litigation, however, may actually represent at least a partial failure for a national law firm—they emphasize preventive law, and their goal is to avoid the courts and the uncertainty of trials in favor of private negotiations. In fact, as Hoffman (1982) notes, these firms are often forced to recruit expert litigators from outside, from government service, for example, or to raid rival firms for such persons.

It should be noted that although the "average" partner in a national law firm earns considerably more than attorneys in general, some Stratum IV attorneys earn considerably more than most partners in elite law firms. This is because personal-injury lawyers usually work on the basis of a **contingency fee**, meaning they receive a portion (usually one-third) of any judgment, which, in some cases, can be quite substantial. Indeed, there is a society of attorneys, the Circle of Advocates, who have won at least one million-dollar judgment, and they earn many times the average income of partners in national law firms (J.

"Yes, sir, I threw it at our legal types, and—uh—they say it's illegal."

Jenkins 1984). The contingency fee is a result of the realization that, without legal counsel, adequate compensation could not be secured for poor persons injured or killed in work- or transportation-related accidents. The contingency fee arrangement was opposed by bar associations dominated by Stratum I, II, and III attorneys who, in addition to having no need for a contingency fee, often represent the defendants in personal injury cases.

Stratum IV Lawyers

The majority of America's more than 700,000 licensed lawyers are at Stratum IV, including the judges, prosecutors, and defense attorneys who are the subjects of the rest of this chapter. Solo practitioners and those practicing in two- or three-lawyer firms constitute about two-thirds of all practicing attorneys. Small firms, those with between four and eleven lawyers, account for about 20 percent of all private practitioners. About ten percent of all lawyers work for government, mostly at the state and local level (Curran 1983). There are roughly 30,000 attorneys who handle criminal cases more than just occasionally, and a substantial number of them work for government as public defenders or prosecutors. Relatively few private attorneys handle only criminal cases, and Paul Wice (1983) states that the absolute number of criminal lawyers in private practice is declining. (We will examine the reasons for this decline later in this chapter.)

THE JUDGE: ROLES AND RESPONSIBILITIES

Sitting on a high bench and attired in formal black robes, criminal court judges are responsible for a variety of pretrial activities:

1. they issue warrants;
2. they insure that defendants are informed of the charge(s) and are represented by counsel;
3. they set and revoke bail;
4. they hold probable cause hearings;
5. they send cases to the grand jury or superior court; and
6. they rule on pretrial motions (e.g., to exclude certain evidence).

Judges preside at criminal trials; in this capacity they serve as referees: they enforce procedural rules and are guarantors of a fair trial. If a defendant opts for a bench trial (waives the right to be tried before a jury), the judge will not only be the final arbiter of the law, but will also act as a factfinder. If the defendant (or the prosecutor who, in most states and in the federal judicial system, has the right to demand a jury trial) chooses a jury trial, the judge explains the substantive principles of law as they are to be applied by the jurors. If a defendant is found guilty after a plea or a trial, the judge must impose a sentence. Trial judges also conduct violation-of-probation hearings (discussed in chapter 13). Appellate court judges review criminal cases on appeal, and all judges have administrative responsibilities that range from setting dates for hearing motions and trials to the more elaborate tasks of presiding judges that were discussed in the last chapter.

How do you judge a judge? A judge must be fair and impartial. As an attorney he or she is expected to understand and adhere to the rules of law and proper judicial procedure. The cases presided over by a trial judge should not be the subject of successful appeals; the frequency of reversals is a measure of judicial competence. The courtroom should be a place of quiet dignity, and a judge is expected to display proper judicial temperament. According to the Task Force on Administration of Justice (1967: 66), "When judges are rude or inconsiderate or permit their courtrooms to become noisy, crowded dispensaries of rapid-fire justice, public confidence in the fairness and effectiveness of the criminal process is diminished."

Selecting Judges

While "judging a judge" is a difficult task, selecting lawyers to be judges presents enormous obstacles. According to the Task Force on Administration of Justice (1967: 66), "Although it is possible to identify such factors as professional incompetence, laziness, or intemperance which should disqualify a lawyer from becoming a judge, it is much more difficult to choose confidently the potentially superior judge from among a number of aspirants who appear generally qualified."

There are three basic methods for selecting judges: executive appointment, election (partisan/nonpartisan), and the merit/ Missouri Plan. Let us examine and compare the advantages and disadvantages of each.

Executive Appointment

In the federal system all judges—district court, court of appeals, Supreme Court—are appointed to lifetime terms by the president, subject to confirmation by the United States Senate. A potential nominee for a federal bench is first subjected to a background check by the FBI. His or her name is then sent to the Senate where the Judiciary Committee holds hearings on the appointment. In most cases the committee recommends that the nominee be approved by the full Senate, and the Senate usually confirms the president's choice. In a few cases, the Senate has refused to confirm a nominee—as was the case with two of the Supreme Court candidates submitted by President Richard Nixon, for example.

The American Bar Association plays an unofficial but often crucial role in the process. The ABA Committee on Judicial Selection reviews the background of potential candidates by consulting with knowledgeable members of the legal profession. It then ranks the candidates: (*a*) exceptionally well-qualified, (*b*) well-qualified, (*c*) qualified, and (*d*) unqualified. Traditionally, in order to avoid nominating a candidate who might be rated "unqualified" by the ABA, the attorney general's office requests the ABA ratings prior to the president's making an official nomination.

Senatorial courtesy requires that the president consult with the senior senator of his or her party before filling a judicial vacancy in that senator's state. If the state with a judicial vacancy does not have a senator of the president's party, the senior member of the party's congressional delegation from that state will be consulted. The failure to do so will make the nomination "personally obnoxious" to the senator, and the Senate, as a "gentlemen's club," will decline to approve the nomination. While senators cannot impose their choices on the president, they can veto a nominee and in practice, the choice of a district court judge is usually left to the senator.

Executive appointment on the state and sometimes municipal levels involves a nomination by the governor, or mayor for some lower courts. The process is basically the same as in the federal system. Potential candidates are investigated by the state police or other state investigators. The governor, usually after conferring with state bar association officials, submits a nomination to the state senate. The senate judiciary committee then holds hearings on the nominee and makes a recommendation to the senate for or against confirmation. State legislators, unlike U.S. senators, do not normally enjoy the prerogative of senatorial courtesy.

Advantages

Executive appointment requires a president or governor or mayor to make a nomination for a judicial vacancy, and the executive becomes closely identified with the candidate. Since most official actions of a chief executive are newsworthy, the nomination of a candidate for judicial office will usually generate considerable coverage by the news media. The nominee's background will be reviewed by reporters, and any defects uncovered will become the subject of newspaper, television, and radio coverage. Thus, the advantage of appointing judges is the accountability that accompanies the process; a chief executive will try to avoid nominating a candidate who may become a political liability or cause personal embarrassment. The chief executive is likely to carefully examine a potential candidate, with not only a background check by investigators but also consultation with knowledgeable members of the legal community—law professors, bar association committees—as well as civic associations, public interest organizations, and community groups.

Disadvantages

The appointment of a judge by a chief executive is often a highly partisan act, meaning that only persons who have made political or financial contributions are likely to be chosen. (As the late Mayor Richard Daley of Chicago said to news media critics of patronage: "What do you expect me to do, appoint my enemies?") Political considerations, as opposed to selecting the best qualified candidate, are the norm for judicial appointments.

Partisan Election

A partisan election means that a candidate for judicial (or any other) office appears on the ballot identified with a particular political party, usually Republican or Democrat. In order to appear on the ballot, an aspiring judge must secure a certain number of signatures of registered voters on a nominating petition—several hundred or several thousand, depending on the size of the jurisdiction and the election laws of the state. If two or more Democrats or Republicans submit qualifying petitions, they must face off in a party primary election, and the winner earns the right to be the Republican or Democratic candidate; his or her name will appear on the general election ballot identified with the party whose primary he or she won. The winner of the general election becomes (or is reelected) a judge.

Advantages

The partisan election of judges is part of the American tradition of participatory democracy. Judges, as public servants, should stand before the voters identified as Democrats or Republicans as do officials in the other branches of government, the chief executives and legislators. Furthermore, as Martin Levin (1977: 15) notes, "popular participation is particularly important in creating legitimacy for the judges' decisions. Since judges are policymakers, . . . removing them from popular control makes the court an undemocratic institution."

Disadvantages

Securing a position on the ballot and winning a primary election requires an organized political effort—the specialty of Republican and Democratic organizations. Winning a primary election for judicial office against an established political organization is always difficult, and often impossible. The backing of a party organization is essential because the electorate is seldom familiar with candidates for judicial office and judicial candidates are restricted by the legal canon of ethics from taking positions on politically controversial issues.

A judge in New York, Samuel I. Rosenman, relates his experience as a partisan candidate:

> I learned at first hand what it means for a judicial candidate to have to seek votes in political club houses, to ask for the support of political district leaders, to receive financial contributions for his campaign from lawyers [which raises the question of conflict of interest] and others, and to make non-political speeches about his own qualifications to audiences who could not care less—audiences who had little interest in any of the judicial candidates, of whom they had never heard, and whom they would never remember. . . . Their concern is centered on the executive and legislative candidates because these candidates are identified with the only issues and causes which interest the voters. Most often, when they reach the judicial candidates down on the ballot, they vote blindly for the party emblem [or they fail to vote for judicial candidates altogether]. (Task Force on Administration of Justice 1967: 66–67)

In practice, it is the local Democrat or Republican leadership that determines who will be "slated" (picked as the party candidate) for judicial office. In areas where one party is clearly dominant, being slated for judicial office by that party is tantamount to being elected. A study of partisan elections in New York revealed that "eighty-seven percent of the elections for New York State Supreme Court [superior court] justice in the last six years were either uncontested or noncompetitive" (Lynn 1984: 18). Thus, in effect, a system of partisan elections usually means the local party leadership selects judges, even though this decision requires ratification by the voters. The party leadership is not accountable to the public, and the selection of judges is invariably based on partisan political considerations; thus, judicial office is simply an important aspect of a larger system of patronage. Highly qualified attorneys who are unwilling to participate in the activities of the dominant political party will not receive serious consideration for judicial office.

Political reporter David Axelrod (1983: 4), in his argument against electing judges, provided an insightful anecdote:

> A few years ago, a Circuit Court judge, who had spent more time with a bottle of blended whiskey than a volume of revised statutes, offered a surprisingly candid self-analysis. "You know, I may not be much of a judge," the boozy jurist cheerily confided . . . , "but I'm one hell of a precinct captain."

Nonpartisan Election

A nonpartisan election for judicial office is much like its partisan counterpart: aspiring candidates must secure a certain minimum number of signatures of registered voters on qualifying petitions in order to have their names appear on the ballot. The only significant difference is that candidates are not identified with a political party on the ballot, and there is no primary election.

Advantages

The nonpartisan election is designed to remove political party politics from the judicial selection process. In theory, at least, being a Democrat or a Republican is irrelevant in nonpartisan elections.

Disadvantages

The lack of a party label nullifies whatever responsibility political party leaders feel to provide competent candidates for judicial office. It is the system with the *least amount of accountability*. In an editorial, the *Journal of the American Judicature Society* (1964:48:124–25) referred to the nonpartisan election of judges as the worst of all the traditional methods used to select judges in the United States; under this system, "having the same name as a well-known public figure, a large campaign fund, a pleasing TV image, or the proper place on the ballot are far more influential in selecting judges than character, legal ability, judicial temperament or distinguished experience on the bench."

Merit/Missouri Plan

The **merit selection** of judges was first adopted for appellate and trial court judges in St. Louis and Kansas City in 1940, thus the name "Missouri Plan." There are a number of variations of the plan in other states, but they all follow a similar formula that includes aspects of executive appointment and nonpartisan election. There is a "blue-ribbon" judicial nominating commission, whose members are lawyers chosen by the bar association, citizen representatives chosen by the governor (e.g., business and labor leaders), and a sitting judge(s) chosen by the state's highest court. The commission submits a list of candidates (usually three names) for each judicial vacancy to the governor, who must appoint one of these persons. The person appointed serves for one year and is then subjected to a retention vote, which permits the public to decide if the judge should remain in office. The judge runs unopposed; the public votes yes or no to the question: "Should Judge _____ be retained?" If the judge is retained, he or she will serve for life or for a very long term.

Advantages

The primary argument in support of the merit plan is that it avoids the disadvantages of the other methods for selecting judges. Says Martin Levin (1977: 13), "The substantive argument is that these expert, nonpolitical, and independent selection procedures will produce higher quality, more efficient, more independent, and therefore more impartial and just judges." The merit plan significantly reduces the influence of political party leadership in selecting judges.

Disadvantages

As noted earlier in this section, it is not an easy task to predetermine whether a person will be a mediocre judge or an outstanding judge; in fact, there is little agreement about specifically what such terms mean. What the merit plan does is remove judicial selection from any type of accountability; "Who picked this judge?" has no real answer. What the merit plan tends to accomplish is not the selection of better judges, whatever that means, but the selection of judges who more closely represent the interests of leadership of the bar association and business. Politics is not absent; it has simply moved from the clubhouse to the private club. Furthermore, during his or her first year on the bench, prior to the retention vote, a judge is likely to keep a low profile and to avoid making any controversial decisions, even if they may be legally correct.

PROSECUTORS

Criminal justice in the United States is based on an adversarial system, and the prosecutor is one of its cornerstones. Like the police, prosecutors are responsible for enforcing the law, and in so doing act in the name of "the people" (actually in the name of the United States or a particular state). Unlike the police, however, prosecutors have an additional responsibility—justice. A police officer who has probable cause of a felony must arrest the suspect. Prosecutors, however, as "officers of the court" and public officials, have a dual role; they must not only enforce the law, but they must also be concerned with the possibility of prosecuting an innocent person. While the police require only probable cause to arrest, a prosecutor requires proof "beyond a reasonable doubt" to convict. This explains why cases brought by the police are often dismissed or *nolle prosequi* (or simply "nol pros") by a prosecutor. Differing levels of proof also play an important role in plea bargaining, which will be discussed in the next chapter.

For three reasons, a prosecutor is the most powerful person in the criminal justice system:

1. The prosecutor is an independent official in the executive branch of government who, in most jurisdictions, is answerable only to the electorate.
2. The prosecutor has virtually unlimited authority to decide

whether or not a person will be prosecuted. Unless corruption or malfeasance can be proved, his or her decision is final.
3. The prosecutor has sole discretion to determine the charges for which an arrestee will be prosecuted.

(How these powers are used is the subject of the next chapter.)

The chief prosecutor for the United States government is the attorney general, a presidential appointee who is a member of the cabinet. The president appoints a United States attorney in each of the ninety-four federal judicial districts. The U.S. attorneys appoint assistant U.S. attorneys in their district.

Within the states—except in Alaska, Connecticut, Delaware, and Rhode Island—the prosecutor is an elected county (or judicial district) official. In order to win an election, the prosecutor obviously needs the support of a political organization, and traditionally the office of prosecutor has been an important source of political patronage. It can also be used to investigate and harass political enemies. The office of prosecutor on a federal, state, or county level can provide the exposure necessary for political advancement. Most prosecutors aspire to higher office, and many important public officials were at one time prosecutors.

Each prosecutor (sometimes called a district attorney, county attorney, or state's attorney) employs a number of assistant or deputy prosecutors, some of whom may be part-time. Most of these assistants are recent graduates from law school who are using the prosecutor's office as an opportunity to gain trial experience. A typical assistant works for about three years and then enters private practice, often to do criminal defense work. The prosecutor's office, then, is characterized by a great deal of turnover, sometimes due to electoral politics, but more often as a result of assistants leaving for more lucrative legal work in private practice.

Most assistants are not graduates of prestigious national law schools, although those in some prosecutor's offices are an exception. The office of the New York (Manhattan) County District Attorney has had an outstanding reputation ever since Thomas E. Dewey was elected to the position in 1937. When Dewey, a Republican, became governor, he was succeeded by his assistant, Frank S. Hogan, a Democrat, who remained district attorney for thirty-four years until his retirement. The nonpolitical nature of the office and its reputation for excellence attracts many law school graduates who might otherwise go into corpo-

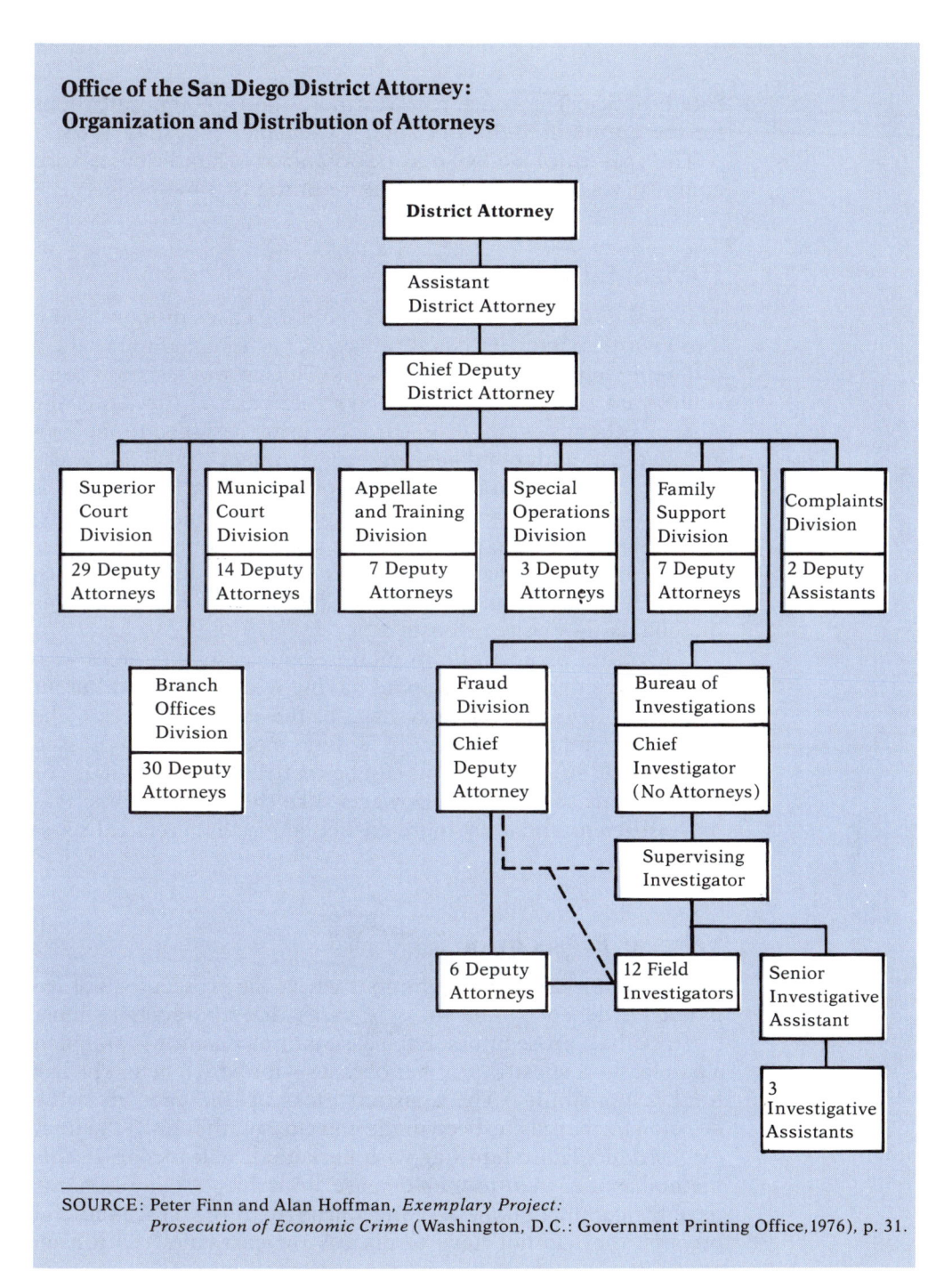

Office of the San Diego District Attorney: Organization and Distribution of Attorneys

```
                          ┌─────────────────────┐
                          │  District Attorney  │
                          └──────────┬──────────┘
                                     │
                          ┌──────────┴──────────┐
                          │     Assistant       │
                          │  District Attorney  │
                          └──────────┬──────────┘
                                     │
                          ┌──────────┴──────────┐
                          │   Chief Deputy      │
                          │  District Attorney  │
                          └──────────┬──────────┘
                                     │
   ┌──────────┬──────────┬───────────┼───────────┬──────────┬──────────┐
┌──┴───┐  ┌───┴───┐  ┌───┴────┐  ┌───┴────┐  ┌───┴────┐  ┌──┴──────┐
│Sup.  │  │Munic. │  │Appell. │  │Special │  │Family  │  │Complaints│
│Court │  │Court  │  │and     │  │Oper.   │  │Support │  │Division  │
│Div.  │  │Div.   │  │Training│  │Division│  │Division│  │          │
│      │  │       │  │Division│  │        │  │        │  │          │
└──┬───┘  └───┬───┘  └───┬────┘  └───┬────┘  └───┬────┘  └────┬─────┘
┌──┴───┐  ┌───┴───┐  ┌───┴────┐  ┌───┴────┐  ┌───┴────┐  ┌────┴─────┐
│29    │  │14     │  │7 Deputy│  │3 Deputy│  │7 Deputy│  │2 Deputy  │
│Deputy│  │Deputy │  │Attorney│  │Attorney│  │Attorney│  │Assistants│
│Attor.│  │Attor. │  │        │  │        │  │        │  │          │
└──────┘  └───┬───┘  └────────┘  └───┬────┘  └───┬────┘  └──────────┘
              │                      │           │
        ┌─────┴─────┐          ┌─────┴────┐ ┌────┴──────────┐
        │Branch     │          │ Fraud    │ │Bureau of      │
        │Offices    │          │ Division │ │Investigations │
        │Division   │          │          │ │               │
        └─────┬─────┘          │Chief     │ │Chief          │
        ┌────┴──────┐          │Deputy    │ │Investigator   │
        │30 Deputy  │          │Attorney  │ │(No Attorneys) │
        │Attorneys  │          └─────┬────┘ └────┬──────────┘
        └───────────┘                │           │
                                     │     ┌─────┴─────┐
                                     │     │Supervising│
                                     │     │Investigator│
                                     │     └─────┬─────┘
                             ┌───────┴──┐  ┌─────┴────┐  ┌──────────┐
                             │6 Deputy  │  │12 Field  │  │Senior    │
                             │Attorneys │  │Investig. │  │Investig. │
                             └──────────┘  └──────────┘  │Assistant │
                                                         └────┬─────┘
                                                         ┌────┴─────┐
                                                         │3 Investig│
                                                         │Assistants│
                                                         └──────────┘
```

SOURCE: Peter Finn and Alan Hoffman, *Exemplary Project: Prosecution of Economic Crime* (Washington, D.C.: Government Printing Office, 1976), p. 31.

rate practice. The office receives more than 1,500 applications for the approximately fifty annual vacancies (Barzilay 1983).

The prosecutor's office may be organized to handle cases horizontally, vertically, or by a mixture of the two methods.

Horizontal Prosecution

This is the predominant mode of handling cases in more populous counties. Each assistant prosecutor is assigned to handle a different step in the judicial process. Thus, some assistant prosecutors are assigned to receive and screen cases as they enter the system; other assistant prosecutors who are assigned to the lower court deal with bond hearings, arraignments, probable cause hearings, offenses, and misdemeanor cases. If a felony case is sent to the grand jury or superior court, it is managed by assistants assigned to the grand jury or superior court. If a case is appealed, it is handled by assistants who specialize in appeals. (Those who are familiar with basketball will recognize this method as the "zone defense.")

Horizontal prosecution in more serious cases—felonies—results in a victim or complainant having to deal with a different assistant prosecutor at each stage of the judicial process. The victim or complainant often feels that he or she is being tossed about in the system, and this can be costly in terms of victim or complainant cooperation. However, like the assembly line it is more efficient and thus more cost-effective than vertical prosecution.

Vertical Prosecution

This system is used in jurisdictions where the prosecutor's office is not burdened by the mass of cases that characterize most metropolitan prosecutors. Each assistant prosecutor is assigned a caseload—a specific number of cases—for which he or she has total responsibility. The assistant picks up the case after the decision to charge has been made and stays with it until the final disposition. (Those familiar with basketball will recognize this method as the "man-to-man defense.") Victims or complainants have the comfort of one assistant throughout the entire judicial process; they do not have to discuss the case anew with each assistant.

Unfortunately, this method can be quite costly in terms of

personnel. As noted in the last chapter, it is often difficult to gather all of the primary and secondary actors in court at the same time, with the necessary files and exhibits needed for a case to move forward. Quite often an assistant prosecutor will be prepared for trial, but other actors or records will be missing, and the case will be rescheduled (a continuance). With horizontal prosecution, the assistant will simply deal with the next case that is called. With vertical prosecution, the entire day may be wasted.

Mixed Prosecution

This system takes advantage of the strengths inherent in horizontal and in vertical prosecution. Most routine cases will be handled in a horizontal (cost-effective) manner—assistants are assigned to different stages of the judical process. Certain targeted cases, however, such as those involving organized crime or serious repeat offenders, will be subjected to vertical prosecution. In using a mixed-prosecution system, prosecutors may set up a *rackets bureau* or a *serious offender bureau*, with assistants and investigators who have special training and skills in dealing with these types of cases. Other special prosecutorial units utilizing a vertical approach may deal with homicide, serious sex offenses, or crimes against the elderly.

Defense counsel

Within the system of adversarial justice the defense counsel has a singular purpose: as an advocate he or she must use every lawful means to exonerate the accused or, failing that, to mitigate punishment. Questions of justice, of guilt or innocence, which should concern the prosecutor, are not the responsibility of **defense counsel**.

The Sixth Amendment provides that "the accused shall enjoy the right . . . to have the assistance of counsel for his defense." In 1928 the Supreme Court ruled (*Johnson v. Zerbst*) that an indigent is entitled to counsel in a federal criminal prosecution. In 1932 the Supreme Court ruled (*Powell v. Alabama*) that an indigent defendant accused of a capital offense in a state court is also entitled to counsel at public expense. In 1963 the Court ruled

In 1931 nine black youths were arrested in Scottsboro, Alabama, and charged with raping two white girls on a freight train. Found guilty in three trials that received international attention, their convictions were reversed twice by the Supreme Court. The Court first ruled in *Powell v. Alabama* that defendants in capital cases must be represented by counsel. The decision, along with *Norris v. Alabama* (which affirmed the right of blacks to serve on grand and trial juries), has become a landmark of U.S. constitutional law.

(*Gideon v. Wainwright*) that all indigent defendants accused of felonies are entitled to counsel at state expense. In 1972 the Court (*Argersinger v. Hamlin*) extended the right to counsel for indigent defendants accused of misdemeanors for which the penalty includes possible imprisonment.

There are three ways to accomplish the right to counsel: engaging a private attorney, using the public defender, or being assigned counsel by the court.

Private Defense Counsel

The professional and private lifestyle of the criminal attorney usually falls far short of the glamourous portrayals in books, in movies, and on television. In his book on criminal lawyers, Paul Wice (1978) presents a portrait that is much more accurate—and rather depressing: he (most criminal defense lawyers are male) must be continually concerned about securing clients, and in some jurisdictions this requires unlawful kickbacks to other persons working in criminal justice, such as police officers and bailiffs, for referrals; he must worry about being paid because his clients are usually poor and, since they are not drawn from the ranks of Boys Scouts, they may refuse to pay when a case is over; the hours are long and a great deal of time is spent simply waiting in, or traveling to, courthouses. Wice (1978: 129) describes a typical daily routine.

> The private criminal lawyer is usually at his office for an hour or two prior to his morning court appearance and will return there in the late afternoon for a few additional hours. He may also be found in his office on weekends and on those rare days when no court appearances are required. For the bulk of the day, however, the criminal lawyer will be in the courthouse. His time will be spent roaming hallways, waiting for appointments, chatting with his fellow practitioners over rancid coffee, and occasionally carrying out his professional responsibilities before a judge.

The private practice of criminal law is not only physically demanding, but, Wice (1978: 91) notes, it has significant social and psychological costs:

> The private criminal lawyer obviously suffers from guilt by association. The public reflexively links the client with his attorney and

fails to appreciate the professional and constitutional responsibility which the latter must exercise. The public seems to reason that if a lawyer chooses to defend a guilty man, then the lawyer must himself also be tainted with some guilt.

Because his clients are poor financial risks, the private criminal attorney usually requires at least part of his fee in advance—"upfront money." In many cases this is the only fee he will receive. Since the fee any single client can afford to pay is relatively low, the criminal attorney must substitute quantity for quality. That is, he must have numerous clients to maintain a profitable criminal practice; and he cannot spend too much time on any single case since the limited funds of most criminal defendants means the fee is rather inelastic—extra time will not necessarily result in additional payment.

It is not unusual for an attorney to find himself prepared for a hearing that fails to take place—for example, when the defendant, a witness, or the complainant fails to appear, or when records are misplaced. Because of the likelihood that at least one of the cases scheduled for a court hearing on a particular day will result in a continuance, private attorneys, like airlines, usually overbook. (Because every empty seat represents lost income, airlines frequently book more passengers for a flight than the plane has seats on the assumption that everyone will not show up for the flight.) Case management becomes a preoccupation as the attorney rushes from courtroom to courtroom juggling his cases, frequently requesting continuances. (The impact of this on plea bargaining will be discussed in the next chapter.)

Public Defender

The **public defender** is a public official who represents indigent defendants in criminal cases, much as the prosecutor represents the state. Unlike most prosecutors, however, the public defender is usually appointed, not elected. The reason for using an appointment system is quite simple: on what would an aspiring candidate base a campaign? While a candidate for prosecutor could engage in a great deal of law-and-order rhetoric, promising to be "tough on criminals," what could a candidate for public defender promise—to free more accused criminals?

11 ▪ THE LAWYERS: JUDGE, PROSECUTOR, DEFENSE COUNSEL

Public defender in court, Oakland, California, 1957.

There are both statewide and local public defender systems. According to *Criminal Defense Systems* (1984: 30),

> Under statewide public defender systems, an individual is designated by statute as the State public defender and is charged with developing and maintaining a system of representation for each of the counties in the State. In such systems, there is usually a governing

board that shares responsibility with the State public defender for the operation of the program. Most statewide systems are part of the executive branch, but others may operate as part of the judicial branch, as independent State agencies, or as independent nonprofit organizations.

Local public defenders are usually part of county government, and they are often appointed by the county legislature or the judges of the county. In a few jurisdictions, such as New York City, the local public defender system is organized as an independent, nonprofit corporation.

While public defenders are the primary providers of criminal defense services in only 34 percent of all counties in the United States, they serve 68 percent of the nation's population, and 43 percent of the largest fifty counties in the nation are served predominantly by a public defender program. Like the prosecutor's office, a public defender's office may be organized horizontally ("zone defense") or vertically ("man-to-man defense") or a combination of the two. Like a prosecutor, the public defender employs assistant or deputy public defenders, who may be full- or part-time, and investigative personnel.

Like other forms of public assistance, the public defender's services may be resented by its recipients. In addition to this generalized attitude toward receiving a necessary beneficence, there is the common folk wisdom that "you only get what you pay for." Jonathan Casper (1978: 4) points out that

> ... what attracts defendants to private lawyers is, for a large number of them at least, the notion that, because of the financial exchange between lawyer and client, the lawyer will be more committed to the defendant's interests. It is money that provides a sense of control, the leverage to insure that lawyers will listen to their clients, take instructions from their clients, and generally exert themselves on their clients' behalf. Moreover, not only does the client fail to pay, and thus lack this leverage over public defenders, but someone else does. And that someone else is "the state"—the very same institution that is proceeding against the defendant. Thus, the public defenders suffer not only from the fact that they are imposed upon defendants rather than being selected, and from the absence of financial exchange, but they are employed by the enemy.

The advantages and disadvantages to a defendant of private counsel as opposed to public defender will be discussed in the next chapter.

Assigned Counsel

About 60 percent of the counties in the United States use **court-appointed attorneys** as the primary method of providing legal representation to indigent criminal defendants. These are primarily rural counties with small populations; their small number of cases do not justify a salaried public defender system. Even in counties that use a public defender system, many defendants will be represented by private attorneys appointed by a trial judge. There are two reasons for this. First, when caseloads are too large for the public defender's office to handle, judges will employ private attorneys. Second, judges will assign private counsel when there is the problem of a conflict of interest. This is the case when a single attorney or a single law firm (including the public defender's office) represents codefendants, since there is always a potential conflict between them; for example, one defendant may agree to testify against another defendant.

Private attorneys in most jurisdictions are assigned by individual judges on a case-by-case basis. In other jurisdictions the assignment of private counsel is more systematic and is done by an administrator who oversees the program and develops standards and guidelines. In a few jurisdictions the public defender or court clerk has responsibility for appointment. In a small number of jurisdictions, a private attorney or a law firm is under contract to provide legal services for indigent criminal defendants (*Criminal Defender Systems* 1984). In most jurisdictions, however, a list of attorneys who have requested to be considered for appointment provides the basis for assigning private counsel. Compensation for assigned counsel is usually based on a fee schedule for in-court and out-of-court hours spent on a case. The hourly fee varies with the jurisdiction and, sometimes, with the type of case being represented. In any event, the hourly fees are typically less than what an attorney would charge to represent a private client.

Attorney Competency

The Sixth Amendment provides for the right to counsel, but as Steven Goldblatt (1983: 226) points out, it "was not traditionally perceived as including the right to a competent lawyer. Once the lawyer was present, the Sixth Amendment was satisfied even if he or she did nothing in the case." Warren Burger (1973: 234), the Chief Justice of the Supreme Court, has stated that "from one-third to one-half of the lawyers who appear in the serious [criminal] cases are not really qualified to render fully adequate representation." The problem is a difficult one—how is legal competence to be decided, and by whom?

Criminal defendants often attempt to overturn their convictions by arguing that they were represented by ineffective counsel. Prior to the 1970s a defendant had to prove that inadequate counsel caused his or her due process rights to be a "farce and mockery." More recently, Paul Wice (1983: 53) notes, the courts have ruled that a defendant is entitled to the "reasonably competent assistance of an attorney who would act as his or her diligent advocate." The difficulties inherent in setting a standard for competency are highlighted by the *United States v. DeCoster* (1976), in which the District of Columbia court of appeals was so divided that justices wrote five separate opinions, each with its own standard.

Goldblatt (1982: 234) notes that there are no comprehensive standards against which to measure attorney competence, and the Supreme Court has not enunciated a clear standard for measuring competence; thus, the courts are "limited to analyzing each case against the bare bones rudiments of representation (e.g., interview and call relevant witnesses)."

The basis of justice in our judicial system is the adversarial process—a competent prosecutor opposed by a competent defense counsel. In practice, however, this process is usually carried out, not in the context of a trial but, instead, through negotiations. In the next chapter we will examine plea bargaining and trials.

KEY TERMS

case method
Cravath system
contingency fee
senatorial courtesy
merit selection

prosecutor
defense counsel
public defender
court-appointed attorneys

REVIEW QUESTIONS

1. What is the basis of English common law?
2. What is meant by the case method, or the study of case law?
3. How did the Cravath system affect the legal profession?
4. What is a contingency fee?
5. What are the responsibilities of trial judges in criminal cases?
6. Why is it difficult to "judge a judge"?
7. What are the advantages and disadvantages of each of the methods for selecting judges?
8. Who is the chief prosecutor for the U.S. government? What is the title of the assistant prosecutors?
9. Why do prosecutors' offices suffer from a great deal of personnel turnover?
10. What is meant by horizontal prosecution? What are its advantages and disadvantages?
11. What is meant by vertical prosecution? What are its advantages and disadvantages?
12. Why would a prosecutor's office use "mixed prosecution?"
13. What are the three powers of a prosecutor?
14. What is the dual role of a prosecutor?
15. What are the three possible kinds of legal counsel in a criminal case?
16. Why is the private practice of criminal law so difficult?
17. Why are public defenders, unlike prosecutors, appointed to their positions?
18. Why do many criminal defendants dislike being represented by a public defender?
19. Why is assigned counsel used in some criminal cases?
20. Why is the question of attorney competence a problem?

CHAPTER 12

Plea Bargaining and Trials

PLEA BARGAINING

PLEA BARGAINING IS UNJUST

PLEA BARGAINING SERVES JUSTICE

PLEA BARGAINING: THE PROCESS

PLEA BARGAINING: LEGAL ISSUES

JURY TRIALS
Jury Selection

THE TRIAL PROCESS
Opening Statements
Prosecution's Case-in-Chief
Cross-Examination
Defendant's Case-in-Chief
Closing Arguments
Charge to the Jury
Jury Deliberations

REVIEW QUESTIONS

Boxes

A Plea Bargaining Session
Selection for a Criminal Trial Jury, Cook County, Illinois
Impeaching Witness Credibility

Our judicial system is based on an adversarial approach to justice. However, while the trial process that we will look at later in this chapter clearly makes use of an adversarial method, most criminal cases are settled without a trial, by a process referred to as plea bargaining. Our system's reliance on plea bargaining raises important and controversial issues in criminal justice, which will be discussed in this chapter.

PLEA BARGAINING

Plea bargaining typically involves an exchange relationship between a defendant, a prosecutor, and a judge. The defendant agrees to plead guilty to a specified charge in return for a lighter penalty than might otherwise result if he or she were found guilty after a trial. For example, the sentence for a residential burglary in Illinois is not less than four years nor more than

A PLEA BARGAINING SESSION

SCENE: Judge's chambers. Participants: judge (**J**), prosecutor (**P**), public defender (**PD**), defendant (**D**), police officer (**PO**).

J to PD: Who is the defendant and what are the facts in this case?
PD to J: The charge is aggravated assault, and the defendant is alleged to have threatened the victim with a knife.
PD to D: Explain the facts of this case to the judge.
D to P: The guy claims that I attacked him, but I didn't. We just had an argument.
PD to J: The victim claimed that my client had a knife.
J to PD: Were there any eye witnesses?
PD to J: No, there were no witnesses. The neighbors heard the argument but didn't see it.
J to D: Did you, in fact, have a knife?
D to J: No, Your Honor, I did not.
J to PO: What do you know about this case?
PO to J: We responded to a neighbor's call. The defendant's parked car had been struck by the victim's car. The two got into an argument. The victim says the defendant got a knife from the glove compartment and started waving it at him.
J to PO: Did you find the knife?
PO to J: No.
J to PD: Does this man have any prior record?
PD to J: Well, yes, there is a pending charge in another case.
J to D: Have you had any prior convictions?
D to J: Yes.
PD to D: Back in 1969, there was a charge of breaking and entering in the Carolinas, was there not?
D to PD: That's correct.
PD to D: How much time did you serve on that charge?
D to PD: Two and a half years.

P to D: Did you have two robbery charges in that case?
D to P: Yes, but they were dismissed. I was only charged with breaking and entering.
J to All: That is not a very good record.
J to D: Are you married?
J to D: Do you have a job?
D to J: I worked at _____ for 14 months but was laid off two months ago.
J to P: What do you think should happen?
P to J: The State wants three years.
J to PD: What do you think should happen?
PD to J: We were looking for time [in jail awaiting trial already] served and probation.
J to PO: Do you have any recommendation?
PO to J: Whatever you think is appropriate is all right with us.
J to All: I can't let him walk on probation. This is a serious charge and I need to protect society as well as look out for the defendant. I am thinking of 18 months and 3 years probation.
PD to J: I'd like to see jail time but not prison. The victim was involved in the argument too.
J to P: Where is the victim?
P to J: The victim is ill today.
J to All: The defendant's record is pretty bad. If the defendant pleads guilty I have to give 18 months [in prison] and probation. This is not the first time he has been in trouble.
PD to J: I'll have to discuss this with my client.
J to PD: When can you report back?
PD to J: I'm back here on April 14th.
J to P: What about you?
P to J: Okay with me.
J to All: Let's reschedule it for sounding on April 6th. Thanks for coming.

SOURCE: Kerstetter and Heinz 1979.

fifteen years—the actual number of years, between four and fifteen, is discretionary with the judge. However, a defendant charged with residential burglary who agrees to plead guilty to a lesser charge, such as possession of burglary tools, will receive a sentence of not less than one year nor more than three years. In fact, most cases in the United States, both criminal and civil, are settled not by trial but by negotiation. On the civil side of justice, this is referred to as an out-of-court settlement; in criminal court it is known as plea bargaining.

Plea bargaining is often criticized as an abuse of discretion that results in leniency for serious criminals. On the other hand, it is also criticized as unfair to defendants who must either waive their constitutional rights or run the risk of a substantially higher sentence if found guilty after a trial (see, for example, Uhlman and Walker 1980). A study in Chicago (Tybor and Eissman 1985b: 1), for example, found that "defendants who insist on jury trials run the risk of being sentenced more severely than if they plead guilty." In order to better understand the reality of plea bargaining, we will examine two opposing views—those who view plea bargaining as unjust, and those who see the process as benign, if not beneficial, in meeting the goals of justice.

PLEA BARGAINING IS UNJUST

Plea bargaining is a process that furthers the needs and interests of the judicial system, rather than the needs or interests of justice. As we noted earlier, police departments are the most heavily funded agencies in criminal justice. This results in an abundance of cases being brought into a judicial system that does not have the resources necessary to provide individualized justice. Justice requires a deliberately slow and exacting concern for due process; it is a luxury the system cannot afford. In response to this dilemma, the key actors—judges, prosecutors, defense attorneys—disregard the goal of justice and, instead, tailor their activities to enable the system to function with a minimum of difficulty or disruption.

Due process is insured through the **adversarial method**, an ideal characterized by a vigorous prosecutor for the state who is opposed by an equally vigorous advocate for the defendant in a courtroom battle before judge and jury. Abraham Blumberg

"My client would like to plead guilty if that would make you feel any better."

(1967: 19-20) argues that the requirements of the judicial system have led to an abandonment of the adversarial ideal. Instead, he says, the practice of criminal law has been reduced to a confidence game.

> Organizational goals and discipline impose a set of demands and conditions of practice on the respective professions in the criminal court, to which they respond by abandoning their ideological and professional commitments to the accused client, in the service of these higher claims of the court organization. All court personnel, including the accused's own lawyer, tend to be coopted to become agent-mediators who help the accused redefine his situation and restructure his perceptions concomitant with a plea of guilty.

How does the system "help" the defendant to "redefine" his or her situation in a manner that induces a plea of guilty? The scenario begins with criminal statutes that prescribe lengthy terms of imprisonment for many felony crimes. Although these sentences are rarely imposed, they serve to generate a great deal of fear in defendants. This fear is aided by the common police practice of **overcharging**, or charging arrestees with every conceivable crime even remotely related to their actions. In addition, notes Michael Cox (1975: 34),

> Prosecutors have great leverage; they draft the charges and generally make recommendations on sentencing. These prosecutorial prerogatives put the defendant at a disadvantage. A prosecutor may "overcharge," either horizontally (e.g., in a bad-check case charge uttering [offering], obtaining by false pretenses, and forgery, even though they may overlap and be multiplicious for sentencing), or vertically (e.g., always charge homicides as first degree murder). Through overcharging, an accused is immediately put on the defensive. If the case is tried on the merits, a jury will often react by thinking (even if only subconsciously), "There are so many charges and they are so serious; the defendant must be guilty of something." The number of charges/specifications and the "degree" [e.g., robbery in the first degree or burglary in the second degree] are at the heart of plea negotiations. As an added incentive to deal, a prosecutor may threaten to recommend a high sentence if conviction is obtained after a trial on the merits.

Thus, at the first meeting with his or her attorney, the defendant is told that if convicted on all of the counts alleged by the police, he or she will be ready for Social Security before being released from prison. The unsettling prospect of a lengthy prison term signals the beginning of a "softening-up" process.

If the defendant is able to secure private counsel, in addition to being concerned about the outcome of the case, he or she must be concerned about paying legal fees. As noted in the last chapter, a private attorney will demand "upfront money," but in most cases this is not sufficient for the hours typically required for a jury trial. Since most criminal defendants can afford only modest fees, attorneys prefer the dependable income from spending a modest amount of time with a large number of clients rather than the risk of devoting many hours on a few clients who may not be able to pay them. Under such circumstances, private defense counsel is likely to recommend that his or her client plead guilty in exchange for leniency. For a defendant who is facing the prospect of a lengthy term of imprisonment, this may appear to be sound advice.

In order to better manipulate the client, defense counsel is assisted by the prosecutor. Albert Alschuler (1968: 95) states that "overcharging and subsequent charge reduction are often the components of an elaborate sham, staged for the benefit of defense attorneys. The process commonly has little or no effect on the defendant's sentence, and prosecutors may simply wish to give defense attorneys a 'selling point' in their efforts to induce defendants to plead guilty."

As opposed to private defense counsel, who must depend on client fees, the public defender is a salaried employee who is paid regardless of how many cases he or she handles. Nevertheless, as Herbert Jacob and James Eisenstein (1977: 26) point out, "Public defender organizations charged with representing all indigent defendants prefer a quick disposition because their manpower barely suffices to handle their case load." Alschuler (1975: 1237) notes that public defenders also experience pressure from trial judges, who are concerned with disposing of as many cases as possible as quickly as possible.

> The process may begin with a judge's suggestion that a certain plea agreement would be fair and if a defender accepts this suggestion, the matter is at an end. Defenders who resist judicial suggestions too often, however, are frequently forced to endure abusive remarks from the bench:
>
> - You're a quasi-public agency. You should be interested in *justice*.
> - Haven't you got any client control?
> - You spend too much time on hardened criminals.
> - No private attorney would take this case to trial.
> - You must be awfully eager for experience.
> - When will you guys bend to reality?
> - You guys believe your clients too much.
> - You're acting like a private lawyer.

The counsel for the defense—whether private, public defender, or assigned—has a great deal in common with prosecutors and judges: a similar educational, professional and, often, political background. Defense attorneys are socialized into this unjust system, and they learn that a price must be paid for failing to understand and abide by system norms. Milton Heumann (1978: 57) notes that "in the process of handling their cases, new defense attorneys learn that the reality of the court differs from what they had expected; through rewards and sanctions, they are taught to proceed in a certain fashion." In particular, they learn to avoid legal challenges that may be seen as frivolous to prosecutors and judges—and that can gain the enmity of both.

> The hostility of prosecutors and judges to these time-consuming motions is communicated to the new attorney. First, the prosecutor or judge may simply call the defense attorney into his office and explain that the motions are needless formalities. If this advice is insufficient to dissuade the newcomer, sanctions such as "hassling" the attorney by dragging the case out over a long period of time, closing all files to the attorney, and even threatening to go to trial on the case, ensue. (Heumann 1978: 62)

The prosecutor can keep a private attorney hopping by objecting to continuances when the attorney overbooks. Usually, if counsel requests a continuance, and the prosecutor does not object, or if he or she agrees, it will be routinely granted. If the prosecutor objects, however, and the judge is also opposed, an attorney with several cases scheduled for the same day is in a serious dilemma. Alan Dershowitz (1983: 355), a Harvard law professor and prominent defense attorney, states, "The prosecutor can make the defense attorney's life pleasant or miserable in countless small, but important ways: by agreeing to or opposing continuances; by opening or closing files for discovery; by waiving or insisting on technical requirements; by recommending or denigrating the attorney to prospective clients; by being generally agreeable or disagreeable."

In this system defense attorneys are forced to abandon their adversarial stance in favor of accommodation. Alschuler (1975: 1179) states that the system of plea bargaining "leads even able, conscientious, and highly motivated attorneys to make decisions that are not really in their clients' interests." Defendants are finessed or coerced, sometimes both, into cooperating with a system that is seeking to punish them. Above all, this system does not have the resources to insure that the innocent do not plead guilty.

Plea bargaining serves justice

When asked to explain the existence of plea bargaining, even informed observers point to the crush of cases that threaten to overwhelm the judicial system and say, "Nobody *likes* plea bargaining, but it is the only way the system can survive." This typical view is contested by Heumann (1978: 157) who points out that guilty pleas have been the outcome of most criminal cases for almost one hundred years, even when courts were not overburdened with too many cases. Trials have not been the central means for resolving criminal (or civil) cases for nearly a century.

> Court personnel simply recognize the factual culpability of many defendants, and the fruitlessness, at least in terms of case outcome, of going to trial. From these perceptions flows the notion that if the obviously guilty defendant cops a plea, he will receive some award. Whether the defendant believes this results from his show of contrition, or, more prosaically, from saving the state time and money, is not of concern here; the fact that he perceives that he receives a reward is the key point. Similarly, prosecutors and judges do not believe that they accord this reward simply to "move the business." They feel that by giving considerations to the defendant who pleads guilty, they are furthering their own professional goals (sorting serious from nonserious cases, obtaining certain [prison] time in serious cases, and so on) . . . [It] is not at all simply an expedient to dispose of "onerously large case loads" (Heumann 1978: 156).

Malcolm Feeley (1979) insists that plea bargaining grows out of the norms of the legal profession. Despite a common perception of combativeness, lawyers actually prefer negotiation, and they prefer events that have a relatively high level of predictability. This is not unique to lawyers; in most businesses, uncertainty is problematic. A grocer needs to know how much milk to buy, because if he orders too much, it will spoil, and if he orders too little, customers will shop elsewhere. An auto manufacturer needs to know how much steel to purchase, how many people to employ, how many cars to produce; uncertainty—which leads to overproducing or underproducing—can bring disaster to the businessman. For attorneys, the trial process lacks the predictability that they favor; it requires a highly educated professional (prosecutor or defense counsel) to relinquish control over the outcome of a case to a jury of twelve persons devoid of legal training. Whether it is a civil or criminal matter, lawyers do not normally find this situation very appealing.

The norms of the legal profession also require cordiality between adversaries. As in the case of professional boxers, attorneys are expected to shake hands before and after a "bout," an act that does not reduce their efforts to emerge victorious. David Neubauer (1974: 78) explains that normative behavior on the part of lawyers requires that they be outgoing and congenial; "if defense and prosecution are on good terms, this does not mean the adversary process has broken down. It may be only a reflection of the normal rules of conduct expected of lawyers. The 'cooperation' of defense and prosecution is a product of such general expectations about how lawyers should conduct themselves."

In practice, defense attorneys—private or public defender—are typically on good terms with their counterparts in the prosecutor's office; they may even be friends. Nevertheless, each is a professional who is expected by the other, as well as by the rest of their legal peers, to behave in a professional manner. This requires a lawyer to engage in vigorous advocacy; anything less can lead to a loss of respect, which can devastate a legal career.

Feeley (1979: 29) insists that the prevalence of plea bargaining does not indicate that the adversarial method has been abandoned in favor of expediency—expediency related to the need to reduce uncertainty. "To infer the lack of an adversarial stance and the existence of bargained settlements—for the pure purpose of administrative convenience—from the absence of trials is to ignore altogether the importance of these other 'truthtesting' and highly combative processes." In place of a trial as the epitome of the adversarial ideal, private plea negotiation has evolved. As Suzann and Leonard Buckle (1977) argue, however, plea negotiation is nonetheless adversarial. In place of two opposing attorneys meeting in a highly dramatic and time-consuming courtroom confrontation, they negotiate in private settings such as the judge's chambers. Each attorney reviews the case, pointing out the strengths of his own position as opposed to the weaknesses of his opponent's; the process continues until an agreement—a "deal"—can be struck. The process is that of an abbreviated "mini-trial" without the formalities required in a courtroom.

PLEA BARGAINING: THE PROCESS

When a prosecutor receives a case from the police, he or she must evaluate its strengths and weaknesses. This is usually accomplished by an assistant prosecutor assigned to an intake (screening) unit. As noted previously, a prosecutor's office frequently has to deal with dozens (more than 125 in Cook County, Illinois) of state, county and municipal police agencies. As would be expected, some perform better than others; some police officers are well trained and conscientious; some are poorly trained and lack motivation. The prosecutor receives cases from them all—the good, the mediocre, and the bad. Rather than waste scarce resources on prosecuting petty or weak cases, prosecutors employ a screening system that generally follows the scheme outlined in the diagram, "Variables Influencing a Prosecutor's Charging Decision":

- *Category I.* A case in which the charges are not serious and the evidence is weak will usually not be prosecuted.
- *Category II.* A case in which the charges are not serious, but the evidence is strong is a good candidate for plea bargaining.
- *Category III.* A case in which the charges are serious but the evidence is weak is a good candidate for plea bargaining.
- *Category IV.* A case in which the charges are very serious and the evidence is strong is a candidate for vigorous prosecution.

In addition to the legal factors that influence a prosecutor's charging decision, there are *extralegal factors*: the defendant's prior criminal record, age, health, marital status, work history, as well as publicity about the case and the background and status of the victim. These factors combine with the evidentiary aspects of a case to determine the charging decision.

The diagram comparing the handling of felony cases in New Orleans, Washington, and Manhattan reveals that felony cases are dealt with differently by prosecutors in different jurisdictions: Why are some cases rejected at screening and others dropped after charges have been filed? As noted above, some cases brought in by the police fail to meet the evidentiary standard necessary to justify prosecution; they are rejected at screening. Barbara Boland and her colleagues (1983) note that a small fraction (8 to 19 percent) of police officers account for

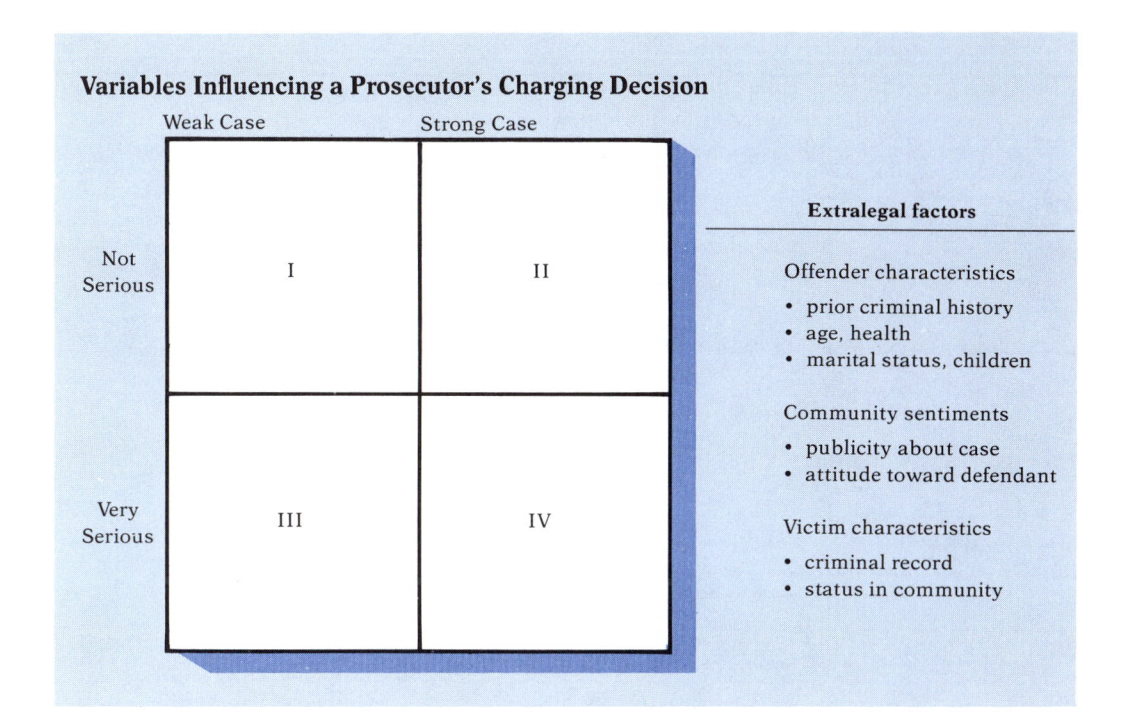

Variables Influencing a Prosecutor's Charging Decision

	Weak Case	Strong Case
Not Serious	I	II
Very Serious	III	IV

Extralegal factors

Offender characteristics
- prior criminal history
- age, health
- marital status, children

Community sentiments
- publicity about case
- attitude toward defendant

Victim characteristics
- criminal record
- status in community

about half of the arrests that end in convictions. These officers are apparently more adept at gathering evidence than their peers.

Some serious cases that appear strong at intake begin to weaken as time passes. They are either dropped after charges have been filed or plea-bargained down to secure a guilty plea.

> The reason why so many cases that come into the system as felonies are not prosecuted as charged is . . . that a high percentage of them, in every crime category from murder to burglary, involve victims with whom the suspect has had prior, often close, relations. Logically, suspects who are known to their victims are more likely to be caught than strangers because they can be identified more easily by the complainants. And this very fact of a previous personal relationship often leads a complainant to be reluctant to pursue prosecution through adjudication. (Vera Institute of Justice 1977: 134)

Tempers cool with the passage of time; a combination of informal mediation, conciliation, and restitution may have been effective; or the complainant may have been intimidated. The

Differences in How Prosecutors Handle Felony Cases
Outcome of felony cases presented to prosecutor

New Orleans, Louisiana

100 cases → 45 rejected at screening; 53 filings of charges; 2 referred to another prosecutor
53 filings → 8 dropped after filing; 45 proceeded
45 proceeded → 8 trials; 37 guilty pleas
8 trials → 2 acquittals; 6 guilty verdicts

Washington, D.C.

100 cases → 17 rejected at screening; 83 filings of charges; 0 referred to another prosecutor
83 filings → 34 dropped after filing; 49 proceeded
49 proceeded → 7 trials; 42 guilty pleas
7 trials → 2 acquittals; 5 guilty verdicts

Manhattan Borough, New York

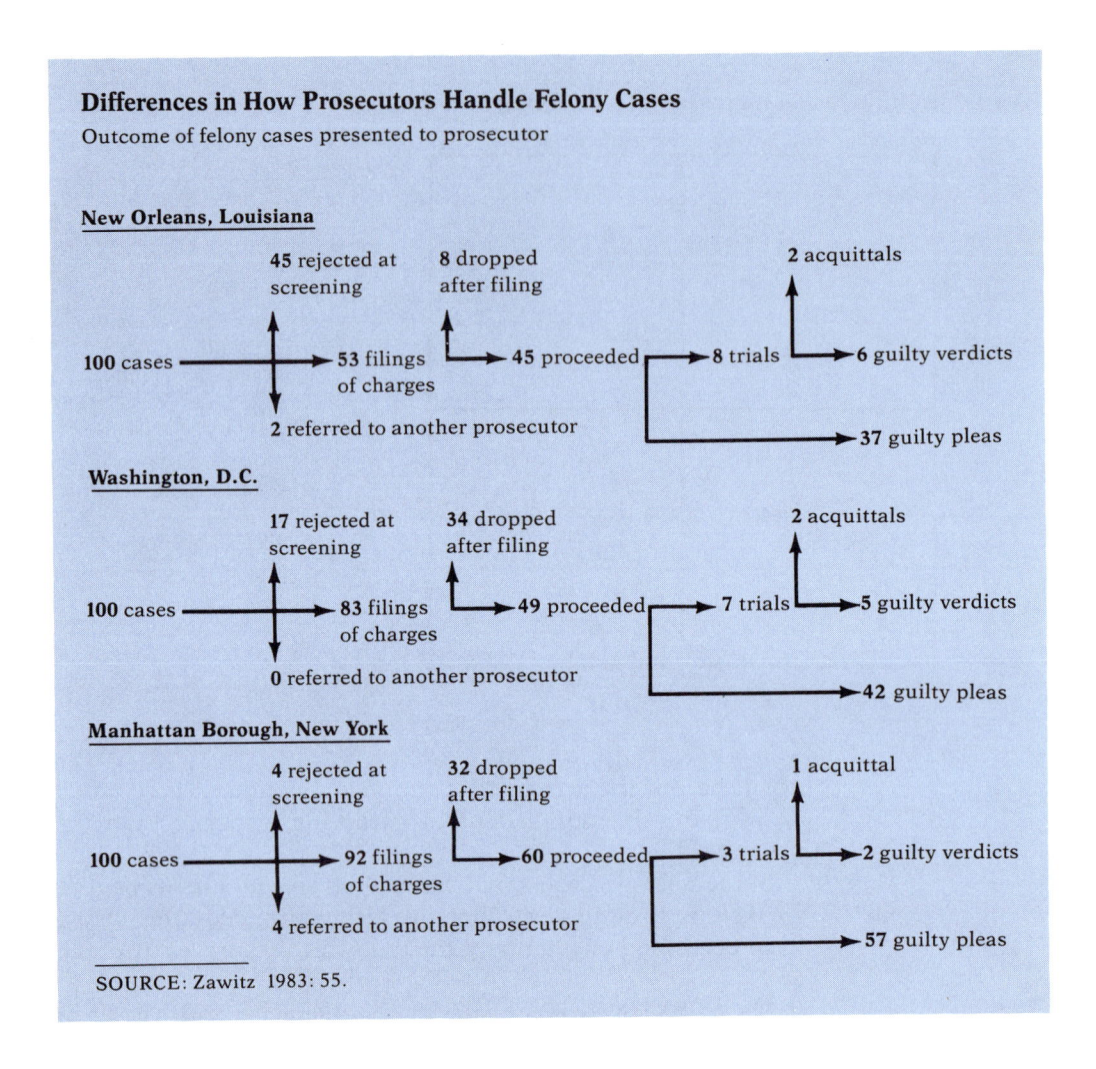

100 cases → 4 rejected at screening; 92 filings of charges; 4 referred to another prosecutor
92 filings → 32 dropped after filing; 60 proceeded
60 proceeded → 3 trials; 57 guilty pleas
3 trials → 1 acquittal; 2 guilty verdicts

SOURCE: Zawitz 1983: 55.

Vera Institute of Justice (1977: 134) notes that "criminal conduct is often the explosive spillover from ruptured personal relations among neighbors, friends and former spouses." Prosecutors are often reluctant to prosecute as full-scale felonies cases that have erupted from personal quarrels. Boland and her colleagues (1983: 6) point out that prosecutors who utilize a more intensive case screening policy (such as New Orleans—see the diagram comparing the handling of felony cases) drop fewer charges after filing.

Cases that are not screened out at intake or dropped after

charges have been filed usually result in a guilty plea. While the guilty plea is most often the result of some form of exchange, the actual process may be so simple that it cannot be accurately described as "negotiation." David Sudnow (1965: 163) explains such transactions by introducing the concept of **normal crimes**: those crimes whose features—for instance, the ways they occur, and the characteristics of the victims and the persons who commit the crimes—are so common that they can be classified as "normal." For example, a "normal burglary" involves a nonprofessional black or Hispanic perpetrator, no weapons, low-priced items, little property damage, and a lower-class victim. Possession of firearms or harm to the occupants, victims who are not lower class, or white perpetrators, for example, would remove the incident from the category of "normal burglary." If the defense attorney and the prosecutor agree that a particular incident is a "normal crime," custom and precedent provide for a settlement without the need for negotiation. In other words, for each crime the statutes provide a penalty; for each "normal crime," however, judicial actors have established their own unwritten penalties, which, because they mitigate statutory penalties, serve to encourage pleas of guilty while insuring a penalty for the perpetrator at a minimum expenditure of scarce legal resources.

Prosecutors, defense attorneys, and sometimes judges, typically constitute a **workgroup** (Jacob and Eisenstein 1977). They are *regular players* who interact frequently and share the common goal of disposing of cases with a minimum of resource expenditure and uncertainty. Judicial systems in which judges, assistant prosecutors, and defense attorneys are shifted frequently will lack the stability necessary for the formation of workgroups, and plea bargaining will be more difficult to accomplish. It should be noted that judges do not participate in plea bargaining in all jurisdictions. Federal district court judges are prohibited by the *Federal Rules of Criminal Procedure* (Rule 11e[1]c) from participating in plea negotiations. However, in Illinois, for example, circuit court judges are routinely involved in plea negotiations.

There have been attempts to limit or to exclude plea bargaining from criminal justice, and the results have been mixed. In New York, for example, laws passed at the behest of Governor Nelson Rockefeller, known locally as the "Rockefeller Laws," severely limited the ability of prosecutors to plea bargain. The

New York State Supreme Court, First District, New York City.

result was a substantial increase in the number of defendants demanding jury trials, and prosecutors and judges soon found ways to circumvent the law (Joint Committee on New York Drug Law Evaluation 1977; Aaronson et al. 1977). In Alaska, on the other hand, when the attorney general, the state's chief prosecutor, issued an order prohibiting the state's district attorneys from engaging in plea bargaining, the number of defendants pleading guilty remained about the same. Prosecutors did not have to waste time on negotiations, and the system became more efficient. There were, however, unanticipated results of the policy (Rubenstein et al. 1980):

- there was absolutely no change in sentences for cases involving violent crimes such as rape, robbery, and felonious assault;

- there was very little change in sentences for most serious property offenders, particularly those with prior felony convictions; and
- the major change was longer sentences for less serious property offenders.

Plea Bargaining: Legal Issues

In order for a plea bargaining agreement to be legally binding on the defendant, the trial judge is required to determine if the defendant fully understands the ramifications of a plea of guilty. Rule 11(c) of the *Federal Rules of Criminal Procedure* requires a judge to determine that the defendant understands:

> 1. the nature of the charge to which the plea is offered, the mandatory minimum penalty provided by law, if any, and the maximum possible penalty provided by law including the effect of any special parole terms; and
> 2. that he has the right to be represented by an attorney at every stage of the proceeding against him and, if necessary, one will be appointed to represent him; and
> 3. that he has the right to plead not guilty or to persist in that plea if it has already been made, and that he has the right to be tried by a jury and at that trial has the right to the assistance of counsel, the right to confront and cross-examine witnesses against him, and the right not to be compelled to incriminate himself; and
> 4. that if he pleads guilty or nolo contendere [no contest] there will not be a further trial of any kind, so that by pleading guilty or nolo contendere he waives the right to a jury trial; and
> 5. that if he pleads guilty or nolo contendere, the court may ask him questions about the offense to which he has pleaded, and if he answers these questions under oath, on the record, and in the presence of counsel, his answers may later be used against him in a prosecution for perjury or false statement.

A judge must also determine that the guilty plea is completely voluntary. Rule 11(d) of the *Federal Rules of Criminal Procedure* provides that

> The court shall not accept a plea of guilty or nolo contendere without first, by addressing the defendant personally in open court, deter-

Inmates' receiving room, Cook County, Illinois, Department of Corrections.

mining that the plea is voluntary and not the result of force or threats or of promises apart from a plea agreement. The court shall also inquire as to whether the defendant's willingness to plead guilty or nolo contendere results from prior discussions between the attorney for the government and the defendant or his attorney.

If a defendant refuses a prosecutor's offer of leniency in return for a plea of guilty, can the prosecutor reindict the defendant on more serious charges? In 1978 the Supreme Court (*Bordenkircher v. Hayes*) said yes. In this case, instead of a sentence of five years, Paul Hayes was convicted of forgery and, as an habitual offender, sentenced to a term of life imprisonment. The Court reasoned that since it had already ruled in prior decisions that plea bargaining is constitutional, it must also accept the "simple reality that the prosecutor's interest at the bargaining table is to persuade the defendant to forego his right to plead not guilty." As long as the procedural safeguards listed above (Rule 11[c]) have been adhered to, a reindictment by the prosecutor on more serious charges does not violate the due process clause of the Fourteenth Amendment.

Does a prosecutor have to live up to the terms of a plea bargain? In 1971 the Supreme Court (*Santobello v. New York*) said yes. In this case the assistant district attorney agreed to permit the defendant to plead guilty to a gambling misdemeanor charge that would carry a maximum prison sentence of one year. The prosecutor agreed to make no recommendation as to the sentence. After the plea of guilty was entered, a sentencing hearing was scheduled at which a different assistant district attorney appeared. In violation of the agreement, this district attorney recommended the maximum sentence. The Court ruled "that when a plea [of guilty] rests in any significant degree on a promise or agreement of the prosecutor, so that it can be said to be part of the inducement or consideration [to plead guilty], such promise must be fulfilled." In 1984, in a modification of *Santobello*, the Supreme Court (*Mabry v. Johnson*) ruled unanimously that a defendant has no constitutional right to enforcement of a *proposed* plea bargain that a prosecutor withdraws before it becomes official.

JURY TRIALS

In order to fully appreciate the efficiency of plea bargaining, we must compare it to the alternative of a jury trial. While the amount of additional time required for trials varies considerably, a Department of Justice study of this question (Bureau of Justice Statistics 1984: 4) in five representative cities determined that "in New Orleans, Portland, and St. Louis, trials take an additional month to 6 weeks to process, while in Manhattan and Washington, D.C., trials take approximately 5 to 6 months longer to dispose than pleas." The jury trial is a relatively infrequent occurrence in criminal justice. An examination in detail will help to explain why; it is a tedious and time-consuming process.

The Sixth Amendment states, "In all criminal prosecutions

the accused shall enjoy the right to a speedy and public trial by an impartial jury." The Supreme Court has not quantified what is meant by a "speedy trial," but it has set down guidelines for assessing if delay in a particular case violates the Sixth Amendment (*Barker v. Wingo*, 1972):

1. the length of the delay
2. the prosecutor's reasons for the delay
3. whether the defendant had demanded a speedy trial
4. the degree of prejudice to the defendant caused by the delay

The court indicated an interest in preventing oppressive pretrial incarceration, minimizing the anxiety and hardship of the defendant, and avoiding hampering the defense. Delay that hampers the defense can result in the denial of a fair trial, a violation of the due process clause of the Fifth and Fourteenth Amendments. In general, a speedy trial is one that takes place between 100 and 120 days after arrest for a defendant in custody, and about 150 days for a defendant on bail.

Jury Selection

The jury selection process has seven steps:

1. The first master list is derived from voting rolls, motor vehicle license records, and the tax rolls.
2. Names selected at random from the master list constitute the first juror list.
3. Questionnaires are mailed to each person on the first juror list to determine if he or she is qualified to serve. In order to be eligible to serve on a jury, a person must be a citizen, at least eighteen years of age, have no felony convictions, and have lived in the court's jurisdiction for some minimum period of time (usually one year), be able to read, write, and understand English, and be free of any physical or mental handicap that would make the person unable to render jury service. Otherwise qualified persons—for example, lawyers, law enforcement personnel, doctors—may be routinely exempted from jury service. Some people may receive temporary postponements based on time-limited hardships—for example, farmers during the harvest season.
4. The second master list contains those persons from the first

Jury Selection

```
(1)                    ┌─────────────────┐
                       │  First          │
                       │  Master List    │
                       └────────┬────────┘
                                │
(2)                    ┌────────┴────────┐
                       │  First Juror List│
                       └────────┬────────┘
                                │
(3)                    ┌────────┴────────┐
                       │  Questionnaires │
                       └────────┬────────┘
        ┌──────────┬────────────┼────────────┬──────────────┐
   Disqualified  Exempt      Excused    Nondeliverables   No Response
                             Qualified
                                │
(4)                    ┌────────┴────────┐
                       │ Second Master List│
                       └────────┬────────┘
                          Summons Mailed
        ┌──────────┬────────────┼────────────┬──────────────┐
   Disqualified  Exempt                   Excused       Nondeliverable
                                │
(5)                    ┌────────┴────────┐
                       │ Report for Service│
                       │    Jury Pool    │
                       └────────┬────────┘
                   ┌────────────┴────────────┐
                Excused                   No Show
                                │
(6)                    ┌────────┴────────┐
                       │   Impaneled     │
                       └────────┬────────┘
                                │
(7)                    ┌────────┴────────┐
                       │   Voir Dire     │
                       └────────┬────────┘
                   ┌────────────┴────────────┐
           ┌───────┴──────┐           ┌──────┴───────┐
           │  Hear Trial  │           │  Challenged  │
           │              │           │  Not Used    │
           └──────────────┘           └──────────────┘
```

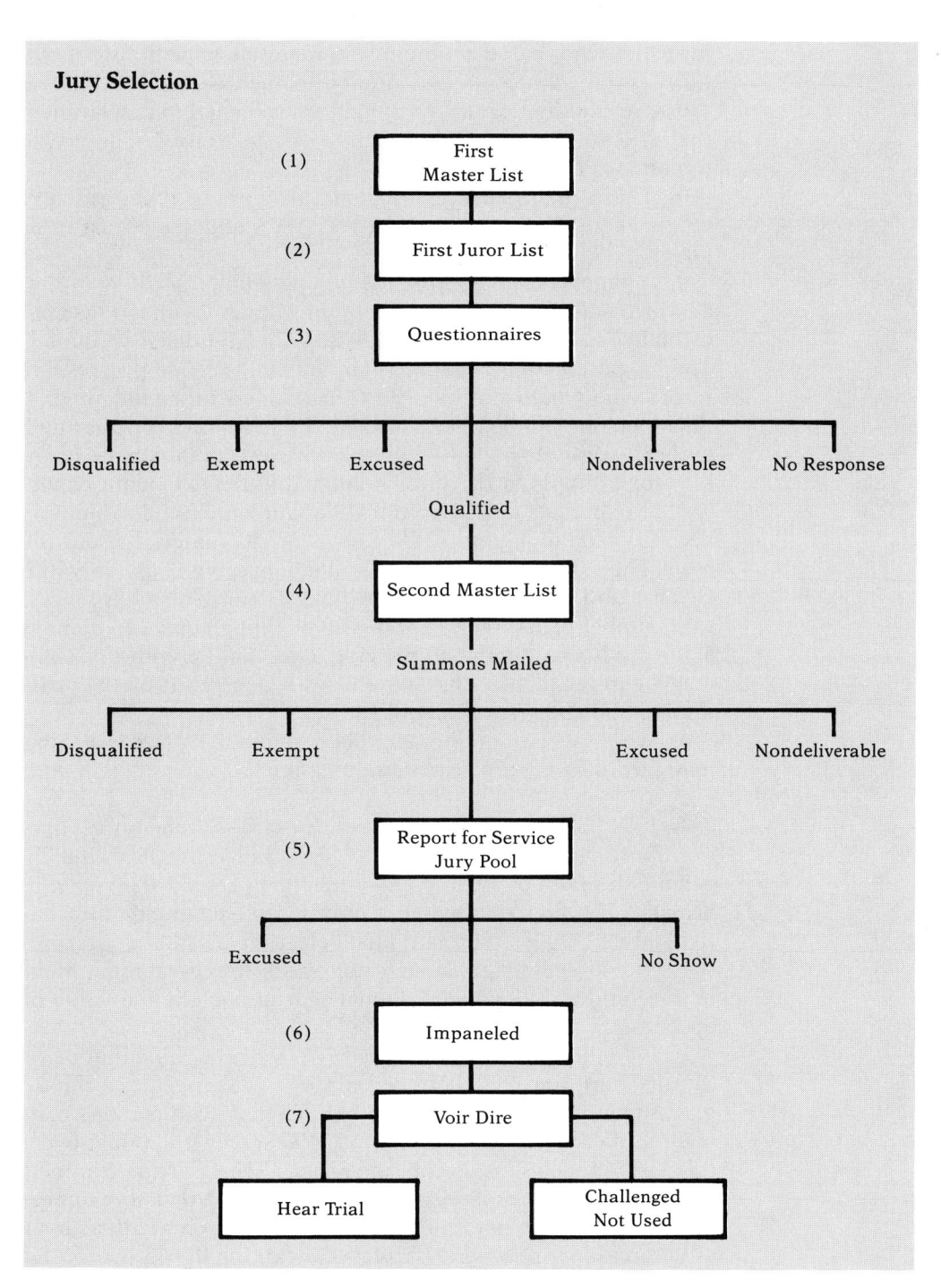

juror list who, based on the questionnaires, appear eligible for jury service. A summons is mailed to each person on this list. Those responding to the summons are screened to determine if they should be disqualified, exempted, or excused. Those who remain are qualified.

5. Those qualified are directed to report to a central jury room where they comprise the **jury pool** and are sworn in as jurors.

6. A panel is selected from the jury pool for a ***voir dire* hearing** at which each prospective juror is questioned by the judge and, in many jurisdictions, by the prosecutor and defense counsel. The purpose of the hearing is to determine those prospective jurors who would not be able to render an impartial verdict. Such persons can be discharged by the judge on his or her own authority or **challenged for cause** by prosecutor or defense counsel—for example, if the juror is related to the defendant or victim, or expresses negative feelings about the defendant, or has been exposed to a great deal of news media material about the case. The judge determines if a challenge for cause is valid. Defense and prosecution, in most jurisdictions, also have a certain number of **peremptory challenges**; that is, they can dismiss a juror without having to provide a reason. Peremptory challenges can range from two to twenty-six, depending on the jurisdiction and the seriousness of the case.

7. When twelve persons are chosen—and in some cases alternate jurors—they are *impaneled* as a jury.

In 1984 the Supreme Court (*Press Enterprise Company v. Superior Court*) ruled unanimously that trial judges must ordinarily permit the public and the news media to attend the *voir dire* hearing. The Court stated that only when less drastic alternatives are not possible, can jury selection be closed; it said, "Closed proceedings, although not absolutely precluded, must be rare and only for cause shown that outweighs the value of openness."

In 1986 the Supreme Court, in a 7–2 decision, ruled that prosecutors may not use their peremptory challenges to exclude blacks from juries because they believe that such persons may favor a black defendant. In *Baston v. Kentucky*, the Court overruled a 1965 decision on the same issue. The Court determined that "Although a prosecutor ordinarily is entitled to exercise permitted peremptory challenges 'for any reason at all, as long as that reason is related to his view concerning the outcome,' the

Equal Protection Clause forbids the prosecutor to challenge potential jurors solely on account of their race or on the assumption that black jurors as a group will be unable impartially to consider the state's case against a black defendant." The decision also made it easier for a defendant to raise the issue: "Once the defendant makes a prima facie showing [that black jurors were excluded], the burden shifts to the state to come forward with a neutral explanation for challenging black jurors." This decision will probably accelerate the move toward abolishing the peremptory challenge in many jurisdictions, a position supported by Justice Thurgood Marshall in his concurring opinion.

A few days after deciding *Baston*, the Court ruled 6–3 that prospective jurors who state that they could not under any circumstances vote for the imposition of the death penalty could be excluded for cause. In *Lockhart v. McCree*, the Court ruled that the so-called death-qualified jury, "unlike the wholesale exclusion of blacks, women or Mexican Americans from jury service, is carefully designed to serve the state's concededly legitimate interest in obtaining a single jury that can properly and impartially apply the law to the facts of the case at both the guilt and sentencing phases of a capital crime." In most states that authorize the death penalty, the jury that decides on guilt or innocence also determines, after a separate hearing, whether the death sentence should be imposed.

THE TRIAL PROCESS

Prior to the trial, a legal formality known as **discovery** occurs. In some jurisdictions, liberal discovery statutes allow the defense attorney access to nearly all of the government's case information, thus permitting counsel to better prepare for trial (or plea bargaining). In some jurisdictions there are restrictive and quite formal discovery rules, which can be time-consuming, but defense counsel on good terms with the prosecutor's office can often avoid these formalities. The right to discovery is reciprocal and, thus, the prosecutor also has access to defense counsel's case information.

A plea of not guilty places the burden of "proof beyond a reasonable doubt" on the prosecutor, who must prove each and every substantive element of the offense(s) charged. The defense,

> ## Selection for a Criminal Trial Jury, Cook County, Illinois
>
> 1. Potential jurors are selected on a random basis from the list of registered voters. They are directed to report to a courthouse assembly room where they become the jury pool.
> 2. The jury pool is randomly divided into panels ranging from 40 to 48, depending on the trial judge's estimated needs.
> 3. A panel is taken to a courtroom, where they form the venire; that is, prospective jurors for a particular trial.
> 4. In the courtroom the judge randomly selects 14 persons from the panel and has them sit in the jury box and two alternative chairs. The judge then begins the *voir dire*, questioning each juror individually in open court about his or her background, experience with courts and law, and ability to be fair and follow the law.
> 5. As a result of the questioning, some jurors are excused by the judge. When the judge is satisfied that the

on the other hand, need only attack the prosecutor's efforts to establish guilt by casting doubt on the accuracy, relevance, and credibility of the prosecutor's proof, usually by a vigorous cross-examination of the government's witnesses. The defense can, however, also offer an affirmative defense such as an alibi or claim self-defense.

Opening Statements

The trial begins with **opening statements** by each side. First, the prosecutor outlines the evidence that will be produced to satisfy the burden of proof, introducing a brief outline of the government's case with the words, "Ladies and gentlemen of the jury, the State intends to prove that on...." Defense counsel is also entitled to an opening statement, although this is sometimes

> prospective jurors who cannot be fair have been removed, the rest are turned over to the prosecutors, usually in groups of four.
>
> **6.** The prosecution exercises peremptory challenges by announcing in open court, "The state excuses Mr. ———, with thanks."
>
> **7.** If the state excuses any jurors from the panel of four, the judge will resume questioning other prospective jurors until the panel again adds up to four, and it is resubmitted to the prosecution. If the state approves, the panel of four is submitted to the defense, who can exercise peremptory challenges.
>
> **8.** The process continues until both sides are satisfied with the panel of four, at which time the jurors are sworn in, and the process begins again until twelve jurors and two alternates have been chosen.
>
> The prosecution and the defense have ten peremptory challenges when the possible sentence is imprisonment. In a death penalty case, each side has twenty peremptory challenges.

waived, the burden of proof falling completely on the government because the defendant is legally innocent until the prosecutor proves otherwise.

Prosecution's Case-in-Chief

The government must now call its witnesses, each of whom is sworn in and questioned by the prosecutor. This is referred to as **direct examination** and consists of a series of questions designed to weave a story. The questions are relatively narrow, and the witness must respond accordingly so that opposing counsel, forewarned by the terms of the question, can object in time to prevent inadmissible statements—for example, hearsay—from being made in front of the jury. A question cannot be *leading*, that is, framed in such a way that it suggests its own answer, nor can it be *loaded*, that is, one that puts an answer in the witness's mouth. In other words, the question, "How was the perpetrator dressed at the time of the incident?" is permissible. But the question, "Was the perpetrator wearing a black leather jacket, blue jeans, and boots when you first saw him?" would be improper. Testimony that cannot be subjected to cross-examination—for example, certain types of **hearsay evidence**—is inadmissible. For example, a third party who testifies, "I was told by the defendant's girlfriend that he . . . ," will not normally be allowed to continue. Although there are a number of exceptions, a witness must restrict testimony to information that is based on *direct* observation or knowledge. The most important exception are admissions made by the accused.

The prosecution, and subsequently the defense, may offer physical, or tangible, evidence. This is done while the witness—usually an investigator or forensic technician—is on the stand. Counsel will pick up the relevant exhibit from a table at the front of the courtroom, request that it be marked by the court reporter for identification—for example, as Exhibit #1—and, after offering it to opposing counsel and the judge, will then ask the witness about the evidence. In some situations a *chain of evidence* must be established by calling a series of witnesses to the stand, each one accounting for the period during which the exhibit was in his or her custody. A missing link can cause the evidence to be inadmissible or to raise doubts in jurors' minds. Opposing counsel can object to admitting any exhibit as evidence, thus requiring the judge to make a ruling on the contested item. Physical evidence, as opposed to **direct** or **eyewitness testimony**, is referred to as **circumstantial evidence**. That is, the evidence is indirect and, while it may support direct testimony, it does not bear directly on the question of guilt or innocence. For example, a bloody knife with the fingerprints of the defendant only proves that he or she had touched the weapon.

Cross-Examination

After each direct examination by the prosecutor, defense counsel has an opportunity to cross-examine the witness (a right granted by the Fifth Amendment). As opposed to direct examination, the restrictive rules against leading or suggestive questions do not apply during **cross-examination**. The attorney may ask leading

IMPEACHING WITNESS CREDIBILITY

Prosecutor: Mr. Lishniss, the defense counsel didn't go into your background in much detail. I'd like to ask you a question or two about your past history.

Mr. Lishniss, isn't it a fact that in April of 1973 you were convicted in Dade County, Florida, of perjury?

A: Yes, that's a fact. And I served some time.

Q: How much time?

A: I was sentenced to a year and a day but I got out in eight months.

Q: The perjury, the lying under oath, was committed before a jury, was it not?

A: That's what they said.

Q: What was it that you lied about?

Defense Counsel: We object, Your Honor. He's getting into the details now and that's improper. We can't retry this witness's Florida case in the middle of our case.

Judge: I would ordinarily allow examining counsel some leeway where the prior conviction was for perjury. Here, however, the witness has readily admitted the conviction and I think that's all you're entitled to, Mr. Prosecutor. Let's not get bogged down in all the details. You've brought out the fact that he was convicted of lying under oath in front of a jury. Go on to something else now.

Prosecutor: Very well, Your Honor.

SOURCE: Jon R. Waltz, *Introduction to Criminal Evidence*. Chicago: Nelson-Hall, 1983, pp. 118-19.

questions as long as he or she is not being argumentative or badgering the witness. During cross-examination, opposing counsel attempts to weaken or destroy the testimony of a witness by questioning his or her knowledge and memory. The attorney may attempt to impeach the credibility of a witness, asking questions about any prior relationship with the defendant, use of alcohol or drugs, or criminal convictions, for example. After cross-examination, the prosecutor is permitted a **redirect**, or questions designed to clarify issues about which the witness has already testified but which have been thrown into doubt by cross-examination. Opposing counsel is then permitted to re-cross-examine, and the process continues until there are no further questions. After each prosecution witness has been subjected to direct examination and cross-examination, the prosecution rests—the government's case has been presented.

At this point, defense counsel may move for a judgment of acquittal, arguing that the government has failed to prove its case beyond a reasonable doubt, in other words, that the government's case lacks sufficient legal substance and therefore is not entitled to further consideration. In most cases this motion is made rather routinely, and is just as routinely denied by the trial judge. However, the motion can serve to lay the foundation for an appeal.

Defendant's Case-in-Chief

The defense need not present any testimony, and if the prosecution's case appears quite weak, the defense counsel may decline to do so, stating that the "defense rests." In most cases, however, the defense opts to present witnesses, one of whom may be the defendant. Each of these witnesses is subjected to direct questioning by the defense counsel and then to cross-examination by the prosecutor. The criminal history of a defendant is usually not admissible. However, if the defendant opts to testify, the prosecutor can ask about prior criminal convictions during cross-examination. After all defense witnesses have testified and have been subjected to cross-examination, redirect, and re-cross-examination, the defense rests.

After the defense has rested, the prosecutor is permitted to call further witnesses for the purpose of *rebuttal*—testimony designed to refute the testimony of defense witnesses. If the prosecution has introduced new evidence or has delved into new matters, the defense is entitled to a *rejoinder*, which is testimony restricted to new defense evidence to refute the prosecutor's rebuttal. It is actually rare for a judge to allow a rejoinder. On rare occasions when there is a surprise witness, it is during rebuttal or rejoinder that he or she is usually called to the stand.

Counsel for the defense delivers closing arguments to the jury.

At this point the defense may again move for a verdict of acquittal by arguing that the government presented insufficient evidence to warrant the case going to the jury for deliberation. The judge can grant the motion, which ends the trial, or deny the motion, which means the case goes to the jury. The judge can also reserve judgment, which means the case will go to the jury, but the judge will retain the power to direct an acquittal, a jury's decision of guilty notwithstanding; in other words, the judge can override a jury's verdict of guilty.

Closing Arguments

If the judge denies the motion for acquittal, each side will have an opportunity to address the jury. The prosecution is often allowed the opportunity to speak twice—once before defense counsel speaks and a second time in rebuttal of the defense argument. During **closing arguments**, lawyers are given rather free rein and they may engage in appeals that are dramatic and emotional. Prejudicial statements by a prosecutor, however, can cause a verdict of guilty to be overturned on appeal. Each side summarizes the testimony and argues for his or her case while pointing out weaknesses in the opponent's case. The case is now ready to go to the jury.

Charge to the Jury

At this point in the trial, the judge must provide the jury with a set of instructions on the law under which they are to reach a verdict. This **charge to the jury** is based both on statutes and appellate decisions and deals with:

1. the nature of the charges against the defendant and the elements the government must prove to the jurors' satisfaction in order to establish the commission of the crime (or *actus reus*, discussed in the first chapter);
2. the impact of rules of evidence relating to such matters as confessions and circumstantial evidence;
3. the meaning of presumption of innocence, burden of proof, the concept of reasonable doubt, and the right of a defendant not to testify; and
4. the legal provisions under which the jury is to deliberate on the case.

An error by the trial judge during the charge to the jury can result in a reversal on appeal.

Jury Deliberations

The jury now retires to deliberate in private in a room set aside for this purpose. At any point in their deliberations, they can ask the judge for help on a point of law or request to review testimony (the court reporter's transcriptions) or to view exhibits that have been entered into evidence. In some cases the jury may be **sequestered**; that is, they may be kept under guard (by bailiffs, court officers, or deputy sheriffs) during the entire trial or only during deliberations that continue for more than one day. In such situations the jurors are housed in a hotel or motel, where they are not able to talk to anyone except fellow jurors; their reading, viewing, and listening matter is monitored to insulate them from publicity about the case. If the jury is unable to reach a verdict despite encouragement from the judge, it is a **hung jury**. The jurors will be discharged, and the government must decide whether to prosecute the accused before a new jury. If the jury reaches a verdict of not guilty, the defendant is released. If the verdict is guilty, there will be posttrial motions by defense counsel for a new trial because of legal errors, for example. If these motions are denied, as they usually are, a sentencing hearing will be scheduled.

In Part II we looked at how society reacts to *crime*, from policing to judging. In Part III we will discuss the last stage of the criminal justice process—how society reacts to *criminals*—sentencing and punishment.

KEY TERMS

plea bargaining
adversarial method
overcharging
normal crimes
workgroup
jury pool
voir dire hearing
challenge for cause
peremptory challenges
discovery
opening statements

direct examination
hearsay evidence
direct or eyewitness testimony
circumstantial evidence
cross-examination
redirect
closing arguments
charge to the jury
sequester
hung jury

REVIEW QUESTIONS

1. Why do some observers consider plea bargaining to be unjust?
2. How does the criminal justice system gain the cooperation of the defendant and get him or her to plead guilty?
3. How can the prosecutor make professional life difficult for a defense attorney?
4. Why do some observers consider plea bargaining to be benign or even beneficial for the goals of justice?
5. What are the most important reasons for the existence of plea bargaining?
6. How can plea bargaining be adversarial?
7. After a suspect has been booked by the police, what are the two legal factors that a prosecutor considers in making a charging decision?
8. What are the extralegal factors that may be considered in a prosecutor's charging decision?
9. Why do so many cases that enter the criminal justice system as felonies fail to be prosecuted as charged?
10. What is meant by the "courtroom workgroup"?

11. What happened as a result of attempts to limit plea bargaining in New York and in Alaska?
12. What has the Supreme Court ruled with respect to plea bargaining?
13. What is meant by "discovery"?
14. What is the difference between challenging a prospective juror for cause and a peremptory challenge?
15. What is the purpose of a *voir dire* hearing?
16. What are the basic requirements to be eligible for jury service?
17. What determines if a defendant is constitutionally entitled to a jury trial?
18. What is meant by a "speedy trial"?
19. Why is a jury trial infrequent in criminal justice?
20. What are the various steps in a jury trial?
21. Why can't hearsay be used as evidence? What is the primary exception to the hearsay rule?
22. What is the difference between "direct" and "indirect" testimony?

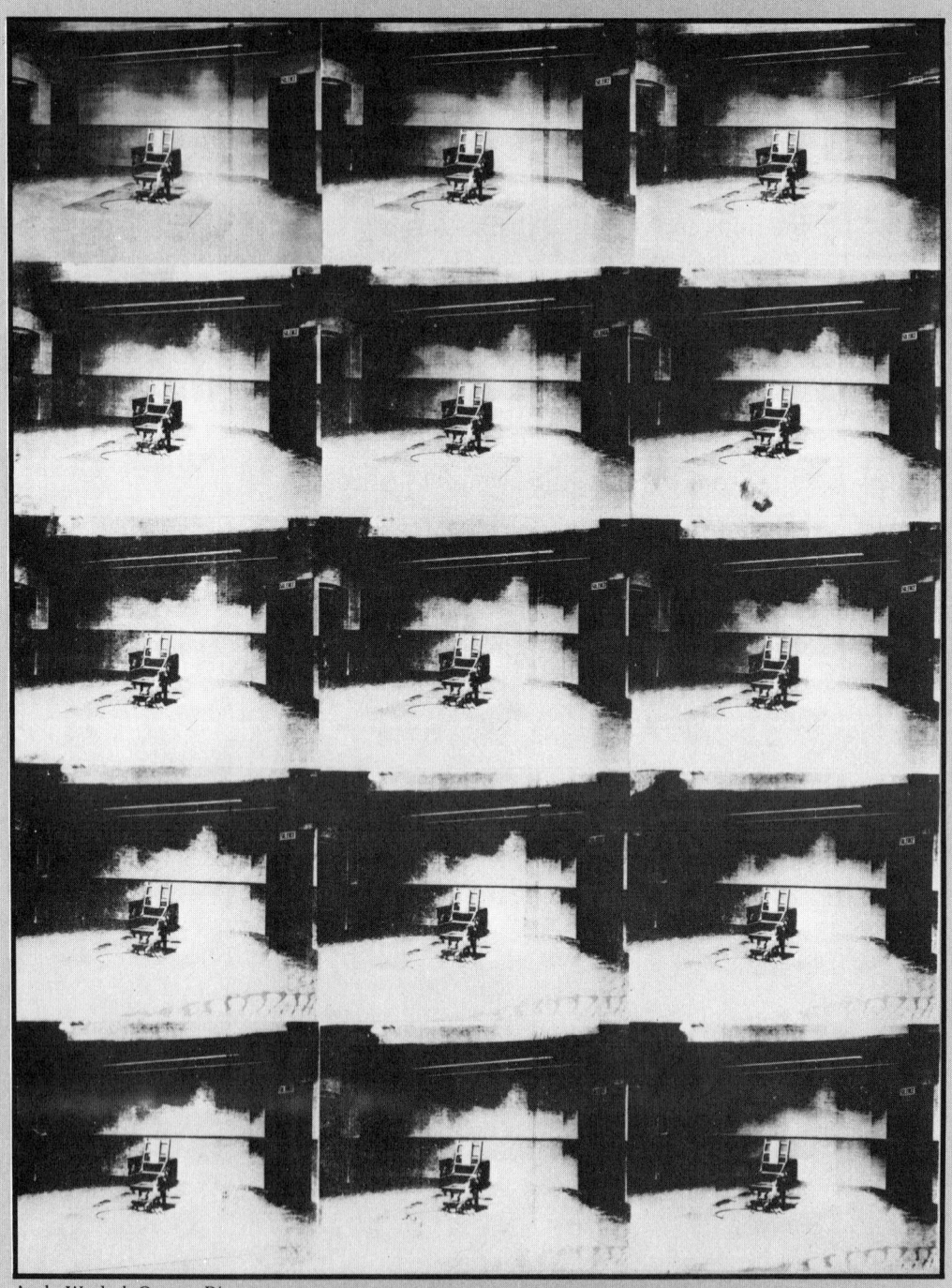

Andy Warhol, Orange Disaster

PART THREE

Reacting to Criminals

13 Sentencing and Probation

14 The Question of Punishment: Jails and Prisons

15 The Question of Punishment: Corrections and Capital Punishment

16 Parole and Community-Based Corrections

CHAPTER 13

Sentencing and Probation

THE OBJECTIVES OF SENTENCING

THEORIES OF CRIME AND SENTENCING
The Classical School
The Positive School

DETERMINATE SENTENCES

INDETERMINATE SENTENCES

SENTENCING GUIDELINES

PRESENTENCE INVESTIGATION

PROBATION
Factors in Granting Probation
Advantages and Disadvantages
Probation Supervision
The Probation Officer

REVIEW QUESTIONS

Boxes

Felony Sentencing Guidelines
Victim Restitution and Community Service
The Probation Officer

A person found guilty after a plea bargain agreement, a bench trial, or a jury trial is entitled to a sentencing hearing. At this hearing the defendant has a right to be represented by counsel in an effort to gain some form of leniency from the court, in particular, to avoid a sentence of incarceration. Alternatives to incarceration can include a fine, restitution, community service, a treatment program for alcoholism or drug addiction and, most frequently, probation. In this chapter we will examine sentencing and probation.

THE OBJECTIVES OF SENTENCING

A sentence can serve one or more objectives: retribution, incapacitation, general or specific deterrence, and rehabilitation.

1. **Retribution**. This most universal of emotions is found in the ancient concept of *lex talionis*—"an eye for an eye"—and

includes such notions as vengeance, punishment, and just deserts; in short, that criminals must "pay" for their transgressions. Ernest van den Haag (1975: 15) states that retribution imposed by courts in proportion to the gravity of the offense serves to vindicate the legal order. If they are to be taken seriously, he says, laws must "threaten, or promise, punishment for crimes. [And] society has obligated itself by threatening. It owes the carrying out of its threats." The Eighth Amendment to the Constitution, by prohibiting "cruel and unusual punishment," limits retribution to fines, imprisonment, and (with severe restrictions) capital punishment—the death penalty.

    2. **Incapacitation.** In some countries, those ruled by Islamic law, for example, thieves have their hands cut off—an obvious impairment to further theft. In our country incapacitation is limited to imprisonment. Since an offender cannot further victimize the public while in prison, some observers, such as James Q. Wilson (1975), have proffered it as a way to lower the amount of crime in the United States.

    3.   a. **General Deterrence.** Does the knowledge that a person has been punished for violating the law deter others from violating the law? To the extent that it does, general deterrence is successful; but, of course, there is no way to measure its success with any certainty.

        b. **Individual Deterrence.** From the discussion of learning theory in chapter 4, we know that behavior that is negatively reinforced tends not to be repeated—unless there are also positive rewards for the behavior that outweigh the negative ones. In any event, individual deterrence assumes that once punished for a crime, the offender is less likely to commit further crimes—the offender has learned his or her lesson.

    4. **Rehabilitation.** As opposed to simply punishing a person who commits a crime, can we "correct" the offender so that his or her future conduct will be law-abiding? In colonial days "correction" was in the form of penalties, fines, and whippings, in an effort to terrorize the offender into correcting his or her ways. Modern rehabilitation, however, refers to the application of some form of "treatment" not based on terror or coercion, although treatment is often applied in the punishing environment of a prison. Treatment can include individual and group counseling, vocational and educational programs, and specialized assistance for persons with a history of alcohol or drug abuse.

In the colonial era "correction" often involved coercing offenders into changing their ways.

Theories of Crime and Sentencing

In order to better understand how the objectives of sentencing are operationalized in the criminal justice system, it is necessary to refer again to the contrasting philosophies represented by the classical and positive schools of thought, which were discussed in chapter 4.

The Classical School

Contrary to the manner in which punishment was inflicted during the seventeenth and eighteenth centuries, the classical school of Rousseau and Beccaria argued that the law should respect neither rank nor station—all men are created equal—and punishment should be meted out with a perfect uniformity. In his *Essay on Crimes and Punishment* (1764), Beccaria stated

A group of prisoners stand with bowed heads as their offenses and sentences are read out to a crowd in Peking. In the People's Republic of China the condemned are customarily brought before the public immediately prior to their execution. These offenders—mostly rapists, murderers, and hardened criminals—will then be driven away to be shot.

that the law should stipulate a particular penalty for each specific crime, and judges should mete out identical sentences for each occurrence of the same offense; this view is the basis for determinate sentences. At a time when laws and law enforcement were unjust and disparate, and often quite brutal, Beccaria was demanding justice, equality, and moderation.

Central to the classical concept of equality before the law is the theory of free will, which maintains that every person has the ability to distinguish and choose between right and wrong, between being law-abiding and being criminal. In this view, criminal behavior is a rational choice made by a person with free will. The classical school holds that since human beings tend towards hedonism, they must be restrained from criminal acts by fear of punishment. Thus, the purpose of the law should not be retribution, but deterrence.

Ian Taylor, Paul Walton, and Jock Young (1973) are critical of the classical approach to crime and criminals and point out that

"The law, in its majesty equality, forbids the rich as well as the poor to sleep under bridges, to beg in the streets, and to steal."—Anatole France, *Crainquebille*.

it supported the interests of a rising eighteenth-century middle class that demanded legal equality with the noble classes and protection from the predations of the lower classes. They note a contradiction between the defense of equality and the emphasis on maintaining an unequal distribution of wealth and property. Taylor, Walton, and Young assert that one's position in society, not free will, determines the degree of choice with respect to committing crimes. They point out that "a system of classical justice of this order could only operate in a society where property was distributed equally," where each person had an equal stake in the system (1973:6). It is irrational for a society that does not offer viable alternatives to criminal behavior to argue that crime is simply a matter of free will. As the French novelist Anatole France noted with some sarcasm in *Crainquebille*, "The law, in its majestic equality, forbids the rich as well as the poor to sleep under bridges, to beg in the streets, and to steal."

The Positive School

The nineteenth-century Venetian physician Cesare Lombroso contributed to the field of criminology by utilizing the tools of science (see chapter 4); the field of inquiry shifted from law and philosophy to empiricism. Basic to this approach is the belief that it is possible to understand why people commit crimes and, moreover, to prevent crime by somehow responding to criminals in a scientific manner. Positivism places emphasis not on the crime, as does classicalism, but on the criminal. It contradicts the theory of free will and, in its most extreme extension, does not recognize the question of legal guilt. In other words, if science determines that the cause of a criminal act is psychological, sociological, or even biological, there is an absense of *mens rea* and, thus, no crime.

For positivists, the purposes of sentencing are not retribution and deterrence; only rehabilitation and incapacitation (for example, early Lombrosians favored castration for sex offenders) are relevant. The views of the positive school form the basis for the *indeterminate sentence*.

In summary, then, do we judge the crime or the criminal? The classical school responds, "the crime." The positivist school says, "the criminal." These contrasting approaches have become part of an American criminal justice system that uses both determinate and indeterminate sentencing.

DETERMINATE SENTENCES

In its most simplistic form, the **determinate sentence** is a specific term—for example, nine years—at the expiration of which the offender is released from custody. A sentencing judge has a "menu" (criminal code) that contains a specific sentence for each crime. The sentencing process is routine and automatic; there is no uncertainty. The judge is required to impose the term that has been set out by the legislature; deviations, in the form of judicial discretion, are not permitted. Thus, all defendants convicted of robbery would receive the same sentence, and all defendants convicted of burglary would receive the same sentence. In practice, it is seldom this simple.

A number of states and the federal government use a variety of so-called *flat* or determinate sentences; the more closely they approximate the above description the more they are determi-

> **Sentencing Ranges for Selected Felony Offenses**
>
> *Forcible Rape/Prior Convictions:* Maine (0-20 years) California (4-6 years) Indiana (6-50 years) Illinois (6-60 years).
> *Forcible Rape/First Offense:* Maine (0-20 years) California (3-5 years) Indiana (6-20 years) Illinois (6-60 years).
> *Narcotic Offense/First Offense:* Maine (0-10 years) California (3-5 years) Indiana (20-50 years) Illinois (4-30 years).
> *Simple Burglary/Prior Convictions:* Maine (0-5 years) California (28-48 months*) Indiana (2-38 years) Illinois (6-60 years[†]).
> *Simple Burglary/First Offense:* Maine (0-5 years) California (16-36 months) Indiana (2-8 years) Illinois (3-14 years).
>
> * Under the California code, one year is added to the base term for each prior prison term for a nonviolent offense; three years are added for violent offenses if the current offense is also violent. This example assumes that one prior prison term was served for a nonviolent felony.
>
> [†] Persons convicted of a class 1 or class 2 felony with two prior convictions of class 1 or class 2 felonies are sentenced as class X offenders under Illinois law.
>
> SOURCE: Based on Lagoy et al., 1978: 399.

nate. In practice, however, each determinate sentencing system provides for some amount of variance, empowering the judge with discretion. Determinate-type sentences can be classified in three categories: narrow discretion, wide discretion, and presumptive sentencing.

1. Narrow Discretion. The legislature provides a specific sentence for each level of offense. For example, all crimes that constitute a certain class of felony require the judge to impose a specific sentence—no deviations permitted. If a Class B or Class 2 felony (e.g., burglary) is punishable by imprisonment for 9–6–0 (a sentence is customarily written in terms of years, months, days; thus, a sentence of nine and a half years and zero days is written: 9–6–0), all judges are required to sentence all defendants convicted of a Class B or Class 2 to 9–6–0.

2. Wide Discretion. The legislature provides for a range of sentences for each level of offense. For example, a Class B felony is punishable with a sentence of from 6–0–0 to 12–0–0. Under this system the judge retains discretion to sentence a Class B offender to 6–0–0, 7–0–0, or 8–0–0, all the way up to 12–0–0. The sentence imposed is determinate—for a specific number of years—but the judge's choice is quite wide.

3. Presumptive Sentencing. The legislature limits discretion to a narrow range of sentences for each level of offense, and for each there is a *presumed* sentence from which the judge cannot deviate unless there are aggravating or mitigating circumstances. In other words, a defendant convicted of a Class B felony would receive a sentence of, for example, 5–0–0. If the prosecutor made a motion for "aggravation," however, the judge could increase the sentence to 6–0–0. On the other hand, if the defense counsel made a motion for "mitigation," the judge could decrease the sentence to 4–0–0.

The table, "Sentencing Ranges for Selected Felony Offenses," compares the ranges in the first four states to adopt determinate sentencing. In Indiana, Illinois, and Maine there is determinate sentencing with wide discretion, while California uses presumptive sentencing. No state utilizes narrow discretion.

INDETERMINATE SENTENCES

The Reverend Enoch C. Wines, secretary of the New York Prison Association and founder of the National Prison Association, organized a National Congress of Penitentiary and Reformatory Discipline, which met in Cincinnati in October 1870. Among the 130 delegates from twenty-four states, Canada, and South America was Zebulon R. Brockway, superintendent of the Detroit House of Correction, who presented a paper that called for a system of indeterminate sentences. Among the principles subsequently adopted by the Congress was one calling for sentences that would be indefinite, "limited only by [the inmate's] satisfactory proof of reformation" (Wines 1975: 205fn).

In 1876, the Elmira Reformatory in New York opened with Brockway as superintendent. Elmira was to be run according to the principles of the Cincinnati congress; inmates would be sentenced to indefinite terms and released upon evidence of their satisfactory progress toward reformation. Rehabilitation, not punishment, was to be the goal of sentencing and imprisonment.

The indeterminate sentence established as part of the experiment at Elmira eventually led to the adoption of a system of parole in the United States (to be discussed in chapter 16). In a system that uses the indeterminate sentence, a judge imposes a term that has both a minimum and a maximum. For example, a defendant convicted of a Class B felony could receive a sentence with a minimum of 3–0–0 and a maximum of 9–0–0; the actual date of release (between 3–0–0 and 9–0–0) is determined by a parole board. The inmate released from prison by a parole board completes the remainder of his or her indeterminate sentence under the supervision of a parole officer.

Under a system of indeterminate sentencing, persons who receive the same sentence for the same class of offense—for example 3–0–0 to 9–0–0 for a Class B felony—will be released at different times, 3–0–0, 4–0–0, or 5–0–0, all the way up to 9–0–0. The indeterminate sentence has been criticized for this differential treatment of persons committing similar crimes, as well as for the problems inherent in "rehabilitating" offenders.

The wide discretion that has characterized judicial sentencing is a source of an apparent injustice, **sentencing disparity.** As Robert H. Jackson, a former U.S. attorney general and associate justice of the Supreme Court (1941–54), has stated, "It is obviously repugnant to one's sense of justice that the judgment meted out to an offender should depend in large part on a purely fortuitous circumstance; namely, the personality of the particular judge before whom the case happens to come for disposition" (President's Commission on Law Enforcement and Administration of Justice 1972: 357).

Sentencing Guidelines

Criticism of disparate sentences in systems that use either determinate or indeterminate sentences has led to the development of **sentencing guidelines** for use by trial judges. Sherwood Zimmerman (1981:69) provides a description:

> The core of sentencing guidelines is a quantitative instrument that defines categories of offenders and indicates the appropriate sentence, or range of sentences for each category. The categories define groups of offenders who are alike on relevant criteria. A penalty schedule attached to the classification instrument indicates the appropriate sentences for each category. Sentencing guidelines thereby specify different sanctions for offenders who are presumed to deserve different sentences and like sanctions for offenders within each category.

Guidelines are usually not binding on judges, although they may be required to provide written reasons for deviating from

Drawing by von Riegen; © 1964 The New Yorker Magazine, Inc.

"*Don't worry about it. One day you're feeling down and you dish out twenty years to some poor devil. The next day you feel great and everybody gets a suspended sentence. It all evens out in the end.*"

FELONY SENTENCING GUIDELINES

Each possible crime is placed in one of five categories, from low to greatest severity of offense. Each of the categories has four possible time spans based on the rehabilitative potential of the offender as revealed in the presentence report.

Offense Severity	Very Good	Good	Fair	Poor
1. Low	Probation	Probation	Probation	2-4 years
2. Moderate	Probation	Probation	2-4 years	3-5 years
3. Very High	3-5 years	4-6 years	5-7 years	6-8 years
4. Greatest	4-6 years	5-7 years	6-8 years	7 years to life

Thus, for example, a defendant whose crime is of *moderate* severity and whose prognosis (rehabilitative potential) is *poor* would receive a sentence of between three and five years. A defendant whose crime is in the *low* severity category and whose prognosis is *very good* would receive probation.

them. Typically, guidelines utilize the past sentencing performance of each judge in a particular jurisdiction to develop the sentencing parameters for the crime and offender scores. Since the suggested sentences are based on the judges' own decisions, there is the likelihood of compliance. Thus, while sentences may vary significantly between jurisdictions, there is little disparity within any one jurisdiction.

A variation of sentencing guidelines is the **sentencing council**. As described by the President's Commission on Law Enforcement and Administration of Justice (1972: 357–58),

The sentencing council consists of several judges of a multijudge court who meet periodically to discuss sentences to be imposed in pending cases.... Foremost among their advantages is the opportunity they give for discussion of sentencing attitudes. From such a discussion a consensus on sentencing standards may emerge. The ultimate responsibility for determining sentences rests with the judge to whom the case is assigned, although the discussion and need to state reasons for a sentence tend to restrain the imposition of unreasonably severe or lenient sentences.

Another variation is **appellate review** of sentences whereby the appellate court can modify downward any sentence that falls beyond some chosen norm. According to the President's Commission on Law Enforcement and Administration of Justice (1972: 358), appellate review encourages

the development of uniform and considered sentencing policies within a jurisdiction. It leads both the trial court and the appellate court to give sustained and explicit consideration to the justification for particular sentences. It provides a workable means of correcting unjust and ill-considered sentences, particularly those in which the punishment imposed is grossly inappropriate.

Carl Imlay and Elsie Reid believe that one of the advantages of this appellate review is "that it can contribute to an offender's rehabilitation by enhancing his belief that the system is fair and not subject to the unchecked caprice of one official" (1975: 15).

PRESENTENCE INVESTIGATION

States utilizing a system of determinate sentencing in which the judge has wide discretion and states utilizing the indeterminate sentence often make extensive use of a presentence investigation (psi) report. The psi is compiled by a probation officer and can play an important part in a judge's sentencing decision.

The presentence investigation report is based on the philosophy of the positive school; it conveys to a sentencing judge information about the criminal, not simply legal information relative to the crime. The psi is prepared by a probation officer at the request of a sentencing judge, and it has four basic purposes.

1. The primary purpose of the psi is to provide a basis for the judge to render an informed sentencing decision, particularly for or against placing an offender on probation.

2. The psi also provides a basis for a plan of probation or, if the defendant is sentenced to imprisonment and paroled, parole supervision.

3. If the defendant is sentenced to a term of imprisonment, the psi assists correctional officials in their classification and rehabilitation planning, and it is usually their main source of information about the new inmate. For example, does he or she present an escape or suicide risk or a threat to other inmates? Is the inmate in need of medical or psychiatric treatment?

4. The psi report can serve as a source of information for research efforts in criminal justice.

The probation officer (PO) typically interviews the defendant, important persons in the defendant's life (such as spouse, parents), the arresting officer, and sometimes the victim or complainant and the defendant's employer(s) or school officials. The PO will review the defendant's arrest record ("rap sheet"), which in many instances is incomplete. Agencies responsible for processing criminals often fail to submit the results of an arrest to the state agency responsible for maintaining individual criminal records. Therefore, arrest data may appear without any information about the disposition. The PO may have to follow up on any arrests for which dispositions are not indicated, because most jurisdictions preclude probation or require additional penalties in cases where a defendant has been convicted of a prior felony. The PO will also review any prior psi reports or those of probation or parole agencies. Based on his or her analysis, the PO may request a psychological or psychiatric exam for the defendant, and the results will be included in the psi report. While the quality and the length of the psi report differs from jurisdiction to jurisdiction, there are standard headings basic to most of them:

- circumstances of the offense (official police version)
- defendant's version of the offense, particularly any mitigating or extenuating circumstances
- complainant's statement

- prior criminal history, including juvenile record
- family and marital history
- employment history
- education
- military service
- mental and physical health
- probation officer's summary, which may include a recommendation.

The degree to which a psi report influences a judge's sentencing decision has been the subject of a great deal of inconclusive research. Most studies reveal a high correlation between the recommendation of a PO and the sentence imposed by a judge. There remains an important question that the research has not adequately answered, however, and it concerns the *direction of influence*. Does the recommendation of the probation officer influence the judge, or does the judge influence the recommendation of the probation officer? In other words, does the opinion of the PO better explain the sentence, or does the judge impose, directly or indirectly, his or her opinion on the PO? For example, if the PO knows that a particular judge has it in for defendants who commit certain crimes, does that influence the PO's recommendation in favor of a lengthy term of imprisonment? While the psi report is usually prepared after a finding of guilty, in some cases it may play a role in plea bargaining arrangements. In such cases a judge may hold in abeyance any decision to accept a plea bargain arrangement until he or she has read the psi report.

Requiring a psi report varies from state to state. Some jurisdictions require one in all felony cases; some make it dependent on the judge's decision; some provide for a short form report. A study (Comptroller General of the United States 1976) of four representative counties in states where the psi is required revealed that in about half the cases a psi had not been done. Additionally, of those reports that had been completed, many were deficient in information and/or verification of information. After having read hundreds of probation reports in several states, and having recently sent for sample reports from several probation departments, this author can corroborate that study's finding that psi reports often lack important information and verification.

Presentence Investigation:
State of Indiana, Marion County Superior Court,
Criminal Division

State of Indiana

    vs.

Sean Browne

                        Bribery, Class C Felony

Date: July 7, 1985
Plea: Guilty As Charged
Finding: Under Advisement
Source of Referral: The Honorable Harold M. Bannerman

SOURCES OF INFORMATION

Sean Browne, Defendant
Indiana Police Division juvenile and adult records
Prosecutor's Office, files
Criminal Court, files
Carol Trayner, deputy prosecutor
Barbara (nee Kirwin) Browne, defendant's wife
Reverend Michael Kirwin, defendant's father-in-law

JUVENILE AND ADULT RECORD

    The defendant has no known juvenile or adult criminal record in Marion County other than a traffic violation filed at the time of his arrest for the Instant Offense. The traffic violation (Driving with a Suspended License) was resolved in Municipal Court Part IV with the defendant receiving a judgment for Seventy-five ($75.00) Dollars fine/costs.

OFFICIAL VERSION

    The defendant is charged with Bribery of a police officer. According to Officer John Singleton's Arrest Report and Affidavit for Probable Cause, the defendant was stopped at about 11:35 P.M. on January 15, 1985, for driving a car with yellow headlights (fog lights). A routine computer check of the defendant's driver's license revealed that it was an Illinois license and had been suspended in July, 1982. The defendant was then arrested for Driving with a Suspended License and placed in the officer's patrol car for transportation to the IPD lock-up. Before the officer had completed his arrest forms, however, the defendant made an offer to give the officer Forty ($40.00) Dollars if he would let him go. Officer Singleton reports he made no reply and, with an assisting officer leaning in the window and listening, asked the defendant to repeat himself. The defendant again made the offer of Forty ($40.00) Dollars for his release and he was then charged with Attempted Bribery.

On February 28, 1985, the defendant was found guilty in Municipal Court of Driving with a Suspended License. On June 15, 1985, the defendant appeared in Marion County Superior Court, Criminal Division, Room V, with the Honorable Harold M. Bannerman presiding. At this time a plea agreement was made known to the effect that the defendant agrees to plead guilty to Bribery (Class C Felony) in exchange for the State's agreement to make no recommendation regarding sentencing.

VICTIM'S VERSION

Other than the officer who filed the charges against the offender, there is no victim for this offense.

DEFENDANT'S VERSION

The defendant agrees basically with the arresting officer's description of the circumstances of his arrest; however, he suggests that his experience in Chicago (where he claims bribery of police officers is commonplace) and his lack of experience in Indianapolis (he and his wife had arrived for their first visit with his wife's father) prompted his actions. The defendant realizes that his actions were wrong, but did not expect that the consequences would be as serious as they have turned out to be.

SOCIAL HISTORY

The defendant was born on May 1, 1960, in Chicago, Illinois, the first of two children of Michael Browne and Sarah (nee Harris) Browne. After his parents' divorce in 1973, the defendant remained with his mother for five years and apparently continues to have a good relationship with her and with his brother, Clyde, who lives with their mother. The defendant's father, who lives in Chicago, has had infrequent contact with the defendant since the divorce.

The defendant completed the 11th grade and expressed an interest in obtaining his G.E.D.

The subject is a (25) twenty-five-year-old Black Male (5'9" and 165 pounds) with no identifying marks and no known current physical or emotional problems. Though he concedes that he had been drinking beer prior to being arrested for the Instant Offense, the defendant claims that alcohol use is not a problem for him, and administration by this officer of the Michigan Alcoholism Screening Test supports this contention.

The defendant claims to be of the Baptist faith but does not now attend church regularly and does not feel that it holds any particular importance in his life. Married since 1983, the defendant lives with his wife Barbara (nee Kirwin) Browne at 2284 S. California in Chicago, Illinois. He has one dependent child from a previous relationship; however, the mother of this child had married and child support is not required of him.

With his car (1979 Chevrolet Malibu) and some furniture as his only assets and two (2) credit balances totalling over Fifteen Hundred ($1,500) Dollars as his only debts, the defendant has a stable work history and has been employed full time as a maintenance worker for Symphonic Works at 2214 N. Ellis in Chicago for the past four (4) years.

EVALUATION

The defendant is before the Court on a charge of Bribery of a police officer. A plea bargain has been offered and accepted, to the effect that the defendant agrees to plead guilty to the Class C Felony charge of Bribery, in exchange for the State's agreement to make no recommendation regarding sentencing. The defendant recognizes the wrongness of his actions, but cites previous experiences in his home state as a factor in his decision to bribe the arresting police officer.

Married, with a steady job and apparently good family and social support in his home (City of Chicago), the defendant appears to have few deficits that would require attention from outside sources.

RECOMMENDATION

Because this is his first offense of a criminal nature, because the Instant Offense is non-violent and suggests no risk to the community, and because the defendant presents little need for supervision provided by this department, this officer recommends suspended sentence with inactive and unsupervised probation.

Respectfully Submitted,

Horace E. Miles
Probation Officer

PROBATION

Probation refers to "the conditional freedom granted by a judicial officer to an alleged or adjudged adult or juvenile offender, as long as the person meets certain conditions of behavior" (*Dictionary of Criminal Justice Data Terminology* 1981). In the United States probation can be traced back to the activities of John Augustus (1784–1859), a successful Boston shoemaker. In 1852, *A Report of the Labors of John Augustus* was published, and in it Augustus wrote, "I was in court one morning . . . in which the man was charged with being a common drunkard. He told me that if he could be saved from the House of Correction, he never again would taste intoxicating liquors: I bailed him, by permission of the Court" (Augustus 1972: 4–5). Like the early probation officers who followed in his footsteps, Augustus was a volunteer who worked without pay. He would appear in court and offer to bail a defendant. If the judge agreed, and he usually did, Augustus would assist the person, helping him or her to find work or a place to live. Like modern probation officers, he kept detailed records of his activities and reported to the court on the progress of his charges.

The work of John Augustus was continued by various prisoner's and children's aid societies. While prisoner's aid societies hired agents to assist adult offenders, children's aid societies employed agents to rescue children from the criminal courts and to assist those who were neglected. In 1878, Massachusetts became the first state to pass a law authorizing the hiring of a probation officer; the mayor of Boston was authorized to hire a probation officer who was supervised by the superintendent of police. The innovation spread slowly; by 1925 probation was available for juveniles in every state, and for adults by 1956 (Task Force on Corrections 1966).

Factors in Granting Probation

A sentence of probation depends upon a number of considerations:

1. The crime for which the defendant has been convicted—most states preclude a sentence of probation for such crimes as

murder, kidnapping, and rape; others extend the list to include robbery, burglary, and arson.
2. The defendant's prior felony record—most states preclude a sentence of probation for a defendant previously convicted of a felony.
3. The probation officer's recommendation—it is doubtful that a judge would render a sentence of probation against the recommendation of the PO for imprisonment.
4. The outcome of plea negotiations—probation may be the sentence agreed upon by the defendant, prosecutor, and judge in exchange for a plea of guilty.
5. The attitude of the prosecutor's office (and possibly the police) toward a sentence of probation.
6. Extralegal considerations, including the amount of publicity in a particular case, public sentiment, and the attitude of the victim(s).

Advantages and Disadvantages

A sentence of probation, as opposed to imprisonment, has some important advantages.

1. It saves the cost of imprisonment.
2. It allows offenders to remain in the community where they can be employed and participate in educational, vocational, and therapeutic (alcohol, drug treatment) programs.
3. It allows offenders to remain with their families and maintain beneficial community ties.
4. It links offenders to a probation agency that can assist their rehabilitative efforts.

A sentence of probation, as opposed to imprisonment, has some important disadvantages.

1. The offender is free to victimize the community.
2. The deterrent value of the law is depreciated.

Probation Supervision

A sentence of probation places an offender under the supervision of a probation agency. Of the more than 1,900 probation agencies supervising adult offenders in the United States, slightly more than half are state-level agencies; the others are county or municipal agencies. In almost half of the states, probation services are administered by the executive branch of government, often as part of a combined probation–parole system. In the other states it is part of the judicial branch. According to the Bureau of Justice statistics, at any given time there are approximately 1.5 million adults under probation supervision in the United States.

A person placed on probation is required to sign a contract agreeing to abide by certain rules or risk being considered in violation of probation, a situation that could result in imprisonment. The rules of probation are fairly standard from agency to agency, although the language may vary. The probationer is cautioned against engaging in criminal conduct, associating with "undesirables," possessing weapons, abusing alcohol or using controlled substances without medical authorization, and leaving the jurisdiction without prior permission. The probationer is required to make in-person, telephone, or mail reports to the probation officer, to seek and maintain lawful employment, to support dependents, to keep the PO advised of any changes in residence or employment, and to report immediately if questioned or arrested by a law enforcement officer. The judge or probation agency may also impose special conditions; for example, an offender with a history of alcohol or drug abuse may be required to attend a treatment program. Victim **restitution** and community service are becoming popular conditions imposed on probationers by sentencing judges.

When a probationer successfully completes the period of supervision, he or she is discharged by the sentencing judge. If a probationer violates probation, usually by absconding (failing to report) or being convicted of a new crime, probation can be revoked by the judge after a hearing. A finding by the judge that a probationer has violated the conditions of probation in an important respect can result in imprisonment. (For details of the probation violation process, see Abadinsky 1987.)

The Probation Officer

After being sentenced to probation, the defendant is required to make an in-person report to the probation agency office, where he or she will be assigned to the caseload of a probation officer. The PO will explain the rules of probation and discuss the probationer's residence and employment plans. The probationer will be placed on a reporting schedule requiring periodic (usually

Common Pleas Court

To .... Docket No.
Address ....

In accordance with authority conferred by Ohio Probation Law, you have been placed on probation this date, ... by the Hon. .... for a period of .... sitting in and for this Court at ....

CONDITIONS OF PROBATION

It is the order of the Court that you shall comply with the following conditions of probation:

(1) You shall refrain from violation of any law (federal, state, and local). You shall get in touch immediately with your probation officer if arrested or questioned by a law-enforcement officer.

(2) You shall associate and communicate only with law-abiding persons and maintain reasonable hours.

(3) You shall work regularly at a lawful occupation and support your legal dependents, if any, to the best of your ability. When out of work you shall notify your probation officer at once.

(4) You shall not leave the county or state without permission of the probation officer.

(5) You shall secure advance approval from the probation officer, in writing, if at any time you wish to:

    a. Purchase or operate a motor vehicle
    b. Incur debts whether by borrowing money or installment buying.
    c. Take on additional responsibilities, such as marrying.
    d. Change employment or place of residence.
    e. Leave the county or state.
    f. Own or carry firearms or other weapons.

(6) You shall follow the probation officer's instructions and advice.

(7) You shall not operate a motor vehicle unless you have liability insurance which has been approved by your probation officer.

(8) You shall not possess, use, sell, distribute or have under your control any narcotic drugs, barbiturates, marijuana, paregoric, or extracts containing them in any form or instruments for administering them except on prescription of a licensed physician. The special conditions ordered by the Court are as follows:

I understand that the Court may change the conditions of probation, reduce or extend the period of probation, and at any time during the probation period or within   years from the date you were placed on probation, may issue a warrant and revoke probation for a violation occurring during the probation period.

I have read, or had read to me, the above conditions of probation. I fully understand them and I will abide by them.

(Signed) ....   (Signed) ....
    Probation Officer   Date   Probationer   Date

CONDITIONS OF PROBATION
INTRODUCTION

The Court has placed you on probation expecting you to use this opportunity to prove to yourself and to others that you are capable of living a socially acceptable life as a productive and responsible, law-abiding member of society. You may earn a final release from probation and retain the privileges and responsibilities of citizenship.

A probation officer will be assigned to work with you, to help you make an acceptable social adjustment. The officer will help you in every way possible, will be available for counselling when problems arise, and will submit regular reports of your progress to the Court.

It is also the probation officer's duty to require you to live by the conditions of probation. The officer has the authority and responsibility to enforce these conditions by notifying the Court of any violation and recommending your appearance before the Court as a probation violator. The probation officer has the power to arrest you without a warrant, or may order your arrest.

Your goal is to terminate your sentence on or before the maximum expiration date. This can be accomplished if you will demonstrate an acceptable attitude and responsible conduct while on probation. After you have completed your period of probation to the satisfaction of the Court, you will receive a written discharge from probation and restoration of all civil rights.

The conditions of probation have been carefully designed as guidelines for acceptable probation behavior. If you should violate one or more of these conditions of probation, the Court has the legal authority to revoke your probation and commit you to a state institution to serve your sentence.

AGREEMENT

In addition to agreeing to abide by the conditions of probation outlined on the reverse side of this paper, I understand and accept that while on probation I do not have the right to vote, serve on juries, or hold public office.

I further understand that if I am granted permission to be in another state, or if I should be there without permission and my return to Ohio is authorized, I hereby waive extradition to the State of Ohio and agree not to contest efforts to effect such return.

The above **INTRODUCTION** and **AGREEMENT** of probation have been explained to me and I understand them.

(Signed) ....
             Probationer   Date   Probation Officer   Date

Victim Restitution and Community Service

Among the conditions of probation, as determined by the court, can be restitution to the victim and/or the community; restitution is an act of restoring, a making good or giving an equivalent for some injury.

Victim Restitution. In addition to paying court costs, fines, and fees, probationers may be required to make restitution or reparation in any sum determined by the court and pay a percentage of their income to compensate the victim for any property damage or medical expenses sustained as a direct result of the offense. The court weighs each case individually and assesses a sum determined to be fair compensation.

Community Service. The Courts may also sentence probationers to a more innovative form of restitution—community service. The offender may be assigned to devote a specific number of hours (anywhere from 24 to 1,000) in service to a local non-profit social agency. Community service restitution may be required in lieu of fines where an offender is unable to pay or in those cases where a fine would have little significance to the offender as punishment. Generally, one hour of community service is valued by the court as equal to one hour of minimum wages in fines.

Fines may be a temporary hardship, but community service can be a valuable rehabilitating experience for offenders. They may be required to serve in an agency where they can see first-hand the destructive results of crime. Or, if they have special skills, the court may make a special effort to put these talents to work for the community.

SOURCE: State of Texas.

13 ▪ SENTENCING AND PROBATION

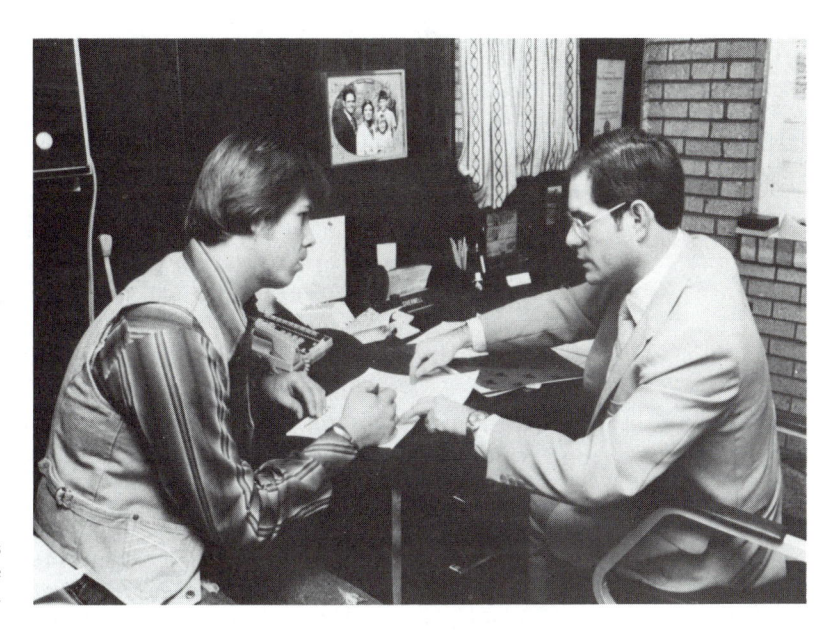

A probation officer helps a probationer complete a job application form.

weekly, monthly) in-person or, in rural jurisdictions, telephone or mail reports to inform the PO of his or her current situation. The PO will make periodic visits to the probationer's residence and place of employment, the frequency of such visits being dependent on the size of the officer's caseload. Unfortunately, in most jurisdictions caseloads run very high, often one hundred to two hundred cases, leaving the PO with very little time to visit clients. Probation supervision is quite often only perfunctory.

Probation officers have a dual responsibility: to provide social services designed to assist in the rehabilitative process and to keep alert for possible indications of criminality (violations of probation rules are supposed to be indicative of more serious—that is, criminal—violations). In practice, however, the size of the PO's caseload often precludes meaningful provision of social services, while control or surveillance functions may be completely discounted.

In many jurisdictions, probation officers (sometimes called probation agents) are required to have at least a bachelor's degree or related experience, and some probation agencies require additional graduate education in a social service discipline such as psychology or social work and/or experience as a counselor in

THE PROBATION OFFICER

Under direction, performs the work as required by any court under the jurisdiction of the New Jersey Supreme Court, but not restricted to, conducting investigations, both predispositional and postdispositional in nature; exercises supervision over defendants adjudicated or convicted offenders, or others who require supervision or assistance by court order; enforces orders for child support and alimony payments; conducts custody investigations; does related work as required and/or mandated by court decision or rule.

Examples of Work. Investigates home and living conditions, neighborhood environment, school record, employment history and other relevant matters pertaining to persons referred to the probation department for investigations.

Interviews relatives, complainants and other persons having knowledge of the life history of defendants/offenders. Prepares presentence, prehearing, pretrial, child custody and other investigations required by the courts.

Supervises and counsels defendants, offenders, probationers and others placed on supervision. Assists in the training and supervision of volunteers. Prepares special reports in connection with violations of court imposed conditions. Assists in the monitoring and collection of court ordered payments. Keeps accurate case records and prepares clear, sound, and informative reports containing findings, conclusions and recommendations. Presides over precourt conferences; performs juvenile intake and referral tasks; and may be required to make arrests in accordance with state law and departmental policy.

SOURCE: State of New Jersey

a social service agency. By law the PO is usually a *peace officer*, a public employee responsible for law enforcement or maintaining the peace. In some agencies this means the PO is responsible for enforcing probation-violation warrants and may carry firearms. Most probation agencies, however, usually restrict the law enforcement activities of their probation officers, and they are seldom allowed to carry firearms. When law enforcement activities are required, they are usually carried out by police officers or deputy sheriffs (or in the federal system, U.S. marshals or FBI special agents). Probation officers attached to a juvenile court have additional responsibilities, which will be discussed in chapter 17.

Convicts who do not receive probation or other alternative to incarceration, and those who receive and subsequently violate probation, enter the bleakest and most troublesome segment of our system of justice, America's jails and prisons.

KEY TERMS

retribution
incapacitation
general deterrence
individual deterrence
rehabilitation
determinate sentence
narrow discretion

wide discretion
presumptive sentencing
sentencing disparity
sentencing guidelines
sentencing council
appellate review
restitution

REVIEW QUESTIONS

1. What are the four objectives of sentencing?
2. According to the classical school, what is the primary purpose of punishment?
3. What are the shortcomings of the classical approach to criminals?
4. How does the positive approach to crime and criminals differ from the classical approach?
5. What was Lombroso's major contribution to criminology?
6. Explain how the positive approach can mean that criminals are not legally responsible for their actions.
7. According to the classical school, should we judge the crime or the criminal?
8. What is a determinate sentence? Is this type of sentence based upon the views of the classical or positive school?
9. What is the presumptive form of determinate sentence?
10. What is meant by an indeterminate sentence?

11. Why can sentencing disparity be considered a problem?
12. What is the purpose of sentencing guidelines? How do they operate?
13. What is a sentencing council, and what is its purpose?
14. What are the four purposes of the presentence investigation report?
15. How does the probation officer develop information for the presentence investigation report?
16. What are two possible explanations for the high correlation between a probation officer's recommendation and the judge's sentencing decision?
17. Why would a presentence investigation report be prepared before a defendant's conviction?
18. A sentence of probation depends on a number of considerations; what are they?
19. What are the advantages and disadvantages of a sentence of probation?
20. What are the dual responsibilities of a probation officer?
21. Why is probation supervision often perfunctory?

CHAPTER 14

The Question of Punishment: Jails and Prisons

HISTORY OF THE AMERICAN JAIL
The Modern American Jail
Problems of Jail Maintenance

HISTORY OF THE AMERICAN PRISON
The Pennsylvania System
The Auburn System
Elmira Reformatory
Prison Labor

The Big House
Prisonization
Maintaining Control

REVIEW QUESTIONS

In this chapter we will go beyond the stone walls of the correctional institution into the melancholy domain of the keepers and the kept, an important piece of American history because the United States has long been a pioneer in the development of jails and prisons. In 1831, for example, Alexis de Tocqueville (1805–59), author of the classic study *Democracy in America* (1835), came from France to the United States primarily to study our prison system (see Beaumont and Tocqueville 1964). We will trace the evolution of jails and prisons as a product of the changing philosophy of criminal justice.

HISTORY OF THE AMERICAN JAIL

A jail is "a confinement facility administered by an agency of local government . . . for adults but sometimes also containing juveniles, which holds persons detained pending adjudication and/or persons committed after adjudication, usually those committed on sentences of a year or less" (*Dictionary of Criminal Justice Data Terminology* 1981). The word *jail* is Latin in origin, and historical documents often use its older spelling (the pronunciation is the same), *gaol*. J.M. Moynahan and Earle Stewart (1980: 9) state that "the American jail, like many other elements in the system of criminal justice in the United States, has its origins in England. The most essential features of the American jail system were brought almost without change to the earliest British colonies and settlements and were modified only slightly to meet peculiar situations in the colonial arena." The colonial jail emerged out of the British experience with three types of institution: (1) jails used to detain those awaiting trial or punishment, (2) houses of correction or bridewells used to house or confine the old and the infirm, vagrants, beggars, homeless children, paupers, and (3) the workhouse, which provided training and work for the unemployed. Local jails emerged throughout the American colonies usually under the management of the sheriff. These poorly constructed institutions, David Rothman (1971: 56) notes, "were not only unlikely places for intimidating the criminal, but even ill-suited for confining him"—escapes were frequent.

British law was severe; many crimes, even petty theft, were punishable by execution. As a result, colonial juries often refused to find a defendant guilty, preferring to free the man rather than condemn him to the gallows. Rothman (1971: 60) notes, "In this way, criminals had escaped all discipline, and the community had allowed, even encouraged, them to persist in their ways." The use of imprisonment provided a way to mete out punishment that was proportionate to the severity of the offense.

In the lengthy history of punishment, the use of incarceration is of rather late vintage. Until the concept of imprisonment as punishment emerged in the latter half of the eighteenth century, American judges utilized fines, stocks, pillories, public cages, whipping, banishment, and hanging. Rothman (1971: 48) notes:

> A sentence of imprisonment was uncommon, never used alone. Local jails held men caught up in the *process of judgment*, not those who had completed it; persons awaiting trial, those convicted but not yet punished, debtors who had still to meet their obligations. The idea of serving time in a prison as a method of correction was the invention of a later generation.

The early American jail emerged out of the British experience with several kinds of institutions, among which was the house of correction, used to house or confine the old and infirm, vagrants, beggars, homeless children, and paupers. *Above*, a prison van unloads at "the Tombs" jail in New York City, ca. 1857.

The ideals of the Enlightenment (out of which developed the "classical school" discussed in chapter 13) and a repugnance for things British following independence inspired Americans to discard corporal punishment and the extensive use of execution in favor of imprisonment, a process that was complete about the time of the Civil War. The jail emerged as a place for the punishment of persons convicted of crimes, but it proved to be inadequate. Jails were not secure enough for more serious offenders, nor were they equipped for the reformation process—strict discipline and hard labor—that became the cornerstone of American penal practices. The jail slowly returned to its former status as a place for persons awaiting trial or punishment, while also housing less serious offenders, except in the South. In the Southern states, where there were few prisons (large state-operated institutions for convicted felons), the county jail and the chain gang were used for all types of offenders.

Some jails, like the famous Walnut Street Jail in Philadelphia,

Until imprisonment emerged as a means of sentencing criminals, American judges often used cages, stocks, pillories, and whipping posts to punish offenders.

were converted to prisons. J.M. Moynahan and Earle Stewart (1980: 38–39) state:

> From the time of the conversion of the Walnut Street Jail to a prison [1790], various prisons began to be constructed in different states. The new emphasis on reform was directed at the prisons and the serious offenders. Interest in the different classes of misdemeanants waned, and conditions in jails lost the reformers' interest. The jails, workhouses, and houses of correction continued to exist, but there were few people concerned with their conditions or that of their

I Am a Fugitive from a Chain Gang (1932) chronicled the story of an ex-soldier (Paul Muni) wrongly condemned to hard labor on a Georgia chain gang. One of Hollywood's earliest social protest films, the movie graphically portrayed the brutalities of the chain gang, resulting in public outcry and major reforms of the system.

inmates. This shift away from the jails had a profound and lasting effect upon these institutions—an effect that is evident today.

The Modern American Jail

The jail continues to be a place of confinement for three types of persons:

1. defendants awaiting trial for misdemeanors and felonies,
2. inmates convicted of a felony awaiting transportation to a state correctional facility (prison overcrowding in many

states has resulted in convicted felons being housed in county jails for indefinite periods of time), and
3. convicts serving a sentence for a misdemeanor.

Other persons who may at times be confined in a jail include probation and parole violators awaiting hearings, persons awaiting extradition to another state or another country, offenders being housed temporarily for federal authorities, material witnesses, persons in protective custody, persons in contempt of court and juveniles (housed in a separate section of the jail).

There are approximately 3,500 jails in the United States under a variety of names: county jail, house of correction, house of detention. Some 2,900 are under county jurisdiction and usually administered by a sheriff; the remainder are operated at the municipal level except in Alaska, Connecticut, Delaware, Rhode Island, and Vermont, where they are under state jurisdiction. On any given day American jails house more than 200,000 persons, about 60 percent of whom are awaiting trial (Bureau of Justice Statistics 1984).

Moynahan and Stewart (1980) note that there is no such institution as a "typical jail" in the United States. Despite the diversity, however, Harry Allen and Clifford Simonsen (1981: 411) offer some generalizations:

> Most jails are fairly uniform in their basic structural arrangements. Usually they are designed to allow for a minimum staff while providing secure confinement for inmates. A large central cagelike structure called the "bullpen" is used for most of the nonviolent prisoners and drunks (the latter use generating another nickname, the "tank"). Larger jails may contain several bullpens and a separate drunk tank. The central area is usually surrounded by rows of cells, facing inward toward the bullpens. Like keepers of caged animals, officials often limit contact with inmates by passing food into the bullpens and cells through slots in the doors.

Generalizations about jail conditions tend to be quite bleak, as this quote from Richard W. Velde, a former federal official with the Law Enforcement Assistance Administration, exemplifies.

> Jails are festering sores in the criminal justice system. There are no model jails anywhere; we know, we tried to find them. Almost no-

where are there rehabilitative programs operated in conjunction with jails. It's harsh to say, but the truth is that jail personnel are the most uneducated, untrained and poorly paid of all personnel in the criminal justice system—and furthermore, there aren't enough of them. The result is what you would expect, only worse. Jails are, without question, brutal, filthy, cesspools of crime—institutions which serve to brutalize and embitter men, to prevent them from returning to a useful role in society. (McGee 1975: 5-6)

While not necessarily typical of all, or even most, jails, the cost of confining an inmate in a New York City jail gives some indication of just how expensive jails can be; according to the Correctional Association of New York, the cost of keeping one inmate incarcerated for one year in New York during 1985 was in excess of $40,000. This includes, in addition to direct operating costs, such indirect but real costs as pension and fringe benefits for correctional employees and debt charges on past capital improvements for the jail system. The relatively high cost of operating a jail compounds the other difficulties endemic to this type of institution.

Problems of Jail Maintenance

Institutions providing twenty-four hour services—nursing homes and mental institutions, as well as jails—are rather expensive to operate. These **total institutions** (Goffman 1961) are responsible for providing for all of the needs of their residents. There is continuous wear and tear on the physical plant, on the plumbing and electrical systems, on floors and doors. Merely keeping the institution sanitary and providing food for residents requires a tremendous effort and expenditure of resources. Staff must be on duty around the clock (168 hours per week), so they serve in shifts; for each staff position the institution may actually have to employ five persons to cover all the shifts seven days a week.

In addition to sharing the problems of other total institutions, jails have several problems peculiar to their genre. First, the jail houses an often hostile and aggressive population of persons who do not want to remain in custody. Internal security—protecting correction officers from inmates and protecting inmates from other inmates—is a continuous problem. Inadequate funding for jails limits the number of officers available during any shift and places both officers and inmates at risk. In addition, recreational facilities are usually limited or nonexistent, and overcrowding is the rule.

Second, the categories of persons housed in a jail makes the population quite unstable; most inmates spend only short periods of time before release or transfer, and new entrants arrive daily. Third, the flow of persons in and out of a jail on a regular basis makes security a continuous problem. During regular business hours (Monday to Friday, 9–5) lawyers and law enforcement personnel enter the jail regularly to consult with or interview inmates. At the same time some inmates are transported to court by correction officers, and others need to be transported to hospitals for medical care. Provisions must be made for inmates to receive visits from spouses and relatives; visitors must be screened and searched, and packages for inmates, containing clothing or toiletries, for example, must be checked. Jail officials who become lax may release the wrong inmates or permit contraband to enter the institution. In one situation, for example, the author was in a jail waiting to transport three inmates to a state prison, only to discover that they had been released. Correction officers had mistaken the three prisoners for three defendants who were being prepared for release on bail.

An unstable total institution with a bored, hostile, crowded population is obviously an unpleasant environment in which to work or be in custody. This fact of life for many defendants tends to make them more amenable to a plea bargain that promises to quickly remove them from jail, even when that only means a transfer to state prison.

Since the 1970s a number of organizations concerned with jails have established **jail standards** for example, the American Bar Association, American Correctional Association, American Public Health Association, National Sheriffs' Association. States have also established minimum standards for jails, although enforcement has sometimes required judicial intervention. The American Correctional Association has a program to "accredit" jails that meet its minimum standards; few have been accredited and some of those have subsequently received court orders requiring them to reduce overcrowding. The standards set by nongovernmental organizations, while not legally binding, provide a standard for litigation and court orders designed to improve jail conditions.

History of the American Prison

In order to better understand the current state of American prisons, there are several historical factors that are worth considering. First, the inhabitants of these institutions have always been members of a disadvantaged underclass. Minority persons, whether immigrant German, Scandinavian, or Irish, Jews, Italians, Poles, or migrant blacks or Hispanics, have, each in their own time, been overrepresented in the prison population. Second, while the humanitarian motivations of criminal justice reformers cannot be dismissed out of hand, they have tended to play a minor role compared to economic motivations. For example, the move away from execution and toward imprisonment for most crimes was certainly a humane reform. Many of those

The Walnut Street Jail in Philadelphia originally combined features of the British gaol, workhouse, and house of correction. In 1790, the Pennsylvania legislature converted the jail into a state prison "for the purpose of confining the more hardened and atrocious offenders."

responsible for these reforms were religious people motivated by their faith; however, they were also economically successful—the Quakers in Philadelphia, for example—and their property interests were at stake. Because the penalty for most property crimes was execution, juries would often refuse to convict defendants. Reducing the level of punishment to incarceration meant juries would be more likely to convict those who victimized propertied persons.

The Pennsylvania System

A prison is a penal institution operated by state government to incarcerate convicts sentenced for felony crimes. They are typically large institutions housing thousands of inmates. The early prisons in America were based on similar institutions in Europe, and the **Walnut Street Jail** in Philadelphia, which was converted to a prison, provides an example. The Walnut Street Jail was the result of legislation enacted on February 26, 1773; it combined all of the features of three types of British institution: the gaol, the workhouse, and the house of correction. That is, it housed a mixture of persons: those awaiting trial, awaiting punishment, the unemployed, debtors, and the destitute. During the Revolutionary War it was used to house military prisoners.

In 1786, a revised penal code substituted sentences of hard labor for capital punishment in all but two major crimes. In response, local sheriffs began to use gangs of convicts to work on public roads and city streets. The prisoners wore bright-colored outfits and were chained to each other or to heavy cannonballs—the ball and chain—"a spectacle disturbing to many sober citizens" (McKelvey 1977: 7). Paul Takagi (1975) states that convicts at work in the city streets drew large crowds of sympathetic people, including friends and relatives of the prisoners. They made contact and, at times, liquor and other goods were given to the prisoners.

In response to these conditions, in 1790 the Philadelphia Society for Alleviating the Miseries of Public Prisons, a Quaker-influenced organization, succeeded in having the Pennsylvania legislature convert the Walnut Street Jail into a state prison "for the purpose of confining there the more hardened and atrocious offenders, who have been sentenced to hard labor for a term of years" (Wines 1975: 152). According to Takagi (1975), this was an historic act; it established the responsibility of state government for prisons.

After the Walnut Street Jail became a state prison, most inmates were confined in separate cells and released to work in the courtyard during the day at a variety of tasks: handicrafts such as weaving and shoemaking, and routine labor such as beating hemp and sawing logwood. The "hardened and atrocious offenders," however, were confined in isolation with nothing but a Bible: "the old Quakers, sensitive as they were to the infliction of bodily pain, seem to have been unable to form in their minds an image of the fearful mental torture of solitude in idleness" (Wines 1975: 152). Solitary confinement was seen as a way of preventing fraternization between prisoners, behavior which would only lead to the spread of evil inclinations among inmates. The concept of penitence that was embroidered into this system led to the use of the term *penitentiary* to describe some penal institutions.

By the time Pennsylvania opened two new prisons in the late 1820s, overcrowding, a problem that is still with us, had caused the demise of Walnut Street; industry and isolation became impossible in the congested prison; discipline lapsed and riots ensued (McKelvey 1972).

To prevent fraternization between prisoners, Pennsylvania extended solitary confinement in the prisons it built in Pittsburgh (Western State Penitentiary opened in 1826) and Philadelphia (Eastern State Penitentiary opened in 1829). These institutions featured massive stone walls around a building that branched out from a central rotunda like the spokes of a wheel. The design prevented prisoner contact, and inmates remained in their cells except for one hour of exercise in a yard also designed to prevent inmate contact. The **Pennsylvania system**

> isolated each prisoner for the entire period of his confinement. According to its blueprint, convicts were to eat, work, and sleep in individual cells, seeing and talking with only a handful of responsible guards and selected visitors. They were to leave the institution as ignorant of the identity of other convicts as on the day they entered. (Rothman 1971: 82)

The Pennsylvania system proved quite expensive; the cost of constructing an institution for solitary confinement was staggering, and there could be little profitable exploitation of inmate labor under such conditions (McKelvey 1972).

The Auburn System

Thomas Eddy (1758-1827), a Quaker from New York who had been briefly imprisoned as a Tory during the Revolutionary War, visited the Walnut Street Jail and was impressed by what he saw (Lewis 1965). As a result of his efforts, in 1796 New York enacted legislation that substituted imprisonment for most corporal and capital punishments and authorized the building of a penitentiary in Greenwich Village, named *Newgate* after the famous English penal institution, and Eddy became its first agent, or warden. Newgate featured congregate rooms and workshops and fourteen cells for solitary confinement. In 1802 there was a bloody riot and a mass-escape attempt that required calling in military personnel. In response to these developments, Eddy suggested that future penitentiaries utilize single cells for all inmates at night, and shops where they would work in strict silence during the day. His suggestions defined what was to be called the **Auburn system** because they were incorporated into the new prison built in Auburn, New York.

While prisoners in the Pennsylvania system were idle, prisoners in the Auburn system were put to work, an innovation that was justified for two reasons:

Auburn Prison (*above*), which opened in upstate New York in 1819, became the prototype for the nineteenth-century American prison. The Auburn system consisted of an unrelenting routine of silence, hard labor, moderate meals, and solitary evenings in individual cells six days per week. *Below*, inmates participate in a relay race in the central yard, surrounded by tiers of cell blocks for which the institution became famous.

If the prisoners were to learn the advantages and satisfactions of hard work and thrift, the New York authorities believed, there could be no better way than to be compelled to work together in harmony. If such a system also offered the potential for inmates to grow and harvest their own vegetables, raise and butcher their own meat, make their own clothes, and manufacture other items for use or sale by the state, such a boon to the state's budget could not be reasonably ignored. (New York State Special Commission on Attica 1972: 8; hereafter, Attica Commission)

Auburn Prison opened in 1819 and was designed by its first agent, William Brittin. It featured a center comprised of tiers of cell blocks surrounded by a vacant area—the yard—with a high wall encircling the entire institution. Each cell measured 7 feet by 3.5 feet and was 7 feet high.

It was designed for separation by night only; the convicts were employed during the day in large workshops, in which, under the superintendency of Elam Lynds, formerly a captain in the army, the rule of absolute silence was enforced with unflinching sternness. Captain Lynds said that he regarded flogging as the most effective, and at the same time the most humane, of all punishments, since it did no injury to the prisoner's health and in no wise impaired his physical strength; he did not believe that a large prison could be governed without it. (Wines 1975: 154)

Instead of replacing flogging with imprisonment, flogging became widespread in the penitentiary system; criminals were punished with imprisonment, and prisoners were punished with flogging and other forms of corporal punishment.

Auburn divided its inmates into three classes. The most difficult inmates were placed in solitary; a less dangerous group spent part of the day in solitude and worked the rest of the time in groups; the least "guilty" worked together throughout the day and were separated only at night when they returned to their individual cells. As in Walnut Street, solitary confinement played havoc on the psyche—inmates jumped off tiers, cut their veins, smashed their heads against walls. According to the Attica Commission (1972: 8), "in addition, there was the issue, perhaps more pressing, of expense to the state. Inmates restricted to their cells 24 hours a day contributed nothing to the cost of their own confinement. The state had to provide all food, clothing, supplies, and materials to its prisoners." Solitary confinement at

Auburn was discontinued except as a punishment for violations of prison rules (Lewis 1965).

At Auburn, inmates dressed in grotesque and ridiculous-looking black-and-white striped uniforms and caps. They marched in complete silence, worked in complete silence, and ate in complete silence. Auburn developed the infamous "lockstep shuffle": inmates stood in line with the right foot slightly behind the left and the right arm outstretched with the hand on the right shoulder of the man in front of him; they moved together in a shuffle, sliding the left foot forward, then bringing the right foot to its position just behind the left, then the left again, then the right. Free citizens were encouraged to visit the prison where, for a small fee, they could view the inmates, an act that was designed to further degrade the prisoners.

The Auburn system consisted of an unrelenting routine of silence, hard labor, moderate meals, and solitary evenings in individual cells six days per week. On Sundays, when there was no work, inmates attended church—in silence—where they were addressed by the prison chaplain, who stressed the American virtues of simple faith and hard work (Attica Commission 1972).

The Auburn system became the prototype for American prisons; such prisons were cheaper to construct than those of the Pennsylvania system and allowed for a factory system that could make profitable use of inmate labor. The concept of reformation gradually disappeared as prisons became bleak and silent factories with labor pools of broken people.

Elmira Reformatory

As noted in the last chapter, the reform efforts of the American Prison Association led to the establishment of Elmira Reformatory, which opened in New York in 1876. The goal of this institution was rehabilitation, and inmates were sentenced to indeterminate terms. A three-grade mark system was established: at admission, each inmate was placed in the second grade; after six months of good behavior the inmate was promoted to the first grade—misbehavior resulted in being demoted to the third grade; an inmate who behaved well for six months in the first grade became eligible for conditional release—parole.

Elmira received inmates who were between the ages of sixteen and thirty. They were housed in Auburn-style cells at night, and during the day were involved in academic and vocational education. They also spent a great deal of time in military drill—an activity that was considered important for the development of discipline and maturity. The institution was organized along military lines with uniforms and a band, swords for inmate officers, and dummy rifles for rank-and-file prisoners.

The reformatory idea spread to other states, but by the first two decades of the twentieth century the movement had floundered. Overcrowding, inadequate and poorly trained staff, and the expense of providing rehabilitative services led to its demise. Reformatories began to resemble the Auburn-style prison in both appearance and practice.

Prison Labor

The use of convict labor often made prisons not only self-supporting institutions but also profit-making enterprises throughout the nineteenth and well into the twentieth century. In Alabama, for example, prior to the Great Depression, prison labor netted the state profits of almost $1 million annually, and just one prison industry manufacturing shirts in Florida netted that state almost $150,000 annually (Gillin 1931). Minnesota's Stillwater Prison netted $25,000 annually as late as 1930, and served as a model for other Northern prisons (Hagerty 1934).

Prison industries, in addition to their economic value, prevented the idleness that plagues many contemporary correctional institutions and helped to maintain prison discipline. There were three types of prison industry:

1. *Contract System.* Inmate labor was sold to private entrepreneurs who provided the necessary machinery, tools, raw materials and, in some cases, the supervisory staff. In many cases the prison was built as a factory with walls around it.
2. *Lease System.* Prisoners were leased out to private business interests for a fixed fee. This system was used extensively in agriculture and mining, particularly in the South.
3. *State-Use System.* Prison inmates produced goods for use or sale by state agencies, for example, office furniture and license plates.

In the latter part of the nineteenth century, there was a series of scandals involving the use of inmate labor. In addition, the growing labor union movement saw inmate labor competing with free labor and undermining employee leverage for increased wages. At times, inmate labor was leased out to break strikes. The National Anti-Contract Association, a manufacturer's group whose members also suffered from having to compete

The use of convict labor has made some prisons profit-making enterprises well into the twentieth century. This photo was taken at the Texas State Prison in 1968.

with prison labor, campaigned against the use of inmate labor as well.

The combination of the scandals and the broad opposition resulted in laws curbing inmate labor in several industrial states such as Massachusetts, New York, and Pennsylvania. The federal government enacted legislation in 1887 that forbade the contracting of any federal prisoners (McKelvey 1977). The use of prison labor, however, continued to be widespread until the Great Depression and the passage of the Hawes-Cooper Act in 1929 and the Ashurst-Sumners Act in 1935. These federal statutes curtailed interstate commerce in goods produced with convict labor.* In the South, where prison labor was used extensively in agriculture and mining, the practice continued.

The curtailing of prison labor had two long-range effects. First, it increased the cost of imprisonment and, thus, encouraged the development of parole (discussed in chapter 16). Sec-

---

*Some of these restrictions were lifted by Congress in 1979 to permit the use of inmate labor on an experimental basis in some correctional institutions. Prison labor is still used on a state-use basis, in the manufacture of license plates, for example.

ond, it forced prison officials to find other ways to deal with prison idleness. As a result many prisons initiated programs to train and educate their inmates.

The Big House

The Great Depression put an end to further construction of Auburn-style prisons; they were too expensive to build and, without exploiting inmate labor, too expensive to maintain. The last of this type of institution was opened in 1931 at Attica, New York (Attica Commission 1972). In its place emerged the **Big House**. Architecturally, the institution John Irwin (1980) refers to as the Big House is an Auburn-style prison: one- or two-man cells clustered in cell blocks stacked in tiers surrounded by high stone walls with guard towers and holding more than 2,000 inmates. Unlike the Auburn-style prison, however, silence, hard labor, the lockstep shuffle, and official use of corporal punishment were absent. The cells had toilets and sinks, were ventilated and heated, and had more space than the typical Auburn cell. In the Big House, inmates were frequently permitted to furnish and decorate their own cells. The better-equipped institutions had recreational facilities, baseball diamonds, basketball and handball courts. Many prisoners were black, but in most Big Houses outside of the South, the inmates were mostly white. Although there were some vocational and educational programs, there was also a great deal of idleness. Rehabilitation programs such as individual and group counseling, psychological and psychiatric services, and vocational training in areas that could provide postrelease employment, were usually absent.

Prisonization

Scholarly studies of the prison environment during the 1930s (for example, Clemmer 1958) noted a phenomenon that became known as **prisonization** and the existence of an **inmate subculture**. Prisonization is the process by which inmates are socialized into the prison milieu. Although they have varying backgrounds, prisoners share a common suspicion and fear of other inmates and guards. Consequently, they tend to align themselves into cliques that serve to counter, if not subvert, the power of prison officials. According to the studies of the 1930s, these cliques form the basis for an inmate subculture that developed and enforced its own rules and emerged in the less rigid environment of the Big House. Contemporary scholars (for example, Irwin and Cressey 1962) argue, however, that the subculture found in the Big House by earlier sociologists did not develop in prison, but was actually brought into the institution by inmates who shared a common subcultural orientation.

Maintaining Control

The Big House guards faced a terrifying problem—they were always vastly outnumbered by inmates who were organized into cliques and who formed a distinct subculture in opposition to the prison administration. While prison officials could request help from outside forces—the state police or National Guard, for example—there was insufficient coercive force immediately available for them to be routinely in effective control at the institution. Corporal punishment was no longer officially permitted, and loss of "good time"—time off for good behavior—or solitary confinement were often insufficient penalties to effectively control behavior in the volatile atmosphere of the Big House.

As a result, Irwin (1980) states, guards developed effective informal control strategies: Personal agreements between guards and inmates were explicit or tacit exchange relationships in which an inmate would refrain from rule-violating behavior in return for some favor or special consideration from a guard. Corrupt favoritism meant that guards granted special privileges to key prisoners—inmate leaders—in return for their support in maintaining order.

In the Big House, inmate leaders helped to maintain order by:

1. keeping their own violations within acceptable limits;
2. supporting the prevailing prison norm that required inmates to "do your own time," that is, mind your own business and "don't make no waves" (which encouraged conformity); and
3. threatening or using violence against prisoners who disrupted the prison routine and thereby endangered the privileged inmate's special arrangements with the guards.

Changes in philosophy led us from Walnut Street to the Big House. After World War II, a new philosophy gained the attention of prison reformers, and the Big House was slowly replaced by the correctional institution, which we will explore in the next chapter.

KEY TERMS

total institutions
jail standards
Walnut Street Jail
Pennsylvania system

Auburn system
Big House
prisonization
inmate subculture

REVIEW QUESTIONS

1. Prior to the use of incarceration, what was the most popular form of punishment under English law?
2. Why did Americans adopt incarceration as punishment after the Revolution?
3. What are the three main purposes of a jail?
4. Why did colonial juries often refuse to find petty thieves guilty?
5. At what level of government are jails usually administered?
6. What is meant by a "total institution," and why is such an institution difficult and costly to maintain and operate?
7. What are the special problems encountered in operating a jail?
8. What was the historic significance of transforming the Walnut Street Jail into a prison?
9. Why did the Walnut Street Jail and the Pennsylvania system utilize solitary confinement?
10. Why was the Pennsylvania system discontinued?
11. What were the characteristics of the Auburn-style prison?
12. What are the three categories of convict labor?
13. What led to the curtailing of convict labor?
14. What were the long-range effects of curtailing convict labor?
15. What led to the demise of the Auburn-style prison?
16. What is meant by the "Big House"?
17. What is meant by "prisonization"?
18. How did the Big House guards deal with the problem of being vastly outnumbered by inmates?

CHAPTER 15

The Question of Punishment: Corrections and Capital Punishment

CORRECTIONAL INSTITUTIONS
Classification
Treatment

DIVISIONS, REBELLIONS, AND RIOTS
Attica
  Riot at Attica

MODERN AMERICAN PRISONS
Prison Violence
  Gangs

Types of Prisons
  Maximum-Security
  Medium-Security
  Minimum-Security
  Prisons for Women
Privately Owned Prisons

THE PRISON AND THE COURTS
Freedom of Religion
Habeas Corpus
Right of Access to the Courts
Prison Conditions
Other Prisoners' Rights

CAPITAL PUNISHMENT
The Arguments Pro and Con

REVIEW QUESTIONS

Boxes

  Inmate Rules
  The Correction Officer
  Valley Women
  Death Penalty Reversals
  The Death Penalty as Deterrent

In this chapter we will discuss the rise of positivism in the decades after World War II, and the impact of this philosophy on the prison system. We will examine the social, political, and legal changes that occurred in the 1960s and 1970s, changes that led us into a period of prison violence and turmoil. Finally, we will review the question of capital punishment in America.

Science made giant strides during World War II with such important developments as the jet plane, streptomycin, radar, sonar, and atomic energy. The possibilities of science appeared to be unlimited, so it was not surprising that, after the war, positivism (discussed in chapter 13) reemerged in penology as the solution to the apparent statistical rise in crime. When wartime production ceased, the possibility of full employment had ceased, but millions of young men, who had been trained to kill and destroy and had done little else for several years, were returning from overseas. Since the allocation of vast societal resources had proven to be successful in the natural sciences, could not a similar commitment of resources prove successful in the behavioral sciences—specifically, in dealing with the problem of crime? Why not a "war against crime"?

Correctional institutions

In order to put the new approach to penology into effect, California adopted an extreme version of the indeterminate sentence. Judges would send criminals with indefinite sentences to the California Adult (or Youth) Authority, which would determine their treatment needs and assign them to the appropriate institution—not a prison, but a **correctional institution** (emphasis on the word "correct"). Convicts would remain incarcerated—"under treatment"—until the Adult Authority determined that they had been rehabilitated, at which time they would be paroled to a community treatment program, that is, supervised by a parole agent. (This approach became known as the "medical model," and will be discussed in greater detail in chapter 16.) There were no longer prisons in California, they became correctional institutions; there were no longer any guards, they became correction officers; there were no longer any wardens, they became superintendents. These correctional institutions had three basic branches, each usually administered by a deputy superintendent (or deputy warden): *administration* (supplies, physical plant, food services, records, etc.), *security* (correction officers), and *treatment* (teachers, counselors, social workers, psychologists, medical staff, etc.).

New institutions were built—medium- and minimum-security correctional facilities. Adult Authority "clients" could be moved from maximum- to medium- to minimum-security correctional facilities and to parole. (The differences among the three will be discussed later in the chapter.) Or if their behavior required, they could be moved from parole supervision back into the institution for further "treatment in a secure setting." Into these correctional institutions came the "treaters"; new superintendents often had extensive education in the behavioral sciences, and their institutions employed teachers, social workers,

Under the leadership of Governor Earl Warren, California reorganized its prison system with rehabilitation rather than punishment as its chief goal.

psychologists, and psychiatrists to implement a rehabilitative regimen. Very slowly, but steadily, the California system was copied, at least in part, by all of the other states; prisons virtually disappeared from America.

Classification

The correctional approach requires a system that can assess the needs of each offender. Based on these needs, inmates are assigned to programs corresponding to existing resources. This process, called **classification,** groups inmates according to certain similarities (e.g., level of security risk, type of treatment) and can be accomplished in one of two ways. Some states use a *reception center,* an institution to which newly sentenced persons are sent for a diagnosis and classification. Once this is accomplished, the inmate is transferred to an appropriate correctional institution. States without a reception center may use *classification committees*, which diagnose and classify each new inmate received at a correctional institution, matching security and treatment needs to available resources.

There are three problematic aspects to the classification process. First, the behavioral sciences do not provide adequate diagnostic tools, nor do they identify the appropriate treatment for criminals. Second, because of the nature of their institutions and clientele, correctional officials are preoccupied with management and security issues, and this often detracts from the classification process. Third, even if the diagnosis and classification are adequate, the required treatment programs are often absent; most of the allocations for correctional institutions are for administration and security; only about 5 percent are for rehabilitation.

Treatment

Treatment is a term used in medicine to refer to a particular method of therapy based on a diagnosis. In correctional institutions, treatment consists of remedial education and high school equivalency classes, vocational training, individual and group counseling, and psychological and psychiatric testing and therapy.

Most prison inmates have not graduated from high school, and they often lack reading and writing skills; some are functional illiterates. Persons unable to correctly fill out a job application are unlikely to secure meaningful employment. Accordingly, postinstitutional adjustment can be facilitated by providing educational opportunities to convicts, and in most correctional institutions there are programs ranging from remedial reading to high school equivalency; sometimes there are courses provided by faculty from nearby colleges. On a more limited basis, select inmates may be permitted to leave the institution for courses at nearby schools. Vocational training in such areas as plumbing, carpentry, and electrical and auto repair can provide the skills necessary for postinstitutional employment. Unfortunately, correctional institutions do not offer such training to many inmates.

Counseling designed to correct antisocial behavior is provided by mental health personnel such as correctional counselors and social workers. It involves verbal interaction either on

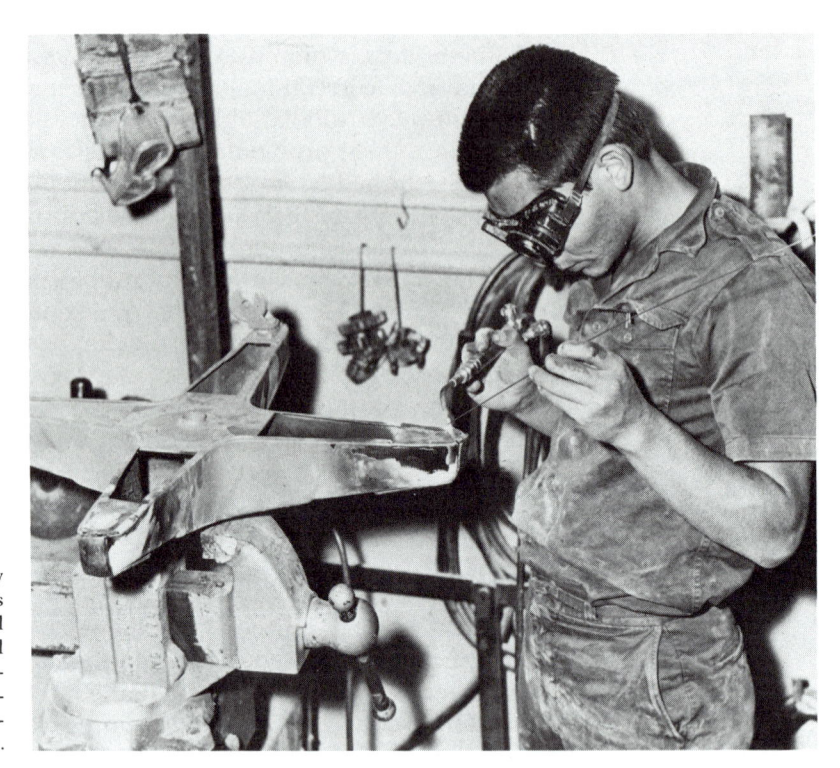

Treatment offered by correctional institutions today includes remedial education, high school equivalency classes, individual and group counseling, therapy, and vocational training.

an individual or group basis, through which inmates explore their attitudes toward specific persons—for example, fellow inmates, spouses, parents—and society in general. Counseling aids in the development of realistic postrelease plans designed to maximize the chances of avoiding further criminal behavior. Counselors may refer inmates to psychologists or psychiatrists for additional testing or therapy when these services are available.

While the intent of treatment programs that offer educational, vocational, and counseling services is worthy, providing such services has always been problematic. The pay is relatively low, and most correctional institutions are located in rural areas not normally attractive to urban graduates trained in therapeutic disciplines. Inadequate funding often results in vocational training that is badly out of date and of little use to ex-convicts seeking employment based on skills developed in the correctional institution. William Parker (1975: 26) argues that the reality of corrections never actually matched the theory: "The theory of rehabilitation has made some changes in the prison: terminology has changed, there are more programs, sweeping floors is now work therapy. . . . The theory of rehabilitation has merely been imposed upon the theories of punishment and control."

In addition, treatment to "correct" criminals is based on two very questionable assumptions: first, that criminals are "sick" and so can benefit from therapy, and second, that behavioral sciences can provide the necessary therapeutic methods. As was noted in chapter 4, there is no agreement on the causes of crime; ways to correct criminal behavior are even more controversial. Experience has shown that criminal "illness" cannot be cured like physical illness.

The problems inherent in a lack of treatment personnel and the questionable assumptions of the correctional approach are compounded by differences between the correction officers and the "treaters." Older staff members, particularly those responsible for prison security, are often resistant to the changes brought in by treaters. This is not surprising, considering their differing backgrounds. Correction officers are typically rural white Protestants, socially and politically conservative, with at best a high school education; they tend to be poorly trained. The treaters tend to be reform-minded urban college graduates, many of whom are Catholics or Jews.

Divisions, Rebellions, and Riots

Despite the corrections revolution, prisoners still lived in overcrowded institutions often pervaded with brutality. They soured on rehabilitative programs that were clearly inadequate or that raised unrealistic expectations among inmates. As John Irwin, a sociologist and former prison inmate, writes (1980: 63), "After prisoners were convinced that treatment programs did not work (by the appearance of persons who had participated fully in the treatment programs streaming back to prison with new crimes or violations of parole), hope shaded to cynicism and then turned to bitterness."

Blake McKelvey (1977: 323) points out that "the prisonization process, which had aligned the great majority of inmates against their keepers, had also divided them from one another, making effective collaboration extremely difficult. Only a rumor of an exceptionally brutal incident or a report of revolts elsewhere could arouse a sense of community sufficient to support a riotous outbreak." During the 1950s, such outbreaks took place at Walla Walla (Washington), Trenton (New Jersey), Jackson (Michigan), Concord and Charlestown (Massachusetts), Soledad (California), Angola (Louisiana), Columbus (Ohio), Western Penitentiary (Pennsylvania), and Jefferson City (Missouri).

Into this environment came thousands of new black and Hispanic inmates. During the 1950s the number of blacks and other nonwhites committed annually to adult federal and state prisons increased from 17,200 to 28,500 (McKelvey 1977). While the predominantly white inmates of the Big House could relate to their keepers, the young urban blacks and Hispanics found no such comfort. In 1954 the Supreme Court ruled in favor of desegregation in the case of *Brown v. Board of Education of Topeka, Kansas* and set off the civil rights revolution in the United States. Rising black consciousness occurring outside the prison took on radical dimensions inside the prison. The Black Muslims emerged as a major separatist organization and confronted prison officials with demands based on religious freedom. The antiwar movement and activities of radical groups such as the Black Panthers stirred and politicized inmates, black and white, who confronted correctional officials with demands often couched in Marxist terminology.

The traditional relationship between inmates and correction officers, based on personal agreements or corrupt favoritism, started to come apart. Inmates became increasingly militant in their refusal to cooperate with their keepers. Correction officials responded in the best tradition of the Big House—with repression—which touched off violence in institutions throughout the country. Correctional institutions simmered throughout the 1960s and into 1971, when, in the month of September, the focus of attention shifted to upstate New York and the last of the Auburn-type institutions to be built.

Attica

The state prison at Attica was a response to an outbreak of prison riots throughout the United States in the late 1920s. (Unless indicated, information in this section is from the New York State Special Commission on Attica 1972.) In 1929, there was a riot at

> ## INMATE RULES
>
> **The Auburn Correctional Facility (NY) requires inmates to abide by 192 rules, including:**
>
> - A weekly shower is mandatory for each inmate.
> - Facility I.D. cards must be carried at all times.
> - The inmate's name and number must be clearly marked on each article of clothing. Green shirts, chino jackets, and coats must have a name tag on the left breast.
>
> **The Clinton Correctional Facility (Dannemora, NY) has an inmate rule book with more than 185 rules. These include:**
>
> - Shirts with tails must be worn inside of the trousers and must be buttoned to the second button from the top.
> - Inmates shall walk in columns of two and to the right of the corridors, and shall move as quietly and orderly as possible while being escorted about the facility.
> - In the visiting room there will be no petting or fondling. Inmates may embrace a visitor once when entering the visiting room and once when leaving.

Clinton Prison in Dannemora, New York, protesting overcrowded conditions; three inmates were killed. In that same year, there was a general riot at the prison at Auburn, New York, in which inmates used firearms; the assistant warden was killed and four inmates escaped before the prison was brought back under control. Typical of prisons in New York and elsewhere, Attica was located in a rural area (in 1971 the town of Attica had a population of less than 3,000) where residents would accept the institution as a basis for employment and other economic benefits.

The institution was completed in 1931 and boasted of being the most secure, escape-proof prison ever built. It has a thirty-foot-high wall that extends twelve feet into the ground and fourteen gun towers. It was constructed with all of the latest advances in maximum-security prisons, including escape-proof cells and unbreakable toilets and washbasins. At the time, it was also the most expensive prison ever built.

In 1970, all of New York's state prisons became "correctional institutions," but reforms were limited to changes in terminology. In September 1971, Attica had more than 2,200 inmates who were locked in their cells for twelve to sixteen hours a day "being rehabilitated," and who spent the remainder of the day with very little to occupy their time. There was no gymnasium, and recreational opportunities were limited. There was almost a total absence of any meaningful rehabilitation programs. Showers were available for most inmates—once a week. Most inmates were black and Hispanic from the downstate New York City area or from upstate urban areas such as Buffalo, Syracuse, and Rochester. Sixty-two percent had been convicted of crimes of violence, and 70 percent had served time previously in a state or federal prison. All but one (a Puerto Rican) of the nearly 400 correction officers were non-Hispanic whites drawn primarily from the rural communities surrounding the prison. While the superintendent had an M.A. degree in correctional administration, correction officers who began their jobs between World War II and the late 1950s had received no formal training. Those who started after that were given two weeks of training. They were expected to enforce the myriad of petty rules typical of correctional institutions.

Attica had a large number of Black Muslims (members of the Nation of Islam) who had difficulty with the lack of ministers and a prison diet that was heavy with pork. Correctional officials would not allow the ministers, many of whom had prison records, into Attica. Black Muslims spent their recreation time together in the yard engaged in worship and highly disciplined physical exercise. The members of the correctional staff, who never understood the Black Muslims, were quite fearful of this group that exhibited military-type discipline and remained aloof from both staff and other inmates.

In Attica, as in other large correctional institutions, "popular conceptions of homosexual advances and assaults in prison were not exaggerated" (1972: 78). Correction officers were unable to protect inmates, who were forced to resort to forms of self-protection, such as carrying a "shiv" (homemade knife), in violation of prison rules. "The irony was not lost on the inmates. They perceived themselves surrounded by walls and gates, and tightly regimented by a myriad of written and unwritten rules; but when they needed protection, they often had to resort to the same skills that had brought many of them to Attica in the first place" (1972: 79).

All of the inmates at Attica (except "lifers") were serving indeterminate sentences, which meant that their release could be obtained in any one of three ways: maximum expiration, conditional or mandatory release, or parole. For example, a convict sentenced to a minimum of three years and a maximum of nine years (3–0–0/9–0–0) faced three possibilities:

1. release after serving 9–0–0, the maximum expiration of his sentence;
2. release at the maximum expiration of his sentence minus any "good time" he had managed to acquire (at the rate of ten days per month, the inmate, as a result of good behavior, could accumulate up to three years of good time and could thus be released after serving 6–0–0); or
3. release by the parole board at any time after completing his minimum sentence of 3–0–0.

Riot at Attica

During the summer of 1971 there were a number of peaceful protests by inmates over conditions at Attica. Leaders of previously antagonistic inmate groups, such as the Young Lords (a Puerto Rican group) and the Black Panthers and Black Muslims, gained greater political awareness, submerged their differences, and joined in a peaceful effort to effect changes at Attica. The new solidarity among inmates frightened officials. The superintendent responded by attempting to transfer the leaders as "troublemakers." He was prevented from doing so by the new Commissioner of the Department of Correctional Services, Russell G. Oswald. Oswald met with inmate representatives at the prison, but was called away on a personal emergency—his wife was seriously ill—before any agreement could be arranged.

On September 8th, when a guard attempted to discipline two inmates who appeared to be sparring, a confrontation ensued, but the incident passed without any action on the part of the

Inmates raise their fists in a show of unity during the 1971 Attica uprising, in which forty hostages were seized following a riot over prison conditions. After the breakdown of negotiations between inmates and correction officers, heavily armed state police retook the prison in a nine-minute assault that left ten hostages and twenty-nine inmates dead.

outnumbered guards. That evening guards appeared and took the two inmates from their cells. The response was a noisy protest, and it was renewed when inmates gathered for breakfast in the morning. A melee broke out, some guards were taken hostage, and a riot quickly ensued. Prison officials had no plan nor had there been any training to deal with such an emergency. As a result, within twenty minutes inmates secured control of the four main cellblocks and seized a total of forty hostages. Guards were beaten, and one died later as a result of his wounds.

The Black Muslims, who had not taken part in the initial uprising, moved to protect the hostages, who were used as the basis for negotiations. An inmate committee for that purpose was formed, although "the tradition in correctional institutions is not to negotiate with inmates holding hostages. This policy is intended to discourage taking hostages, an ever-present danger in institutions in which sometimes as many as 80 inmates are in the custody of one officer" (1972: 208).

Commissioner Oswald found that when he returned to Attica the police were not prepared to immediately retake the prison. By the time sufficient forces had gathered, negotiations were under way, and Oswald chose to continue them in an effort to prevent bloodshed. At the request of the inmate committee, a number of outside observers were permitted to enter Attica, including reporters, lawyers, and politicians. The negotiations were quite spontaneous and quite disorganized. Nevertheless, Oswald agreed to most of the inmate demands for improved conditions at Attica. The negotiations broke down, however, over the issue of complete amnesty—one guard had died after the negotiations began—and the inmates' insistence that Governor Nelson Rockefeller himself come to Attica.

On the morning of September 13th, in a poorly planned and uncoordinated nine-minute assault, heavily armed state police and correction officers retook the prison. The results of the carnage were two hostages seriously injured by the inmates, and ten hostages and twenty-nine inmates killed by correction officers and state troopers. Three hostages, eighty-five inmates, and one trooper were wounded (Wicker 1975).

In the aftermath of the rebellion at Attica, there were a number of official investigations by state and federal bodies, and a number of books and articles emerged, some written by participants (e.g., Oswald 1972; Badillo and Haynes 1972; Wicker 1975). Despite the diversity of the authors, one assessment is constant: the inmates at Attica made a serious error in judgment. They failed to realize that to those in charge of state government the lives and safety of correction officers were only slightly more important than the lives and safety of inmates. In the end, neither the lives of inmates nor those of correction officers were sufficient to prevent state officials from making their point: the state is sovereign, and rebellious prisoners must not be permitted to challenge that sovereignty. Did the rebellion at Attica result in any lasting changes? Observers of the current state of our prisons would be hard pressed to document any positive substantive changes.

Exacerbating the lack of reform is a "get tough" philosophy

that is resulting in a prison-building boom. The United States is experiencing the biggest prison-building campaign in history despite the questionable relationship between the rate of serious crime and imprisonment. North Carolina's rate of imprisonment, for example, is five times that of Minnesota's, but the two states have roughly the same rate of serious crime (Brisbane 1985). Texas and Pennsylvania have similar sized populations, but Texas imprisons three times as many offenders as Pennsylvania. From 1983 through 1984 crime in Texas grew 2 percent, while at the same time it declined 1.9 percent in Pennsylvania. The Washington, D.C. rate of incarceration is three and one-third times that of the rest of the country. Yet while crime declined nationally 3 percent from 1983 through 1984, in Washington it dropped less than 1 percent (Velie and Miller 1985).

Modern american prisons

Who will we find upon entering America's prisons? Almost half a million persons, 97 percent of whom are male, about half black or Hispanic, and more than 60 percent under thirty years of age. In America's prisons are persons who are poorer, darker, younger, and less educated than the rest of the population. The United States has the dubious distinction of being third when it comes to incarcerating citizenry; only the Soviet Union and South Africa imprison a higher percentage of their populations. This is accomplished at an annual cost in excess of $10 billion dollars—about $20,000 per inmate. At a time when the rate of crime, as measured by the Uniform Crime Report and National Crime Survey (see chapter 2), has been declining, the prison population has increased dramatically; most state prison systems are badly overcrowded, and many are under court order to reduce their prison populations.

There are several reasons for this dramatic rise in the prison population. Many states have increased their sanctions for a variety of crimes, and they often include mandatory minimum terms of imprisonment. There are claims of better law enforcement and prosecution, and some states have shifted to determinate sentencing and have abolished parole release, which can obviously impact on the prison population.

Prison Violence

The perennial problem of prison discipline and violence—mostly inmate against inmate—has been exacerbated by three factors: overcrowding, judicial orders limiting punishment (to be discussed later in the chapter), and gangs. A particularly grisly outbreak of violence occurred at the New Mexico State Penitentiary, which was built in 1957 to house 850 inmates. On February 1, 1980, the prison had nearly 1,000 inmates and was badly understaffed; there were only eighteen correction officers on duty when prisoners took over the institution. Although the prison was quickly retaken by police and National Guard, it was only after inmates had systematically slaughtered thirty-three of their fellow prisoners—many were tortured, burned with blowtorches, and had their eyes gouged out and limbs cut off. Prisons in Texas experienced a wave of stabbings and killings. There were 25 murders and 409 stabbings in 1984, and 27 murders and 219 stabbings in 1985. Much of this violence has been linked to gangs (Reinhold 1986).

Gangs

Some gangs developed in prison, while others were brought into the prison by convicted gang members. In either event, the contemporary prison has provided fertile soil for the growth of these often dangerous groups. In most instances gangs are organized along racial or ethnic lines. Instead of the politicized groups of the 1960s, such as the Black Panthers, there is an array of gangs with such exotic-sounding names as La Nuestra Familia, Latin Kings, Aryan Brotherhood, Royal Family, and Black Guerillas. The gangs have increased the potential for prison violence because members use the power of their gang affiliations for various extortionate practices. Inmates without the protection of a gang are often easy prey for the violence-prone gang members. Attempts by prison officials to dissipate the power of the gangs by transferring their leadership to other institutions have only served to spread the phenomenon.

The gangs often transcend the prison, with members active inside and outside the institution and bound together by secret blood oaths and organized along strict hierarchical lines. Inside the prison, leaders of gangs, some of whom are middle-aged, are often able to exert control over important aspects of institution-

The New Mexico State Penitentiary, site of one of the bloodiest riots in prison history, offered photographer Bob Saltzman a unique opportunity to portray life inside a maximum-security prison. Saltzman, who visited the institution over a period of fifteen months, shot nearly 500 photographs depicting inmates, staff, and the day-to-day workings of the facility itself. From these he selected 28 images, printed them in color, mounted them with wide margins, and returned the photographs to those he portrayed, asking that they use the space around the image in any way they chose. The resulting collaborations formed the basis for the exhibition "La Pinta: Doing Time in Santa Fe." *La Pinta* (the Spanish slang name for the state prison) was first shown publicly in 1983, and has since traveled widely throughout the country.

> # THE CORRECTION OFFICER
>
> On the front line of prison work is the "hack," "screw," "turnkey," the guard whose official title is "correction officer." The rural location of most prisons means that the surrounding population is usually white, Protestant, socially and politically conservative. Since the prison is a primary employer in such areas, correction officers are often recruited from the local population.
>
> At the historically important Auburn prison in New York, Lucien Lombardo (1981) notes, most of the approximately 350 correction officers were born in the area. Auburn is a city of about 35,000, and the prison population is approximately 1,500. Correction officers at Auburn wear standardized, nonmilitary apparel, blazers or jackets; they do not carry any of the paraphernalia associated with policing—such as handcuffs and nightsticks. Lombardo (1981: 36) describes the transition made by newly assigned officers: "As the naive citizens of Auburn become the guards of the prison community, . . . they quickly learned

al life. In any number of institutions the correction officers have conceded to them power to rule the cellblocks. The prison provides the gang with an available population for recruiting new members. Outside of the institution, the released gang members are welcomed into the ranks of their comrades and quickly become part of the drug trafficking or other criminal activities in which these groups are involved (Lindsey 1985).

Types of Prisons

Contemporary prisons can be grouped into categories according to their level of security or the gender of the inmates:

Maximum-Security

The typical **maximum-security prison** has a high concrete wall with gun towers surrounding an open yard. From the towers,

> to identify with and appreciate the convicts over whom they would stand guard and learned that convicts had to be judged by behavior and not as stereotypes."
>
> Lombardo (1981: 39) describes the job of an officer in charge of a cell block housing from 300 to 400 prisoners: "During the evening shifts, when inmates are locked in their cells, the tasks of the block officer are fairly routine: making the rounds to inspect cells for fires, watching for signs of self-destructive behavior and handling inmate problems as they arise." On the day shift, however, the tasks are more complex and include keeping the block orderly and on schedule. Lombardo (1981: 39) quotes an officer:
>
>> Let them in and out on time, made regular counts [physically accounting for each inmate]. Let those in coming from work. Give out medication. Lock them in and count again. Then let them out into the yard. All the while I have to handle all kinds of problems, personal, plumbing or electrical. I hand out newspapers and mail. I make check rounds to make sure there's no two in a cell. Let some in at seven o'clock and after eight o'clock let those in from the yard. Then I made the final count.

correction officers armed with an array of firearms have a clear view of the yard and the outside perimeter of the institution. In the center there are buildings containing individual cells facing long corridors. Cells are grouped together into cellblocks, and tiers of cellblocks are stacked one on top of the other. These institutions typically house more than 1,000 inmates.

There is no privacy. Correction officers are able to patrol along the corridor and view each inmate behind the bars of his cagelike cell, but inmates are unable to see into other cells. Each cellblock is partitioned off from the others by a series of gates. An inmate who is able to escape from his cell would thus be confined to the cellblock. In effect, the maximum-security prison is a series of mini-prisons, and movement within the institution involves short trips between locked gates or doors.

Maximum-security prisons of a later vintage do not have walls but instead use a series of high fences topped with razor wire or similar devices. The modern prison also uses closed

Maximum-security prisons frequently employ "shakedowns"—searches of inmates for weapons and other contraband.

television monitors and infrared sensing devices to keep track of inmates. There are frequent "counts" (inventories to account for each inmate) and "shakedowns" (searches of inmates and cells for weapons and other contraband).

Maximum-security prisons require their inmates to abide by numerous rules. Visits are closely supervised (except those with attorneys), and physical contact is often prohibited; communication is often by way of special communication devices.

In theory, maximum-security prisons are used to house the most dangerous offenders and escape risks. In practice, however, in many states this may be the only type of institution available for convicted felons, whether or not they pose a security risk.

Medium-Security

Medium-security institutions, unless they are converted Big Houses, do not have high stone walls. They are enclosed with a double fence topped by razor wire and gun towers. Instead of high-security "inside cells," their cells face out, away from the prison. Medium-security prisons also utilize dormitories and other congregate types of housing. The security and, thus, the atmosphere of a medium-security prison is considerably less rigid than that of a maximum-security institution. This type of institution is for inmates who do not pose a serious security or escape risk. It may also serve as part of a system to reward the good behavior of maximum-security inmates by reducing the level of confinement. They usually contain fewer inmates than the maximum-security prison.

Minimum-Security

There are a variety of **minimum-security** and open-type **institutions**. They may be camps where inmates are employed in the raising of crops and livestock, or forestry camps where inmates perform such tasks as maintaining public park lands and combatting forest fires. A minimum-security prison may be composed of cottage-type housing and not even be surrounded by a wall or a fence topped by razor wire. The minimum-security institution is reserved for inmates who pose no security risk, nonviolent offenders such as white-collar criminals, and persons with short sentences or whose release is imminent.

Prisons for Women

There are relatively few prisons for women. Prior to the twentieth century, women accounted for only about 1 percent of the adults convicted of felonies. While the number of women in this category has increased more than 500 percent, the total female prison population remains relatively small; women account for only 3 percent of the prison population. There were no separate prisons for women until one was opened in Indianapolis, Indiana, in 1873, followed by ones in Massachusetts (1877) and New York (1887). Until that time women were confined together with men in a congregate prison, or housed in a separate section of a male institution. By 1940, twenty-three states had established separate prisons for women, and by 1975 only sixteen states did not have them. The first federal prison for women was a cottage-style reformatory opened in 1927 in rural Alderson, West Virginia (Freedman 1981). Today, women prisoners are usually housed in cottage-type minimum-security facilities.

> # Valley Women
>
> Although the name of the place is Huron Valley Women's Correctional Facility, the women locked up inside just call it "The Valley." Located seven miles outside of Ypsilanti, Michigan, Huron Valley is the state's only prison for female felony offenders, many of whom are incarcerated for murder (usually of a husband or boyfriend). It consists of a group of single-story brick structures surrounded by fences of chicken wire topped by a strand of electrified wire. There are three towers with correction officers carrying high-powered rifles. The facility has three levels of custody: minimum, medium, and closed.
>
> New inmates are processed in "the tank," a bright yellow cinder-block room with windows and two large electrified doors. As papers are processed, a correction officer stamps inmate street clothes with a six-digit number and checks belongings for contraband. The door of the tank booms open, and inmates, one at a time, are told to undress behind a shower curtain. Each is handed a towel and disappears

Estelle Freedman (1981: 153) points to a serious deficiency in the separate prison for women.

> Because sex is the primary criterion for commitment, it has been difficult to provide specialized treatment on other grounds. Almost every state maintains a variety of institutions for men, depending on age, offense, and previous record. A young male misdemeanant could serve in an institution with similar offenders. A young woman, though, must enter a reformatory which houses all types of women offenders. She is treated there as a woman, not as a misdemeanant, youth, or recidivist.

Privately Owned Prisons

The most recent innovation in prisons is a response to budgetary problems encountered in providing cell-space for a rapidly increasing inmate population. Government is constrained by the

> into the line of shower stalls. The inmate showers, using a shampoo designed to combat lice and ticks. She is then fingerprinted and photographed. Each inmate is kept in quarantine for the next forty-eight hours until the clinic determines that she is free of any infectious diseases. She is tested to determine her educational level, assigned to one of the three levels of custody, issued sheets, towels, and prison clothing. A fortunate inmate is assigned to a cell of her own. Often, however, a new inmate winds up in a cell with two other inmates.
>
> At 6:30 A.M. the public address system announces "wake-up time." Cells remain dark for another half hour until the electricity is turned on. Groups of thirty inmates march to the showers and afterwards into the cafeteria. They are served toast with margarine and milk. Another day is about to begin for the "Valley Women," where the reality includes being preyed upon to engage in sex, to steal, and to smuggle.
>
> SOURCE: Adapted from Marney Rich, "Valley Women: Life Inside a Prison for Female Felons." *Chicago Tribune Magazine* (May 19, 1985: 25-36).

need for legislative action, competitive bidding, civil service statutes, and general bureaucratic lethargy. Private industry, on the other hand, can accomplish the construction and staffing of a correctional facility in a relatively short period of time. While the use of private facilities for the custody of juveniles has a long history, private facilities for adult criminals is a recent phenomenon. According to the American Correctional Association, by 1985 there were about two dozen major correction facilities being operated by private groups (Tolchin 1985). The largest of these is the Correction Corporation of America, headquartered in Nashville, Tennessee. The largest customer for the privately owned facilities is the United States Immigration and Naturalization Service, which uses them to house illegal aliens (Wiedrich and Rowley 1985).

The use of private correctional facilities is controversial. While the profit motive has been seen by some as a way of providing cost-effective correctional facilities, it is viewed by others (for example, the National Sheriffs' Association) as detrimental to the government's responsibility for the care of prisoners—cost-effective need not mean safe, healthy, or secure. (Of course, many, if not most, public correctional facilities also fail to provide an environment that is safe, healthy, and secure.) Pay scales of employees of private institutions, if they are to hire qualified personnel, must be competitive with that of government service. Yet, cost-effectiveness often means lower employee compensation. In response to this problem, private facilities have established a profit-sharing incentive for their employees; the greater the profit, the greater the employee income.

Additional issues are legal and ethical. What are the powers and limitations of private correctional personnel ("resident supervisors") who are not peace officers subject to standards of conduct and discipline set out by law? Is it proper for government to turn over its responsibility for the incarceration of prisoners to private persons for profit? Whatever the answers, they would also be applicable to other basic services such as policing and fire protection.

THE PRISON AND THE COURTS

Throughout most of our history, the courts have been unwilling to intervene in matters pertaining to prisons and prisoners. Once the requirements of due process were fulfilled with respect to arrest, trial, and sentencing, the courts have exercised a hands-off policy. This was based on three considerations:

1. The doctrine of **sovereign immunity** precludes legal action against a sovereign government (this originally meant the king, but in the United States it came to refer to the state). More recently, however, this doctrine has been largely abrogated.

2. Since prison inmates cannot vote and do not usually have the sympathy or support of the public, they lack any significant ability to force their grievances to be addressed—except via the prison riot. (However, as noted in chapter 5, the least democratic branch of government is the federal judiciary because its members are selected, not elected, for lifetime terms. Thus, the lack of political power on the part of prisoners had little effect on the federal judiciary considering their grievances.)

3. The difficulties encountered in administering penal institutions have made judges reluctant to impose their legal standards in place of the expertise of prison administrators. Indeed, by the 1960s it appeared that only this issue of prison administration was keeping the courts out of the prison.

Freedom of Religion

In 1961, a question of religious liberty signaled the end of judicial indifference. If there is a single constitutional right that represents the most basic American value, it is the First Amendment's guarantee of the free exercise of religion. Even prison officials could not be allowed to abrogate *this* right. As noted earlier in this chapter, prison officials viewed the Nation of Islam as a dangerous group. In many states they denied the legitimacy of the Black Muslims and forbade them the religious privileges typically granted Jewish and Christian groups. In 1961, the Black Muslims began to fight back, litigating their First Amendment claims in New York, California, and the District of Columbia. As Claire Cripe (1977) notes, these cases served to "open the floodgates" of litigation; once the courts became involved in prisons, there was no way to withdraw. Neal Shover (1979: 245) states that "newly cognizant of their rights and how to seek redress for violations of them, prisoners not only have won decisions from the courts expanding their formal rights but modification of administrative laws of corrections in virtually every state."

Habeas Corpus

During the post-Civil War Reconstruction period, Congress enacted the Civil Rights Act of 1871, which enabled blacks deprived of their civil rights to avoid state courts; this legislation, particularly Section 1983, has provided the basis for prisoners to move directly into federal court. While Section 1983 can be used to challenge prison practices and provides for money damages, it does not provide for release from imprisonment. The release remedy can only be obtained by a **writ of habeas corpus,** which can also be used to challenge prison practices. The Supreme Court has been inundated with such writs.

Derived from the Latin, meaning "you shall have the body," a writ of habeas corpus directs a prison official to bring an inmate before a judicial officer to determine the lawfulness of the imprisonment. As Stephen Schlesinger writes in *Habeas Corpus* (1984: 1), "Article III of the Constitution extends 'the great writ' of habeas corpus to Federal prisoners; the right of State prisoners to obtain Federal review of State court convictions was legislatively established by the Congress in 1867," and further strengthened by the Civil Rights Act of 1871.

In the past thirty years there has been an almost 700 percent increase in filings by state prisoners. This, no doubt, has been tied to the increased availability of law books and related materials for prisoners resulting from the *Younger* decision (to be discussed shortly). Although petitions that were granted relief in whole or in part amount to less than 3 percent, the volume of petitions has burdened the courts with endless postconviction litigation. Providing finality to a case after appeals have been exhausted, while protecting the rights of individuals, has made this a dilemma of efficiency vs. liberty, and there have been various legislative and administrative proposals to limit the habeas corpus rights of inmates (*Habeas Corpus* 1984).

Right of Access to the Courts

Prison officials frequently prevented inmates—"jailhouse lawyers"—from assisting other inmates with their legal challenges to prison practices. These "troublemakers" upset the prison routine, and prison officials responded in the traditional manner—with repression. Instead of viewing these activities as a welcome alternative to violence and riot, prison officials denied inmates the only lawful means to redress perceived grievances. In response to litigation on this point, prison officials argued that they were merely upholding the law; namely, persons who are not admitted to the bar cannot practice law. The Court responded by offering prison officials the option of providing licensed attorneys to inmates—at state expense—an option that proved quite unattractive. In its 1969 decision (*Johnson v. Avery*), the Court ruled that prison officials must permit prisoners to assist their fellow inmates with legal work. In 1971 (*Younger v. Gilmore*), the Court expanded this right by requiring prison officials to provide legal materials such as law books and legal forms for inmates.

Prison Conditions

There has been a great deal of litigation over prison conditions. Federal courts in many jurisdictions have ordered prison officials to reduce inmate populations at overcrowded institutions and to take other corrective steps to bring their institutions into line with constitutional provisions prohibiting cruel and unusual punishment. In 1976, for example, Frank Johnson, a federal district court judge in Alabama, found that state's entire prison system in violation of the Eighth Amendment and appointed a committee of penal experts to oversee sweeping changes.

In 1979 (*Bell v. Wolfish*) and 1981 (*Rhodes v. Chapman*), however, the Supreme Court overturned lower court decisions that had found prison overcrowding to be unconstitutional. The Court ruled the Constitution does not require that inmates be housed in single cells. Double-bunking was to be permitted even for those persons awaiting trial—persons who are legally innocent. In *Chapman*, the Court ruled that prison conditions were constitutional as long as the totality of these conditions is not "grossly disproportionate to the severity of the crime warranting punishment" and does not "involve the wanton and unnecessary infliction of pain."

Other Prisoners' Rights

In 1968, fourteen years after segregation in public schools was declared unconstitutional, the Supreme Court ruled (*Lee v. Washington*) that the racial segregation of prisoners violated the Fourteenth Amendment. In 1974 (*Procunier v. Martinez*), the Supreme Court limited the power of prison officials to censor inmate letters. In 1977 (*Jones v. North Carolina Prisoners' Labor Union, Inc.*), the Court began to draw the line by rejecting the notion that prisoners had a right under the First Amendment to organize inmate unions.

In a 1974 decision (*Wolf v. McDonnell*), the Supreme Court held that prisoners are entitled to minimal due process protections whenever disciplinary action threatens their "liberty" by imposing solitary confinement or loss of privileges or good time. In *Hutto v. Finney* (1978), the Court ruled that solitary confinement in a harsh setting for more than thirty days constitutes cruel and unusual punishment.

In 1986 (*Davidson v. Cannon* and *Daniels v. Williams*), the

Court limited the liability of prison officials for negligence that caused unintentional injury to inmates. In a 6–3 decision, the Court ruled that the Civil Rights Act of 1871 is not violated by negligent conduct on the part of prison officials. The Court distinguished between carelessness, which does not violate due process, and acting recklessly, even if not intentionally, which does.

Capital Punishment

As noted earlier, until the use of imprisonment as a punishment became widespread, execution was the preferred penalty for many types of criminal activity. In colonial America, the hangman was often quite busy dispatching criminals; in prerevolutionary New York, for example, more than 20 percent of the sentences handed down were for execution (Bernes 1979). While the use of imprisonment reduced the number of offenses that were punishable by death, capital punishment continued into the twentieth century, during which time it emerged as a matter of great controversy.

Thorsten Sellin (1980) notes that during the second decade of the twentieth century, reformers were successful in having eight states abolish the death penalty. A few years later some of these states restored capital punishment, while others abolished the practice. In 1967 the Supreme Court declared a virtual moratorium on the use of capital punishment. In 1972 the Court (*Furman v. Georgia*) ruled against capital punishment for three black defendants who had been convicted by a jury, two for rape and one for murder, and sentenced to death. In the opinion of five justices, the death penalty laws of thirty-nine states and the District of Columbia were too arbitrary and discriminatory to be constitutional. The Court ruled that "the imposition and carrying out of the death penalty in these cases constitutes cruel and unusual punishment in violation of the Eighth and Fourteenth Amendments." However, each of the nine justices wrote a separate opinion, which left the states in some confusion over the use of capital punishment: four justices held that capital punishment per se is not unconstitutional; two justices said that it was; and three justices, while agreeing that the Georgia statute was invalid as applied, left open the question of whether such punishment may ever be applied.

The 1986 execution of James Terry Roach in South Carolina brought to light a new issue in the unending debate over capital punishment: Should the death penalty be imposed on juveniles who commit capital crimes? Roach was seventeen when he and two friends raped and murdered two women and killed a young man. The issue of juvenile executions is currently up to the states: sixteen have no minimum age for the death penalty, and fourteen others have set limits under eighteen. At ten, Indiana has the lowest age.

In response to *Furman*, thirty-five states and the federal government revised their capital punishment statutes. In a review of the revised statutes of the state of Georgia in 1976 (*Gregg v. Georgia*), the Supreme Court ruled that capital punishment was constitutionally permitted if the statute guided and restricted sentencing so that the judge and the jury considered aggravating and mitigating circumstances in each case. In response to *Gregg*, some states modified their statutes, many instituting a two-stage trial system. First, the jury decides on the question of guilt.

If the defendant is found guilty of a crime which is punishable by execution, the jury then determines in favor of imprisonment or death. Most states make appeals of the death sentence mandatory, and it often takes several years before the process is exhausted and an execution takes place.

The first post-*Gregg* execution was the celebrated case of Gary Mark Gilmore, who was executed by firing squad in Utah in 1977. Since that execution, the pace has quickened; while there was only one execution in 1981, there were twenty-one in 1984. By the end of 1985 there were thirty-five states permitting capital punishment, and public opinion polls showed that most Americans, as many as 85 percent, favored capital punishment for certain crimes.

In 1985, the Court ruled (*Wainwright v. Witt*) that jurors can be excused if their views on capital punishment would prevent or substantially impair them in the performance of their duties in cases where the imposition of capital punishment is a possibility. Until this decision, only jurors who made it unmistakably clear that they would automatically vote against the imposition of capital punishment or would be unable, regardless of the evidence, to find the defendant guilty could be removed for cause. In other words, persons who indicate that they oppose capital punishment can be challenged for cause by prosecuting attorneys. The result is a "death-qualified" jury, discussed in chapter 12.

The Arguments Pro and Con

As the number of executions increased, so did the number of articles and books on the subject of capital punishment. The arguments about capital punishment can be reduced to issues of morality and deterrence. Proponents generally argue that the death penalty upholds the sanctity of life by requiring the execution of a murderer: "And he that killeth any man shall surely be put to death" (Lev. 24:17). They also argue that capital punishment, in addition to obviously deterring the offender from further criminality, has a positive effect on general deterrence; in other words, it deters potential murderers from carrying out their crimes.

Opponents argue that the taking of life (except in self-defense) is immoral, and that capital punishment decreases the value of life and makes the state a murderer. There is also the possibility of a mistake. According to one controversial study (Margolick

> ## DEATH PENALTY REVERSALS
>
> **In 1902, J.B. Brown was sentenced to death in Florida, but was saved by a technicality—the wrong name had been entered on the death warrant. Eleven years later a man gave a deathbed confession clearing Brown.**
>
> **In 1915, Charles Stielow received a stay of execution forty minutes before he was to be executed. Three years later he was exonerated and released.**
>
> **In 1926, Anastarico Vargas' head had been shaved in preparation for his execution in the electric chair; he received a last-minute commutation. Four years later he was released with $26,500 in compensation.**
>
> **In 1933, Charles Bernstein of Washington, D.C., had his death sentence commuted minutes before his scheduled execution. Two years later he was declared innocent and released from prison.**
>
> **SOURCE: Simon 1985.**

1985), in the twentieth century 343 people were wrongfully convicted of offenses punishable by death, and 25 were actually executed. In addition, research into the deterrent value of capital punishment is inconclusive. Indeed, if this were a serious argument, we would have public, perhaps televised, executions.

There is an interest in the technology of execution. During 1983, for example, six states changed those sections of the law relating to methods of execution by adding "lethal injection." Fourteen states provide for more than one method, leaving the choice up to the condemned prisoner (*Capital Punishment in 1983* 1984).

There is some controversy over the question of capital punishment for crimes committed by juveniles. Twenty states cite a minimum age that ranges from ten (only Indiana) to eighteen (six states). Age is not a factor in three states, and in eleven states

The Death Penalty as Deterrent

Paris, 1757

The victim was taken to the front of the Paris City Hall which was surrounded by thousands of Parisians. The prisoner was placed on the scaffold and tied with ropes applied to his arms and legs. His hand was then burned in a brazier filled with flaming sulphur, and he was pinched with red-hot tongs on his arms, thighs, and chest. On his open wounds was poured molten lead and boiling oil. The procedure was repeated several times as the victim let out excruciating cries of pain, all to the satisfaction of the enthralled masses who pressed to get a better view of the spectacle. Then, four big horses, whipped by four attendants, pulled the ropes and the arms and legs became more and more distorted, but remained attached to the body. The executioners then cut some of the tendons, and with some more pulling two legs and one arm separated from the body. The victim was still breathing which stopped only after the second arm was separated from the torso.

London, 1817

In the center of a great crowd gathered for the occasion, the infamous executioner Calcraft slipped the noose around Brandreth's neck, then quickly sent him swinging. That was not the end of it. Brandreth was cut down after a half an hour, still not dead, since in those days hanging caused death through strangulation. He was carried to the block where the executioner took one mighty swipe with an ax that had been ordered specially for the job. But his aim was not true, and he only partly severed the head. His assistant finished the job with a butcher's knife.

SOURCE Maestro 1973; Newman 1983.

Beheaded in Bordeaux, 1377.

there is no minimum age but it is a factor to be considered in sentencing. The United States is a signator to an international agreement that forbids execution for crimes committed at ages younger than eighteen. However, the agreements have never been ratified by the Senate (Reinhold 1985).

Most persons sentenced to prison are eventually released on parole. However, some states have done away with parole—why? The next chapter will provide some answers. The apparent failure of correctional institutions to "correct" criminals led to the rise of a system of alternatives to incarceration that became known as community-based corrections, an issue we will also examine in the following chapter.

KEY TERMS

correctional institution
classification
treatment
maximum-security prison

medium-security institutions
minimum-security institutions
sovereign immunity
writ of habeas corpus

REVIEW QUESTIONS

1. Why did scientific advancements during the Second World War set the stage for the advent of "correctional institutions"?
2. What were the revolutionary changes in penology that occurred in California toward the end of World War II?
3. What are the purposes of classification in a correctional institution?
4. What are the problematic aspects of classification?
5. Why is it difficult to provide treatment in a correctional institution?
6. What are the assumptions upon which the treatment of criminals in corrections is based?
7. What are the differences between the correction officers and the "treaters"?
8. How did the civil rights and antiwar movements affect the correctional institution?
9. What social and political conditions led up to the riot at Attica prison?
10. Contemporary prisons suffer from a number of problems in addition to overcrowding. What are these problems?
11. What are the characteristics of a maximum-security prison?
12. What distinguishes a medium-security prison from a maximum-security prison?
13. What are the characteristics of a minimum-security prison?
14. Why have the courts traditionally been reluctant to intervene in matters pertaining to prisons?
15. What issue led to the end of the Supreme Court's "hands off" policy with respect to prisons, and why?
16. What rights have been granted to prisoners by the Supreme Court?
17. What are the arguments for and against capital punishment?

CHAPTER 16

Parole and Community-Based Corrections

THE HISTORY OF THE INDETERMINATE SENTENCE AND PAROLE
Elmira Reformatory

THE MEDICAL MODEL
Criticisms of the Medical Model

THE PAROLE BOARD
Parole Guidelines

PAROLE SUPERVISION

PAROLE VIOLATIONS
Parole Violation Hearings

THE ABOLITION OF PAROLE

INTENSIVE SUPERVISION

EXECUTIVE CLEMENCY

COMMUNITY-BASED CORRECTIONS
Diversion
Pretrial Release
Deferred Sentencing
Halfway Houses
Work Release

THE DEMISE OF COMMUNITY CORRECTIONS

REVIEW QUESTIONS

Boxes

The Parole Officer
The Pardon in California
Brooke House Multi-Service Center

In the last two chapters we examined jails and prisons and their attendant problems: overcrowding, violence, and limited educational, recreational, and rehabilitation opportunities. Parole and community-based corrections are two responses to these problems.

THE HISTORY OF THE INDETERMINATE SENTENCE AND PAROLE

Time spent in prison after conviction varies considerably from offense to offense and state to state. One of the reasons for this variation is the indeterminate sentence and parole that we began looking at in chapter 13. The use of indeterminate sentences and parole release derives from the English experience with the

ticket-of-leave. In 1853, Parliament enacted the Penal Servitude Act, which enabled prisoners to be released—or paroled—on a ticket-of-leave. Sir Walter Crofton, who in 1854 became head of the Irish prison system, adopted the ticket-of-leave as the last of three stages of penal servitude that he established in Ireland. In order to qualify for a ticket-of-leave under the Irish system, inmates had to evidence signs of reformation. The releasees (parolees) were supervised by the police in rural districts and in Dublin by the Inspector of Released Prisoners, forerunner of the modern parole officer. The system established by Crofton was widely publicized in the United States.

Elmira Reformatory

In 1869 a reformatory was authorized for Elmira, New York, to receive male first offenders between the ages of sixteen and thirty. The following year, prison reformers meeting in Cincinnati urged New York to copy the Irish system when the new institution was completed. When the Elmira Reformatory opened in 1876, one of the leading reformers, Zebulon R. Brockway, was appointed superintendent. He drafted a statute for the state legislature directing the sending of young first offenders to Elmira under an indeterminate sentence not to exceed the maximum term for nonreformatory offenders. The actual date of release was set by the reformatory's Board of Managers based on the inmate's institutional behavior. According to a historical account by the Division of Parole of the State of New York (1984: 6): "After the inmate accumulated a certain number of marks based on institutional conduct and progress in academic or vocational training, and if the investigation of his assurance of employment was positive, he could be released."

Frederick Wines (1975: 230), a colleague of Brockway, described the principles of the Elmira system:

> [that] criminals can be reformed; that reformation is the right of the convict and the duty of the State; that every prisoner must be individualized and given special treatment adapted to develop him to the point in which he is weak—physical, intellectual, or moral culture, in combination, but in varying proportions, according to the diagnosis of each case; that time must be given for the reformatory process to take effect, before allowing him to be sent away, uncured; that his cure is always facilitated by his cooperation, and often impossible without it.

The founders of the Elmira Reformatory, which opened in 1876, were among the first to acknowledge that young offenders can be reformed and that it is the state's responsibility to do so.

Cooperation was fostered by a system of inmate classifications, according to which privileges were dispensed. Behavior judged to be "reformative" was rewarded by reclassification and, thus, by increased privileges, which eventually led to release on parole. Upon being admitted to Elmira, each inmate was placed in the second grade of classification. Six months of good conduct meant he could be promoted to the first grade, and misbehavior caused him to be placed in the third grade from which he would have to work his way back up. Continued good behavior by inmates in the first grade resulted in their being released—America's first parole system. Paroled inmates remained under the jurisdiction of reformatory authorities for an additional six months, during which time parolees were required to report on the first day of every month to their appointed guardian (from which parole officers evolved) and provide an account of their situation and conduct. If it was judged that they had or were likely to revert to criminal behavior, their parole would be revoked and they would have to return to the reformatory.

The system used at Elmira was quickly copied by reformatories in some states, such as the Massachusetts Reformatory at Concord, and made applicable to all or part of the prison population in other states such as Pennsylvania, Michigan, and Illinois (Wines 1975). In 1907, New York extended indeterminate sentencing and parole release to all first offenders except those convicted of murder. The great impetus for the expansion of parole, however, did not occur until the Great Depression of the 1930s. The large numbers of unemployed workers during the Depression led to legislation that effectively abolished the economic exploitation of prison labor. This was accompanied by the prohibitive cost of constructing prisons, prison overcrowding, and an outbreak of prison riots. A 1931 federal report by the National Commission of Law Observance and Law Enforcement described the overcrowding of American prisons as "incredible"; Michigan, for example, had 78.6 percent more inmates than its original capacity; California, 62.2 percent; Ohio, 54.1 percent; and Oklahoma, 56.7 percent.

Economic conditions and the need to reduce prison populations led to the widespread acceptance of indeterminate sentencing and parole release. As noted in chapter 15, at the end of World War II the indeterminate sentence and parole became intertwined with the idea of corrections and a medical model approach to dealing with criminal offenders.

THE MEDICAL MODEL

The positive approach to crime and criminals seeks to explain and respond to criminal behavior using the principles and methods of science, much as physical illness is treated by a physician. As Donal MacNamara (1977: 439) states, "In its simplest (perhaps oversimplifed) terms, the **medical model** as applied to corrections assumed the offender to be 'sick' (physically, mentally, and/or socially); his offense to be a manifestation or symptom of his illness, a cry for help." The medical mataphor is often extended to the postconviction process, with parallels between the following terms:

- examination = presentence report
- diagnosis = classification
- treatment = correctional programs

The effects of treatment are reviewed and analyzed by the parole board, which determines if the offender is sufficiently rehabilitated to be discharged from the correctional institution. Treatment continues on an outpatient basis in the form of parole supervision. The American Friends' Service Committee (1971: 37) sums up the rationale for this medical approach:

> It rejects inherited concepts of criminal punishment as the payment of a debt owed to society, a debt proportioned to the magnitude of the offender's wrong. Instead it would save the offender through constructive measures of reformation, [and] protect society by keeping the offender locked up until the reformation is accomplished.

Criticisms of the Medical Model

Although there was a paucity of systematic research supporting this approach to criminal behavior, the medical/corrections model continued without serious criticism into 1970. Opposition to the use of indeterminate sentencing and parole came primarily from the political right, as exemplified by the attacks of J. Edgar Hoover, who saw parole as a way to "coddle" criminals (see, for example, Hoover's "The Faith of Free Men" in *Vital Speeches of the Day*, November 5, 1965).

During the 1970s this changed; the political left also began to criticize the corrections approach. In 1971, the American Friends' Service Committee (AFSC) published the first comprehensive attack on the indeterminate sentence and parole. AFSC noted that the indeterminate sentence and parole rest on a view of crime as the result of *individual* pathology that can best be "cured" by "treating" *individual* criminals. Such an approach, it noted, discounts environmental factors such as poverty, discrimination, and unemployment. Furthermore, AFSC argued, even if the medical model approach is valid, the behavioral sciences are not precise enough to offer a scientific basis for treatment.

The work of AFSC had only limited impact and no practical effect on corrections until 1974. In that year Robert Martinson published "What Works?" to which he answered, virtually nothing! "What Works?" was a synopsis of the research findings of Martinson, Douglas Lipton, and Judith Wilks; the complete work was published in the following year (Lipton et al. 1975). While the synopsis was more critical of the correctional system than the larger report, both lent credence to the arguments of the AFSC. The three researchers surveyed 231 studies of correctional programs up until 1967 about which Martinson (1974: 25) concluded, "With few and isolated exceptions, the rehabilitative efforts that have been reported so far have had no appreciable effect on recidivism."

Criticism of the indeterminate sentence, corrections, and parole increased. David Fogel (1975: 192) presented a *justice model* in which he criticized the unbridled discretion exercised by correctional officials.

> It is evident that correctional administrators have for too long operated with practical immunity in the backwashes of administrative law. They have been unmindful that the process of justice more strictly observed by the visible police and courts in relation to rights due the accused before and through adjudication must not stop when the convicted person is sentenced. The justice perspective demands accountability from all processors, even the "pure of heart."

Although they believe that the rehabilitative approach, properly administered, has merit, Francis Cullen and Karen Gilbert (1982: 246) note, "There can be little dispute that the rehabilitative ideal has been conveniently employed as a mask for inequities in the administration of criminal penalties and for brutality behind the walls of our penal institutions."

THE PAROLE BOARD

A target of much of the criticism was the **parole board**. Parole boards evolved out of the power of governors to issue pardons to selected convicts, often for the purpose of relieving prison overcrowding. Today, parole boards make pardon recommendations to the governor. Their primary function, however, is to decide how long an inmate is to remain in prison. In states with indeterminate sentencing laws, the judge sets a minimum and maximum term, leaving it up to the parole board to determine when the convict is to be released—or paroled—from prison.

A parole board consists of anywhere from three to twelve members, who are usually appointed by the governor for terms ranging from three to six years. Parole board appointments are usually part of the patronage powers enjoyed by a governor, and few states require specific professional qualifications for the position; "the only real qualification may be the political responsiveness and reliability of the board member to the appointing power" (Parker 1975: 30).

Typically, several members of the parole board hold hearings in the state's correctional institutions. The members examine the presentence investigation (probation) report, institutional records, and any information gathered by parole field staff, such as interviews with a spouse, an employer, and parents. Usually, the inmate appears before the board in a brief question-and-answer session, after which the board, in private, renders its decision. In some states, however, hearing officers interview inmates and make recommendations to the board, and the inmate never appears before members of the parole board.

Questionable qualifications of parole board members and brief hearings have been two criticisms leveled at parole boards. The criteria used by parole board members in making release decisions have also been criticized for their subjectivity and lack of uniformity—a basic denial of equality before the law. In response to these criticisms, many parole boards have developed guidelines to structure discretion.

Parole Guidelines

Parole guidelines use severity and salient factor scores to determine the length of time an inmate is to remain incarcerated. The *severity score* is determined by the nature of the offense—for example, low to greatest—from minor theft to robbery. In some parole guideline schemes, very serious crimes such as murder are not included. The *salient factor score* is a prognosis of the inmate's potential for rehabilitation and parole, an educated guess about future conduct. Thus, as noted in the table, "Federal Parole Guidelines," an inmate with a severity score of "Moderate" and a salient factor score of "Good" would serve 14–18 months before being released on parole.

Parole guidelines go well beyond the rehabilitative medical model on which the indeterminate sentence is presumed to be based. Indeed, satisfactory progress in the institution does not necessarily affect the parole decision; good institutional behavior is expected, not rewarded. In fact, institutional adjustment

Guidelines of the United States Board of Parole

Offense Severity (examples)	Parole Prognosis			
	Very Good	Good	Fair	Poor
Low: property offenses and tax violations of less than $2000	6*	6-9	9-12	12-16
Low/Moderate: Small scale drug law violations and property offenses over $2000.	8	8-12	12-6	16-22
Moderate: auto theft with value of less than 20,000; small scale drug trafficking; property offenses over $2000 and under $20,000	10-14	14-18	18-24	24-32
High: counterfeiting ($20,000 to $100,000); medium level drug sales; involuntary manslaughter; property offenses from $20,000 - 100,000.	14-20	20-26	26-34	36-44
Very High: robbery; residential burglary; large-scale drug trafficking; extortion; property offenses of $100,000 - 500,000.	24-36	36-48	48-60	60-72
Greatest-I: robbery with injuries; very large-scale drug trafficking; espionage; voluntary manslaughter; limited duration kidnapping.	40-52	52-64	64-78	78-100
Greatest II: murder; robbery with serious injury; highest level drug trafficking; treason; air piracy; kidnapping for ransom or terrorism.	— no limits —			

*Figures in number of months

has never been an accurate guide for predicting postrelease behavior. Certain offenders, such as professional criminals, most often perform well in prison, but tend to return to crime as soon as they are released. Instead, the parole board evaluates such items as the inmate's prior criminal record, employment history, military record, and marital history. The use of guidelines enables a parole board to base its decisions on uniform standards while incorporating the "just deserts" criterion—the amount of time an offender deserved—of those who support determinate sentencing. In practice then, the nature of the offense is the prime factor in making a parole release decision.

PAROLE SUPERVISION

Inmates may be released from prison by the parole board or they may be released after reaching their maximum sentence minus "good time." In states with determinate sentencing (and thus without parole boards), inmates can usually earn one day of good time for every day served—50 percent off their sentence. In

Convicted mass murderer Charles Manson at a parole hearing in early 1986. Manson, who was sentenced to life in prison for the 1969 killing of actress Sharon Tate and five others, was refused a sixth bid for parole.

either event, whether paroled or released on good time (referred to as **mandatory** or **conditional release**), the offender is usually supervised by a parole officer. As with probation supervision, offenders are required to abide by a set of parole or conditional release regulations that require them to report at regular intervals, to seek and maintain employment, to support dependents, to avoid "undesirable" persons and places and, of course, to refrain from law-violative behavior. A violation of the rules of parole can result in a hearing before the parole board and the offender's return to prison. The period of supervision varies from state to state; it may continue until the remainder of the sentence is completed, or until the parole board decides to release the offender from supervision as a result of satisfactory behavior, whichever comes first.

Parole supervision has two purposes:

1. helping the offender to reintegrate into the community; and
2. protecting the community from recidivism—that is, from the offender.

Typically, parolees (or conditionally released offenders) visit their parole officer once a month, during which time the officer briefly interviews them. During the visit the parolee will apprise the officer of his or her situation—residence, employment activities—and the officer will provide advice and guidance, and possibly admonitions.

Parole agencies may have employment services, or parolees may be referred to other agencies for assistance with employment or other services such as vocational training. Most offenders released from prison have few marketable skills, and employment for parolees is an ongoing problem, particularly when unemployment is widespread. Many, probably most, employers will not knowingly hire an ex-convict. Thus, in order to secure employment, parolees usually have to lie to cover up the fact of their conviction or remain unemployed. Except when the employment is in a sensitive area—for example, in a school or hospital—parole officers will usually cast a blind eye to the deception.

Parole officers "enter the field" to visit their parolees at home or at work, to verify residence and employment, and to maintain contact with family and friends of the parolees. The policy of agencies that stress control—or community protection—is for

> **Statement of Conditions Under Which Parole Is Granted**
>
> This Certificate of Parole shall not become operative until the following Conditions are agreed to by the prisoner, and violation of any of these Conditions may result in revocation of Parole.
>
> 1. I shall report immediately to the Parole Officer under whose supervision I am paroled by personal visit.
>
> 2. I shall not change my residence or employment or leave the State without first getting the consent of my Parole Officer.
>
> 3. I shall, between the first and third days of each month, until my release from parole, make a full and truthful report to my Parole Officer in writing.
>
> 4. I shall not use narcotic drugs, or frequent places where intoxicants or drugs are sold, dispensed, or used unlawfully.
>
> 5. I shall avoid injurious habits and shall not associate with persons of bad reputation or harmful character.
>
> 6. I shall in all respects conduct myself honorably, work diligently at a lawful occupation, and support my dependents to the best of my ability.
>
> 7. I shall not violate any law.
>
> 8. I hereby waive all extradition rights and process and agree to return when the State Board of Pardons and Paroles directs at any time before my release from parole.
>
> 9. I shall promptly and truthfully answer all inquiries directed to me by the State Board of Pardons and Paroles and my Parole Officer and allow that Officer to visit me at my home, employment site or elsewhere, and carry out all instructions my Parole Officer gives.

these visits to be unannounced; thus, they serve to let the parolees know that they may be under observation by their parole officer at any time. Since parolees often reside in high-crime neighborhoods, and parole officers may be required to make arrests, some agencies allow the officers to carry firearms. In many agencies, parole officers work closely with law enforcement personnel and share information about parolees who represent a potential danger to the community.

Typically, as with probation officers, parole officers are burdened with excessive caseloads, often making supervision per-

10. If at any time it becomes necessary to communicate with my Parole Officer for any purpose and that Officer is not available, I shall contact the State Board of Pardons and Paroles.

11. I shall not marry without first seeking the advice and counsel of my Parole Officer.

12. Immediately upon release from the service of sentence in _____ and if prior to _____, I will report directly to the State Board of Pardons and Paroles, 750 Washington Avenue, Montgomery, AL 36130, either by telephone, correspondence or in person.

13. I shall pay fifteen dollars ($15.00) per month to the State Board of Pardons and Paroles as required by law.

14. I shall not own, possess or have under my control a firearm or ammunition of any kind, nor any other deadly weapon or dangerous instrument as defined by Alabama law.

15. I shall participate in alcoholic, drug treatment, or other therapeutic programs when instructed to do so by my Parole Officer.

16. I shall pay $ _____ Restitution as ordered by the sentencing court or the State Board of Pardons and Paroles.

I hereby certify that this Statement of Conditions of Parole has been read and explained to the Parolee.

This _____ day _____ 19 _____ _____
                                 Signature of Parolee

_____   _____
Member of Board or Warden   (Give full address at which you can be reached)

functory. Caseloads ranging from 100 to 200 are not unusual. To deal with this problem, some agencies have developed a system of classifying parolees according to the level of supervision required. This enables officers to allocate their time accordingly and pay more attention to offenders who are the greatest threats to the community and to those who require the most services to become reintegrated into the community. Parole agencies may also have specialized units whose officers supervise parolees with special problems such as a serious history of drug or alcohol abuse, mental illness, or retardation.

THE PAROLE OFFICER

Under close and periodic supervision of a Senior Parole Officer, supervises parolees by providing individual and group counseling and surveillance; helps secure employment and vocational opportunities; makes referrals to community service agencies; maintains contact with family, friends, employers, etc.

Conducts placement, arrest and violation investigations; develops plans for rehabilitation within the community or within the institution in accordance with correctional recommendations; dictates supervision progress reports, placement reports, etc.

Issues arrest, hold and release orders; arrests parole violators; conducts searches and seizes contraband and/or secures search warrants; delivers subpoenas as directed; testifies at violation hearings; transports parole violators.

Develops sound working relations with community agencies, citizen groups and criminal justice agencies through authorized speaking engagements, memberships on community council and committees, etc.

SOURCE: State of Ohio.

PAROLE VIOLATIONS

Although parole officers are supposed to be diligent in uncovering parole violations, this is often impossible given their large caseloads. Furthermore, there may be a reluctance to return offenders to prisons, which are already overcrowded, for violations of the technical rules of parole. In practice, then, parolees in some states are returned to prison only when their behavior constitutes a new crime for which they may or may not be convicted. When parolees are accused of new criminal offenses, it is easier to send them back to prison for a rule violation than it is to convict them for the new crime—the level of evidence is significantly less, and parole violations are handled administratively, not before a judge in a court of law.

Parole Violation Hearings

Based on the 1972 Supreme Court decision in *Morrissey v. Brewer*, an accused parole violator who is in custody is entitled to two hearings. The first, a *preliminary hearing*, is similar to the probable cause hearing in a criminal court. The parolee is able to defend against the charges, to be represented by an attorney, and to present witnesses. If the hearing officer determines that the parolee has violated one or more of the rules of parole in an important respect, he or she finds "probable cause" and the offender remains incarcerated until a *revocation hearing* is held. Otherwise the parolee is restored to supervision. The revocation hearing is usually conducted by members of the parole board, but otherwise follows the same format as that of the preliminary hearing. At this hearing, in addition to considering the charges against the parolee, the board will hear information about the totality of the parolee's situation, such as mitigating circumstances and employment while on parole. Thus, even if the allegations are sustained, the parolee can be returned to supervision—or returned to prison.

THE ABOLITION OF PAROLE

Beginning in the mid-1970s, criticism of parole increased to the point that a number of states abolished the practice and instituted determinate sentencing. Critics on the right complained about parole-as-leniency, while critics on the left saw it as an abuse of government discretion. By 1980, eight states, including California, the state that pioneered the corrections approach, abolished parole release. In the late 1970s the attack that had centered on the indeterminate sentence and the parole board shifted to parole/post-prison supervision. About one-third of the state prisoners released from prison were found to recidivate within three years; there was very little evidence that supervision was accomplishing either of the two purposes that justified its existence. Research into the effectiveness of parole supervision was inconclusive. Deborah Star (1979), who conducted research in California, found that releasees who received a significantly reduced level of supervision did no worse than those subjected to normal supervision. Mark Jay Lerner (1977) found that parole supervision in New York markedly reduced the post-release criminal activity of a group of conditional releasees, however, and a similar study in Connecticut (Sachs and Logan 1979) found that parole supervision resulted in a modest reduction in recidivism.

Intensive supervision

One of the trends in parole (and probation) has been the proliferation of so-called **intensive supervision** as an alternative to incarceration. In parole, intensive supervision is viewed as risk management—allowing for a high-risk inmate to be paroled, but under the most restrictive of circumstances. In either case, intensive supervision is a response to prison overcrowding. The basic premise of intensive supervision in parole is that *more* of whatever it is that the agency does with routine cases will have a salutory effect on cases at greater risk. While a number of research studies have challenged this premise, there is a strong (if unproven) belief in probation and parole that "more is better."

The intent of intensive supervision is to discourage offenders from committing parole violations by closely monitoring them. Probation and parole officers are portrayed as making unannounced visits to offenders and monitoring offenders around-the-clock, ready to take immediate action to prevent danger to the community. For agencies whose officers are armed and trained in law enforcement, this approach is a natural extension of the services they already provide. However, agencies whose officers do not have adequate law enforcement training or authority, cannot live up to the image. Indeed, agencies that adopt a meaningful form of intensive supervision, but fail to equip their officers accordingly, are placing them in potential danger.

Executive clemency

Every chief executive—the president and all fifty governors—can exercise some form of **executive clemency**, which includes reprieve, commutation, and pardon. Parole officers usually in-

> # THE PARDON IN CALIFORNIA
>
> Any person who has been convicted of an offense in California may apply to the governor for a pardon. Once an application has been filed, the Board of Prison Terms [formerly the board of parole] undertakes an investigation. The case is then presented to the full Board for a recommendation. The governor reviews the case and has complete discretion in deciding whether to grant a pardon, and a pardon is not granted to every person who applies.
>
> A governor's pardon restores citizenship rights to the individual who has demonstrated a high standard of constructive behavior following conviction for an offense: individuals who have made a sincere and successful effort to complete a prescribed period of rehabilitation have proved to themselves and others that they have earned the restoration of rights to citizenship.
>
> If a full and unconditional pardon is granted, the person pardoned may own and possess any type of weapon that may lawfully be possessed and owned by other citizens unless that person has been convicted of any offense which involved the use of a dangerous weapon. A California pardon may not permit the possession of weapons under the laws of another state or federal laws.
>
> A person who has been pardoned cannot state that he or she has never been convicted of a felony. A pardon does not seal or expunge the record of the conviction. The granting of a pardon does not affect the right of a licensing agency to consider the conviction which has been pardoned in its determination of whether a license to practice a profession should be granted or restored.
>
> **SOURCE:** State of California

vestigate requests for executive clemency, and the parole board usually provides the chief executive with a report and recommendation.

The **reprieve** is a temporary suspension of the execution of a sentence—usually in cases of capital punishment—to give the prisoner time to seek further legal redress or amelioration of the sentence. The commutation is a reduction in sentence that results in an immediate eligibility for parole or release from incarceration. Commutation does not generally connote forgiveness; it is usually used to shorten an excessively long sentence, or as a reward for some exemplary service on the part of an inmate, such as saving a correction officer from harm. It may also be used to release an inmate suffering from a terminal illness. A pardon completely and unconditionally absolves a convict from all of the consequences of a criminal conviction. Although it is an act of forgiveness, it is often used when there is serious doubt about the guilt of an inmate and not only when new evidence shows that the convict is innocent. There is also a limited form of pardon that does not imply forgiveness nor absolve the person from all of the consequences of a criminal conviction. Instead, it rewards exemplary postinstitutional behavior by providing a restoration of certain rights typically lost by convicted felons.

Community-Based Corrections

By the 1960s it was becoming obvious that the rehabilitative ideal was impossible to accomplish in the prison setting. The "correctional" expectations of prisons were not being fulfilled. As Paul Hahn (1976: 6) remarks, "The spending of years in confined quarters, perhaps as small as eight by ten feet, in a setting dominated by a toilet and a possibly criminally aggressive cellmate, can hardly be considered conducive to encourage socially acceptable behavior upon release." The failure of corrections was often blamed on the counterproductive influences of the prison subculture and the very destructive aspects of these total institutions. "Even the most well-developed treatment program," notes Paul Cromwell (1978: 68), "if totally contained within the institution, will lack one ingredient essential to an inmate's success after release. The missing factor is contact with the community and family." Instead of abandoning the rehabilitative ideal, supporters argued for a new approach that they referred to as community-based corrections

Vernon Fox (1977) defines community-based corrections as that part of corrections, other than traditional probation, prison

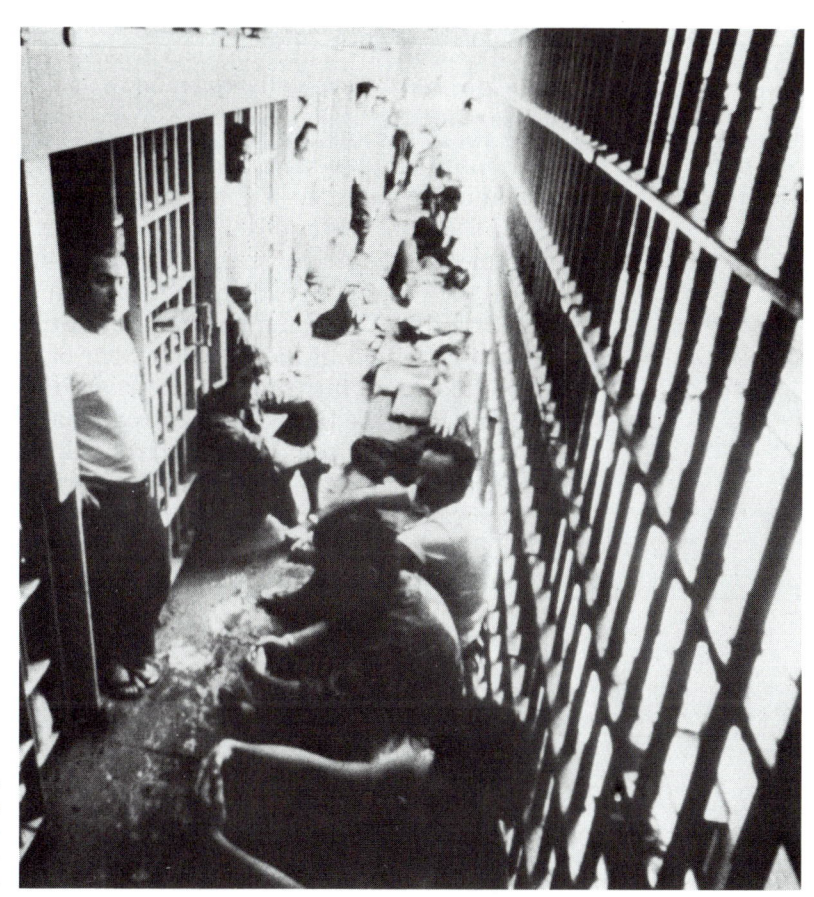

Community-based corrections are a response to prisons as an inadequate setting for rehabilitation.

and parole, that makes use of community resources to assist the more traditional functions. Fox (1977: 1) states that the purposes of community-based corrections are "the mobilization and management of community resources to assist in the rehabilitation of offenders" and "the provision of alternatives to incarceration in a way that is compatible with the public interest and safety."

The case for community-based corrections was summed up by the President's Commission on Law Enforcement and Administration of Justice (1972: 398):

> Institutions tend to isolate offenders from society, both physically and psychologically, cutting them off from schools, jobs, families, and other supportive influences and increasing the probability that

the label of criminal will be indelibly impressed upon them. The goal of reintegration is likely to be furthered much more readily by working with offenders in the community than by incarceration.

The commission added that the cost of incarceration also made community-based corrections attractive.

In 1965, the Federal Rehabilitation Act authorized programs designed to aid in the rehabilitation of offenders while holding down the number of persons in prison. In 1968, Congress passed the Omnibus Crime Control and Safe Streets Act which subsequently resulted in the establishment of the Law Enforcement Assistance Administration (LEAA). With encouragement and funding from the LEAA, state correctional officials began to look outside of the prison for ways to rehabilitate offenders. The approach they adopted, community-based corrections, centered on reintegrating offenders into the community. A number of programs are generally offered as being part of such a system of community-based corrections, in addition to probation and parole, including diversion, pretrial release, deferred sentencing, halfway houses, and work-release.

Diversion

The President's Commission on Law Enforcement and Administration of Justice (1972) noted that for many persons who come to the attention of the criminal justice system, criminal sanctions are excessive, but these persons are often in need of treatment or supervision. Since the courts are overburdened with cases, a system—**diversion**—that provides needed services for nonserious offenders while easing court congestion is quite attractive.

Police have traditionally exercised the unofficial discretionary power to warn or reprimand offenders or to refer them to various service agencies instead of arresting them. Police diversion is an official response, through the use of a program specifically designed to deal with certain marginal cases. In one Maryland county, for example, the police are authorized to issue juvenile citations for certain juvenile offenses. The citation must be signed by the juvenile and his or her parent, and this avoids an arrest. The juvenile is required to appear at an arbitration hearing seven days later, and if a settlement can be reached, there will be no court action (Blew and Rosenblum 1977). In the Night Prosecutor's Program in Columbus, Ohio, law students serve as hearing officers for cases referred by the police. Arrests are avoided, and the hearings, which are informal, allow for the settlement of interpersonal disputes without official court action (Palmer 1974). In some police diversion programs, sworn or civilian personnel arrange referrals to social agencies for persons with alcohol, drug, marital, or other problems that have needed police intervention. In order to avoid being sent to court for prosecution, the offender must agree to accept the referral, and a failure to adhere to diversion program rules can result in prosecution.

When an arrest is made, the prosecutor decides if the case is to be prosecuted; a diversion program provides the prosecutor an option between dismissal of the charges and full prosecution. In more elaborate programs, the prosecutor has a diversion unit staffed with social workers. They screen cases and recommend defendants for diversion and, if the defendant agrees, they will provide social services. In Dade County, Florida, for example, certain defendants can avoid prosecution by agreeing to participate in a program that involves individual and group counseling and vocational and educational support. If the defendant completes that program, charges are dismissed by the prosecutor. Those who fail to respond to the offer of help or fail to cooperate with the program are subjected to prosecution (Mullen 1975).

The use of diversion has been criticized for extending the "criminal justice net." Frederick Howlett (1973) argues that in the absence of a diversion program, police officers usually return errant children to their homes, which to some extent requires parents to deal with them. When the diversion alternative is available, children become the subject of an official file and suffer from the negative labeling that results. Franklin Dunford (1977: 344) argues, "The police in their diversionary zeal succeeded, in this instance, in increasing rather than reducing the number of youth falling under their jurisdiction." Moreover, youngsters often have no other choice than to participate when the alternative is adjudication. Dunford (1977: 350) is particularly critical of this coercive element because it "potentially leads youth to view diversion programs as extensions of the justice system." In sum, criticism is based on research that indicates that persons who are diverted, juveniles or adults, would often not be arrested in the first place or would soon be diverted from the criminal justice system as the result of failure to prosecute, dismissal, or receiving a fine or suspended sentence.

Pretrial Release

As we noted in earlier chapters, persons who lack the funds necessary to be released on bail and so are detained pending trial suffer significant handicaps. The jail experience itself is punishing. In addition, people in jail are separated from their community—from family, friends, employment. Not only does this handicap the defendant, but it also burdens the criminal justice system whose limited funds must be used to detain large numbers of persons awaiting trial. **Pretrial release** programs developed as a response to these problems. One of the earliest, the Manhattan Bail Project, was established by the Vera Institute of Justice of New York in 1961. Pretrial investigators (PTIs) were hired from among law students at New York University. PTIs interviewed defendants before their arraignment and gathered and verified information about residence, employment, family—in short, community ties. This information was conveyed to the judge who could, in appropriate cases, use it to release a defendant without bail—a **release on recognizance** (ROR). By 1965, forty-two jurisdictions had programs enabling defendants with community ties to remain free pending trial without the need for bail (McCarthy and McCarthy 1984).

The pretrial release concept was expanded to provide a host of services, including supervision, to persons released without bail. **Supervised release** serves those defendants who, because of their lack of community ties and/or their more serious criminal background, would ordinarily be denied ROR. The Des Moines Pre-Trial Services, for example, utilizes a unit with counselors and job development personnel. Candidates for the program are interviewed by law students and, if released to the program by a judge, are supervised by the release unit during the pretrial stage. Supervised release programs are designed not only to release the maximum number of persons consonant with public safety but also to assist the released defendant to become qualified for probation if convicted (Boorkman et al. 1976).

Deferred Sentencing

Deferred sentencing usually involves a plea of guilty followed by either restitution or some form of community service, both of which can also be made conditions of a sentence of probation. Under deferred sentencing, however, there is no supervision by a probation officer. The failure to live up to the conditions of a deferred sentence can lead to a sentence of incarceration.

Proponents of deferred sentencing argue that restitution and community service are appropriate responses to less serious offenses in which there has been a loss or damage to public or private property. Vernon Fox (1977: 57) points to the advantage of face-to-face contact between offender and victim; it "helps make the victim a real person to the offender, rather than just a faceless entity. This type of contact can expiate guilt on the part of the offender and perhaps even change his attitude about committing further property crime." Belinda McCarthy and Bernard McCarthy (1984: 133-34) further observe that "requiring offenders to work off their crime in proportion to the damage done may be more merciful and more fair than requiring periods of incarceration or community supervision [probation] unrelated to the injury or the offense." It is also cheaper than either probation supervision or incarceration.

Restitution has been criticized, however, because it has the potential of increasing the disparity of treatment between persons committing similar offenses. Thus, a defendant with financial resources may receive a sentence of restitution, while one without resources suffers a sentence of incarceration.

Halfway Houses

A **halfway house** may be operated by a private or public agency. As a transition between the structures and supervision of a total institution and living independently in the community, some provide room, board, and help with employment, while others also provide a whole range of social services. The first such facility was opened in Boston in 1864 "to provide shelter, instruction, and employment to the discharged female prisoners who are either homeless or whose homes are only scenes of temptation" (Edwin Powers, cited in Allen et al. 1984: 318). The use of halfway houses was widespread until the Great Depres-

> # Brooke House Multi-Service Center
>
> **Brooke House, established in 1965, is the oldest halfway house for adult ex-offenders in New England, as well as one of the oldest in the country. Located in Boston's South End, Brooke House is a 65-bed co-educational multi-service center for ex-offenders. Its four stories house the Massachusetts Half-Way Houses Inc. Temporary Housing Program, the Massachusetts Community Assistance Parole Program, and the Women's Program. In addition is the Brooke House program which consists of a community residence for pre- and postreleasees from state, county, and federal correctional institutions.**
>
> **Brooke House provides a program of structured guidance and a supportive environment through which ex-offenders can take their lives into their own hands and develop the skills and discipline necessary for productive lives. The women's program consists of five beds for female residents who share kitchen and dining room facilities with the male residents. The women come from state and federal institutions on pre- and postrelease status, or from the courts on pretrial diversions.**
>
> SOURCE: Massachusetts Half-Way Houses, Inc.

sion, when funding dried up and there was a lack of facilities for the many homeless Americans who were not ex-convicts. The indeterminate sentence and the requirement that an inmate have an offer of employment to qualify for parole release took the place of the halfway house into the 1950s. In 1963, renewed interest in penal reform led to the founding of the International Halfway House Association.

A halfway house can involve two basic functions, "half-way in" and "half-way out." Donald Thalheimer (1975: 1) describes them:

> The very name halfway house suggests its position in the corrections world: halfway-in, a more structured environment than probation

Brooke House, Boston.

and parole; halfway-out, a less structured environment than institutions. As halfway-in houses they represent a last step before incarceration for probationers and parolees facing or having faced revocation; as halfway-out houses, they provide services to prereleasees and parolees leaving institutions. Halfway houses also provide a residential alternative to jail or outright release for accused offenders awaiting trial or convicted offenders awaiting sentencing.

Talbot House is a model halfway house that was founded by Jack Brown, a professor of psychiatry at the University of Cincinnati, to aid parolees. The three Talbot House residences provide the security of a homelike setting where an ex-offender can get professional assistance to aid with reintegration into the community. In addition to the professionals, Talbot House has staff members who are themselves ex-offenders and former residents of the program. As opposed to the acceptance Talbot House has received in Cincinnati, halfway houses typically suffer from community opposition. "It's a good idea, but not in my neighborhood!" is the prevalent response to proposals for halfway houses (see, for example, Krajick 1980b).

Work Release

Like the halfway house, **work release** is designed to prepare inmates for the freedom of community living. Typically an inmate leaves the institution or work-release center during the day for employment and returns at the end of the workday. Nonworkdays are spent in the institution, although there may be furloughs built into the program. Work release enables the inmate to support dependents and to accumulate funds necessary for community living. Work release may also be granted to secure employment or to attend job training or educational programs.

All states are authorized to grant work release, although the criteria for eligibility varies from state to state. Most have general criteria such as "not a high security risk" or "not likely to commit a crime of violence," and some automatically exclude those serving a life sentence or who have a **detainer** (a warrant to be activated upon the inmate's release) filed against them. In some states, work release must be authorized by the sentencing court.

Work release has sometimes been combined with restitution. The Minnesota Restitution Center, for example, receives adult male property offenders who have served four months of their state prison sentence. While in prison, the inmate meets with his victim face to face and, with the assistance of institutional staff, develops a restitution agreement. When the inmate is paroled, he resides in the Restitution Center where, with the assistance of the staff, he gains employment and fulfills the terms of the restitution agreement.

There are a number of problems with work release, not the least of which is the difficulty encountered by offenders seeking employment. Most are unskilled, and the prison provides little useful job training. Since most prisons are located in rural areas

Work-release programs are designed to prepare inmates for the freedom of community living.

far from industry, work-release centers are often opened near to areas where there is a demand for labor. This sometimes means that the center is located in or near residential communities, whose inhabitants may strongly oppose having criminals living nearby. In Illinois, for example, in 1985 the Department of Corrections abandoned efforts to set up new work-release centers because of community opposition across the state. There are fifteen still operating in the state, with six located in Chicago.

Work release can also be problematic with respect to administration and security. Inmates may fail to abide by regulations—by using intoxicating beverages, for example, or failing to return on time, or at all, to the facility. Field staff, such as parole officers, can lessen such problems because the inmates' employment can be investigated and absconders can be more easily apprehended. Lax programs inevitably result in bad press and a negative public reaction that can jeopardize work-release programs in general.

THE DEMISE OF COMMUNITY CORRECTIONS

David Greenberg is among the criminologists who have questioned the basic assumptions of community-based corrections. He says (1975: 4), "One might ask why, if the community is so therapeutic, the offender got into trouble there in the first place? Indeed, an offender's home community, where he is already known as a delinquent or criminal, might pose more obstacles to the abandonment of criminal activity than some new residential location." Furthermore, Greenberg argues, to the extent that criminal behavior is a rational response to the lack of lawful employment opportunity, it is beyond the ability of community-based corrections to "correct."

The impetus for an expansion of community-based corrections programs was the availability of federal funding. Andrew Scull noted in 1977 (p. 45) that "since the creation of the Law Enforcement Assistance Administration [LEAA, in 1969], efforts have been under way to manipulate federal funding and support for state and local law enforcement so as to provide sizeable financial incentives for the development of community corrections programs." During the early 1980s, however, funding through the LEAA dried up and the agency itself was dismantled. State and local governments, already severely pressed to maintain the services they traditionally provided and at the same time trying to maintain the reins on taxes, slowly abandoned the often costly programming that adequate community-based corrections required. Disillusionment with community-based corrections increased with public concern over a rising rate of crime (as reported by the Uniform Crime Reports). The result was a shift toward a more punitive approach to dealing with criminals and the demise of community-based corrections as an important programmatic response to criminal behavior.

KEY TERMS

ticket-of-leave
medical model
parole board
parole guidelines
mandatory or conditional release
intensive supervision
executive clemency
reprieve
commutation
pardon

community-based corrections
diversion
pretrial release
release on recognizance
supervised release
deferred sentencing
halfway house
work release
detainer

REVIEW QUESTIONS

1. Why is there so much variation between states with respect to the amount of time inmates spend in prison?
2. What were the principles underlying the indeterminate sentence established for the Elmira Reformatory?
3. What four factors provided the impetus for the expansion of parole in the United States?
4. What is meant by the "medical model" approach to corrections?
5. What are the arguments against the medical model of corrections?
6. What is the relationship between the indeterminate sentence and the parole board?
7. What are the reasons parole boards have been criticized?
8. What are the two factors used in determining parole release according to parole guidelines?

9. What are the responsibilities of a parole officer?
10. What are the various forms of executive clemency and what do they provide?
11. What led to the widespread adoption of community-based corrections?
12. What is meant by community-based corrections?
13. What are diversion programs?
14. What is the purpose of a pretrial release program?
15. What is deferred sentencing?
16. What are the purposes of a halfway house?
17. What is the most significant problem in establishing a halfway house?
18. What is a work-release program?
19. What led to the demise of community-based corrections as an important response to criminal behavior?

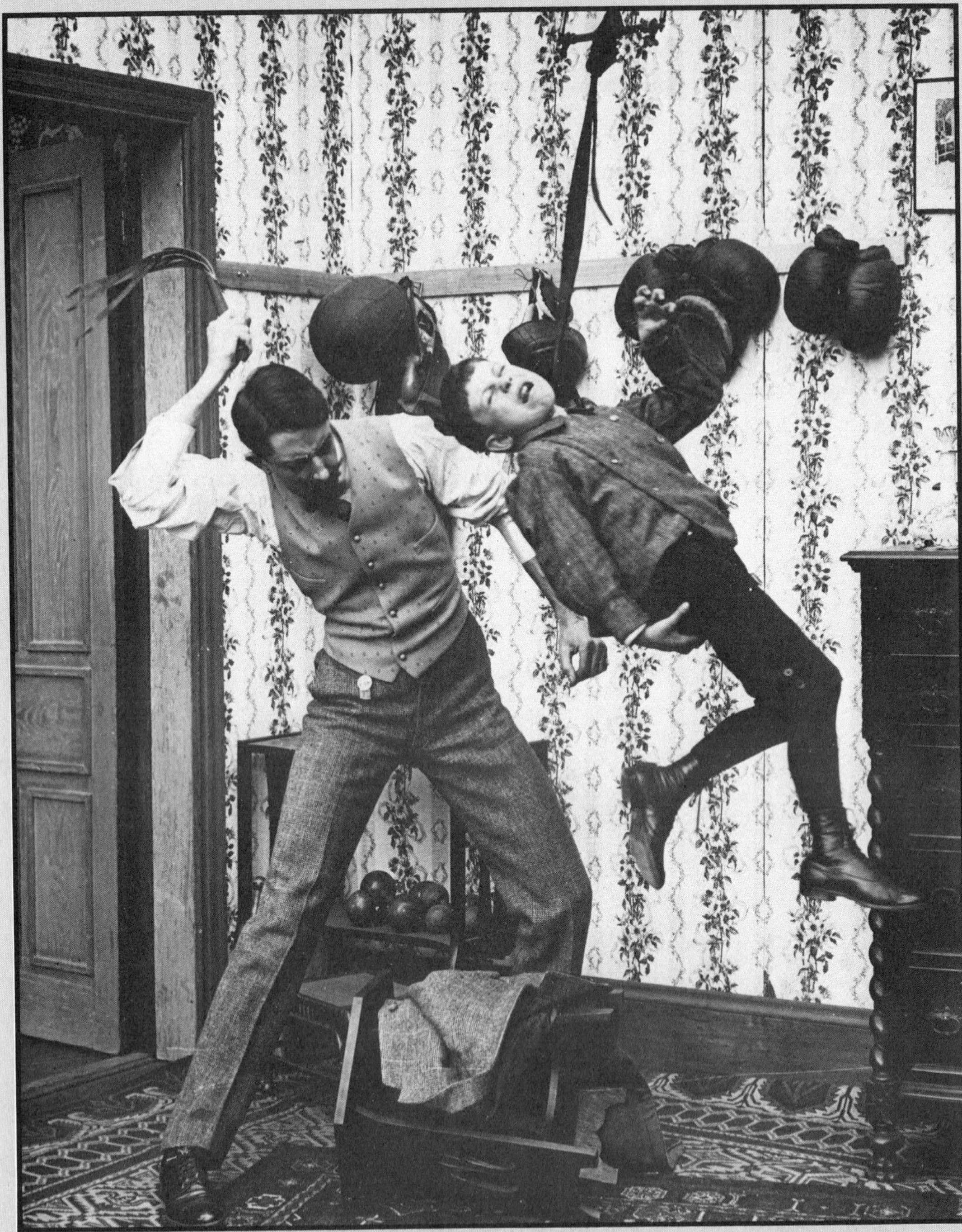

PART FOUR

Juvenile Justice

17 Juvenile Justice and the Juvenile Court

CHAPTER 17

Juvenile Justice and the Juvenile Court

THE HISTORY OF JUVENILE JUSTICE
The Child-Savers

JUVENILE COURT

THE RIGHTS OF JUVENILES
Due Process
Standards of Evidence
Jury Trial
Double Jeopardy
Preventive Detention

THE JUVENILE JUSTICE PROCESS
Delinquency
Status Offenses
Neglect, Abuse, and Dependency

JUVENILE COURT PROCEDURES
Preliminary Hearing
Adjudicatory Hearing
Dispositional Hearing
  Delinquents
  Status Offenders
  Abused or Neglected Children
  Dependent Children

JUVENILE INSTITUTIONS

REVIEW QUESTIONS

The system of justice used in response to juveniles in the United States is based on a philosophy so dramatically different from that of the adult system of criminal justice that it will be treated in a separate chapter in this book.

THE HISTORY OF JUVENILE JUSTICE

Societal attitudes toward children have varied throughout the ages, from early Christian beliefs that stressed their innocence and frailty to the eighteenth-century view of children as potential "little devils" in need of close supervision and strict discipline. The novels of Charles Dickens, particularly his *Oliver Twist* (1838), dramatized the plight of children in nineteenth-century England. In America, too, children were creatures for exploitation.

Child labor was an important part of economic life, and the children of the poor labored in mines (where their size was an advantage), mills, and factories under unsanitary and unsafe conditions. Laws prohibiting the hiring of children under twelve and limiting the workday of those over twelve to ten hours were routinely disregarded. Increased immigration, industrialization, and urbanization changed American society. The ten- to twelve-hour workday for adults left many children without parental supervision; family disorganization was becoming widespread. Many children lived in the streets, where they encountered the disorder and rampant vice of the new urban environments. Boys formed street gangs, committed crimes to survive, and provided the manpower for what later became known as organized crime. For girls, the situation was even worse.

Concern for the plight of children led to the establishment of the House of Refuge in New York in 1825, quickly followed by others in Boston and Philadelphia. These institutions provided housing and care for troublesome children who might otherwise be left in the streets or, if their behavior brought them into serious conflict with the law, sent to jail or prison.

> Houses of refuge were to become family substitutes, not only for the less serious juvenile criminal, but for runaways, disobedient children, or vagrants. Well-run institutions that incorporated both parental affection and stern discipline could only work to the child's benefit. Orphan asylums would likewise serve the same purposes for abandoned or orphaned children, for the children of women without husbands, or for those children whose parents were unfit. (Empey 1979: 25–26)

Although these institutions were run by private charities, Samuel Walker (1980: 78) notes that their publicly granted charters included the first statutory definitions of juvenile delinquency:

> The New York law designated the refuge for "children who shall be taken up or committed as vagrants, or convicted of criminal offenses" where the judge thought they were the "proper objects" for such treatment. The Massachusetts law was broader, including "rogues, vagabonds, common beggars, and other idle, disorderly and lewd persons," as well as "all children who live an idle or dissolute life, whose parents are dead or if living, from drunkenness, or other vices, neglect to provide any suitable employment, or exercise salutary control over said children."

The Barnardo Homes, one of the largest charity organizations in England, opened as institutions for wayward and vagrant children in the late nineteenth century. Their founder, Dr. Thomas John Barnardo, kept a photographic record of every child admitted to the homes. These images—some 55,000 were made between 1870 and 1905—are remarkable today both for their documentary value and as an illustration of middle-class response to the plight of outcast children in Victorian England.

These early laws, states Walker, provided the basis for the state to intervene in the cases of children who were neglected or in need of supervision, as well as those who committed crimes. The philosophy embodied in these statutes was that of **parens patriae**, a term that originally referred to the feudal duties of the overlord toward his vassals and later to the legal duties of the king toward his subjects who were in need of care, particularly children and the mentally incompetent. When they rejected the monarchy but kept the English common-law system, the Americans substituted the state for the crown as the *parens patriae* of all minors, including those who were delinquent. James Finckenauer (1984: 111) states that in 1838 a Pennsylvania case (*Ex parte Crouse*) based on *parens patriae* had the effect of allocating to the state "almost complete authority to intervene in parent-child relationships, and to deprive children of certain constitutional liberties guaranteed adults in the Bill of Rights. This was to remain the dominant philosophy in juvenile justice for the next 125 years."

The Child-Savers

As both immigration and urbanization continued unabated, the specter of masses of undisciplined and uneducated children gave rise to the **child-saving movement.** Led by upper-class women of earlier American stock, the child-savers were influenced by the nativist prejudices of their day and, later, by social Darwinism. Something had to be done to save the children from their environment of ignorance and vice; otherwise they would be led into poverty and crime and in turn become progenitors of the same.

There is some controversy surrounding the interests and motivations of the child-savers. Anthony Platt (1974: 3) argues that these women, although they "viewed themselves as altruists and humanitarians dedicated to rescuing those who were less fortunately placed in the social order," were actually motivated by boredom and middle- and upper-class social, economic, and political interests. "The child savers were concerned not with championing the rights of the poor against exploitation by the ruling class, but rather integrating the poor into the established social order and protecting 'respectable' citizens from the 'dangerous classes'" who might otherwise be drawn into social revolution (Platt, quoted in Empey 1979: 31). The juvenile court would serve to protect propertied and commercial classes from the predation of lower-class youngsters. It would also insure an adequate supply of disciplined and vocationally trained labor by sending youngsters to special institutions where they would be taught skills and the proper habits of a working class. Platt argues that the child-savers also "invented" a new category of delinquent: the status offender (to be discussed later in this chapter). David Rothman (in Empey 1979: 37) places the dispute in perspective; he states that the juvenile court movement "satisfied [both] the most humanitarian of impulses and the most crudely self-interested considerations." The orphan asylum, the house of refuge, and the reformatory were all the result of the dual motivations of this movement, but the most important accomplishment was the juvenile court.

Juvenile Court

In addition to helping neglected children, the child-savers wanted those accused of crimes to avoid being processed by the adult criminal justice system. While a juvenile might be sent to the house of refuge or the reformatory instead of jail or prison, he or she could also be arrested, detained, and tried as would any adult accused of a crime. Herbert Lou (1972) reports that the earliest modification of the trial process with respect to juveniles occurred in Massachusetts in 1869. A statute provided for an agent of the state board of charity to be present during court cases involving juveniles. The agent was notified of every criminal action against a child under sixteen so that he could investigate the case, attend the trial and, as an advocate for the child, make recommendations to the judge. In 1877 Massachusetts authorized separate trials for children, the "session for juvenile offenders." New York followed the lead of Massachusetts and prohibited the placing of any child under sixteen in any institution or courtroom in the company of adults charged with criminal offenses. Massachusetts also inaugurated a system of probation under which young offenders were supervised by an officer instead of being confined. However, notes Herbert Lou (1972: 19), "it was left to Illinois to pass the first comprehensive law to create the first specially organized juvenile court."

The first juvenile court was established in Cook County, Illinois, on July 1, 1899, as the result of the Juvenile Court Act of April 14, 1899. Consistent with the concept of *parens patriae*, the juvenile court was given jurisdiction over neglected and dependent children as well as those who were delinquent (that is, those who were under sixteen and had violated the criminal law). The Illinois statute defined the neglected child as

> any child who for any reason is destitute or homeless or abandoned; or has not proper parental care or guardianship; or who habitually begs or receives alms; or who is found living in any house of ill fame or with any vicious or disreputable person; or whose home, by reason of neglect, cruelty or depravity on the part of its parents, guardian or other person in whose care it may be, is an unfit place for such a child.

Because the purpose of the juvenile court was to aid, not punish, children, the proceedings of the court were designed to

Cook County, Illinois, juvenile court and detention home (1907). The court maintains jurisdiction over delinquent as well as neglected and dependent children.

be informal rather than adversarial and the due process guarantees of the adult criminal process were absent. In his pioneering work on juvenile courts, which was first published in 1927, Herbert Lou wrote (1972: 2):

> These principles upon which the juvenile court acts are radically different from those of the criminal courts. In place of judicial tribunals, restrained by antiquated procedure, saturated in an atmosphere of hostility, trying cases for determining guilt and inflicting punishment according to inflexible rules of law, we have now juvenile courts, in which the relations of the child to his parents or other adults and to the state and society are defined and adjusted summarily according to the scientific findings about the child and his environments. In place of magistrates, limited by the outgrown custom and compelled to walk in the paths fixed by the law of the realm, we have now socially-minded judges, who hear and adjust cases according not to rigid rules of law but to what the interests of society and the interests of the child or good conscience demand. In place of juries, prosecutors, and lawyers, trained in the old conception of law and staging dramatically, but often amusingly, legal battles, as the necessary paraphernalia of a criminal court, we have now probation officers, physicians, psychologists, and psychiatrists, who search for the social, physiological, psychological, and mental backgrounds of the child in order to arrive at reasonable and just solutions of individual cases.

> **Juvenile Court proceedings outlined**
>
> In Illinois minors under the age of 17 and 13 or older, who are charged with crimes, are handled under the Juvenile Court Act. Only 15 and 16-year-olds who are accused of murder, aggravated criminal or deviate sexual assault, or armed robbery with a firearm are automatically prosecuted as adults.
>
> Minors 13 or older may be tried as adults under criminal proceedings at their request, or by order of the juvenile court after an adult transfer hearing.
>
> Juvenile court terminology reflects civil rather than criminal law. Matters are initiated by petition rather than indictment. The term respondent is used instead of defendant. The state must prove charges at an adjudicatory hearing, not at a trial. A minor is found delinquent rather than guilty and receives a disposition, not a sentence.
>
> These are the purposes of the Juvenile Court Act:
>
> - Secure care and guidance in the minor's own home. Serve the moral, emotional, mental and physical welfare of the minor and the best interests of the community.
> - Preserve and strengthen the minor's family ties and remove him/her from the custody of parents only when the minor's welfare or safety—or the protection of the public—cannot be adequately safeguarded without removal.
> - Secure for the minor removed from the family the custody, care and discipline equivalent to that which should be given by parents, or to place the minor in a family home so that the child can become a member of a family.

The juvenile court in Illinois with this unstructured and informal system of justice quickly became the standard for the United States; by 1924, all but two states had specialized courts for children (Finckenauer 1984). The noncriminal nature of the proceedings extended to the nomenclature used:

Adult Criminal Court	*Juvenile Court*
defendant	respondent
charges/indictment	petition
arraignment	hearing
prosecution/trial	adjudication
verdict	finding
sentence	disposition

> Proceedings may begin under the provision of the Juvenile Court Act if a boy or girl falls into these categories:
>
> - **Delinquent minor**—one who, prior to the 17th birthday, has violated or attempted to violate any federal or state law or municipal ordinance. However, a juvenile 13 years of age or older charged with delinquency can be tried in criminal proceedings either at the minor's request or after an adult transfer hearing. Juveniles 15 years of age or older charged with murder, aggravated criminal sexual assault or armed robbery with a firearm are automatically tried under criminal proceedings.
> - **Minor requiring authoritative intervention (MRAI)**—one under 18 absent from home without permission or beyond control of parent or guardian and who, 21 days after being taken into limited custody and having been offered interim crisis intervention services, refuses to return home, and parents and minor cannot agree to voluntary residential placement.
> - **Addicted minor**—one who is an addict as defined in the Alcoholism and Substance Abuse Act or an alcoholic as defined in the Alcoholism and Intoxification Treatment Act.
> - **Neglected or abused minor**—one under 18 who is abandoned, not receiving proper support, education, medical or other attention necessary for the minor's well-being. An abused minor is one under 18 who has been physically or sexually abused, at risk of such abuse, or in an environment harmful to the minor's welfare.
> - **Dependent minor**—one under 18 without a parent, guardian or legal custodian or without proper care because of disability of a parent or guardian or not receiving medical or other care through no fault of the parent or whose parent or guardian wishes to be relieved of responsibility for the minor.

THE RIGHTS OF JUVENILES

The nature of the juvenile court remained unchanged until the 1960s, when the Warren Court began to pay increasing attention to questions of due process, as indicated by decisions in the cases of *Mapp*, *Gideon*, and *Miranda*. The first case in which the Supreme Court reviewed the operation of the juvenile court occurred in 1966 (*Kent v. United States*). Morris Kent, age sixteen, was convicted in an adult criminal court of raping a woman in her Washington, D.C., apartment; he received a sentence of 30–90 years in prison. The case, as mandated by federal statutes, had first been referred to the juvenile court where, over the objections of defense counsel, it was waived to the adult criminal court. On appeal, the Supreme Court ruled that before juveniles can be tried in criminal court, they are entitled to a waiver hearing with counsel and, if jurisdiction is waived, a statement of the reasons.

Due Process

The most important juvenile court case, *In re Gault*, was decided in 1967. Gerald Gault, age fifteen, and a friend were arrested by the police on the complaint of a female neighbor that they had made lewd and indecent remarks over the telephone. The youngster's parents were not notified of their son's arrest and did not receive a copy of the petition; Gerald was not advised of his right to remain silent or his right to counsel. At a second juvenile court hearing, Gerald was declared to be a juvenile delinquent and committed to a state industrial school for a maximum of six years—until his twenty-first birthday. Had Gerald been over the age of eighteen, the maximum sentence would have been a fine of not more than $50 or imprisonment for not more than two months. The complainant was not present at either hearing and the judge did not speak with her on any occasion. No record was made of the court proceedings. Since no appeal in juvenile cases was permitted under Arizona law, Gerald's parents filed a petition of habeas corpus, which was dismissed by state courts. In its decision, the U.S. Supreme Court acknowledged the helping—that is, noncriminal—philosophy that led to the establishment of the juvenile court, but it also expressed outrage over what had transpired in the case of Gerald Gault. "Under our Constitution," said the Court, "the condition of being a boy does not justify a kangaroo court."

With the *Gault* decision, the Court defined due process requirements for the juvenile court.

1. *Notice* shall be given to the child and parents or guardians "in writing, of the specific charge or factual allegations to be considered at the hearing ... at the earliest practicable time, and in any event sufficiently in advance of the hearing to permit preparation."

2. The *right to counsel* requires that "the child and his parents must be notified of the child's right to be represented by counsel retained by them, or if they are unable to afford counsel, that counsel will be appointed to represent the child."

3. *Protection against self-incrimination* "is applicable in the case of juveniles as it is with respect to adults." The Court stated, "It would be surprising if the privilege against self-incrimination were available to hardened criminals but not to children."

4. The *right to confront/cross-examine adverse witnesses*, like the right to remain silent, was found to be essential. The justices said, "No reason is suggested or appears for a different rule in respect to sworn testimony in juvenile courts than in adult tribunals."

5. The *right to appellate review and transcripts of proceedings* cannot be denied: "As the present case illustrates," said the Court in its *Gault* decision, "the consequences of failure to provide an appeal, to record the proceedings, or to make findings or state the grounds for the juvenile court's conclusion may be to throw a burden upon the machinery for habeas corpus, to saddle the reviewing process with the burden of attempting to reconstruct a record, and to impose upon the Juvenile Judge the unseemly duty of testifying under cross-examination as to the events that transpired in the hearings before him."

Standards of Evidence

Because of the noncriminal nature of the juvenile court, instead of the standard of proof beyond a reasonable doubt, the level of evidence required for a finding of delinquency was typically that used in civil proceedings: a preponderance of the evidence. In the 1970 case of *In re Winship*, the Supreme Court noted, "The reasonable-doubt standard plays a vital role in the American scheme of criminal procedure. It is a prime instrument for reducing the risk of conviction resting on factual error." Accordingly, the Court ruled that "the constitutional safeguard of proof beyond a reasonable doubt is as much required during the adjudicatory stage of a delinquency proceeding as are those constitutional safeguards applied in *Gault*."

Jury Trial

The right to an impartial jury in all criminal prosecutions under federal law is guaranteed by the Sixth Amendment, and through the Fourteenth Amendment it is imposed upon the states. The due process guarantee of a jury trial, afforded adults in criminal cases, had not been granted to juveniles and became the basis of a Supreme Court decision in 1971. In *McKeiver v. Pennsylvania*, the Court held that a juvenile-court proceeding is not a criminal prosecution within the meaning of the Sixth Amendment. While saying that the rights already accorded juveniles in the earlier decisions such as *Gault* and *Winship* were "a necessary component of accurate factfinding," the Court held that "the imposition of the jury trial on the juvenile court system would not strengthen greatly, if at all, the factfinding function." In denying the right to a jury trial in juvenile proceedings, the court concluded, "If the formalities of the criminal adjudicative process are to be superimposed upon the juvenile court system, there is little need for its separate existence. Perhaps that ultimate disillusionment will come one day, but for the moment we are disinclined to give impetus to it."

Double Jeopardy

In 1975 the Supreme Court was faced with the question of double jeopardy with respect to the juvenile court. *Breed v. Jones* concerned a seventeen-year-old who had been arrested for armed robbery; a juvenile petition alleging the same was filed. After taking testimony from two prosecution witnesses and the respondent, the juvenile court sustained the petition. At a subsequent disposition hearing, the court ruled that the respondent was "not . . . amenable to the care, treatment and training program available through the facilities of the juvenile court," and ordered that he be prosecuted as an adult. He was subsequently found guilty of armed robbery in criminal court. The Supreme Court stated, "We hold that the prosecution of respondent in Superior Court, after an adjudicatory proceeding in Juvenile Court, violated the Double Jeopardy Clause of the Fifth Amendment, as applied to the States through the Fourteenth Amendment."

Preventive Detention

In 1984 the Supreme Court (*Schall v. Martin*) upheld the constitutionality of the preventive detention of juveniles—a strong affirmation of the concept of *parens patriae*. *Schall* upheld a New York statute that authorizes the detention of a juvenile arrested for an offense if there is "serious risk" that before trial the juvenile may commit an act that if committed by an adult would constitute a crime. The Court found that juveniles, unlike adults, "are always in some form of custody." That is, "by definition, [they] are not assumed to have the capacity to take care of themselves."

THE JUVENILE JUSTICE PROCESS

Children may fall under the jurisdiction of the juvenile court if they are charged with a criminal offense (except those charged with certain serious offenses such as murder); if they are runaways, habitually truant, beyond the control of parents, or addicted to drugs; or if they are abused, neglected, or dependent. While there are some variations in the juvenile-court process from state to state and even from jurisdiction to jurisdiction, they all approximate the basic model that will be presented in this chapter.

Juvenile justice involves four types of cases:

1. **Delinquency**, or behavior that if engaged in by an adult would constitute a crime.
2. **Status offense**, or behavior that if engaged in by an adult would not constitute a crime, but that (based on *parens patriae*) provides the basis for governmental intervention in the life of a child, for example, truancy, being beyond the control of parents or guardians, running away, or being addicted to drugs.
3. **Neglect or abuse**, or the lack of proper care as the result of some action or inaction by parents or guardians.
4. **Dependency**, or the lack of parents or guardians available to provide proper care.

Before we further discuss the four types of juvenile cases, we should note that, although our focus here is the juvenile court system, many of these cases are often handled outside the formal justice apparatus. School officials or the police, for example, may refer juvenile cases directly to public or private social welfare agencies or child protective agencies.

The Flow of Juvenile Justice

```
   police        parents        school        agencies
                         ↓    ↓
                       Intake
   unofficial  ←─────────┼─────────→  reject
     case                ↓                case
                      petition
                         ↓
                    preliminary    • custody
                      hearing      • protection
                                   • transfer
                                   • etc.
                         ↓
   finding   ←─── adjudicational ───→  no finding
   of fact         hearing               of fact
         │              
         ↓              
              dispositional    • foster care
                hearing        • community service
                               • probation
                               • group home
                               • residential treatment
                                 center
                               • training school
                               • reformatory
                               • etc.
```

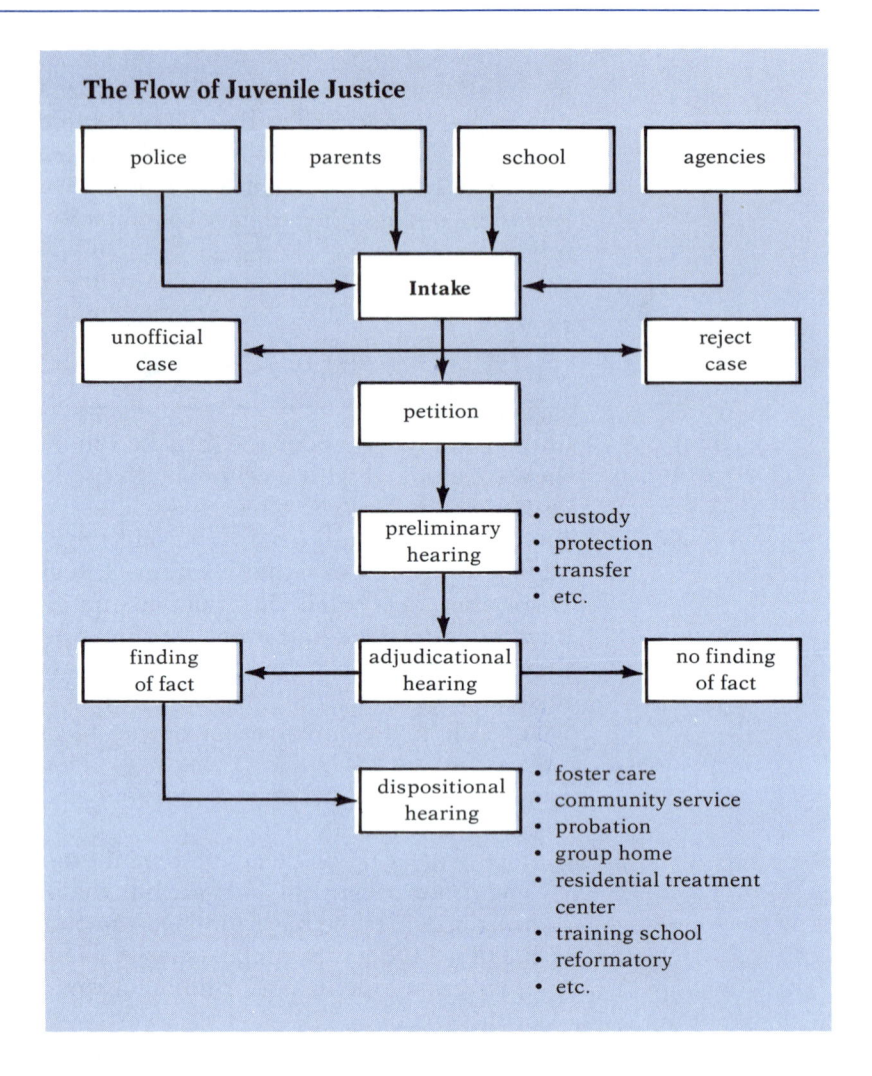

Delinquency

Most cases that come to the attention of the juvenile court involve delinquent acts, and the referrals are typically made by the police, usually juvenile or youth division officers. In such cases, after apprehending a child and informing the child of his or her rights, the officer generally has several options:

1. If the crime is a serious one—murder, rape, armed robbery—statutes may require that the case be referred directly to the prosecutor's office for processing as an adult offender.

2. If the problem is minor, the officer may simply give the child a verbal warning, with nothing being entered in the record.
3. The officer may make a *station adjustment*; that is, the action is recorded but the child is allowed to return home with his or her parents with no further action taken.
4. The officer may refer the case to juvenile court, while allowing the child to remain with his or her parents.
5. In cases of delinquency where the officer has reason to believe that the parents cannot control the child, that the child is a danger to self or to the community, or that the child requires protection, after informing the parents, the officer may have the child placed in a *juvenile detention center*.

Status Offenders

Status offenders are referred to by a number of different acronyms: **MINS**(Minor in Need of Supervision), **MRAI**(Minor Requiring Authoritative Intervention), **PINS**(Person in Need of Supervision), **CHINS**(Child in Need of Supervision) and **JINS** (Juvenile in Need of Supervision). There has been a great deal of controversy surrounding juvenile court jurisdiction over status offenders. More than a decade ago, this author (Abadinsky 1976) argued that the juvenile court is unable to provide sufficient services for children who violate the law; jurisdiction over status offenders compounds this problem and, furthermore, stigmatizes children whose behavior does not constitute a crime. Those who favor juvenile court jurisdiction over status offenders argue that such children are not essentially different from those youngsters committing delinquent acts; they are children in need of services, and without juvenile court intervention, these services would not be forthcoming. However, a number of European countries provide services to status offenders without using the judicial system.

The procedure in status offense cases is usually as follows.

1. The officer may take the child into "limited custody" (not more than a few hours) and, if the child agrees to return home, transport and release the child to parents or guardians; the officer may also assist the family in contacting a social service agency.
2. If the child refuses to return home or if the parents are unavailable, the officer may transport and release the child to a

social agency offering crisis intervention services and shelter for the child. The social agency will contact the parents and, if the child agrees, transport and release the child to the parents. If the child still refuses to return home or the parents are unavailable, the agency may place the child in a temporary shelter for a specified period of time—for example, two weeks—unless the parents and the child agree to continue the alternative living arrangement.

3. If the parents refuse to allow the child to return home, the social agency will file a neglect petition in juvenile court, which will result in a hearing on the matter. Or, if after the specified period of time—for example, two weeks—the parents and the child remain in disagreement, the agency, the parents, or the child may request the filing of a petition in juvenile court for the purpose of having a judge decide the outcome.

Neglect, Abuse, and Dependency

Most cases involving abused, neglected, and dependent children are referred to the juvenile court by the department of child welfare, sometimes after being notified by the police or neighbors. The law requires certain professionals—medical doctors, teachers, social workers, nurses, and police officers, for example—to report cases of suspected abuse or neglect to the child welfare agency for investigation. A caseworker may draft a petition which refers the case to court for a hearing, since the court has the sole authority to ensure the protection and treatment of the child through various judicial orders.

JUVENILE COURT PROCEDURES

Cases enter the juvenile court by way of the *intake section*, which is usually staffed by juvenile probation officers. The intake officer determines if the case is to be referred to a courtroom for a hearing, or if services should be provided by another source. He or she also must determine if the youngster is in need of immediate shelter or detention. The intake officer will interview the referring agent (e.g., police officer), the child, the parents or guardians, and any other interested parties such as victims or witnesses. The files of any previous court contact will be reviewed, and the intake officer, especially in serious cases, will often consult with the prosecutor's office before making a determination.

In less serious cases, a nonjudicial alternative is often the first choice, making it an "unofficial case." If all parties are amenable, the child and the parents will be referred to a social service agency, and the child may be placed on "unofficial probation" for a period of time, usually ninety days.

If unofficial handling is not successful, or if the case is too serious for such treatment, it will be sent to court by way of a petition. The petition results in a court hearing during which a corporation counsel (municipal attorney) or assistant prosecutor will represent "the people." Children whose families are unable to pay for legal services are represented by an attorney from the public defender's office.

Preliminary Hearing

Matters considered at preliminary hearings are those that must be dealt with before the case can proceed further. Hearings in juvenile court are confidential; unlike those in the adult justice system, spectators are not permitted to attend. At the first preliminary hearing, the judge will inform the parties involved of the charges in the petition and of their rights in the proceedings as per the *Gault* decision. If the case involves an abused, neglected, or dependent child, a guardian will be appointed to act as an advocate for the child.

The judge may also issue an *order of protection*, which directs a potential abuser or assailant to refrain from further contact with the child or others in danger. A violation of the order constitutes contempt of court, which is punishable by summary imprisonment.

If the case involves a charge of delinquency, the hearing will be used to determine whether the child should remain in detention, or custody. Such *custody hearings* are usually held within twenty-four hours (excluding weekends and court holidays) of apprehension. If it is determined that there is "an urgent and immediate necessity" to continue detention, the judge issues a *hold-in-custody order*. If continued custody is unnecessary, the judge orders the child to be released.

Status offenders and dependent and neglected children may

be placed into foster care or residential shelters. Within a few days a *shelter hearing* will be held at which a judge must determine if continued out-of-home placement is necessary. If so, the judge will appoint a temporary custodian for the child, usually from the child welfare agency, but sometimes a relative or friend of the family. During a custody or shelter hearing, probable cause must be established; that is, the judge must determine if there is enough evidence to believe that the charges stated in the petition justify a full hearing.

Transfer hearings (as per *Kent*) are also held during the preliminary stage of the juvenile-court process. The purpose of such a hearing is for the juvenile-court judge to consider the request of a prosecutor that a youth be transferred to criminal court to be tried as an adult. The judge hears all evidence and decides whether it is in the best interests of the public and the child to transfer the minor for prosecution as an adult or to continue the case in juvenile court.

Adjudicatory Hearing

The **adjudicatory hearing** parallels that of an adult criminal trial. The purpose is for the judge to decide ("adjudge") whether the child should be made a ward of the juvenile court because he or she is delinquent, a status offender, abused, neglected or dependent. There are three phases common to adjudicatory hearings.

    1. If appropriate, a plea is entered in the form of an admission or a denial of the charges made in the petition.

    2. In cases of delinquency or status offenses, if a denial is made, evidence must be presented to prove "beyond a reasonable doubt" (as per *Winship*) that a delinquent act occurred or, in the case of a status offense, with a simple "preponderance of evidence" that the child is a MINS/CHINS/PINS/JINS/MRAI. Cases of abuse, neglect, or dependency require the same level of proof as a status offense—preponderance of evidence.

    3. If the charges are sustained, the judge enters a **finding** that the child is an "adjudicated delinquent," MINS/CHINS/PINS/

JINS/MRAI, abused, neglected, or dependent and declares him or her to be a ward of the court.

Dispositional Hearing

If the judge makes a positive finding, the probation department will prepare a pre-disposition report (officially a **social investigation**) containing the social and psychological factors affecting the child and his or her family; clinical evaluations may be requested from a court-related mental health unit or child welfare agency. The report will include the PO's recommendation as to what disposition would best serve the child and the community. (It parallels the presentence investigation report in criminal cases.) The purpose of the dispositional hearing is to determine what outcome (or **disposition**) of the case will serve the interests of the child and the community. Unlike the more demanding levels of evidence required in adjudicatory hearings, any kind of evidence that may be helpful in determining the disposition may be taken into consideration. This includes any written or oral reports from the parties involved or from anyone who has a personal or professional interest in the case.

Delinquents

There are several types of disposition for delinquent youngsters.

1. *Commitment to the juvenile division of the department of corrections* (or division for youth agency) for children who are at least thirteen years old and whose offense would be punishable with incarceration if the case were tried under criminal law for adults. The period of this commitment is indeterminate, but may not last longer than the delinquent youth's twenty-first birthday. The actual date of release is determined by department of corrections juvenile officials or those of the division for youth agency.

2. *Probation* for adjudicated delinquent children of any age for a period not beyond the age of twenty-one. A child placed on probation will be released to parents or placed out of the home and will receive supervision and services by a PO. Conditions of probation, as with adults, are set by both the judge and the probation department.

These photographs are from a series completed by Jay Paris of youths in correction centers across the country. *At right,* a detention center in Canton, Ohio, sets forth hall regulations for its young residents; below, an eight-year-old arsonist peers out from behind the fence of a training center for delinquent children in Birmingham, Alabama.

3. *Conditional discharge* and release to parents on the condition that no further delinquent acts will take place.

4. *Out-of-home placement,* often in the form of a commitment to the child welfare agency, which will arrange for a foster home or residential treatment setting where counseling and education can be provided to help the child behave in a more constructive manner.

5. *Referral* to a public or private agency with specialized services, such as a drug treatment program for children who are addicted to controlled substances.

6. *Detention,* usually for no more than thirty days in a juvenile detention facility.

In addition to the dispositional options listed above, the judge may order protective supervision of the parents or guardians in whose custody the child was released. The child can also be required to make monetary or public service restitution whenever appropriate.

Status Offenders

There are several dispositional alternatives for status offenders.

1. *Probation* supervision by a PO who provides services similar to those that would be provided to a delinquent on probation.
2. *Out-of-home placement* in a foster home or residential treatment facility, with or without supervision by a PO.
3. *Referral* to the child welfare agency for placement and counseling.
4. *Emancipation* of the child as a "mature minor."

Abused or Neglected Children

For children who are adjudicated as abused or neglected, the judge can choose the disposition that is best able to protect the child and to help overcome the ill effects of the neglect or abuse.

1. *Out-of-home placement* in a foster home or group home with the assignment of a guardian, usually a child welfare agency representative or a concerned relative or friend. This form of guardianship includes full authority and responsibility for ensuring that all appropriate care and services are provided to the child.

2. *Continued in-home placement* with the parents or guardians only after a special fitness hearing is held to determine whether the abusive or neglectful parents or guardians have sufficiently improved themselves or the conditions of the home to justify this disposition. This disposition is often accompanied by court-ordered protective supervision and services provided by social service agencies.

3. *Emancipation* of the child as a "mature minor" who will often be assisted by a public welfare agency.

Dependent Children

The dependent child is by definition without parents or guardians available to provide proper care, and dispositions are limited to out-of-home placement with the assignment of a guardian, or emancipation. As in cases involving delinquents, status offenders, or neglected or abused children, the judge may also order protective supervision. In many jurisdictions, the juvenile court also has jurisdiction over cases of adoption.

JUVENILE INSTITUTIONS

There are a number of different institutions to which juveniles can be sent by the juvenile court or, sometimes, by which they can be received through a voluntary process initiated by a parent or guardian. In general juvenile institutions are either public or private, although many private institutions receive a great deal of public funding.

Shelters are nonsecure facilities designed to provide temporary emergency care for youngsters who are neglected, abused, or status offenders. **Group homes** provide short-term residential housing for seven to thirteen youngsters who have been adjudicated as delinquent, in need of supervision, neglected or abused. The home is usually located in a residential area, allowing youngsters to attend public schools and use other educational and recreational services located in the community. House parents, usually trained social workers who reside in the home, attempt to replicate the domestic environment of a natural home, while offering the resi-

In 1983 Martin Bell, Mary Ellen Mark, and Cheryl McCall scouted the streets of Seattle's waterfront and interviewed several dozen teenagers who survive as prostitutes, pimps, muggers, panhandlers, petty thieves, and small-time drug dealers. *Streetwise*, the documentary that resulted from their interviews, offers a rare glimpse into an urban subculture, in which the subjects' stories are told by the children themselves.

dents the structure and care they are unable to receive in their own homes. Youngsters assigned to group homes are those who do not suffer from severe pathology or present a danger to themselves or others.

The **residential treatment center (RTC)** is a private institution that offers a wide range of enriched educational, vocational, and recreational opportunities. The facility also provides a therapeutic milieu that is implemented by social workers, psychologists, and other child treatment specialists. While the RTC is often associated with a particular religious denomination, it receives most of its funding from public sources and accepts youngsters on a nondenominational basis.

Youngsters who are not amenable to the RTC program, or for

whom there is not enough room, and those who require a secure facility, are sent to the training school, usually a state or county institution. Like the RTC, the training school has a variety of services from basic remedial education to group therapy. The security at a training school is usually more than that at an RTC and less than that at a reformatory. Youngsters who are tried as adults are usually sent to reformatories, high-security institutions under the auspices of the state department of corrections.

KEY TERMS

parens patriae
child-saving movement
delinquency
status offense
neglect or abuse
dependency
MINS, MRAI, PINS, CHINS, JINS
adjudicatory hearing

finding
social investigation
disposition
shelters
group homes
residential treatment center (RTC)
training school
reformatories

REVIEW QUESTIONS

1. How would you characterize the situation of poor urban children in the United States during the early years of industrialization?
2. What is *parens patriae*, and how does it provide a basis for juvenile justice?
3. How did the concept of *parens patriae* justify a lack of due process for children sent to juvenile court?
4. Who were the "child-savers"?
5. What conditions led to the establishment of the juvenile court?
6. Provide examples of how the nomenclature of the juvenile court reflects its noncriminal nature.
7. What are the due process rights provided juveniles by the *Gault* decision?
8. What level or standard of proof is required for a finding of delinquency in juvenile court?
9. What did the Supreme Court say with respect to the right of a jury trial in juvenile court (*McKeiver v. Pennsylvania*)?
10. What are the options of a police officer with respect to a youngster who presents a behavior problem that does not constitute a serious crime?
11. What are the responsibilities of an intake unit in juvenile court?
12. There are three stages of hearings in juvenile court. What are they and what are their purposes?
13. What does the pre-disposition report contain and what is its purpose?
14. What are the various dispositions available for children adjudicated in juvenile court?
15. What are the various types of institution available for juveniles who are delinquent or status offenders?

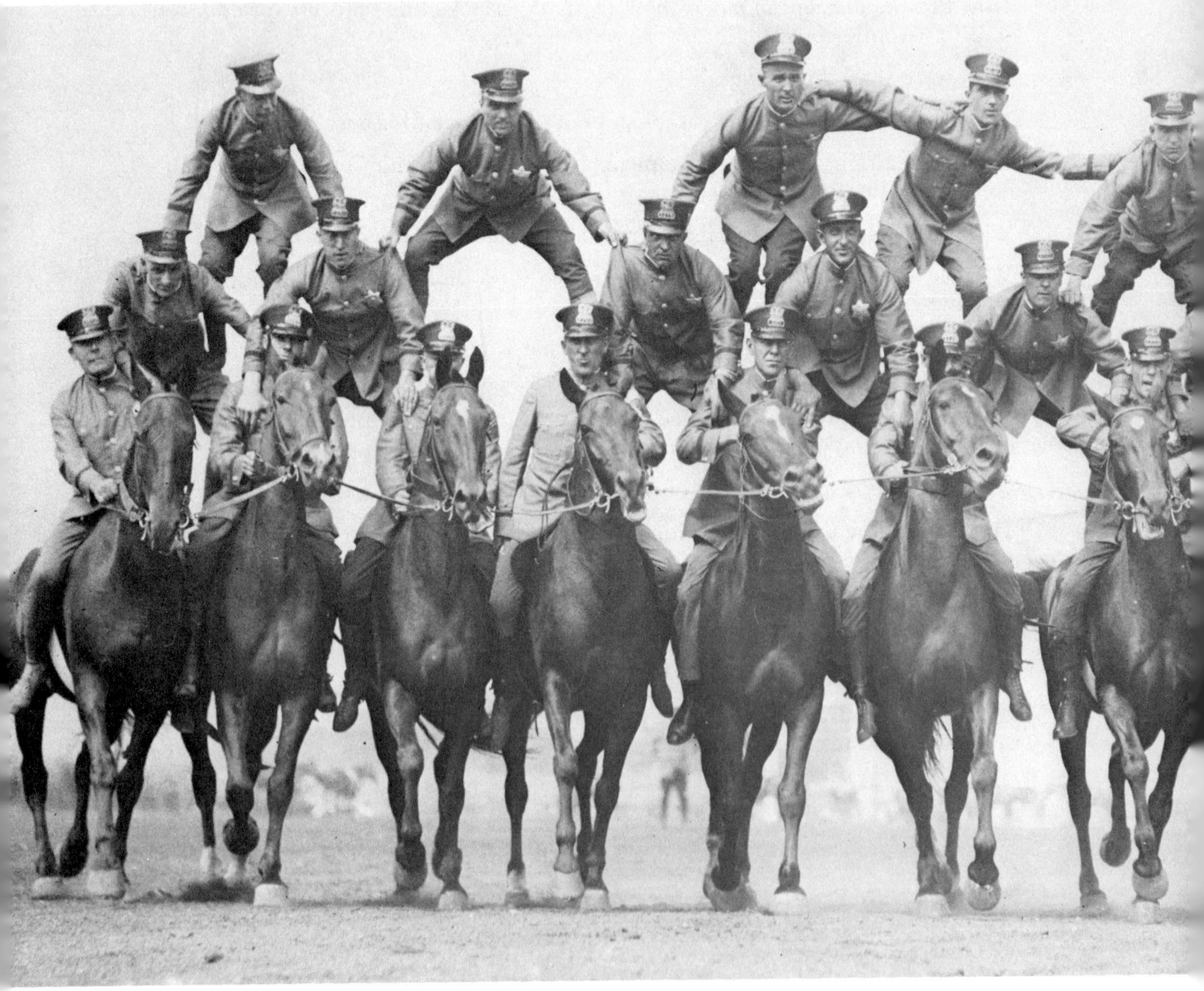

Postscript

This book has come to an end. Hopefully, it has been informative and thought-provoking. In class I explain to my students that if the teacher has been successful, they should be more confused at the end of this course than they were at the start—better-informed, perhaps, but more confused. Questions of crime and criminal behavior defy simple answers. We saw how difficult it is even to define "crime," and once we defined it, to determine the amount of crime. Then, we were confronted by the often contradictory explanations for criminal behavior.

When we entered the system of criminal justice, we found out that it is not supposed to be "systematic," that our Founding Fathers left us with a structure of government whose division of powers ensures both liberty and inefficiency. We noted that the police, the most visible representative of governmental authority, are fragmented into several levels and thousands of jurisdictions but they are, nevertheless, expected to control crime and disorder while being restrained by the severe limitations imposed on policing in a democratic society.

We examined the courts and the education and professional qualities of key actors in the courtroom. We "listened" to a debate over plea bargaining between those who see it as a distortion of justice and those who see it as a normal, benign extension of the way lawyers "do their thing."

We reviewed the philosophies upon which the sentencing of criminals is based and the logical extension of one of them into a way of relieving prison overcrowding. We noted the swinging pendulum of history that moves from vengeance-to-reformation-to-punishment-to-treatment-to-just-deserts.

We looked at the history of jails and prisons, especially the pioneering role that the United States played in the development of these alternatives to corporal and capital punishment. We traced how this history has led to the present sorry state of modern correctional institutions.

Finally, we examined the system of justice used for juveniles, a system very different from that of the adult criminal justice system, one where only recently some of the rights of due process have eroded the traditional concept of *parens patriae*.

If this book has served its purpose, it should have whetted your appetite for further study and, perhaps, for further courses on crime and justice. In any event, I would welcome your comments and suggestions, and I can be reached at Saint Xavier College, Chicago, IL 60655.

Glossary

Actus reus See *corpus delicti*.

Adjudicatory hearing In juvenile court, a trial.

Adversarial method System of fact-finding used in American trials in which both sides are represented by attorneys who act as adversaries in the attempt to prove a defendant's guilt or innocence.

Affirmative defense Without denying the charge, defendant raises extenuating or mitigating circumstances such as insanity, self-defense, or entrapment to avoid criminal responsibility.

Anomie From the Greek word meaning "lack of law," refers to a condition in society or in individuals characterized by "normlessness," or a feeling of being adrift due to a breakdown of social controls.

Appeal Legal challenge to a decision by a lower court.

Appellate review The consideration of a case by a court of appeals.

Area surveillance Intensive, covert police observation of a limited geographic area.

Arraignment Early stage in the judicial process during which the defendant hears the charges and enters a plea of not guilty, *nolo contendere*, or guilty.

Arrest The physical taking into custody of a suspected criminal or juvenile.

Arrest warrant A document issued by a judicial or administrative officer authorizing the arrest of a specific person.

Atavism Manifestation in a human being of physical and mental characteristics of an earlier evolutionary state.

Auburn system Prison system developed in nineteenth-century New York and characterized by a daily routine of silent, hard labor in group settings followed by isolation in solitary cells at night.

Authoritarianism A personality state characterized by rigidity of thinking, opposition to change, and prejudicial attitudes toward minority persons.

Bail Money or other security placed in custody of the court in order to ensure the return of a defendant to stand trial.

Behaviorism An approach to psychology that views human behavior as being shaped by reward and punishment.

Bench trial A trial conducted without a jury.

Big House An Auburn-style prison that permits inmates some personal comforts in cells and provides recreational facilities but minimal educational or rehabilitational programs.

Bond Document signed by a defendant in which he or she agrees to return to court at a subsequent date to stand trial.

Bond hearing An appearance before a judicial officer who determines the conditions for release—bail—pending trial.

Booking The process of photographing, fingerprinting, and recording identifying data of a suspect following arrest.

Career criminals Criminals whose income is derived primarily from criminal activities.

Case law Law based on previous decisions of appellate courts, particularly the Supreme Court.

Case method Teaching method commonly used in law schools that emphasizes the reading and analyzing of appellate court cases as a means of developing judicial thinking and understanding the law.

Case study Qualitative research technique involving in-depth examination of one or at most several cases.

Certiorari Requirement that four justices must agree to hear a case before it can be considered by the Supreme Court.

Challenge for cause Counsel's objection to a prospective juror on the grounds that circumstances, such as prejudice against the defendant, make the juror unable to render an impartial verdict. Occurs at a *voir dire* hearing.

Charge to the jury The instructions of a judge to the jury after the trial is complete and deliberations are about to begin.

Child-saving movement An organized effort of middle- and upper-class women of the late nineteenth century that led to the establishment of the juvenile court.

Circumstantial evidence Physical evidence, such as fingerprints, from which an inference can be drawn. Circumstantial evidence is indirect, as opposed to eye-witness testimony, which is direct.

Civilian review board An administrative board made up largely of civilians which reviews the activities of police officers, usually on a complaint from a civilian source.

Civil law Body of law whose primary objective is the resolution of disputes between individuals or organizations.

Classical theory of crime An outgrowth of Enlightenment philosophy which stresses equality before law—"All men are created equal"—and provides a basis for the determinate sentence.

Closing arguments Summary statements to a judge or jury by attorneys for the state and the defense at the end of a trial.

Commission on Accreditation for Law Enforcement Agencies A nonprofit agency established by national police organizations to accredit police and sheriff's departments.

Common law A legal system inherited from England and based on tradition or precedent rather than statutory law or fixed legal codes.

Community-based corrections Programs and services for offenders outside of the traditional prison, including probation, parole, halfway houses, and work release.

Commutation Shortening of a sentence by a governor or president by virtue of his or her powers of executive clemency.

Conditional release The release of an inmate from prison, at the end of his or her sentence minus time off for good behavior, after which the releasee is required to abide by certain regulations.

Conflict theory A theory closely identified with the writings of Karl Marx and Max Weber that societies are characterized by competing class interests which are the inevitable result of the stratification of society.

Consensual crime An offense that has no victim but has nevertheless been outlawed, such as the possession of heroin or certain sexual activities.

Corporate crime Illegal behavior engaged in by executives on behalf of their firms.

Corpus delicti In legal parlance, refers to the three basic requirements for a crime: *actus reus*, or proof that a criminal act has occurred; *mens rea*, or the "guilty mind" necessary to establish criminal responsibility; and concurrence, a timely relationship between the two.

Courtroom workgroup The regular participants in the daily activities of a courtroom: judge, prosecutor, defense attorney, and possibly clerk and bailiffs.

Criminalistics The science of crime detection; refers to the examination of physical evidence of a crime such as footprints, weapons, bloodstains.

Cross-examination Questioning by an attorney of an opposing witness aimed at discrediting the witness's courtroom testimony.

Cravath system A method used by national law firms to train graduates of elite law schools in the practice of corporate law.

Crime A term applied to any violation of the criminal law.

Crime control model A model of the criminal justice system that emphasizes efficiency in handling criminal cases over protecting the rights of the accused. Proponents of this model view crime control as the criminal justice system's most important function and due process as an impediment to efficiency.

Crime rate The number of index crimes reported to the police divided by the population and multiplied by 100,000.

Criminal informant An active criminal who provides information to the authorities for some personal benefit.

Criminal law Body of law intended to control wrongful behavior of citizens. Unlike civil law, it is not available to individuals and is invoked by government on behalf of the people.

Criminal man theory The belief that there are certain recognizable characteristics that determine if a person will commit crimes.

Criminology The scientific study of criminal law, criminal behavior, and the criminal justice system.

Cultural transmission A theory that explains how a tradition of delinquent and/or criminal behavior may be transmitted from one cultural group to another as they interact in close physical proximity in a community.

Deadly force A term applied to that force which is likely to cause serious injury or death, usually used in reference to the discharge of a firearm.

Decoy operation Proactive police tactic which deploys disguised officers as targets of crime in order to apprehend criminals.

Deferred sentencing A process by which, in exchange for a plea of guilty, the judge postpones imposing sentence on the defendant, who then must adhere to certain rules and participate in certain programming, at the successful completion of which sentencing is dropped.

Delinquent A child whose behavior would be considered criminal if he or she were an adult.

Detainer A judicial or administrative document which orders that an inmate be turned over to specific authorities when his or her sentence or period of detention is over.

Determinate sentence A fixed term of imprisonment for a specific crime, for example 9–0–0 or nine years for burglary, which is set by a legislature and from which a judge cannot deviate in sentencing criminals.

Determinism A doctrine stressing humans' lack of choice, particularly the belief that one's behavior is "determined" by physiological or environmental variables, devoid of criminal intent.

GLOSSARY

Differential association A theory that views criminal behavior as the result of learning that occurs within intimate groups and is based on the intensity, duration, and frequency of association with such groups.

Differential opportunity A combination of anomie and differential association theory that notes that criminal opportunity, like legitimate opportunity, is not evenly distributed throughout the population.

Direct examination Questioning of a friendly witness by counsel at trial.

Direct or eye-witness testimony Testimony by an eye-witness to a crime.

Discovery A pretrial procedure allowing each counsel access to information held by opposing counsel.

Discretion The lawful ability of an agent of government to exercise choice in making a decision.

Disposition The decision of a juvenile court judge after a positive finding has been made—for example, placing the juvenile on probation.

Diversion Permitting a person charged with an offense to avoid prosecution in exchange for participation in a rehabilitation or restitution program.

Double jeopardy Subjecting a defendant to prosecution more than once for the same offense, prohibited by the Fifth Amendment.

Due process Those procedural guarantees to which every criminal defendant is entitled under the Constitution and its interpretation by the Supreme Court, including, for example, the right to remain silent or to a trial by jury.

Due process model A model of the criminal justice process that emphasizes the rights of the accused and due process protections over speed and efficiency in the system. Proponents of this model presume that the criminal justice system is subject to errors and abuse of power and thus seek to slow down and regulate the process to protect the innocent.

Durham Rule A test of responsibility which holds that if a defendant's criminal behavior was the product of a mental disease or illness, he or she cannot be held legally accountable.

Electronic stakeouts The use of video systems, alarms, and sensing devices to alert police to the presence of suspects.

Embezzlement Unauthorized, systematic appropriation of company funds by an employee, usually one who has access to the company's financial records.

Employee crime Theft by an employee from his or her employer; can range from minor pilferage to embezzlement.

Entrapment Behavior of an agent of government which encourages the committing of a criminal act by a person who was not predisposed to do so. Constitutes an affirmative defense.

Exclusionary rule A legal doctrine prohibiting the use at a trial of evidence secured in an improper manner.

Executive clemency The power of a governor or president to grant pardons, commutations, and reprieves.

Experimental design Type of quantitative research in which at least two groups, a control group and an experimental group, are analyzed after the experimental group is exposed to a test variable.

Federal system Governmental system unique to the United States in which power is divided between a central (federal) government and state governments, with the central government supreme.

Felony The more serious of the two basic types of crime, usually bearing a penalty in excess of one year in prison.

Field interrogation The questioning of civilians by law enforcement officers in the street or a location other than a governmental facility.

Finding The verdict in a juvenile court.

Fleeing felon rule In common law, a rule that allows a peace officer to use deadly force to prevent the escape of a suspect in a felony case when the officer believes there is substantial risk that the suspect will cause death or serious harm if apprehension is delayed. The Supreme Court prohibits use of deadly force in cases where suspects are neither armed nor dangerous.

Fraternal Order of Police (FOP) Oldest of the national police unions with lodges representing police officers in many jurisdictions.

Free will Concept based on the classical theory that each person has the opportunity to be law-abiding or criminal and, therefore, the person who opts to commit a crime is deserving of punishment commensurate with the offense.

Functionalism An approach to sociology that examines how particular social phenomena (such as criminality) "fit into," or function within, the larger society. Functionalists, unlike other theorists, view crime as an indispensable aspect of society.

General deterrence The belief that punishing one criminal deters other would-be criminals.

Good time A reduction in sentenced time in prison as a reward for good behavior; usually one-third to one-half off the maximum sentence.

Grand jury A group of citizens, usually numbering twenty-three, who are assembled in secret to hear or investigate allegations of criminal behavior.

Group home Residential treatment facility for a small number of young offenders.

Guilty but insane The legal concept that a person who was suffering from a mental illness but was not insane at the time of the commission of the crime is not relieved of criminal responsibility.

Habeas corpus, writ of A legal document that forces law enforcement authorities to produce a prisoner they are holding and to legally justify his or her detention.

Halfway house A residential facility for offenders who have been released from jail or prison (halfway out), or who have been placed on probation in lieu of incarceration (halfway in).

Hearsay evidence Testimony from a third party who is not a witness, about a statement made to him or her regarding a crime or suspect, the veracity of which cannot be subjected to cross-examination and is therefore usually not admissible.

Hierarchy rule A rule utilized by the Uniform Crime Report according to which only the most serious crime committed in a single incident is counted.

Hung jury A jury which cannot reach a unanimous verdict.

Impaneling The selection and swearing in of a jury.

Incapacitation Physically preventing an offender from committing further criminal acts; in the United States, it is achieved by imprisonment.

Indeterminate sentence A sentence which has both a minimum and maximum term of imprisonment, for example, three to nine years for burglary, with the actual length determined by a parole board.

Index crimes The eight crimes that comprise part I of the Uniform Crime Report: criminal homicide, forcible rape, robbery, aggravated assault, burglary, larceny-theft, motor-vehicle theft, and arson.

Individual deterrence The belief that once punished, a criminal will tend not to engage in further criminal behavior.

Inevitable discovery An exception to the exclusionary rule that permits the use of evidence that was secured in an improper manner on the grounds that it would have been discovered eventually anyhow.

Infancy A legal age above which a person can be held criminally responsible.

Information Accusatory document, filed by the prosecutor, detailing the charges against the defendant. Used in states that do not have grand juries, it serves to bring a defendant to trial.

Inmate subculture A social system which develops among prisoners in opposition to the prison administration.

Insanity In law, the lack of criminal responsibility; also, incompetence, or the inability to stand trial.

Insanity defense Affirmative defense, based on the proposition that the accused lacked capacity to understand the criminal nature of his actions, offered to avoid accountability for criminal behavior.

Internal affairs (IA) A unit of a law enforcement agency that investigates wrongdoing on the part of other officers within the same agency.

Irresistible impulse test Affirmative defense in which the subject is considered to have known that his or her actions were wrong, but was unable to control them.

Jail A municipal or county institution housing those awaiting trial, those convicted of a misdemeanor, and those convicted of a felony and awaiting transfer to a prison.

Judicial review The power of the judicial branch to declare acts of the executive and legislative branches unconstitutional.

Jury pool Persons summoned and sworn to serve on a jury who have not yet been subjected to a *voir dire* hearing.

Just deserts Punishment that fits the crime.

Kansas City Study A research project undertaken in Kansas City, Missouri in the early 1970s designed to test the effectiveness of preventive patrol strategies in preventing crime.

Labeling The branding by society of those individuals who have undergone arrest or conviction with a stigma that may possibly exert a controlling influence on their future behavior.

Learning theory *See* Behaviorism.

Mala in se "Evil in itself"—behavior that is universally regarded as criminal, for example, murder.

Mala prohibita "Wrong because prohibited"—behavior that is criminal only because a society defines it as such, for example, the manufacture of alcoholic beverages, during Prohibition.

Managing criminal investigations (MCI) Method by which cases reported to the police are quantified on the basis of available evidence or solvability factors to determine whether they are to be investigated or classified as inactive.

Mandatory release *See* Conditional release.

Medical model The attempt to rehabilitate criminals by employing methods similar to those used by medical doctors: examination, diagnosis, and treatment.

Mens rea *See corpus delicti.*

Merit selection Appointment of governmental employees, including judges, on the basis of a written examination which is supposed to measure competency.

Misdemeanor Lesser of the two basic types of crime; usually punishable by no more than one-year of imprisonment.

Missouri Plan The "merit selection" of judges by the governor from a slate of three candidates chosen by a panel which has been appointed by the governor or selected by the bar association. After serving one year, each judge so chosen must stand for retention in a general election.

M'Naghten Rule A test of criminal responsibility, taken from English common law, requiring proof of an *inability to distinguish* between right and wrong as a result of mental defect.

National Crime Survey (NCS) A survey conducted by the U.S. Census Bureau for the Department of Justice which uses household interviews to determine the rate of criminal victimization.

Neutralization A social-psychological technique that permits offenders to express general support for law while at the same time violating the law in specific instances.

Nolle prosequi A decision by the prosecutor declining to prosecute a specific defendant.

Normal crimes Crimes that fall into certain frequent and routine patterns that are viewed as "normal" by prosecutors and defense attorneys.

Opening statements Statements made to the jury by attorneys at the start of a trial.

Order maintenance The noncriminal aspects of police work.

Organized crime Ongoing criminal conspiracies which may persist indefinitely involving persons whose goals are personal gain.

Overcharging A practice, sometimes used by police, of charging arrestees with as many crimes as can apply, even remotely, to their actions.

Panel survey method A research technique utilized in the National Crime Survey which involves interviewing a set number of households over a period of time at regular intervals.

Pardon An act of executive clemency releasing an inmate from prison or removing certain legal disabilities from persons convicted of crimes.

Parens patriae Common law concept that recognizes the obligation of the state toward persons who are unable to care for themselves, such as children or the mentally ill.

Parole The release of a prison inmate by a parole board, followed by a period of supervision by a parole officer.

Parole board An administrative body whose members are chosen by the governor to review the cases of prisoners eligible for release on parole. The board has the authority to release such persons and to return them to prison if they violate the conditions of parole.

Parole guidelines An attempt to structure the discretionary powers of parole boards by providing guidelines which set the time to be served by inmates based on the seriousness of the crime and the parole prognosis or salient factors score.

Participant observation A qualitative research technique in which the researcher joins and participates in a group's activities in order to observe them firsthand.

Pennsylvania system Prison system developed in the nineteenth century in Pennsylvania and characterized by isolation of inmates in solitary cells and forced idleness intended to promote penitence in inmates.

Peremptory challenge The prerogative of opposing attorneys to excuse prospective jurors without having to state a reason.

Physical stakeouts A procedure in which law enforcement officers wait either in hiding or in disguise for the expected appearance of criminal suspects.

Plain view doctrine Legal concept that admits evidence that is seized by police without a warrant as admissible, if such evidence was in "plain view" and could be seen from a public area, for example, through the window of an automobile stopped for a traffic infraction.

Plea bargaining A legal transaction in which a defendant pleads guilty in exchange for some form of leniency.

Political crime Criminal behavior that is motivated by political, as opposed to personal, concerns. Sometimes refers to crimes committed by government.

Positivism The use of the scientific method to study crime; the theory of positivism attributes crime to poor social and economic conditions, rather than free will.

POST (Police Officer Standards and Training) Commission An official state agency responsible for setting minimum levels of training for law enforcement officers in that state.

Presentence investigation report (psi) A report submitted by a probation department to a judge, containing information about a defendant. The judge can base his or her sentencing decision on the psi report.

Presumptive sentence A determinate form of sentencing which allows for some discretion in the form of mitigation or aggravation.

Pretrial release Release of a defendant without bail pending trial; release on recognizance, or ROR.

Preventive detention Holding a defendant in custody pending trial on the belief that he or she is likely to commit further crimes.

Preventive patrol The primary service of a police department, which involves uniformed police officers patrolling randomly in assigned areas on foot or in police vehicles.

Prima facie case A case that is sufficient, that is, has the minimum amount of evidence necessary to allow it to continue in the judicial process.

Prisonization Process by which inmates are socialized into the prison subculture.

Proactive policing Police activities designed to discover crime, such as undercover operations.

Probable cause The minimum level of evidence needed to make a lawful arrest or secure certain warrants; a level of information that would lead a prudent person to believe that a crime was being, or had been, committed by a specific perpetrator.

Probable cause hearing A court hearing to determine if the arresting officer had sufficient evidence—probable cause—to justify the arrest.

Probation A sentence in lieu of imprisonment which brings a defendant under supervision of a probation officer. The probationer must abide by a set of regulations or be incarcerated.

Professional criminals Persons highly skilled at a criminal trade.

Prosecutor The attorney, who is also a public official, who represents the state in a criminal action.

Protective search A warrantless search by police that is permitted by law under certain circumstances: for example, when it is likely that suspects will escape before a warrant is secured, or to protect the public or the police.

Psychoanalytic theory An approach to psychology that stresses the importance of unconscious mechanisms in determining conscious behavior.

Public defender An attorney, who is also a public official, who represents indigent defendants.

Public safety exception An exception to the exclusionary rule, on the grounds that an action which resulted in securing evidence that would normally be suppressed was necessary to protect the public from some immediate danger.

Reactive policing Police strategy of maintaining readiness to respond to citizen complaints.

Reasonable mistake exception An exception to the exclusionary rule, which justifies the admission of evidence it is reasonably believed was obtained without Fourth Amendment violations.

Recidivate To repeat criminal behavior.

Redirect The questioning of a friendly witness after he or she has been subjected to cross-examination by opposing counsel.

Reformatory A high-security correctional facility for young offenders.

Rehabilitation The restoration of an individual to society; the goal of corrections or the medical model.

Release on own recognizance: *See* Pretrial release.

Reprieve A temporary stay of the execution of a sentence to allow more time for judicial review.

Residential treatment center (RTC) A private facility for the treatment of juveniles which offers a broad range of educational, vocational, and therapeutic programs.

Restitution Reimbursing the victim of a crime.

Retribution That portion of a criminal penalty which is based on vengeance or just deserts.

Self-defense Affirmative defense based on the right to use physical force to protect oneself or others in imminent danger.

Self-incrimination Forcing a suspect to provide evidence against himself or herself, which is prohibited by the Fifth Amendment.

Self-report study Research technique in which subjects are asked to respond in confidence to questions about their criminal activities.

Senatorial courtesy Tradition which allows a senator to veto the appointment of a judge in his or her state.

Sentencing council A device intended to reduce disparate sentencing by having judges from a single court meet to decide jointly on the proper sentences to be imposed for pending cases.

Sentencing disparity The phenomenon of offenders who commit similar crimes receiving vastly different sentences.

Sentencing guidelines A series of nonbinding guidelines intended to reduce sentencing disparity by providing judges with a range of sentences for offenders based on crime and on other relevant factors.

Separation of powers The division of government into three branches: executive, legislative, and judicial.

Sequester Placing a jury in protective custody, insulated from media coverage of a trial, until they complete their deliberations.

Shelters Temporary residential facilities for children in need of emergency care.

Social investigation A study prepared by a probation officer in juvenile court describing social and psychological factors affecting a case and intended to provide the judge with information upon which to base a disposition.

Status offense An action that would not constitute a crime if the actor was an adult (e.g., truancy) but, in accord with *parens patriae*, can subject a youngster to the juvenile court process.

Statutory law The enactments of legislative bodies.

Substantial capacity test A legal test for criminal responsibility that examines whether a person "lacks substantial capacity to appreciate the criminality of his conduct" as a result of mental defect. It has replaced the M'Naghten test in many states.

Supervised release An alternative to cash bail in which the defendant is supervised while in the community awaiting trial.

Supremacy clause The constitutional provision that the federal government has powers which cannot be exercised by the states, or to which the states must conform.

Survey research Quantitative research technique of selecting a sample from a larger population and using a survey instrument—a series of questions requiring answers that can be analyzed by computer—to determine something about the larger population, for example, attitudes toward the death penalty, the police, or building more prisons.

Suspect surveillance Tailing and otherwise maintaining direct observation of a suspect.

SWAT Team A special weapons and tactics unit of the police which responds to hostage, barricade, and sniper situations.

Sworn officer A public official who according to law has certain powers not entrusted to civilians; for example, to arrest on probable cause, or to carry concealed weapons.

Symbolic interactionism An approach to sociology concerned with how individuals assign meaning to themselves, their interactions, and society through symbols such as language.

Temporary insanity Affirmative defense which argues that although the defendant is currently sane, he or she was suffering from insanity at the time of the offense.

Ticket-of-leave Early form of parole used in England and Ireland.

Tort A private wrong which is the subject of a lawsuit.

Total institutions Public and private institutions which provide for the totality of residents' needs; these include prisons, mental institutions, and monasteries.

Training school A residential facility operated by the state or the county to treat juvenile delinquents.

Trial Examination in court of the facts of a case, where each side is represented by counsel and can call witnesses. Results in a verdict of guilty or not guilty.

True bill The handing up of an indictment by a grand jury.

Uniform Crime Reports (UCR) An annual report of crime statistics, produced by the FBI, that divides crime into two parts: part I offenses (called index crimes), which are more serious, occur more frequently, and are reported to the police; and part II offenses, which are less serious, occur less frequently, and are often victimless.

Uniformed Tactical Patrol (UTP) A police strategy which frees a select number of uniformed police officers from routine duties and answering calls for service in order for them to concentrate on street crime.

Venire Process by which jurors are summoned to service.

Venue Proper jurisdiction for considering a particular case.

Victimization studies Studies used by the National Crime Survey to determine how many households are victimized by crime each year.

Victimless crime A crime which normally does not have a complainant(s), for example, drug trafficking, gambling, or prostitution.

Victimology The study of crime victims.

***Voir dire* hearing** A judicial procedure during which opposing counsel have an opportunity to challenge prospective jurors.

Workgroup. *See* Courtroom workgroup.

Work release Program which enables select inmates to leave prison during the day for employment, vocational training, or education.

Writ of *certiorari*. *See Certiorari.*
Writ of habeas corpus. *See* Habeas corpus, writ of.

XYY chromosome theory A belief that males with an extra Y chromosome are predisposed to criminal behavior.

References

Aaronson, David E., Nicholas N. Kittrie, David J. Saari and Caroline S. Cooper
- 1977 *Alternatives to Conventional Criminal Adjudication: Guidebook for Planners and Practitioners*. Washington, DC: U.S. Government Printing Office.

Abadinsky, Howard
- 1987 *Probation and Parole: Theory and Practice*. 3d Ed. Englewood Cliffs, NJ: Prentice-Hall.
- 1985 *Organized Crime: Second Edition*. Chicago: Nelson-Hall.
- 1984 *Discretionary Justice: An Introduction to Discretion in Criminal Justice*. Springfield, IL: Charles C. Thomas.
- 1983 *The Criminal Elite: Professional and Organized Crime*. Westport, CT: Greenwood Press.
- 1976 "The Status Offense Dilemma: Coercion and Treatment." *Crime and Delinquency* 22 (October): 456–60.

Allen, Carol Baley-
- 1984 "Border Patrol Officers Attempt to Stem the Alien Tide." *Police Product News* (December): 30–31, 44–49.

Allen, Harry E. and Clifford E. Simonsen
- 1981 *Corrections in America: An Introduction*. 3d Ed. New York: Macmillan.

Allen, Harry E., Helen H. Bowman, Eric W. Carlson and Richard P. Seiter
- 1984 Halfway Houses in the United States. In *Probation, Parole and Community Corrections*, edited by Robert M. Carter, Daniel Glaser and Leslie T. Wilkins, 318–22. New York: Wiley.

Alschuler, Albert
- 1975 "The Defense Attorney's Role in Plea Bargaining." *Yale Law Review* 84: 1179–1314.
- 1968 "The Prosecutor's Role in Plea Bargaining." *University of Chicago Law Review* 36: 50–112.

American Friends Service Committee
- 1971 *Struggle For Justice*. New York: Hill and Wang.

Andreski, Stanislav, ed.
- 1971 *Herbert Spencer: Structure, Function and Evolution*. New York: Scribner's.

Applebome, Peter
- 1984 "Black Is Cleared by New Arrest in Texas Holdup." *New York Times* (March 22): 10.

Attica Commission. *See* New York State Special Commission on Attica.
Augustus, John
    1972 *John Augustus, First Probation Officer.* Montclair, NJ: Patterson-Smith.
Axelrod, David
    1983 "Judicial Bench No Place to Practice Party Loyalty." *Chicago Tribune* (August 28): Sec. 4, p. 4

Badillo, Herman and Milton Haynes
    1972 *A Bill of Rights: Attica and the American Prison System.* New York: Outerbridge and Lazard.
Barker, Tom and Robert O. Wells
    1982 "Police Administrator's Attitude Toward the Definition and Control of Police Deviance." *FBI Law Enforcement Bulletin* (March): 8–16.
Barzilay, Jonathan
    1983 "The D.A.'s Right Arms." *New York Times Magazine* (November 16): 119-230.
Beaumont, Gustave de and Alexis de Tocqueville
    1964 *On the Penitentiary System in the United States and Its Application in France.* Carbondale, IL: Southern Illinois University Press.
Beigel, Herbert and Allan Beigel
    1977 *Beneath the Badge: A Story of Police Corruption.* New York: Harper and Row.
Bernes, Walter
    1979 *For Capital Punishment.* New York: Basic Books.
Binder, Arnold and Gilbert Geis
    1983 *Methods of Research in Criminology and Criminal Justice.* New York: McGraw-Hill.
Blew, Carol H. and Robert Rosenblum
    1977 *The Community Arbitration Project: Anne Arundel County, Maryland.* Washington, DC: U.S. Government Printing Office.
Blok, Anton
    1975 *The Mafia of a Sicilian Village: 1860–1960.* New York: Harper and Row.
Blumberg, Abraham S.
    1967 "The Practice of Law as Confidence Game: Organizational Cooptation of a Profession." *Law and Society Review* 1: 15–39.
Boland, Barbara, Elizabeth Brady, Herbert Tyson, and John Bassler
    1983 *The Prosecution of Felony Arrests, 1979.* Washington, DC: U.S. Government Printing Office.
Boorkman, David, Ernest J. Fazio, Jr., Noel Day, and David Weinstein
    1976 *Community-Based Corrections in Des Moines.* Washington, DC: U.S. Government Printing Office.
Brantingham, Paul and Patricia Brantingham
    1984 *Patterns in Crime.* New York: Macmillan.

Brashler, William
    1977 Introduction to Herbert Beigel and Allan Beigel, *Beneath the Badge: A Story of Police Corruption*. New York: Harper and Row.
Brighton, L. D.
    1983 "The United States Army's C.I.D." *Police Product News* (November): 44–47.
Brisbane, Arthur S.
    1985 "A Get-Tough Policy Starts a Building Boom." *Washington Post* (March 3): 1, 14–15.
Buckle, Suzann R. and Leonard Buckle
    1977 *Bargaining for Justice: Plea Disposition in the Criminal Courts*. New York: Praeger.
Buder, Leonard
    1986 "A Prison Nightmare Is Over." *New York Times* (July 4): 18.
Bureau of Justice Statistics
    1984 *The Prevalence of Guilty Pleas*. Washington, DC: Bureau of Justice Statistics.
Burger, Warren
    1973 "The Special Skills of Advocacy: Are Specialized Training and Certification of Advocates Essential to Our System of Justice?" *Fordham Law Review* 42: 227–42.
Burgess, Robert L. and Ronald L. Akers
    1969 "Differential Association–Reinforcement Theory of Criminal Behavior." In *Behavioral Sociology*, edited by Robert L. Burgess and Don Bushell, Jr. New York: Columbia University Press.
Burkhart, W. Robert, Shirley Melnicoe, Annesley K. Schmidt, Linda J. McKay, and Cheryl Martorana
    1982 *The Effects of the Exclusionary Rule: A Study in California*. Washington, DC: U.S. Government Printing Office.

Campane, Jerome O., Jr.
    1984 "The Constitutionality of Drunk Driver Roadblocks." *FBI Law Enforcement Bulletin* (July): 24–31.
Capital Punishment 1983.
    1984 Washington, DC: Bureau of Justice Statistics.
Casper, Jonathan
    1978 *Criminal Courts: The Defendant's Perspective*. Washington, DC: U.S. Government Printing Office.
Central Office of Information
    1976 *The Legal System of Britain*. London, England: Her Majesty's Stationary Office.
Chambliss, William
    1973 *Functional and Conflict Theories of Crime*. New York: Modular Publications.
    1972 *The Box-Man: A Professional Thief's Journey*. New York: Harper and Row.

Chevigny, Paul
   1969 *Police Power: Police Abuses in New York City*. New York: Pantheon.
Clemmer, Donald
   1958 *The Prison Community*. New York: Holt, Rinehart and Winston.
Clinard, Marshall B., ed.
   1964 *Anomie and Deviant Behavior*. New York: Free Press.
Clinard, Marshall B. and Peter C. Yeager
   1980 *Corporate Behavior*. New York: Free Press.
Clinard, Marshall B. and Richard Quinney
   1967 *Criminal Behavior Systems: A Typology*. New York: Holt, Rinehart and Winston.
Clinard, Marshall B., Peter C. Yeager, David Petrashek and Elizabeth Harries
   1979 *Illegal Corporate Behavior*. Washington, DC: U.S. Government Printing Office.
Cloward, Richard A. and Lloyd E. Ohlin
   1960 *Delinquency and Opportunity*. New York: Free Press.
Cohen, Albert K.
   1965 *Delinquent Boys*. New York: Free Press.
Comptroller General of the United States
   1976 *State and County Probation Systems in Crisis*. Washington, DC: U.S. General Accounting Office.
Cox, Michael P.
   1975 "Discretion: A Twentieth Century Mutation." *Oklahoma Law Review* 28: 311–32.
Cressey, Donald R.
   1953 *Other People's Money*. New York: Free Press.
   1950 "The Criminal Violation of a Financial Trust." *American Sociological Review* 15 (December): 738–43.
Criminal Defense Systems.
   1984 Washington, DC: Bureau of Justice Statistics.
Criminal Justice Careers Guidebook.
   1982 Washington, DC: U.S. Government Printing Office.
Cripe, Claire A.
   1977 "Religious Freedom in Prisons." *Federal Probation* 41 (March): 31–35.
Cromwell, Paul F., Jr.
   1978 "The Halfway House and Offender Reintegration." In *Corrections in the Community. 2d Ed.*, edited by George C. Killinger and Paul F. Cromwell, Jr., 66–72. St. Paul, MN: West Publishing Co.
Cullen, Francis T. and Karen E. Gilbert
   1982 *Reaffirming Rehabilitation*. Cincinnati, OH: Anderson.
Cunningham, William C. and Todd H. Taylor
   1984 *The Growth of Private Security*. Washington, DC: U.S. Government Printing Office.

Curran, Barbara A.
   1983 "The Legal Profession in the 1980's: The Changing Profile of the Legal Profession." Paper presented at a research seminar of the American Bar Association, July 30, in Atlanta, GA.

Deitch, L. I. and L. N. Thompson
   1985 "The Reserve Officer: One Alternative to the Need for Manpower." *Police Chief* (May): 59–61.

Denzin, Norman K.
   1970 *The Research Act*. Chicago, IL: Aldine.

"The Department of Defense Hotline: Report Suspicions of Waste, Fraud or Abuse by Telephone."
   1985 *Police Chief* (May): 34.

Dershowitz, Alan M.
   1983 *The Best Defense*. New York: Vintage Books.

Dictionary of Criminal Justice Data Terminology.
   1981 Washington, DC: U.S. Government Printing Office.

Dilworth, Donald C., ed.
   1976 *The Blue and the Brass*. Gaithersburg, MD: International Association of Chiefs of Police.

Division of Parole of the State of New York
   1984 *Annual Report: 1982–83*. Albany: Division of Parole.

Dobyns, Fletcher
   1932 *The Underworld of American Politics*. New York: Fletcher Dobyns.

Donohue, William B.
   1982 "Summertime Cops." *FBI Law Enforcement Bulletin* (February): 2–9.

Dunford, Franklin W.
   1977 "Police Diversion: An Illusion?" *Criminology* 15 (November): 335–52.

Durkheim, Emile
   1966 *The Rules of the Sociological Method*. New York: Free Press.

Edelman, Bernard
   1979 "Blending." *Police Magazine* (September): 53–58.

Efficient Use of Police Resources.
   1984 Washington, DC: U.S. Government Printing Office.

Eliot, Charles W., ed.
   1910 *American Historical Documents: 1000–1904*. New York: P. F. Collier and Son.

Empey, LaMar T., ed.
   1979 *Juvenile Justice: The Progressive Legacy and Current Reforms*. Charlottesville, VA: University Press of Virginia.

Erikson, Kai T.
   1966 *Wayward Puritans*. New York: Wiley.

Federal Register
  1984 *The United States Government Manual, 1983/84*. Washington, DC: U.S. Government Printing Office.
Feeley, Malcolm M.
  1979 *The Process Is Punishment: Handling Cases in a Lower Court*. New York: Russell Sage Foundation.
Finckenauer, James O.
  1984 *Juvenile Delinquency and Corrections: The Gap Between Theory and Practice*. New York: Academic Press.
Fishman, Mark
  1978 "Crime Waves as Ideology." *Social Problems* 25: 531–43.
Fogel, David
  1975 *We Are the Living Proof: The Justice Model for Corrections*. Cincinnati: Anderson.
Fogelson, Robert M.
  1977 *Big City Police*. Cambridge, MA: Harvard University Press.
Fooner, Michael
  1985 *A Guide to Interpol*. Washington, DC: U.S. Government Printing Office.
Forst, Brian E. and Jolene C. Hernon
  1985 *Research in Brief: The Criminal Justice Response to Victim Harm*. Washington, DC: National Institute of Justice.
Fox, Vernon
  1977 *Community-Based Corrections*. Englewood Cliffs, NJ: Prentice-Hall.
Franklin, Tim
  1985 "State to Seek Funds to Replace Bungling Lab." *Chicago Tribune* (August 18): Sec. 3, p. 1.
Frantz, Joe B.
  1969 "The Frontier Tradition: An Invitation to Violence." In *The History of Violence in America*, edited by Hugh David Graham and Ted Robert Gurr, 127–54. New York: Bantam.
Freedman, Estelle B.
  1981 *Their Sisters' Keepers: Women's Prison Reform in America, 1830–1930*. Ann Arbor, MI: University of Michigan Press.
Friedman, Lawrence M.
  1973 *A History of American Law*. New York: Simon and Schuster.
Fyfe, James J.
  1979 "Deadly Force." *FBI Law Enforcement Bulletin* (December): 7–9.

Garrow, David J.
  1981 *The FBI and Martin Luther King, Jr.: From "Solo" to Memphis*. New York: Norton.
Gay, William G., Theodore H. Schell, and Stephen Schack
  1977 *Routine Patrol*. Improving Patrol Productivity, vol. 1. Washington, DC: U.S. Government Printing Office.

Gifis, Steven H.
   1975 *Law Dictionary*. Woodbury, NY: Barron's.
Gillin, John T.
   1931 *Taming the Criminal*. New York: Macmillan.
Glick, Henry R.
   1983 *Courts, Politics, and Justice*. New York: McGraw-Hill.
Goffman, Erving
   1961 *Asylums: Essays on the Social Situation of Mental Patients and Other Inmates*. Garden City, NY: Doubleday.
Goldblatt, Steven H.
   1983 "Ineffective Assistance of Counsel: Attempts to Establish Minimum Standards." In *The Defense Counsel*, edited by William F. McDonald, 221–46. Beverly Hills, CA: Sage.
Goldstein, Herman
   1977 *Policing a Free Society*. Cambridge, MA: Ballinger.
Gontarz, Christopher S.
   1984 "*Delaware v. Prouse:* Guidelines for Drunk Driver Roadblocks." *Journal of Police Science* 12 (June): 177–85.
Gracey, James S.
   1985 "Winning the War at Sea." *Police Chief* (October): 63–67.
Greenberg, Bernard, Carola V. Elliott, and H. Steven Procter
   1977 *Felony Investigation Decision Model: An Analysis of Investigative Elements of Information*. Washington, DC: U.S. Government Printing Office.
Greenberg, David F.
   1975 "Problems in Community Corrections." *Issues in Criminology* 10 (Spring): 1–34.
Greenberg, David F., Ronald C. Kessler and Colin Loftin
   1983 "The Effect of Police Employment on Crime." *Criminology* 21 (August): 349–74.
Greenberg, Ilene and Robert Wasserman
   1979 *Managing Criminal Investigations*. Washington, DC: U.S. Government Printing Office.
Greenwood, Peter, Jan Chaiken, and Joan Petersilla
   1975 *Summary and Policy Implications*. The Criminal Investigation Process, vol. 1. Santa Monica, CA: Rand Corporation.
Grunson, Lindsey
   1983 "Second Opinions on Medical Examiners." *New York Times* (May 15): E6.

Habeas Corpus.
   1984 Washington, DC: U.S. Bureau of Justice Statistics.
Hagerty, J. E.
   1934 *Twentieth Century Crime, Eighteenth Century Methods of Control*. Boston, MA: Stratford.

Hahn, Paul
    1976 *Community-Based Corrections and the Criminal Justice System*. Santa Cruz, CA: Davis Publishing Co.

Hall, John C.
    1984 "Deadly Force: The Common Law and the Constitution." *FBI Law Enforcement Bulletin* (April): 26–31.

Halper, Andrew and Richard Ku
    n.d. *New York City Police Department Street Crime Unit*. Washington, DC: U.S. Government Printing Office.

Hanewicz, Wayne B.
    1978 "Police Personality: A Jungian Perspective." *Crime and Delinquency* 24 (April): 152–72.

Harrell, Mary Ann and Burnett Anderson
    1982 *Equal Justice Under Law: The Supreme Court in American Life*. Rev. Ed. Washington, DC: National Geographic Society for the Supreme Court Historical Society.

Hart, Peter M.
    1977 "Mountain Rescue." *FBI Law Enforcement Bulletin* (December): 2–6.

Heumann, Milton
    1978 *Plea Bargaining*. Chicago: University of Chicago Press.

Hoffman, Paul
    1982 *Lions of the Eighties: The Inside Story of the Powerhouse Law Firms*. Garden City, NY: Doubleday.

Howlett, Frederick
    1973 "Is the YSB All It's Cracked Up to Be?" *Crime and Delinquency* 19 (October): 485–92.

Hunt, Jennifer
    1985 "Police Accounts of Normal Force." *Urban Life* 13 (January): 315–41.

Ianni, Elizabeth Reuss-
    1983 *Two Cultures of Policing*. New Brunswick, NJ: Transaction Books.

Ianni, Francis A. J. with Elizabeth Reuss-Ianni
    1972 *A Family Business: Kinship and Social Control in Organized Crime*. New York: Russell Sage Foundation.

Illinois Revised Statutes.
    1985 St. Paul, MN: West Publishing Co.

Imlay, Carl H. and Elsie L. Reid
    1975 "The Probation Officer, Sentencing and the Winds of Change." *Federal Probation* 39 (December): 9–17.

Inciardi, James A.
    1977 "In Search of the Class Cannon: A Field Study of Professional Pickpockets." In *Street Ethnography: Selected Studies in Crime and Drug Use in Natural Settings*, edited by Robert S. Weppner, 55–77. Beverly Hills, CA: Sage.

Irwin, John
   1980 *Prisons in Turmoil*. Boston: Little, Brown.
Irwin, John and Donald R. Cressey
   1962 "Thieves, Convicts, and the Inmate Culture." *Social Problems* 10 (Fall): 142–55.

Jacob, Herbert and James Eisenstein
   1977 *Felony Justice*. Boston: Little, Brown.
Jenkins, John A.
   1984 "Betting on the Verdict." *New York Times Magazine* (November 25): 86-99.
Jenkins, Philip
   1984 *Crime and Justice: Issues and Ideas*. Belmont, CA: Brooks/Cole.
Johnson, Edwin S.
   1981 *Research Methods in Criminology and Criminal Justice*. Englewood Cliffs, NJ: Prentice-Hall.
Johnson, Elmer
   1969 "Police: An Analysis of Role Conflict." Paper presented at a symposium on criminology, Indiana State University at Terre Haute, July 24.
Johnson, Thomas A., Gordon E. Misner, and Lee P. Brown
   1981 *The Police and Society*. Englewood Cliffs, NJ: Prentice-Hall.
Joint Committee on New York Drug Law Evaluation
   1977 *The Nation's Toughest Drug Law: Evaluation of the New York Experience*. New York: Association of the Bar of the City of New York.
Josephson, Matthew
   1962 *The Robber Barons*. New York: Harcourt, Brace.

Kelling, George L., Tony Pate, Duane Dieckman, and Charles E. Brown
   1974 "The Kansas City Preventative Patrol Experiment." Reprinted in the *Aldine Crime and Justice Annual*. Chicago: Aldine.
Kerstetter, Wayne A., and Anne M. Heinz
   1979 *Pretrial Settlement Conference: An Evaluation*. Washington, DC: U.S. Government Printing Office.
Krajick, Kevin
   1980a "Police vs. Police." *Police Magazine* (May): 7–20.
   1980b "Not on My Block." *Corrections Magazine* (October): 15–27.

Lagoy, Stephen P., Frederick A. Hussey, and John H. Kramer
   1978 "A Comparative Assessment of Determinate Sentencing Structures." *Crime and Delinquency* 24 (October): 385–400.
Lemert, Edwin M.
   1951 *Social Pathology*. New York: McGraw-Hill.
Lerner, Mark Jay
   1977 "The Effectiveness of a Definite Sentence Parole System." *Criminology* 15 (August): 211–24.

Letkemann, Peter
   1973 *Crime as Work*. Englewood Cliffs, NJ: Prentice-Hall.

Levin, Martin A.
   1977 *Urban Politics and the Criminal Courts*. Chicago: University of Chicago Press.

Lewis, Peter and Kenneth D. Peoples
   1978 *The Supreme Court and the Criminal Process: Cases and Comments*. Philadelphia, PA: W.B. Saunders.

Lewis, W. David
   1965 *From Newgate to Dannemora*. Ithaca, NY: Cornell University Press.

Lindsey, Robert
   1985 "They're Behind Bars But Not Out of Business." *New Times* (June 2): 2E.

Lipton, Douglas, Robert Martinson and Judith Wilks
   1975 *The Effectiveness of Correctional Treatment: A Survey of Treatment Evaluation Studies*. New York: Praeger.

Lloyd, Henry Demarest
   1963 *Wealth Against Commonwealth*. Edited by Thomas C. Cochran. Englewood Cliffs, NJ: Prentice-Hall.

Lombardo, Lucien X.
   1981 *Guards Imprisoned: Correctional Officers at Work*. New York: Elsevier.

Lombroso, Cesare
   1968 *Crime: Its Causes and Remedies*. Montclair, NJ: Patterson-Smith. Originally published in 1911.

Loth, David
   1938 *Public Plunder: A History of Graft and Corruption in America*. New York: Carrick and Evans.

Lou, Herbert H.
   1972 *Juvenile Courts in the United States*. New York: Arno Press. Originally published in 1927.

Lubasch, Arnold H.
   1986 "Postal Inspectors Shun Frills as They Take on Big Cases." *New York Times* (June 16): 13.

Lundman, Richard J.
   1979 "Organizational Norms and Police Discretion: An Observational Study of Police Work with Traffic Law Violators." *Criminology* 17 (August): 159–71.

Lynn, Frank
   1984 "Group Finds Voters Lack Choices in Many Supreme Court Elections." *New York Times* (October 14): 18.

Maas, Peter
   1974 *Serpico*. New York: Bantam.

McCarthy, Belinda Rogers and Bernard J. McCarthy
   1984 *Community-Based Corrections*. Monterey, CA: Brooks/Cole.

McGee, Richard A.
   1975 "Our Sick Jails." In *Jails and Justice,* edited by Paul F. Cromwell, Jr., 5–18. Springfield, IL: Charles C. Thomas.

McGowan, Robert H.
   1978 "Pasadena Police Make Alarming Progress." *FBI Law Enforcement Bulletin* (January): 2–5.

McKelvey, Blake
   1977 *American Prisons: A History of Good Intentions.* Montclair, NJ: Patterson-Smith.
   1972 *American Prisons: A Study in American Social History Prior to 1815.* Montclair, NJ: Patterson-Smith.

MacNamara, Donal E. J.
   1977 "The Medical Model in Corrections: Requiescat in Pace." *Criminology* 14 (February): 439–48.

Maestro, Marcello
   1973 *Cesare Beccaria and the Origins of Penal Reform.* Philadelphia, PA: Temple University Press.

Mancini, Joseph
   1983 "NYPD's Hero Cops." *The National Centurion* (August): 21–25, 34.

Margolick, David
   1985 "25 Wrongfully Executed in U.S. Study Finds." *New York Times* (November 14): 13.
   1984 "The Rights of Suspects." *New York Times* (September 21): 19.
   1983a "The Trouble with Law Schools." *New York Times Magazine* (May 22): 20–25, 30, 32, 36, 38.
   1983b "The Blue-Chip Firms Remain Mostly White." *New York Times* (February 13): 18E.

Martin, Thomas C.
   1978 "Seattle Police Department's 'Decoy Squad'." *FBI Law Enforcement Bulletin* (February): 16–20.

Martinson, Robert
   1974 "What Works? Questions and Answers About Prison Reform." *The Public Interest* 35 (Spring): 22–54.

Matulia, Kenneth J.
   1982 *A Balance of Forces.* Gaithersburg, MD: International Association of Chiefs of Police.

Matza, David
   1964 *Delinquency and Drift.* New York: Wiley.

Maurer, David W.
   1940 *The Big Con: The Story of the Confidence Man and The Confidence Game.* Indianapolis: Bobbs-Merrill.

Mayer, Martin
   1969 *The Lawyers.* New York: Dell.

Melanson, Philip H.
   1984 *The Politics of Protection: The United States Secret Service in the Terrorist Age.* New York: Praeger.

Merton, Robert K.
 1938 "Social Structure and Anomie." *American Sociological Review* 3: 672–82.
Miller, Walter B.
 1958 "Lower Class Culture as a Generating Milieu of Gang Delinquency." *Journal of Social Issues* 14: 5–19.
Mintz, Morton
 1986 *At Any Cost: Corporate Greed, Women, and the Dalkon Shield*. New York: Pantheon.
Moley, Raymond
 1929 *Politics and Criminal Prosecutions*. New York: Minton, Balch.
Monkkonen, Eric
 1981 *Police in Urban America: 1860–1920*. Cambridge, England: Cambridge University Press.
Moore, Mark H., Susan R. Estrich, Daniel McGillis and William Spellman
 1984 *Dangerous Offenders: The Elusive Target of Justice*. Cambridge, MA: Harvard University Press.
Morgan, Richard E.
 1982 "Federal Bureau of Investigation: History." *Encyclopedia of Crime and Justice*. New York: Free Press.
Moynahan, J. M. and Earle K. Stewart
 1980 *The American Jail: Its Growth and Development*. Chicago: Nelson-Hall.
Mullen, Joan
 1975 *The Dilemma of Diversion*. Washington, DC: U.S. Government Printing Office.
Murphy, Patrick V. with Thomas Plate
 1977 *Commissioner: A View From the Top of American Law Enforcement*. New York: Simon and Schuster.
Myers, Gustavus
 1936 *The History of Great American Fortunes*. New York: Modern American Library.

National Commission on Law Observance and Law Enforcement
 1931 *Report on Penal Institutions*. Washington, DC: U.S. Government Printing Office.
Neubauer, David W.
 1974 *Criminal Justice in Middle America*. Morristown, NJ: General Learning Press.
Newman, Graeme
 1983 *Just and Painful: A Case for the Corporal Punishment of Criminals*. London, England: Macmillan.
New York Special Commission on Attica
 1972 *Attica*. New York: Praeger.

Niederhoffer, Arthur
   1969 *Behind the Shield: The Police in Urban Society*. New York: Random House.

O'Connor, Richard
   1962 *Gould's Millions*. Garden City, NY: Doubleday.
Oswald, Russell G.
   1972 *My Story*. Garden City, NY: Doubleday.

Packer, Herbert L.
   1968 *The Limits of the Criminal Sanction*. Stanford, CA: Stanford University Press.
Palmer, John W.
   1974 "Pre-Arrest Diversion: Victim Confrontation." *Federal Probation* 38 (September): 12–17.
Parker, William
   1975 *Parole*. College Park, MD: American Correctional Association.
Pascoe, Michael A.
   1985 "The Naval Investigative Service." *National Sheriff* (December–January): 34–37.
Pennsylvania Crime Commission
   1980 *A Decade of Organized Crime: 1980 Report*. St. Davids, PA: Pennsylvania Crime Commission.
Platt, Anthony M.
   1974 *The Child Savers: The Invention of Delinquency*. Chicago: University of Chicago Press.
Polsky, Howard W.
   1965 *Cottage Six: The Social System of Delinquent Boys in Residential Treatment*. New York: Wiley.
President's Commission on Law Enforcement and Administration of Justice
   1972 *The Challenge of Crime in a Free Society*. New York: Avon.

Quadagno, Jill S. and Robert J. Antonio
   1975 "Labeling Theory as an Oversocialized Conception of Man: The Case of Mental Illness." *Sociology and Social Research* 60 (October): 30–41.

Raab, Selwyn
   1985 "Man Wrongfully Imprisoned by New York to Get $600,000." *New York Times* (January 20): 1, 19.
Rand, Michael R.
   1981 *The Prevalence of Crime*. Washington, DC: U.S. Government Printing Office.

Reid, Sue Titus
    1985 *Crime and Criminology, 4th Ed*. New York: Holt, Rinehart and Winston.

Reinhold, Robert
    1986 "Killings Prompt Texas Prisons to Halt Inmates' Mail." *New York Times* (January 20): 11.
    1985 "Execution for Juveniles: New Focus on Old Issue." *New York Times* (September 10): 8.

Reppetto, Thomas A.
    1978 *The Blue Parade*. New York: Free Press.

Rich, Marney
    1985 "Valley Women: Life Inside A Prison for Female Felons." *Chicago Tribune Magazine* (May 19): 25–36.
    1983' "Doing Time for No Crime: Can the State Ever Right Unrightable Wrongs?" *Chicago Tribune* (December 12): Sec. 5, pp. 1, 2.

Rich, William D. and L. Paul Sutton
    1981 "Compliance with Sentencing Guidelines." In *Corrections at the Crossroads: Designing Policy*, edited by Sherwood E. Zimmerman and Harold D. Miller, 85–108. Beverly Hills, CA: Sage.

Richardson, James F.
    1974 *Urban Police in the United States*. Port Washington, NY: Kennikat Press.

Rimer, Sara
    1985 "Special Job that Mixes Boredom and Terror." *New York Times* (February 11): 14.

Roberts, Sam
    1985 "For One Zealous Judge, Hard Bargaining Pushes Cases Through the Courts." *New York Times* (April 29): 13.

Robertson, John A.
    1974 *Rough Justice: Perspectives on Lower Courts*. Boston: Little, Brown.

Rockel, Henry
    1984 "Sobriety Checkpoints." *Police Chief* (July): 38–41.

Roebuck, Julian and Stanley C. Weeber
    1978 *Political Crime in the United States: Analyzing Crime by and Against Government*. New York: Praeger.

Ross, Irwin
    1980 "How Lawless Are the Big Companies?" *Fortune* (December): 57–64.

Rothman, David J.
    1971 *The Discovery of the Asylum: Social Order and Disorder in the New Republic*. Boston, MA: Little, Brown.

Rousseau, Jean Jacques
    1954 *The Social Contract*. Henry Regnery.

Rubin, H. Ted
    1984 *The Courts: Fulcrum of the Justice System*. New York: Random House.

1980 "The Emerging Prosecutor Dominance of the Juvenile Court Intake Process." *Crime and Delinquency* 26 (July): 299–318.

Rubinstein, Jonathan
1973 *City Police*. New York: Farrar, Straus and Giroux.

Rubinstein, Michael L., Stevens H. Clarke, and Teresa J. White
1980 *Alaska Bans Plea Bargaining*. Washington, DC: U.S. Government Printing Office.

Russell, Francis
1975 *A City in Terror, 1919: The Boston Police Strike*. New York: Viking.

Sachs, Howard R. and Charles H. Logan
1979 *Does Parole Make a Difference?* West Hartford, CT: University of Connecticut Law School.

Sanders, Robert E.
1981 "National Response Teams: ATF's Coordinated Effort in Arson Investigation." *FBI Law Enforcement Bulletin* (December): 1–5.

Schack, Stephen, Theodore H. Schell and William G. Gay
1977 *Specialized Patrol*. Improving Patrol Productivity, vol. 2. Washington, DC: U.S. Government Printing Office.

Schafer, Stephen
1974 *The Political Criminal: The Problem of Morality and Crime*. New York: Free Press.

Scharf, Peter and Arnold Binder
1983 *The Badge and the Bullet: Police Use of Deadly Force*. New York: Praeger.

Schmeck, Harold M., Jr.
1985 "Brain Defects Seen in Those Who Repeat Violent Acts." *New York Times* (September 17): 17.

Schneider, Anne L.
1981 "Differences Between Survey and Police Information About Crime." In *Current and Historical Perspectives*, edited by Robert G. Lehnen and Wesley G. Skogan, The National Crime Survey: Working Papers, vol. 1., 39–46. Washington, DC: U.S. Government Printing Office.

Schur, Edwin M.
1973 *Radical Non-Intervention: Rethinking the Delinquency Problem*. Englewood Cliffs, NJ: Prentice-Hall.

Schwendinger, Herman and Julia Schwendinger
1981 "Social Class and the Definition of Crime." In *Crime and Social Justice*, edited by Tony Platt and Paul Takagi, 59–81. Totowa, NJ: General Learning Press.

Scull, Andrew T.
1977 *Decarceration*. Englewood Cliffs, NJ: Prentice-Hall.

Seligman, Joel
1978 *The High Citadel: The Influence of Harvard Law School*. Boston: Houghton Mifflin.

Sellin, Thorsten
   1980 *The Penalty of Death*. Beverly Hills, CA: Sage.

Shaw, Clifford and Henry McKay
   1972 *Juvenile Delinquency and Urban Areas*. Rev. ed. Chicago: University of Chicago Press.

Shenon, Philip
   1984 "Errors Led to Innocent Man's Murder Conviction." *New York Times* (March 15–16): 18 and 16.

Sherman, Lawrence W.
   1982 "Execution Without Trial: Police Homicide and the Constitution." In *Readings on Police Use of Deadly Force*, 88–117. Washington, DC: Police Foundation.
   1978 *Scandal and Reform: Controlling Police Corruption*. Berkeley, CA: University of California Press.

Sherman, Lawrence W. and Richard A. Berk
   1984 "The Minneapolis Domestic Violence Experiment." *Police Foundation Reports* 1: 1–8.

Sherman, Lawrence W. and Robert H. Langworthy
   1982 "Measuring Homicide by Police Officers." In *Readings on Police Use of Deadly Force*, 12–41. Washington, DC: Police Foundation.

Shipp, E. R.
   1983 "$1 Million is Awarded to Man Wrongly Imprisoned 24 Years." *New York Times* (June 1): 1, 14.

Short, James F., Jr.
   1968 *Gang Delinquency and Delinquent Subcultures*. New York: Harper and Row.

Shover, Neal
   1979 *Sociology of Corrections*. Homewood, IL: Dorsey.
   1971 "Burglary as an Occupation." Ph.D. dissertation, University of Illinois at Urbana-Champaign.

Sigler, Jay A.
   1968 *An Introduction to the Legal System*. Homewood, IL: Dorsey Press.

Silverman, Charles E.
   1978 *Criminal Violence, Criminal Justice*. New York: Random House.

Simon, David R. and D. Stanley Eitzen
   1982 *Elite Deviance*. Boston: Allyn and Bacon.

Simon, Roger
   1985 "What If Dotson Got the Chair?" *Chicago Tribune* (May 26): 5.

Sinai, Arthur and E. Edward Dahl
   1985 "Who Investigates Crime Against the Department of Education?" *Police Chief* (May): 30–33.

Sinclair, Andrew
   1962 *The Era of Excess: A Social History of the Prohibition Movement*. Boston: Little, Brown.

Skogan, Wesley
  1981 *Issues in the Measurement of Victimization*. Washington, DC: U.S. Government Printing Office.
Skolnick, Jerome H.
  1975 *Justice Without Trial: Law Enforcement in a Democratic Society*. New York: Wiley.
Smigel, Erwin O.
  1964 *The Wall Street Lawyer*. Glencoe, IL: Free Press.
Smith, Richard Austin
  1961a "The Incredible Electrical Conspiracy." *Fortune* (May): 161ff.
  1961b "The Incredible Electrical Conspiracy." *Fortune* (April): 132ff.
Star, Deborah
  1979 *Summary Parole: A Six and Twelve Month Follow-Up Evaluation*. Sacramento, CA: California Department of Corrections.
Steffens, Lincoln
  1958 *The Autobiography of Lincoln Steffens*. New York: Harcourt, Brace, Jovanovich. Originally published in 1931.
  1957 *The Shame of the Cities*. New York: Hill and Wang. Originally published in 1902.
Stewart, James B.
  1984 *The Partners*. New York: Warner Books.
Stolz, Barbara Ann
  1984 "Interest Groups and Criminal Law: The Case of Federal Criminal Law Revision." *Crime and Delinquency* 30 (January): 91–106.
Sudnow, David
  1965 "Normal Crimes: Sociological Features of the Penal Code." *Social Problems* 12 (Winter): 255–64.
Surette, Ray, ed.
  1984 *Justice and the Media*. Springfield, IL: Charles C. Thomas.
Sutherland, Edwin H.
  1973 *On Analyzing Crime*. Edited by Karl Schuessler. Chicago: University of Chicago Press.
  1972 *The Professional Thief*. Chicago: University of Chicago Press. Originally published in 1937.
  1949 *White Collar Crime*. New York: Dryden Press.
  1940 "White Collar Criminality." *American Sociological Review* 5: 1–12.
Sutton, Willie and Edward Linn
  1976 *Where the Money Was*. New York: Viking.
Swanberg, W. A.
  1959 *Jim Fisk: The Career of an Improbable Rascal*. New York: Scribner's.
Sykes, Gresham M. and David Matza
  1957 "Techniques of Neutralization: A Theory of Delinquency." *American Sociological Review* 22 (December): 664–70.

Takagi, Paul
    1975 "The Walnut Street Jail: A Penal Reform to Centralize the Powers of the State." *Federal Probation* 39 (December): 18–26.

Task Force on Administration of Justice
    1967 *Task Force Report: The Courts*. Washington, DC: U.S. Government Printing Office.

Task Force on Corrections
    1966 *Task Force Report: Corrections*. Washington, DC: U.S. Government Printing Office.

Taylor, Ian, Paul Walton, and Jock Young
    1973 *The New Criminology*. New York: Harper and Row.

Texas Criminal Justice Council
    1974 *Model Rules for Law Enforcement Officers: A Manual on Police Discretion*. Gaithersburg, MD: International Association of Chiefs of Police.

Thalheimer, Donald J.
    1975 *Halfway Houses*, vol. 2. Washington, DC: U.S. Government Printing Office.

Then . . . and Now
    n.d. Washington, DC: Department of Justice.

Tolchin, Martin
    1985 "Private Guards Get New Role in Public Law Enforcement." *New York Times* (November 29): 1, 4.
    1985 "Privately Operated Prison in Tennessee Reports $200,000 in Cost Overruns." *New York Times* (May 22): 8.

Turner, Jonathan H.
    1974 *The Structure of Sociological Theory*. Homewood, IL: Dorsey.

TVI Interview
    1985 "Commander Ray Kendel, Secretary-General of Interpol." *TVI Journal* 6 (Summer): 8–13.

Tybor, Joseph R. and Mark Eissman
    1986 "Illegal Evidence Destroys Few Cases." *Chicago Tribune* (January 5): 1, 13.
    1985a "Plea Bargaining Declines." *Chicago Tribune* (November 3): 1, 18.
    1985b "Judges Penalize the Guilty for Exercising the Right to a Jury Trial." *Chicago Tribune* (October 13): 1, 6.
    1985c "City Bail System Unfair, Unsafe." *Chicago Tribune* (June 2): 1, 8.

Uhlman, Thomas M. and N. Darlene Walker
    1980 "He Takes Some of My Time, I Take Some of His: An Analysis of Judicial Sentencing Patterns in Jury Cases." *Law and Society Review* 14 (Winter): 323–41.

Vanagunas, Stanley and James F. Elliott
  1980 *Administration of Police Organizations*. Boston: Allyn and Bacon.
Van den Haag, Ernest
  1975 *Punishing Criminals*. New York: Basic Books.
Velie, Lester and Jerome G. Miller
  1985 "More Prisons Aren't the Answer." *New York Times* (July 30): 31.
Vera Institute of Justice
  1977 *Felony Arrests: Their Prosecution and Disposition in New York City's Courts*. New York: Vera Institute.

Walker, Samuel
  1980 *Popular Justice: History of American Criminal Justice*. New York: Oxford University Press.
Waltz, Jon R.
  1983 *Introduction to Criminal Evidence*. 2d Ed. Chicago: Nelson-Hall.
Werner, Leslie Maitland
  1985 "An Agency Steps Out of Obscurity." *New York Times* (January 27): 22E.
  1984 "3000 Fugitives Are Caught in 8 States." *New York Times* (November 20): 7.
Westley, William A.
  1978 *Violence and the Police: A Sociological Study of Law, Custom, and Morality*. Cambridge, MA: MIT Press.
Whyte, William F.
  1961 *Street Corner Society*. Chicago: University of Chicago Press.
Wice, Paul B.
  1983 "Private Criminal Defense: Reassessing an Endangered Species." In *The Criminal Defense Counsel*, edited by William F. McDonald, 39–64. Beverly Hills, CA: Sage.
  1978 *Criminal Lawyers: An Endangered Species*. Beverly Hills, CA: Sage.
Wicker, Tom
  1975 *A Time to Die*. New York: Quadrangle.
Wiedrich, Bob and Storer Rowley
  1985 "Prisons for Profit." *Chicago Tribune* (May 19): 1, 21.
Williams, Gregory Howard
  1984 *The Law and Politics of Police Discretion*. Westport, CT: Greenwood Press.
Williams, P. K.
  1984 "How to Build a S.W.A.T. Team." *Police Product News* (July): 30–33.
Wilson, James Q.
  1980 "Police Use of Deadly Force." *FBI Law Enforcement Bulletin* (August): 16–21.

1978 *The Investigators: Managing FBI and Narcotic Agents.* New York: Basic Books.
1976 *Varieties of Police Behavior.* New York: Atheneum.
1975 *Thinking About Crime.* New York: Basic Books.

Wines, Frederick Howard
1975 *Punishment and Reformation: A Study of the Penitentiary System.* New York: AMS Press. Originally published in 1919.

Wiviott, Margaret B.
1984 "Police Traffic Training." *Police Product News* (May): 42–45.

Wizner, Stephen
1984 "Discretionary Waiver of Juvenile Court Jurisdiction: An Invitation to Procedural Arbitrariness." *Criminal Justice Ethics* 3 (Summer/Fall): 41–50.

Zawitz, Marianne W.
1983 *Report to the Nation on Crime and Criminal Justice.* Washington, DC: U.S. Government Printing Office.

Zimmerman, Sherwood E.
1981 "Developing Sentencing Guidelines." In *Corrections at the Crossroads: Designing Policy*, edited by Harold D. Miller, 69–84. Beverly Hills, CA: Sage.

Case Index

Apodaca v. Oregon, 406 U.S. 404 (1972), **128**
Argersinger v. Hamlin, 407 U.S. 525 (1972), **127, 325**

Baldwin v. New York, 399 U.S. 66 (1970), **127**
Ballew v. Georgia, 435 U.S. 233 (1978), **128**
Barker v. Wingo, 407 U.S. 514 (1972), **350**
Baston v. Kentucky, No. 84–6263 (1986), **352–53**
Bell v. Wolfish, 441 U.S. 520 (1979), **439**
Bordenkircher v. Hayes, 434 U.S. 357 (1978), **348**
Breed v. Jones, 421 U.S. 519 (1975), **490**
Brewer v. Williams, 430 U.S. 387 (1977), **132**
Brown v. Board of Education, 347 U.S. 483 (1954), **280, 420**
Burch v. Louisiana, 441 U.S. 130 (1979), **128**

California v. Carney, No. 83–859 (1985), **237**
California v. Ciraolo, No. 84–1513 (1986), **132–33**
Chapman v. Rhodes, 101 S.Ct. 2392 (1981), **439**
Chimel v. California, 395 U.S. 752 (1969), **239**
Crane v. Kentucky, No. 85–5238 (1986) **123**
Ex parte Crouse, 4 Wharton, Pa., 9 (1838), **482**

Daniels v. Williams, 106 S.Ct. 662, 667 (1986), **439**
Davidson v. Cannon, No. 84–6470 (1986), **439**
Delaware v. Prouse, 440 U.S. 648 (1979), **199**

Dow Chemical Company vs. United States, 106 S.Ct 1819 (1986), **132–33**
Duncan v. Louisiana, 391 U.S. 145 (1968), **127**

Furman v. Georgia, 408 U.S. 239 (1972), **440**

In re Gault, 387 U.S. 1 (1967), **488–89**
Gideon v. Wainwright, 372 U.S. 335 (1963), **127, 325**
Gregg v. Georgia, 428 U.S. 204 (1976), **441**

Heath v. Alabama, No. 84–5555 (1985), **128–29**
Hutto v. Finney, 437 U.S. 678 (1978), **439**

Johnson v. Avery, 393 U.S. 483 (1969), **438**
Johnson v. Louisiana, 406 U.S. 356 (1972), **128**
Johnson v. Zerbst, 304 U.S. 358 (1928), **323**
Jones v. North Carolina Prisoners' Labor Union, 433 U.S. 119 (1977), **439**

Katz v. United States, 389 U.S. 347 (1967), **239**
Kent v. United States, 383 U.S. 541 (1966), **487**

Lee v. Washington, 390 U.S. 333 (1968), **439**
Lo–Ji Sales, Inc. v. New York, 442 U.S. 319 (1979), **239**
Lockhart v. McCree, **353**

Mabry v. Johnson, No. 83–328 (1984), **349**
Malley v. Briggs, No. 84–1586 (1986), **133**
Mancusi v. DeForte, 392 U.S. 354 (1968), **239**
Mapp v. Ohio, 357 U.S. 643 (1961), **130**
McKeiver v. Pennsylvania, 403 U.S. 441 (1971), **490**
Michigan v. Bladel, No. 84–1539 (1986), **122–23**
Michigan v. Jackson, No. 84–1531 (1986), **122–23**
Michigan v. Long, No. 82–256 (1983), **236**
Miranda v. Arizona, 384 U.S. 436 (1966), **122, 123, 124**
Moran v. Burbine, No. 84–1485 (1986), **124–26**
Morrissey v. Brewer, 408 U.S. 471 (1972), **361**

New York v. Quarles, No. 82–1213 (1984), **123**
Nix v. Williams, No. 82–1651 (1984), **132**

Oregon v. Elstad, No. 83–773 (1985), **124**

Powell v. Alabama, 287 U.S. 45 (1932), **323**
Press Enterprise Co. v. Superior Court, No. 82–556 (1984), **352**
Procunier v. Martinez, 417 U.S. 817 (1974), **439**

Santobello v. New York, 404 U.S. 257 (1971), **349**
Schall v. Martin, No. 82–1248 (1984), **490**

Schmerber v. California, 384 U.S. 757 (1966), **126**
Stacey v. Emery, 97 U.S. 642, 645 (1878), **235–36**

Tennessee v. Garner, No. 83–1035 (1985), **225**
Terry v. Ohio, 392 U.S. 1 (1968), **236**

United States v. DeCoster, 624 F2d 196 (1978), **330**
United States v. Johns, 105 S.Ct. 881 (1985), **239**
United States v. Leon, 82 U.S. 667 (1984), **129, 130–31**
United States v. Ross, 456 U.S. 789 (1982), **239**
United States v. Wade, 388 U.S. 218 (1967), **126**

Wainwright v. Witt, 83–1427 (1985), **442**
Weeks v. United States, 232 U.S. 383 (1914), **129**
Williams v. Florida, 399 U.S. 78, 102 (1970), **128**
In re Winship, 397 U.S. 358 (1970), **489**
Winston v. Lee, No. 83–1334 (1985), **126–27**
Wolf v. McDonnell, 418 U.S. 539 (1974), **439**

Younger v. Gilmore, 404 U.S. 15 (1971), **438**

Author Index

Aaronson, David E., 346
Abadinsky, Howard, 5, 23, 35, 41, 42, 107, 211, 246, 385, 493
Akers, Ronald L., 89
Allen, Carol Baley-, 253
Allen, Harry E., 469
Alschuler, Albert, 338, 339
Anderson, Burnett, 273, 279n
Andreski, Stanislav, 80–82
Antonio, Robert J., 96
Applebome, Peter, 121
Augustus, John, 383
Axelrod, David, 317

Badillo, Herman, 425
Barker, Tom, 216, 219
Barzilay, Jonathan, 322
Beaumont, Gustave de, 394
Beigel, Allan, 216
Beigel, Herbert, 216
Berk, Richard A., 106
Bernes, Walter, 440
Binder, Arnold, 77, 222, 224
Blew, Carol H., 467
Blok, Anton, 106
Blumberg, Abraham S., 335
Boland, Barbara, 342
Boorkman, David, 468
Brantingham, Patricia, 58
Brantingham, Paul, 58
Brashler, William, 216
Brighton, L. D., 265
Brisbane, Arthur S., 426
Buckle, Leonard, 341
Buckle, Suzann R., 341
Buder, Leonard, 121
Burgess, Robert L., 89
Burkhart, W. Robert, 133

Campane, Jerome O., Jr., 199
Casper, Jonathan, 325
Chaiken, Jan, 195
Chambliss, William, 5, 35

Chevigny, Paul, 222
Clemmer, Donald, 411
Clinard, Marshall B., 25, 27, 29, 31, 32, 33, 87
Cloward, Richard A., 89, 90–91, 93
Cohen, Albert K., 91–92, 93
Cox, Michael P., 337
Cressey, Donald R., 412
Cripe, Claire A., 437
Cromwell, Paul F., Jr., 464
Cullen, Francis T., 453
Cunningham, William, 233, 235
Curran, Barbara A., 312

Dahl, E. Edward, 266
Deitch, L. I., 206
Dershowitz, Alan M., 339
Dilworth, Donald C., 159, 167
Dobyns, Fletcher, 38
Donohue, William B., 204
Dunford, Franklin W., 467
Durkheim, Emile, 87, 98–99

Edelman, Bernard, 185
Eisenstein, James, 338
Eissman, Mark, 133
Eitzen, Stanley, 33, 443
Eliot, Charles W., 6
Empey, LaMar, 481, 483
Erikson, Kai T., 96

Feeley, Malcolm M., 286, 340, 341
Finckenauer, James O., 482
Fishman, Mark, 47
Fogel, David, 453
Fogelson, Robert M., 162, 164
Fooner, Michael, 269, 270
Forst, Brian E., 146
Fox, Vernon, 464, 465, 469
Frantz, Joe B., 157

Freedman, Estelle B., 433, 434
Friedman, Lawrence M., 6, 284, 301, 302, 304, 305, 306, 307
Fyfe, James J., 224

Gay, William G., 178–79, 182
Geis, Gilbert, 77
Gifis, Steven H., 3, 281
Gilbert, Karen E., 453
Gillin, John T., 409
Glick, Henry R., 273
Goffman, Erving, 401
Goldblatt, Steven H., 329, 330
Goldstein, Herman, 194
Gontarz, Christopher S., 200
Gracey, James S., 264
Greenberg, Bernard, 195, 196
Greenberg, David F., 210, 474
Greenberg, Ilene, 195, 196
Greenwood, Peter, 195
Grunson, Lindsey, 56
Guerry, A. M., 80

Hahn, Paul, 464
Halper, Andrew, 185
Hanewicz, Wayne B., 215
Harrell, Mary Ann, 273, 279n
Hart, Peter M., 256
Haynes, Milton, 425
Heinz, Anne M., 334n
Hernon, Jolene C., 146
Heumann, Milton, 339, 340
Hoffman, Paul, 310
Hoover, J. Edgar, 452
Howlett, Frederick, 467
Hunt, Jennifer, 221, 222
Hussey, Frederick A., 372

Ianni, Elizabeth Reuss-, 107, 228
Ianni, Francis, 107
Imlay, Carl, 377

545

AUTHOR INDEX

Inciardi, James A., 35
Irwin, John, 411, 412, 419

Jacob, Herbert, 338
Jenkins, John A., 310–11
Jenkins, Philip, 82
Johnson, Elmer, 169
Josephson, Matthew, 42

Kelling, George L., 182
Kerstetter, Wayne A., 334n
Kessler, Ronald C., 210
Krajick, Kevin, 200, 201, 472
Kramer, John H., 372
Ku, Richard, 185

Lagoy, Stephen P., 372
Langworthy, Robert H., 223
Lemert, Edwin M., 96
Lerner, Mark Jay, 462
Letkemann, Peter, 35
Levin, Martin A., 316, 318
Lewis, Peter, 405, 408
Lindsey, Robert, 430
Lipton, Douglas, 452
Lloyd, Henry Demarest, 42
Loftin, Colin, 210
Logan, Charles H., 462
Lombardo, Lucien X., 430, 431
Lombroso, Cesare, 82, 101
Lou, Herbert H., 484, 485
Lubasch, Arnold, 257
Lundman, Richard J., 197
Lynn, Frank, 317

Maas, Peter, 216
McCarthy, Belinda Rogers, 468, 469
McCarthy, Bernard J., 468, 469
McGee, Richard A., 400
McGowan, Robert H., 190
McKay, Henry, 88
McKelvey, Blake, 404, 405, 410, 419
MacNamara, Donal E. J., 451
Mancini, Joseph, 202
Margolick, David, 118, 308, 442
Martin, Thomas C., 187
Martinson, Robert, 452, 453
Matulia, Kenneth J., 162, 224
Matza, David, 94–95
Maurer, David W., 35
Mayer, Martin, 304

Melanson, Philip H., 247
Merton, Robert K., 87
Miller, Jerome G., 426
Miller, Walter B., 92–93
Mintz, Morton, 33
Monkkonen, Eric, 160, 161–62, 168
Moore, Mark H., 30
Morgan, Richard E., 262
Moynahan, J. M., 395, 397, 399
Mullen, Joan, 467
Myers, Gustavus, 42

Neubauer, David W., 341
Newman, Graeme, 414
Niederhoffer, Arthur, 215, 226

O'Connor, Richard, 42
Ohlin, Lloyd E., 89, 90–91, 93
Oswald, Russell G., 425

Packer, Herbert L., 10, 113, 116
Palmer, John W., 467
Parker, William, 418, 454
Pascoe, Michael A., 265
Petersilia, Joan, 195
Platt, Anthony M., 483
Powers, Edwin, 469

Quadagno, Jill S., 96
Quetelet, Adolphe, 80
Quinney, Richard, 25, 27, 29, 31

Raab, Selwyn, 120
Rand, Michael R., 62
Reid, Elsie, 377
Reid, Sue Titus, 15
Reinhold, Robert, 427, 446
Reppetto, Thomas A., 155, 167
Rich, Marney, 435
Richardson, James F., 162
Rimer, Sara, 202
Robertson, John A., 286
Rockel, Henry, 199
Roebuck, Julian, 31
Rosenblum, Robert, 467
Ross, Irwin, 32
Rothman, David J., 395, 405, 483
Rousseau, Jean Jacques, 78
Rowley, Storer, 435

Rubin, H. Ted, 287, 288, 291, 294–95
Rubinstein, Jonathan, 164, 182, 346
Rubinstein, Michael, 346
Russell, Francis, 165, 229

Sachs, Howard R., 462
Sanders, Robert E., 251
Schack, Stephen, 178, 184, 185, 191
Schafer, Stephen, 31
Scharf, Peter, 222, 224
Schell, Theodore H., 178
Schmeck, Harold M., Jr., 84
Schneider, Anne L., 60
Schur, Edwin M., 96
Schwendinger, Herman, 97
Schwendinger, Julia, 97
Scull, Andrew T., 474
Seligman, Joel, 301, 304
Sellin, Thorsten, 440
Shaw, Clifford, 88
Shenon, Philip, 121
Sherman, Lawrence W., 106, 218, 219–21, 223, 224
Shipp, E. R., 119
Short, James F., Jr., 91
Shover, Neal, 35, 437
Sigler, Jay A., 301
Silverman, Charles E., 210
Simon, David R., 33, 443
Simonson, Clifford E., 469
Sinai, Arthur, 266
Sinclair, Andrew, 240
Skinner, B. F., 86
Skogan, Wesley, 67, 68, 69
Skolnick, Jerome H., 169
Smigel, Erwin O., 308
Smith, Richard Austin, 32
Star, Deborah, 462
Steffens, Lincoln, 164
Stewart, Earle K., 395, 397, 399
Stewart, James B., 309, 310
Stolz, Barbara Ann, 4
Sudnow, David, 345
Surette, Ray, 47
Sutherland, Edwin H., 32, 33, 34, 35, 88–89, 106–7
Swanberg, W. A., 42
Sykes, Gresham M., 94–95

Takagi, Paul, 404
Taylor, Ian, 79, 80, 87, 369, 370

AUTHOR INDEX

Taylor, Todd, 233, 235
Thalheimer, Donald J., 470
Thompson, L. N., 206
Tolchin, Martin, 233, 435
Turner, Jonathan H., 77
Tybor, Joseph R., 133

Uhlman, Thomas M., 335

Van den Haag, Ernest, 367
Velde, Richard W., 399
Velie, Lester, 426

Walker, Darlene, 335
Walker, Samuel, 160, 162, 164, 481
Walton, Paul, 79, 80, 87, 369, 370
Waltz, Jon R., 144, 357n
Wasserman, Robert, 195, 196
Weeber, Stanley C., 31
Wells, Robert O., 216, 219
Werner, Leslie Maitland, 250
Westley, William A., 215
Whyte, William F., 107
Wice, Paul B., 312, 325
Wicker, Tom, 425
Wiedrich, Bob, 435
Wilks, Judith, 452

Williams, P. K., 201, 202
Wilson, James Q., 169, 170, 192, 194, 223, 367
Wines, Frederick H., 373, 404, 407, 449, 451

Yeager, Peter C., 33
Young, Jock, 79, 80, 87, 369, 370

Zawitz, Marianne W., 172, 173
Zimmerman, Sherwood, 374

Subject Index

Abortion, 4
Abscam, 20
Actus reus, 11–12, 13, 360
Affirmative defense, 18–19
American Academy for Professional Law Enforcement, 229
American Bar Association, 307, 314, 402
American Correctional Association, 402
American Prison Association, 408, 449
Anomie, 87–88
Appeals, 148–49, 288–93
Arrest, 137
Arson, 52
Ashurst–Sumners Act, 410
Assault, 52
Atavism, 82
Attica Prison, 411, 420–26
Auburn Prison 405–8, 411, 421, 430
Augustus, John, 383
Auto theft, 56

Bail, 127, 141, 468
Beccaria, Cesare, 78–79, 368
Behaviorism, 85–86
Biology, and crime, 80–84
Black Muslims, 420, 422, 423, 426, 437
Black Panthers, 420, 423, 427
Blackstone, William, 301, 302
Booking, 137–39
Border Patrol, 252–53
Boston Police Strike, 164, 229
Brittin, William, 407
Brockway, Zebulon, 449
Brooke House, 470–71
Brown, Jack, 471
Bugging. *See* Electronic surveillance

Bureau of Alcohol, Tobacco and Firearms, 250–51
Burglary, 22–23, 35, 52

Capital punishment, 353, 396, 402–3, 440–46
  juveniles, 441, 443, 446
Capone, Al, 38
Case law. *See* Law: case
Case method, 303–4
Child–savers, 483
Civilian review boards. *See* Police: civilian review boards
Civil law. *See* Law: civil
Classical theory, 76–77, 78–80, 368–70, 396
Clinton Prison, 421
Coast Guard, 264
Coke, Edward, 301
Commission on Accreditation for Law Enforcement Agencies, 228
Common law. *See* Law: common
Comte, Auguste, 80, 86
Community-based corrections. *See* Corrections: community–based
Community service, 385, 388, 469
Conflict theory, 96–98
Cook County Juvenile Court, 484
Coolidge, Calvin, 165
Corpus delicti, 10, 11–13
Correction officers, 412, 415, 419, 430–31
Correctional institutions. *See* Prisons
Correction Corporation of America, 435
Corrections
  classification, 416–17
  community–based, 464–75

medical model, 415–16
officers, 412, 415, 419, 430–31
treatment, 417–19
Counsel, right to, 127
Counterfeiting, 112
Court reform, 295
Court workgroup, 345
Courts, 272–97. *See also* Juvenile court; Supreme Court
  administering, 294–95
  appellate, 287–88, 289–91
  of general jurisdiction, 287
  of last resort, 288
  of limited jurisdiction, 285–86
  and reform, 295
  state, 282–88
  U.S. Appeals, 277–78
  U.S. District, 273–77
  U.S. magistrates, 276–77
Cravath, Paul D., 308
Crime. *See also* Organized crime
  career, 29–30
  categories of, 10
  causes of, 78–99
  corporate, 32–34, 55
  defined, 2–6
  employee, 28–29
  occasional, 27
  political, 30–31, 269–70
  theories of, 78–99
  UCR categories, 49–52
  victimless, 37
  violent personal, 25–27
  white-collar, 33
Crime, theories of
  classical, 78–80
  positivism, 80
  biological, 80–84
  psychological, 84–86
  sociological, 86–99
Crime control, versus due process, 113–16

549

550 SUBJECT INDEX

Crime statistics, 46–73
  NCS, 60–71
  and perceptions of crime, 46–49
  problems with, 71–73
  UCR, 46–60
Crime victims, 146–47
Criminal Investigation Command, 264–65
Criminal investigations, 135–36, 192–98. *See also* Managing Criminal Investigations
Criminal law. *See* Law, criminal
Criminal man, 82, 101
Criminal responsibility, 13–18
Criminal subculture. *See* Subcultural theory
Crofton, Walter, 449
Cross–examination, 128, 356–58
Cultural transmission, 88
Customs Service, 353–54

Darwin, Charles, 82, 483
Defense counsel, 289, 323–30, 358
  role of, in plea bargaining, 335–39
Deferred sentencing, 469
Delinquency, 491, 492–93
Des Moines Pretrial Services, 468
Determinism, 83
Deterrence, 9–10
Dewey, Thomas E., 320
Dickens, Charles, 480
Differential association, 34, 88–89
Differential opportunity, 89–91
Diversion, 466–68
Double jeopardy, 128–29, 289
Drift, 95
Drug Enforcement Administration, 257–59
Drugs, 37, 88
Drunk driving, 197, 198–200
Due process, 113–23, 127–29
Durham Rule, 15

Eddy, Thomas, 405
Eisenhower, Dwight D., 280
Electronic surveillance, 112–13, 162, 239

Elmira Reformatory, 408–9, 449–50
Entrapment, 19–20
Exclusionary rule, 129–34, 234
Executive clemency, 462–64

Federal Bureau of Investigation (FBI), 20, 31, 49, 58, 112, 259–64, 268
Federal law enforcement agencies, 242–70
Felony, 10
France, Anatole, 270
Fraternal Order of Police, 230–31
Fraud, 28
Free will, 79, 80
Freud, Sigmund, 84–85, 106
Fugitive Slave Act, 3
Functionalism, 98–99

Gambling, 37
General Services Administration, 255
Gilmore, Gary, 442
Grand jury, 142, 286, 287, 289

Habeas corpus, 274, 437–38, 488, 489
Halfway houses, 469–72
Hawes–Cooper Act, 410
Hearsay, 356
Hickok, James Butler ("Wild Bill"), 157–58
Hinckley, John W., 17
Hitler, Adolph, 83
Hogan, Frank S., 320
Homicide, 50–51, 56
Hoover, J. Edgar, 31, 259, 268, 452
House of refuge, 481
Huron Valley Women's Correctional Facility, 434–35

Immigration and Naturalization Service, 251–53
Index crimes. *See* Uniform Crime Report: index crimes
Innovation, criminal, 88
Insanity defense, 14–18

Inspector General, 266
Internal Revenue Service, 255–56
International Association of Chiefs of Police, 167, 228
International Brotherhood of Police Officers, 231
International Brotherhood of Teamsters, 231 232
International Union of Police Associations, 231
INTERPOL, 268–70

Jails, 146, 398–402
Jefferson, Thomas, 273, 301
Johnson, Frank, 439
Johnson, Lyndon B., 93
Judges
  roles and responsibilities of, 312–13
  role of, in plea bargaining, 338, 339, 340, 345, 347–48
  selection of, 275–76, 313–19
  and sentencing, 371–77
Jurisdiction, 111–13
Jury, right to trial by, 127–28
Jury trials, 350–61
Justice model, 453
Juvenile court, 484–87, 494–500
Juvenile Court Act of 1899, 484
Juvenile justice
  courts, 484–87
  history, 480–83
  institutions, 500–502
  proceedings, 494–500
  rights of juveniles, 487–91
  types of cases, 491–94

Kansas City Study, 105
Kennedy, John F., 262
Kennedy, Robert, 262
King, Martin Luther, Jr., 31, 262
Knapp Commission, 218
Ku Klux Klan, 31, 247

Labeling. *See* Societal reaction theory
Langdell, Christopher Columbus, 302–4
Larceny, 52

SUBJECT INDEX 551

Law
  case, 6
  civil, 6–7
  common, 6, 282, 301, 304, 482
  criminal, 7–10
  schools, 301–6
  sources of, 8–9
  statutory, 6, 301
Law enforcement, amount spent on, 154
Law Enforcement Assistance Administration, 466, 474, 475
Lawyers. *See also* Defense counsel; Prosecutors; Public defenders
  education, 300–306
  and practice of law, 306–12, 341
Learning theory, 85–86
Legal counsel, right to, 127
Legal education
  case method, 303–4
  elite schools, 305
  history of, 301–5
  stratification of, 305–6
Legal impossibility, 12
Lincoln, Abraham, 301
Lindsay, John V., 222
Lombroso, Cesare, 82–83, 371
Lynds, Elam, 407

Mala in se, 3
Mala prohibita, 3–4, 37
Managing Criminal Investigations, 195–96
Marshall, John, 280
Marshals. *See* United States Marshals Service
Marx, Karl, 96
Medical model, 415, 451–53, 454
Mens rea, 12–13, 83
Military law enforcement, 264–65
Minneapolis Domestic Dispute Project, 105–6
Minnesota Restitution Center, 472
Miranda decision, 122
Misdemeanor, 10
Missouri Plan, 318–19
M'Naughten Rule, 14–15
Murder. *See* Homicide

National Anti-Contract Association, 409–10
National Association of Police Organizations, 231
National Crime Survey (NCS), 60–71
  crime categories, 61
  compared to UCR, 60, 70
  findings, 62–67
  problems with, 67–69, 71
  sample victimization study, 63–66
National Organization of Black Law Enforcement Executives, (NOBLE), 228
National Rifle Association, 251
National Sheriffs' Association, 228, 402, 436
Naval Investigative Service, 265
Nazis, 3
NCS. *See* National Crime Survey
Neutralization, 94–95
Newgate, 405
New Mexico State Penitentiary, 427–29
Night Prosecutor's Program, 467

Office of Special Investigations, 265
Opportunistic criminal, 23, 25
Organized crime, 5, 37, 38–44, 262, 270, 323, 481
Oswald, Russell G., 423, 425
Overcharging, 337

Palmer, H. Mitchell, 259
Pardon. *See* Executive clemency
Parens patriae, 482–83, 484, 490
Park Rangers, 266–67
Parole, 147–48, 408, 415, 448–64
  abolition of, 461–62
  board, 453–54
  conditions/rules, 458–59
  criticism of, 452, 461–62
  guidelines, 454–56
  intensive, 462
  officers, 457–60
  supervision, 456–60
  violations, 460–61
Part-time criminal, 23

Patrolmen's Benevolent Association, 231
Pennsylvania system, 403–5, 408
Pinkerton Detective Agency, 233, 244, 259, 260
Piracy, 112
Plain view doctrine, 239
Plea bargaining, 143, 332–49, 384, 402
  legal issues, 347–49
Police, municipal, 159–76
  accreditation, 228
  affirmative action, 232–33
  alienation, 215–16
  authoritarianism, 215–16
  auxiliaries, 203–6
  brutality, 221–23
  calls for service, 179–80
  civilian review boards, 222–25
  civilians in policing, 216
  collective bargaining, 231–32
  community relations, 206
  corruption, 216–21, 228
  deadly force, 223–25
  decoy operations, 185–88
  discretion, 211–214, 466
  goals, 169–70
  history, 159–68, 228, 229
  internal affairs, 200–201
  investigations. *See under* Criminal investigations
  juvenile bureau, 206
  legal issues, 235–40
  licensing, 227–28
  organization, 172–76
  patrol, 178–84
  proactive policing, 192–93
  professionalism, 226–29
  reactive policing, 193–95
  specialized patrol, 184
  styles of policing, 170–71
  subculture, 215, 216
  SWAT teams, 201–3
  tactical patrol. 184–85
  traffic, 196–97
  unionism, 229–32
Police, state. *See* State police
Police Executive Research Forum, 228
Political crime. *See* Crime, political
Positivism/positive school, 80, 371, 414
Postal Inspection Service, 256–57

SUBJECT INDEX

Presentence investigation report, 377–82, 454
Pretrial release, 468
Prisonization, 411–12, 419–20, 464
Prisons, 146–47, 402–12, 414–40. *See also* Auburn Prison; Pennsylvania system
   California, 415–16
   gangs in, 427–30
   and labor, 409–11
   legal decisions, 436–40
   maximum-security, 430–32
   medium-security, 432–33
   minimum-security, 433
   overcrowding, 398–99, 404, 409, 426, 434, 439, 451, 460, 462
   privately owned, 434–36
   riots, 419–26
   as treatment facilities, 417–19
   violence in, 427, 430
   women's, 434–35
Private security 233–35
Proactive policing. *See* Police, proactive policing
Probable cause, 135, 142, 319
Probation, 145–46, 383–91, 468, 497
   intensive, 462
   officers, 385–91, 494–95
   supervision, 384–91, 484
Professional crime, 22–23, 30, 34–36
Prohibition, 5, 38
Prosecutors, 289, 319–23, 355–56
   role of, in plea bargaining, 337–39, 340
Prostitution, 37
Psychoanalytic theory, 84–85, 86
Psychological theory of crime, 84
Psychopaths, 85
Public defenders, 326–28
   role of, in plea bargaining, 338

Quakers, 403, 404, 405

Rape, 51
Reagan, Ronald, 17, 76, 251
Red Scare, 259
Rehabilitation, 453. *See also* Medical model
Research, 104–7
Reserved powers, 112
Restitution, 385, 388, 469
Retreatism, 88
Rice, Fred, 209
Robbery, 51
Rockefeller, Nelson, 425
Roosevelt, Franklin D., 262
Rousseau, Jean Jacques, 78

Saltzman, Bob, 428
Searches, warrantless, 236–39
Secret Service, 247–49
Self-defense, 18–19
Sentencing, 145, 366–82
   deferred, 469
   determinate, 371–73, 426, 456, 461
   guidelines, 374–77
   indeterminate, 373–74, 408, 423, 448–51, 454
   objectives, 366–67
Serpico, Frank, 216, 220
Sheriff, 76, 155–59, 230, 395, 399, 402, 404
Situational criminal, 23–24
Skinner, B. F., 86
Sobriety checkpoints, 198–200
Social contract, 78
Societal reaction theory, 95–96
Sociology, 86
Sociopaths, 85
Spencer, Herbert, 80
Stare decisis, 281, 301
State police, 155, 156–57, 230
Status offense, 491, 493–94, 499
Statutory law. *See* Law: statutory
Subcultural theory, 89–94
Supremacy clause, 112
Supreme Court, 277–82, 288, 291

Talbot House, 471–72
Theft, 52

Theories of crime. *See* Crime, theories of
de Tocqueville, Alexis, 394
Trial, 143–45. *See also* Jury trials

Uniform Crime Report (UCR), 46–60
   compared to NCS, 70
   crime categories, 49–52, 54–55
   hierarchy rule, 53
   index crimes, 49–52
   problems with, 57–60
United States Marshals Service, 243–46

Vera Institute of Justice, 343, 468
Victimization studies. *See* National Crime Survey
Vollmer, Auguste, 167

Walnut Street Jail, 396–97, 404, 407
Warrant, 137
Warren, Earl, 416
Weber, Max, 96
White-collar crime. *See* Crime: white–collar
Wildlife Law Enforcement Agents, 266
Wilson, Woodrow, 229
Wiretapping. *See* Electronic surveillance
Witnesses, right to confront, 128
Workgroup. *See* Court workgroup
Work-release, 472–74

XYY chromosome theory, 83–84

PHOTO CREDITS 553

Photograph Credits

xv, Courtesy Phyllis Kind Gallery, Chicago; 4, Archives of the Yivo Institute for Jewish Research; 5, Copyright 1929 the Detroit News; photo: Milton Brooks; 16, (left) AP/Wide World; (right) Museum of Modern Art/Film Stills Archive; 24, (top) Art Resource/VAGA/S.P.A.D.E.M.; 24, (bottom) AP/Wide World; 26, (top and bottom) AP/Wide World; 39, The Print Archive, San Francisco; 40, AP/Wide World; 48, Copyright © 1976 by The New York Times Company. Reprinted by permission; 59, © John Waldvogel/the New York Post; 68, Courtesy New York Women Against Rape; 72–73, Chicago Historical Society; 81, (left) AP/Wide World; 81, (right) Museum of Modern Art/Film Stills Archive; 90, Milton Rogovin/Photo Researchers; 102–3, (left) UPI; (right) AP/Wide World; 114, The Print Archive, San Francisco; 115, AP/Wide World; 117, UPI/Bettmann Newsphotos; 138, Courtesy Richard J. Elrod, Sheriff's Office, Cook County, Illinois; 140, Courtesy Federal Bureau of Investigation; 148, © 1981 Jim Nachtwey/Black Star; 152, Courtesy Kennedy Galleries; 158, Bettmann Archive; 161, The Print Archive, San Francisco; 163, The Print Archive, San Francisco; 166, Chicago Historical Society #DN 739; 171, Courtesy Oakland Museum/Dorothea Lange Art Fund neg# 80.103.339; 183, © 1981 Andy Levin; 198, Courtesy U.S. Dept. of Transportation, National Highway Traffic Safety Administration; 203, AP/Wide World; 204, 205, Courtesy Illinois Department of State Police; 212, Chicago Historical Society #ICHi 19703 photo: Fred Korth; 217, AP/Wide World; 220, AP/Wide World; 223, UPI; 230, Bettmann Archive; 238, Jack Prelutsky/Stock, Boston; 244, The Print Archive, San Francisco; 248, AP/Wide World; 252, Courtesy U.S. Immigration and Naturalization Service; 260–61, National Archives; 263, Courtesy Federal Bureau of Investigation; 267, © Roger Robinson; 276, © Jan Lukas/Photo Researchers; 279, Supreme Court Historical Society; 281, AP/Wide World; 283, The Print Archive, San Francisco; 303, Harvard Law Art Collection; 324, Brown Brothers; 327, Courtesy Oakland Museum/Dorothea Lange Art Fund neg# 80.103.338; 346, © Rhoda Galyn 1973/Photo Researchers; 384, Courtesy Richard J. Elrod, Sheriff's Office, Cook County, Illinois; 359, © James H. Pickerell; 364, Courtesy Solomon R. Guggenheim Museum, New York. Photo: Robert E. Mates; 368, The Print Archive, San Francisco; 369, AP/Wide World; 370, Walker Evans/Library of Congress; 389, Courtesy Texas Adult Probation Commission. Photo: John Munro; 396, The Print Archive, San Francisco; 397, The Print Archive, San Francisco; 398, Museum of Modern Art/Film Stills Archive; 400, Cornell Capa/Magnum; 403, American Correctional Association; 406, (top) American Correctional Association; (bottom) Courtesy New York State Department of Correctional Services; 410, Danny Lyon/Magnum; 416, UPI; 418, National Criminal Justice Reference Service; 424, AP/Wide World; 428, 429, © Bob Saltzman; 432, Danny Lyon/Magnum; 441, The State Newspaper, Columbia, S.C.; 445, The Print Archive, San Francisco; 450, American Correctional Association; 456, AP/Wide World; 465, National Criminal Justice Reference Service; 471, (left and right) Courtesy Massachusetts Half-Way Houses, Inc. Photo: John Kyper; 473, © Robert L. Smith/Buffalo News; 478, Bettmann Archive; 482, Barnardo's Photographic Archives, Ilford, Essex, England #D146; 485, (top and bottom) Chicago Historical Society; 498, © Jay Paris; 504, Chicago Historical Society.